THE SPIV AND THE ARCHITECT

THE SPIV AND THE ARCHITECT

Unruly Life in Postwar London

RICHARD HORNSEY

UNIVERSITY OF MINNESOTA PRESS

MINNEAPOLIS • LONDON

An earlier version of chapter 1 was published as "'Everything Is Made of Atoms': The Reprogramming of Space and Time in Post-War London," *Journal of Historical Geography* 34, no. 1 (2008): 94–117; copyright 2008; reprinted with permission from Elsevier Ltd. An earlier version of chapter 2 was published as "The Queer (Spatial) Economies of *The Lavender Hill Mob*," *Journal of British Cinema and Television* 5, no. 1 (2008): 38–52; reprinted by permission of Edinburgh University Press, http://www.euppublishing.com/journal/jbctv. An earlier version of chapter 3 was published as "Francis Bacon at the Photobooth: Facing the Homosexual in Post-War Britain," *Visual Culture in Britain* 8, no. 2 (2007): 83–104; reprinted by permission of Manchester University Press. An earlier version of chapter 4 was published as "The Sexual Geographies of Reading in Post-War London," *Gender, Place, and Culture* 9, no. 4 (2002); reprinted by permission of Taylor & Francis, Ltd., http://www.tandf.co.uk/journals, and as "Of Public Libraries and Paperbacks: 'Deviant' Masculinities and the Spatial Practices of Reading in Post-War London," in *Posting the Male: Masculinities in Post-War and Contemporary British Literature,* ed. Daniel Lea and Berthold Schoene-Harwood (New York and Amsterdam: Editions Rodopi, 2003), 35–54.

Published by the University of Minnesota Press
111 Third Avenue South, Suite 290
Minneapolis, MN 55401-2520
http://www.upress.umn.edu

Library of Congress Cataloging-in-Publication Data

Hornsey, Richard Quentin Donald.
The spiv and the architect : unruly life in postwar London / Richard Hornsey.
p. cm.
Includes bibliographical references and index.
ISBN 978-0-8166-5314-0 (hc : alk. paper) — ISBN 978-0-8166-5315-7 (pb : alk. paper)
1. Homosexuality—England—London—History—20th century. 2. Reconstruction (1939–1951)—England—London. 3. Urban policy—England—London—History—20th century. 4. London (England)—Social conditions—20th century. 5. London (England)—Social life and customs—20th century. I. Title.
HQ76.3.G72L655 2010
363.4'90942109045—dc22
2009052922

CONTENTS

Introduction: Social Modernism and Male Homosexuality in Postwar London   1

1. Reconstructing Everyday Life in the Atomic Age   39

2. The Perversity of the Zigzag: The Criminality of Queer Urban Desire   81

3. Trial by Photobooth: The Public Face of the Homosexual Citizen   117

4. Of Public Libraries and Paperbacks: The Sexual Geographies of Reading   163

5. Life in the Cybernetic Bedsit: Interior Design and the Homosexual Self   201

Conclusion: City of Any Dream   247

Acknowledgments   263

Notes   265

Index   293

introduction

SOCIAL MODERNISM AND MALE HOMOSEXUALITY IN POSTWAR LONDON

London is there, waiting indifferently for her poets; and so long as she exists, and they, the challenge of her aloofness to their intention will remain.

—COLIN MACINNES, "City of Any Dream," 1962

In the summer of 1954, Sir David Maxwell Fyfe, the Conservative Home Secretary, asked John Wolfenden to form a Departmental Committee to make recommendations on the twin problems of male homosexuality and female prostitution. During the previous half-decade, both of these phenomena had become popularly perceived as virulent metropolitan threats, stoked by frequent tabloid exposés and mounting calls for political intervention. One of the new committee's first actions was to invite various doctors, policemen, youth leaders, and military personnel to submit written evidence detailing their own experiences of queer men and their thoughts concerning what could and should be done about them. These documents can now be read as part of the Home Office files in the National Archive in Kew, where one of the researcher's pleasures comes from reading Wolfenden's own comments, handwritten in the margins, as he responds to the various arguments being made.

Among those to submit a report was the journalist Peter Wildeblood, who had shot to public notoriety in the spring of 1954 when he was found guilty (alongside Lord Montagu of Beaulieu and the landowner Michael Pitt-Rivers) of conspiring to incite acts of gross indecency and buggery with a pair of younger airmen. Wildeblood's statement remains a rare and valuable attempt by a well-known homosexual to justify his way of life within an official public forum. His overall presentation situated homosexuality as an unfortunate medical condition, a view derived from both nineteenth-century sexology and the interwar psychiatry that was becoming increasingly familiar by the mid-1950s.[1] But within this document there is one particularly interesting passage, in which he writes:

> Havelock Ellis once compared homosexuality to colour-blindness. You do not punish people for being colour-blind, and you do not force them to take medical treatment, for none exists. Is it any more logical, or just, to punish people like me?[2]

In the margin alongside, Wolfenden has written: "Yes, if colour-blindness results in them driving cars across traffic lights."

This brief exchange between Wildeblood's typewriter and Wolfenden's pencil encapsulates many of the themes with which this book is concerned. On one level Wolfenden, as the head of a public Departmental Committee, was countering Wildeblood's liberal defense with a more communitarian framework typical of British policy makers during the early postwar period. Sometimes, he was suggesting, the wider interests of society must be privileged over those of certain disruptive individuals who threaten the stability of its underlying norms. Indeed, Wildeblood had already anticipated this kind of maneuver by grounding his apology in medical science—a move that, on its own terms, shifted the fact of a man's homosexuality beyond the boundaries of individual culpability and thus opened the way for some form of social realignment.[3]

Yet Wolfenden's rejoinder had an even more timely significance. The automated traffic light had been introduced onto London's streets during the early 1930s, as part of a series of measures to combat the exponential rise in road accidents and congestion brought on by the arrival of the motorcar. As a technology with regular and predictable effects, it strove to manage— in an impersonal and equitable manner—the ordered flows of vehicles and pedestrians. As such, the traffic light was an early example of a wider approach to the administration of metropolitan life that would come to sudden prominence as Britain emerged from the Second World War. In the mid-1940s, the swift ascendency of town planning ideology would firmly embed such strategies of spatial management within public visions of post-war reconstruction. As this became disseminated via the popular media, it helped to reinforce an emphatic moral imperative around the use and experience of everyday urban space, sustaining a prescriptive notion of ordered civic life that would dominate official thinking well into the 1950s. Wolfenden's reply to Wildeblood, therefore, by casually invoking the mode of spatial governance through which social consensus was then being sought, unwittingly articulated the very terms through which queer male behavior had already become constituted as a metropolitan threat. Homosexuality, his comment understood, challenged the social stability of the postwar metropolis precisely because of its inability—or perhaps its unwillingness—to respect the spatial and temporal orders through which peace and civic harmony were currently being pursued.

This book is partly about those attempts to reorganize everyday space and time within postwar London, their foundational importance to dominant projections of social order, and the various ways in which male same-sex desire was demonized, defended, and negotiated in relief. After the devastation of the blitz, promissory accounts of a reformed metropolis would repeatedly equate good urban behavior with a specific way of moving through, socializing within, and appreciating the built environment—a logic that insinuated itself across a range of spatial scales and that came to saturate almost all aspects of ordinary everyday life. Yet London's queer men—already existing as a diverse agglomeration of different identities, lifestyles, and ways of engaging with the city—found themselves, to varying degrees, at odds with these new prescriptions of urban citizenship. To this extent, the early postwar decades witnessed a complex set of cultural contestations around the dynamics of metropolitan male same-sex desire, as certain practices became confirmed in their criminality, new forms of queer subjectivity took shape, and alternative modes of resistance emerged. Only by recognizing the centrality of these imperatives within wider programs of social reconstruction—with all their intricate prescriptions concerning space, time, and urban perception—can we understand the parameters within which various forms of queer subjectivity and experience coalesced during this period, the lingering traces of which can still be discerned within the more familiar contours of queer lives today.

Disorder and Desire: The Queer Landscapes of Interwar London

The crucial importance of this postwar moment lay in its concerted attempts to realign many of the dynamics of metropolitan life and address what was now becoming recognized as the multiple crises facing mid-century London. The physical destruction so recently wrought by German bombers proved something of a catalyst, a moment of opportunity that would be seized by a range of affiliated actors whose agendas for social reform had been gathering momentum throughout the 1930s. The cultural force of postwar reconstruction must thus be understood in relation to a developing perception of a connected range of metropolitan crises and disorders that was largely in place already by 1939.

For its planners and administrators, London's postwar rebuilding would provide the mechanism through which to finally repair the contradictory legacies of Victorian capitalism, itself the driving force which had produced the metropolis, but one whose potent defects remained catastrophically embedded within its basic material fabric. The most obvious point of crisis, again only exacerbated by the devastation of the blitz, was the chronic disparity between the living conditions of London's richer inhabitants and those of its very poorest. On one level, the city's wealth seemed visibly concentrated in its commercial West End—particularly those districts around Mayfair, Piccadilly, and St. James's. In the early nineteenth century, this area had been consolidated as a site of luxury bachelor apartments and gentleman's clubs, but it became progressively opened up to more feminine forms of bourgeois leisure and consumption in the 1880s and 1890s.[4] In the early twentieth century, its status had been confirmed as large parts of it were demolished and ostentatiously rebuilt according to the dominant taste for Edwardian neoclassicism. The Ritz Restaurant and Hotel, for instance, had opened on Piccadilly in 1906, to be followed by Selfridge's department store on Oxford Street in 1909—two notable instances within a succession of grand commercial redevelopments that would continue right up until the piecemeal clearance of Park Lane at the close of the 1920s to make way for the majestic American-style Grosvenor House and Dorchester Hotels.[5]

Yet in the older industrial areas of the city, particularly around the docklands to the east and south, large expanses of Victorian slum housing continued to provide an obvious point of contrast to the West End's luxurious modernity. Imagined since the mid-nineteenth century as a disquieting zone in which economic, physical, moral, and racial forms of destitution were alarmingly intermingled, the largely unaltered continuation of these districts into the twentieth century provoked increasingly insistent calls for more systematic intervention.[6] After the Interdepartmental Committee on Physical Deterioration published its report in 1904, the slum dweller's body became firmly identified as a portentous symbol of Britain's industrial decline and imperial weakness.[7] In the decades that followed, piecemeal legislation would seek to improve the health and living conditions of the urban working classes. Yet, although the 1930 Housing Act would make slum redevelopment a statutory duty of local authorities, the fall of the

Labour government in the following year, coupled with financial pressures on the municipal purse, helped ensure that radio and press features on the appalling situation of life in the slums continued throughout the prewar decade.[8] During the 1930s, then, a broad-based coalition emerged among those invested in social reform, producing what the architectural historian Elizabeth Darling has termed a "narrative of modernity." At its root was a belief that the amelioration of poverty in London was inseparable from the reconstruction of the physical environment within which it took shape. Thus, a generation of young architects open to the philosophies of Continental modernism came together with various medical professionals, eugenicists, and voluntarist housing associations to forge a progressive agenda for tackling the slums. Not only did modern architecture offer a radical means for reforming the domestic environment of London's poor, but by aligning themselves with each other's projects, modernist architects, health reformers, and philanthropic organizations could feed off the attention and support garnered by their associates. To this end, the 1930s witnessed the construction of a number of key modernist public buildings—for example, the Pioneer Health Centre in Peckham (1935), Kensal House in Ladbroke Grove (1937), and the Finsbury Health Centre (1938)—that came to encapsulate this pragmatic fusion of social and architectural reform. More important, the coverage of these projects across the media, coupled with ongoing propaganda campaigns in booklets, films, and public exhibitions, helped shape the rhetoric of social modernization that would dominate progressive thinking in the period after the Second World War.[9]

Yet, aside from the obvious degradations of urban poverty, a more nuanced set of blights were seen to be sapping London's vitality by the end of the 1930s. Between the wars, the city made its uneven transition to an economy based on corporate rationalization and mass production, a shift that left a radical imprint on both its landscapes and its streets. Modern electrically powered factories producing a range of consumer durables and foodstuffs had sprung up on its northwestern fringes. But, perhaps more troublingly, vast acres of speculative suburban housing had been built on London's outskirts, helping to consolidate the middle-class identities of its new ranks of clerks and supervisors and stabilizing the kind of domestic consumption on which this economic expansion depended.[10] Encouraged by the rapid expansion of the London Underground network during the 1930s, London's surface area more than doubled between the wars.[11] But the speed of its development provoked widespread alarm among cultural commentators, not only for the apparent impoverishment of the inner city as young affluent couples moved outwards, but for the rapid and seemingly unstoppable encroachment of the metropolis on the surrounding country-side. In 1926, Patrick Abercrombie founded the Campaign for the Preservation of Rural England and, although the 1938 Green Belt Act would begin to set limits to London's outward growth, interwar concern about its size would dominate postwar programs of social renewal.[12]

Further, as if to compound fears about the social decline of London's central districts, large areas of Georgian and Victorian housing on the fringes of the old inner city were visibly changing in character. As their present inhabitants migrated to the suburbs, increasing numbers of residences were converted into rented "furnished rooms," home—among others—to a new generation of transient migrants attracted to London by the promise of employment in its expanding service and leisure industries. The physical dilapidation of districts such as Islington, Paddington, Bayswater, and Pimlico seemed to testify to a state of moral uncertainty, a gathering of young and rootless individuals whose access to the pleasures of the commercial metropolis was perilously unmoored from the stabilizing influences of familial home life or traditional neighborhood communities.[13]

Concerns about the impact of such working-class mobility were only exacerbated by the attendant democratization of the commercial West End. Responding to the general rise in working people's wages, the city had seen a rash of new chain stores, restaurants, cinemas, and dance halls, proffering greater opportunities for leisure, entertainment, and urban performance to an expanded clientele.[14] To many observers, this generation's investments in Hollywood, syncopation, cheap fashions, and makeup revealed a malignant and highly sexualized submission to the entreaties of American commercial mass culture.[15] Newly visible within what had, until recently, remained a predominantly bourgeois terrain, such individuals appeared disquietingly out of place and an obvious form of cosmopolitan disorder against the imperial splendor of London's landmark district.

Importantly, within this unruly metropolitan panorama, one figure notably stood out. In the mid-1920s, the weekly journal *John Bull* drew panicked attention to what it termed the "painted boy menace"—the presence of young men wearing makeup on the streets around Piccadilly and the Strand. Here, it seemed, was a pertinent confirmation of national degeneration—a rotting of the manhood at the heart of Britain's imperial might—

and a timely warning about the feminization caused by the commercial superfluities of the central metropolis.[16] The historian Matt Houlbrook has traced the lives of these interwar "queans" in much more detail. Typically employed in the service sector, they tended to live in those furnished rooms around Bayswater and Paddington, but looked to the streets of the West End as a more conducive space in which to forge a more amenable—if never particularly easy—subjectivity and sexual sociability. Without the resources needed to access either their own secure private space or the city's more discreet commercial queer venues, their lives existed in constant tension with those regulatory authorities for whom—alongside the city's female prostitutes and other working-class participants in forms of public courtship—they remained an insistent affront to normative bourgeois codes of public comportment and sexual discretion.[17]

The situated nature of the quean's metropolitan practices had clear historical precedents. In 1870, the spectacular trial of Frederick Park and Ernest Boulton—or, more specifically, the public revelation of their West End lives as "Fanny" and "Stella"—revealed how the district's thoroughfares, arcades, and theaters could provide wealthy young bachelors with the resources needed to create their own queer formations of self.[18] In many ways, London's interwar queans marked the persistence of this model into the Fordist era, while reflecting the wider economic transformations that were altering the district's social landscape. Crucially, they also inherited an understanding of self that read same-sex desire as an essentialized form of gender inversion, which not only intersected productively with the interwar retail expansion in clothing and cosmetics, but also brought them into more obvious public conflict with hegemonic notions of sexual difference. As Houlbrook notes, for many people the West End quean defined queer activity within London, ensuring that such men were in perpetual tension with both the forces of metropolitan law and order and an ambivalent, and sometimes openly hostile, general public. For both of these groups, they remained very much at the limits of the district's permissive cosmopolitanism.

Yet although such queans were certainly the most visible, they were not the only men to engage in queer activity in interwar London.[19] Across the city, in the dockside pubs, lodging houses, and hostels that clustered around the Thames to the south and east, a rugged bachelor street culture had developed among young laborers drawn to the city by its promises of casual employment. Within this milieu, opportunistic sex with more obviously queer men was considered an acceptable form of sexual relief that didn't necessarily pose a threat to a lad's normal masculinity. Further, since many middle-class queers would habitually offer their working-class partners some form of material reward, any such encounters were available to be read as an enviable display of streetwise prowess.[20]

Again, these configurations looked back to an earlier historical period. In the 1890s, two notable press scandals announced the existence of an entrenched network of interclass male vice in London, which confirmed for their late-Victorian readership a familiar set of narratives about the habitual abuse of aristocratic privilege and the perils facing vulnerable youths at risk within the unruly metropolis.[21] The Cleveland Street affair of 1890–91 revealed how wealthy and prominent personages were routinely buying the services of young telegraph delivery boys in a private West End brothel; and—most notoriously of all—the 1895 trials of the playwright Oscar Wilde would further attest to how richer older men could use diffuse forms of patronage to lure young working lads into committing foul and despicable acts.[22]

Putting to one side the melodramatic tone and political agendas of such radical "new journalism," that such forms of contact should persist throughout the first half of the twentieth century reveals how—for both sets of partners—young working-class men were impervious to charges of essentialized queerness, providing they retained a visible distance from more recognized forms of effeminate behavior. At the same time, earlier anxieties about class exploitation and the corruption of the young would surface again in the postwar period as an important dynamic within the wider drive to combat metropolitan sexual disorder.

Yet, in other quarters of interwar metropolitan society, a more modern form of homosexuality was developing, in direct tension with these older (and increasingly working-class) models of queer subjectivity. For many of London's more affluent men, the disordered performances and mercantile encounters that seemed endemic to the city's more manifest forms of queerness were anathema to their own sense of class privilege. Instead, they invested in those same dynamics through which this status was distinguished—public discretion, domestic propriety, and companionate monogamy. Refuting both the commercial blatancy of West End street life and the dissolute trade of the dockyards and barracks, they forged a more exclusive social network of private homes, expensive restaurants, and private members' clubs, across which they pursued a more selective and less obvious form of queer sociality, protected by the capital on which such access depended.[23]

Again there were intimations of something similar in the later nineteenth century. Certain groups of socially advantaged men had previously been able to exploit their wealth and levels of education to reframe their desires and situate themselves away from the public arenas of the decadent West End. Knowledge of Hellenism, for instance, had authorized investments in the muscular male body—often played out around the Serpentine at Hyde Park or in the classical sculpture galleries at the British Museum—while, from the late 1880s, the Settlement House movement allowed men with investments in notions of social progress to forge relationships with others in the poorer districts of the East End.[24] Yet, during the first half of the twentieth century, such intellectual sources would become eclipsed by a progressive interest in the ideas of several notable sexologists (such as Richard von Krafft-Ebing, Henry Havelock Ellis, and ultimately Sigmund Freud) who proposed models of "homosexuality" as an irrevocable medical affliction.[25] For many men, such approaches offered a persuasive and pragmatically insular framework through which to approach their own desires, in tune with bourgeois cultural lifestyles and in opposition to more popular schemata that rooted queer sexual practices in willful sin or national degeneracy. Of course, access to these ideas remained heavily selective in practice, requiring a level of cultural capital, certain social connections, or the money to pay for one's own therapeutic treatment. Before 1939, therefore, they remained very much the province of a minority.

Thus, as London entered the Second World War, it already facilitated a plurality of queer male behaviors, rooted in different parts of the city and sustaining distinct and contrasting understandings of self. These remained in obvious tension; many middle-class homosexuals, for instance, while seeking to repudiate public sexual conduct, found working-class bodies a persistent site of available temptation. Yet, after 1945, the cultural climate of social reconstruction would intersect with these formations to significant and lasting effect. On the one hand, attempts to reorder the metropolitan landscape would identify both the effeminate quean and the procurable working lad as explosive evidence of public disorder—a form of defiance at once social, economic, geographic, and sexual. In the early 1950s, mounting outrage at such "male vice" and "perversion" would make the capital's streets increasingly inhospitable for its queans, while continuing to drive more affluent homosexuals into discreet commercial spaces in which they could socialize more safely, uncontaminated by the diffuse degradations of public queer life.[26]

In addition, the liberal counterdiscourses that arose in response to this mounting moral panic would serve to disseminate those sexological notions of "homosexuality," previously only the province of a privileged few. As a result, the more varied gender identifications that operated within interwar London became channeled into a narrower binary between the "homosexual" and the "heterosexual." Because this was the notion around which campaigners would build their case for legislative reform, it further stigmatized more feminized forms of overt queer behavior. Moreover, for London's workingmen, it became much more difficult to have sex with queers without similarly becoming tainted by the shadow of homosexuality, while—at the same time—the greater affluence of the later 1950s would remove one of the prime motivations for doing so in the first place.[27]

During the late 1940s and 1950s, as anxieties about metropolitan disorder became embedded within wider programs of postwar urban renewal, these manifold queer ways of inhabiting the city would appear—to differing degrees— emphatically out of place. Yet, at the same time, an awkward rapprochement had already begun between certain middle-class homosexuals and those social modernists who were professionally invested in notions of domestic reform, psychological health, and forms of public order. Within this climate, the meaning, significance, and political implications of queer urban behavior became heavily contested, in a battle that was fought out between many cultural agents across a wide range of discursive, material, and spatial domains.

Social Reconstruction and the Design for Community Living

To appreciate what was at stake within these fraught negotiations, it is necessary to recognize exactly how crucial the administration of everyday space and time was to the mechanics of postwar reconstruction. Only on these terms can the multiple threats posed by the machinations of London's various queer men be properly understood. At root, London's planners sought to actively ameliorate the pressing contradictions of mid-twentieth-century capitalism and expunge its most obvious forms of social disharmony. The reformed urban environment was the vehicle through which such tensions might be resolved, producing in its wake a more vibrant city in which the continuation of basic economic disparity would no longer be in conflict with the authorized performance of collective civic life.

By tacitly orchestrating the individual's daily practices and managing the conditions under which they ordinarily lived, disordered activities and moments of dissent might effectively be precluded. This, in effect, involved not only managing observable urban behavior, but a careful reformation of citizens' basic orientation to their quotidian surroundings. Reconstruction planners sought to instill in ordinary Londoners a specific spatial sensibility, a purposive appreciation of their remodeled city that would propel them into an ongoing mode of active participation and consensus. All of this involved firmly demarcating the boundaries of acceptable metropolitan desire, a project pursued not only by planners, but by other state agencies such as the newly formed Council of Industrial Design (COID), which sought to train the public in how to recognize good design and respond to its entreaties for appropriate behavior. Within this program of social renewal, the city and the commodity appeared as two volatile entities to be subjected to bureaucratic administration. If social order was to be both established and maintained, citizens had to be reoriented away from the pernicious temptations of the unstable metropolis via the prescriptive inculcation of a more controlled—and controllable—form of metropolitan sensibility.[28]

Ultimately, here was being developed a new mode of liberal urban governance.[29] To understand it in more detail, it is useful to return to "Citizenship and Social Class," an influential essay by the sociologist T. H. Marshall that was first delivered as a series of lectures in 1949. Within this piece, Marshall traced a genealogy of citizenship from the present welfare state back toward feudalism, seeking to locate its historical development within the structural transformations of industrial capitalism. Citizenship, he argued, was an essentially variable concept, always defined as the set of fundamental rights and duties shared by all members of the community, but with shifting notions of who those members were and in what those entitlements actually consisted. During the earliest phases of the industrial revolution, Marshall noted, citizenship had been equated with the twin civic rights of mobility and contract, as required by a developing wage-labor system, which in turn precipitated the political right to parliamentary representation. Then, at the end of the nineteenth century, spurred on by free education and the ambitions of the trade-union movement, citizenship had been expanded to include the social right to welfare. To Marshall writing in 1949, the recent raft of postwar welfare legislation marked the end point of this progression. Citizenship had reached its most expansive formulation—now far in excess of any mere civil or political entitlements—as the right to fully participate in the social and cultural heritage of the nation.

Here, then, citizenship was revealed to have its own internal logic. Always a normative concept, it sought the progressive fulfillment of its own ideals by extending ever-richer entitlements to an ever-greater sector of the populace. Yet, Marshall's primary interest lay in understanding how such an egalitarian and expansive social system could have evolved as part of an industrial configuration inherently structured by class inequalities and economic disparity. His eventual answer came via a recognition of the basic difference between "citizenship" and "class" as two distinct conceptual categories. While the former consisted in an official conferment of status and was thus emphatically a social institution, the latter was merely a theoretical conceit for describing an outcome of social imbalance—a by-product of other social institutions, but not an actual institution in and of itself. Theoretically at least, therefore, class and citizenship were not necessarily in conflict, such that—by the mid-twentieth century—the latter had become deployed as an instrumental device for stabilizing the ongoing inequalities of the former. As Marshall expressed it:

> Equalisation [under the welfare state] is not so much between classes as between individuals within a population which is now treated for this purpose as though it were one class. Equality of status is more important than equality of income.[30]

Those recent measures that promoted such an equality of status—paying the lowest earners a wage beyond their market worth, for instance, or supplying every child with an appropriate free state education—thus extended to the poorest sectors of the population a feeling of inclusion, which would bring them more successfully into the social life of the collective. If such concessions were coupled with the removal of both absolute poverty and intolerable living conditions, then they should lessen the incentives for political dissent. Hence the capitalist economy, while still structured around wage differentials and their attendant hierarchies of class, could renew its legitimacy, soothed by a new form of social consensus that would discourage the kind of bitter class conflict that had marred earlier phases of its existence. In effect, Marshall concluded, the postwar extension of citizenship and welfare, by clipping the wings of the free market and ameliorating its more visible excesses, looked to secure the continuation of capitalism within the decades to come.

Within the present context, the real value of Marshall's analysis lies less in his articulation of this reformist logic than in his astute—if somewhat underplayed—recognition of how such measures gained their cultural force. This had less to do with raw economics than with their manifestation as a set of collective performances carefully interwoven into the fabric of everyday life. As he put it:

> Even when benefits are paid in cash, this class fusion is outwardly expressed in the form of a *new common experience*. All learn what it means to have an insurance card that must be regularly stamped (by somebody), or to collect children's allowances or pensions from the post office.[31]

It was the crystallization of these measures as a universal set of ordinary rituals that bound even those wealthy individuals without need of such benefits within what Marshall termed a "superstructure of legitimate expectations," or the "details in a design for community living."[32]

Insinuated thus into daily life, postwar enactments of quotidian social citizenship can be seen as the culmination of an already developing movement within twentieth-century British culture. As Alison Light and others have noted, during the 1920s and 1930s, the traumatic experience of the First World War and the ongoing erosion of imperial power had produced a general retreat from the expansionist ideologies of earlier decades and a shift toward a softer, more homely rhetoric that found an essential national character to be expressed within the ordinary and the domestic.[33] By recognizing the significance of the weekly visit to the post office, Marshall echoed, for instance, George Orwell's location of "all the culture that is most truly native" within the communal foci of "the pub, the football match, the back garden, the fireside and the 'nice of cup of tea,'" as well as Mass-Observation's attention to quotidian detail as the site for its anthropology of the British people.[34] At the same time, however, when Marshall wrote that "citizenship has itself become, in certain respects, the *architect* of legitimate social inequality," he implicitly recognized the strategic importance that such rituals had assumed for the nascent welfare state.[35] After the Second World War, such everyday practices could no longer be seen as the spontaneous expressions of some innate national character, for they had now become a set of infrastructural supports that sought to sustain, however covertly, the material disparities of social democratic capitalism.

As part of his analysis, Marshall was astute as to the links between such designs for community living and the ascendancy of town-planning doctrine with which they had coincided. Urban reform, as widely disseminated across a range of popular media from the mid-1940s, was presented to the public as a heroic continuation of national wartime struggle and a unique opportunity to make good the devastation of Britain's cities, by replacing its squalid Victorian slums with the most advanced social housing, parkways, and precincts. Yet, already by 1949, Marshall observed the conservatism within this drive, which was aimed less at ameliorating the misery of the poor per se than at preventing the class conflict that such misery might provoke. These schemes of "total planning," he argued, had found a way to stabilize their own structural inequalities. The planner's celebrated ideal of the "balanced community" was "not a classless society, but a society in which class differences are legitimate in terms of social justice, and in which, therefore, the classes cooperate more closely than at present to the common benefit of all."[36]

Indeed, Patrick Abercrombie's hugely influential vision for rebuilding the capital—divided between his *County of London Plan* (1943; with J. H. Forshaw) and his *Greater London Plan* (1944)— focused on creating precisely this kind of hierarchical interclass cooperation through the promotion of a revitalized and collective civic life. Imagining a metropolis that had been successfully remolded back into its original network of archaic village communities, Abercrombie recast the capital as a network of local neighborhoods, each one centered on a cluster of municipal buildings to which its residents would congregate "for physical culture, dancing, dramatics, handicrafts, discussion groups, lectures, etc."[37] Such buildings, and the benign communal activities they were designed to foster, would infuse the fabric of everyday life with just that type of new common experience that Marshall saw as crucial to the peaceful maintenance of postwar class inequality. Further, Marshall also sensed how the efficacy of such activities was rooted in their grounding as neighborhood acts of community participation, for their inherent sense of local collectivism worked to disavow its more impersonal production at the level of national policy by institutional technologies of state.[38]

This dialectic between the national coordination of social citizenship and its localized public performance on the ground dominated the early period of postwar reconstruction. This was particularly evident in the repeated use of public exhibitions to promulgate official visions of reformed national cohesion. Events such as *Britain Can Make It* (the COID's showcase of good British design, held at the Victoria and Albert Museum in 1946) and the various components of the Festival of Britain (which took place during the summer of 1951) promoted the values of one-nation ideology via a controlled mode of spatial participation. Such exhibition sites provided a distilled experience of affiliatory citizenship, because the visitor became part of a localized collective that enacted in microcosm the larger national community invoked by the displays. The strikingly modern plazas and pavilions of the *South Bank Exhibition*—the centerpiece of the whole festival—famously emulated the precincts and communal buildings sketched out within Abercrombie's London plans, thus making explicit the prescriptive pleasures and performative duties already embedded within these new urban environments.

The type of remodeled space here being offered contained two important mechanisms through which a future of social order and community cohesion might be pursued. On one level, their functional, accessible, and open designs were understood by their architects to clearly express a legible set of civic virtues that would instill in the viewer the required sensibility of willful consensus.[39] Yet, far less overtly, such sites were quietly being programmed with a more insidious form of strategic social management. Abercrombie's London plans, for instance, were foundationally organized through the discrete spatialization of everyday activities, separated out into a series of monological zones that were sequentially arranged according to the imagined routine of a generic Londoner. By thus attending to the everyday repetitions of the abstract individual, planners could project a form of managed social order in which the careful provision of all aspects of life precluded the possibility of disruption or dissent. This London of the future—already built around circuitous trajectories—was thus a city in which malignant social practices would, quite literally, be unable to take place. These endless cycles of atomized routines would safeguard the city from any collective dissension or unforeseen events. By projecting a highly programmed space, the planners and administrators of the early reconstruction could offer the public a comforting framework for imagining a metropolis protected from the possibility of conflict or trauma. And while town-planning documents propagated this form of spatial orchestration, the managed choreographies built into the design of both *Britain Can Make It* and the *South Bank Exhibition* supported this project by offering visitors a more concrete experience of just what this new form of urban citizenship would feel like to perform within a rebuilt metropolis.

Very little of Abercrombie's plans was ever properly implemented, and the sympathetic visions of both *Britain Can Make It* and the *South Bank Exhibition* soon foundered amid the social and economic contradictions of the ensuing postwar decades. But the timely force of these pedagogical endeavors gave them a cultural momentum that far exceeded their limited realization on the ground.[40] Attached to a persuasive projection of a unified and peaceful social democracy, these sanctioned ways of looking at, responding to, and circulating around the built environment became morally identified with a form of spatial citizenship at once localized and national. But it is important to note how they were already deeply at odds with the everyday experiences of many of London's queer men, who—across their range of divergent and class-marked subject positions—had developed their own, more selective, ways of operating within the city. These queer dynamics had brought men into conflict with the forces of metropolitan law and order long before the war, but against the urgent agendas of postwar reconstruction, this friction swiftly intensified. Already culturally marginalized by renewed social invest-ments in the child and the nuclear family, the equation of national citizen-ship with a mode of spatial and temporal conformity further criminalized queer metropolitan cultures, as such illicit ways of operating within the built environment became forcefully recast as willful acts of antisocial opposition.

Of Spivs and of Architects

To explore this conflict further, it is worth returning to an insightful article on the *South Bank Exhibition* by Owen Gavin and Andy Lowe, which ap-peared in the pioneering visual culture journal *Block* in 1985. During a wider exploration of the prescriptive visual logics embedded within the site, they made a brief but incisive comparison between "what must seem like the odd-est pairing—the spiv and the architect, the deviant and the expert." This opposition—from which the present book borrows its title—has proven extremely productive for thinking through exactly what was at stake in the various postwar reformulations of the queer male subject. As Gavin and Lowe explain:

> In terms of the London of the post-war forties and the early fifties [the spiv and the architect] are not obvious "opponents", certainly did not confront each other directly, but within the rhetoric of planning and reconstruction, within the promise of a brave new world, environmentalism poses these two figures at opposite extremes.[41]

The postwar architect, of course, was the key cultural agent in urban reconstruction, poised to reform both the citizen's spatial environment and—by extension—his or her consensual orientation toward the performance of civic life. Thus, at *Britain Can Make It,* a "young architect-painter" was found among the assortment of fictitious families used to humanize its presentation of well-designed "Furnished Rooms." Here, posted above his "kitchen plus dining space," a cartoon by Nicholas Bentley revealed a dynamic young father eager to play his part within the vibrant national community of modern postwar Britain (Figure 1). As his wife talks into the telephone and his son plays with a toy plane—London Airport opened to civilians at around the time of the exhibition's opening—here was a family brimming with domestic fulfillment, while also looking outwards to the confident advances of the technocratic world. Significantly, among all of Bentley's drawings, this young architect was the only character to gaze out of the frame and engage the visitor's eye. Looking up from a set of blueprints—for a new neighborhood precinct, perhaps, or maybe his own kitchen diner—he interpellated the viewer into the progressive nation that he both encapsulated and made available, a model citizen within whom the latest in modern living, a loving nuclear family, and a purposive appreciation of functional design all happily coalesced.

As the darker counterpoint to this celebrated figure, the spiv was more elusive and harder to pin down. The word itself seems to have come to public prominence during the summer of 1947, as correspondents to the *Daily Mail* and *Daily Telegraph* debated its etymology and the Tory MP Ralph Assheton accused the Labour government in the House of Commons of creating a "spiv-economy."[42] A recognizable but essentially protean figure, the spiv came to express a complex range of anxieties and wish fulfillments about metropolitan society in the immediate postwar period. At one end of the spectrum, he remained an opportunistic and largely harmless crook. His street-corner existence was seen to provide an illicit point of access to the forbidden fruits of the illegal black market, in defiance of austerity and the ever-tightening strictures of state-imposed rationing. Always depicted in a voluminous snazzy suit, whose excessive cut signaled both his ill-gotten spoils and his desire to cut a dash amid the drabness of the city, he became a stock character within Osbert Lancaster's satirical "pocket cartoons" on the front page of the *Daily Express* (Figure 2). And, as a figure of affectionate release, he was an established presence on popular radio, where Arthur English's "Prince of the Wide Boys" was a firm favorite on *Variety Bandbox,*

Figure 1. The steady gaze of the social modernist: Nicholas Bentley, "Young architect–painter. Wife, keen on amateur dramatics. One son." Cartoon for the Furnished Rooms section at *Britain Can Make It*, 1946. Courtesy of Design Council/University of Brighton Design Archives.

and in such popular Ealing comedies as *Passport to Pimlico* (Henry Cornelius, 1949), in which the shady dealings of Benny Spiller (Roy Carr) are never dark enough to undermine the plucky residents of Miramont Gardens or the wider national community they clearly came to symbolize.

Yet, against such softly comic incarnations, the spiv was also a much more troubling cultural figure. During the late 1940s, Britain witnessed what the media hailed as a violent postwar crime wave, encapsulated by a series of headline-grabbing incidents, such as the Charlotte Street shooting of April 1947 in which a gang of young armed robbers shot and killed a passing motorcyclist who tried to prevent their escape.[43] Such incidents seemed to confirm multiple fears about the hordes of young wartime deserters still

Figure 2. Excessive consumption, suspect masculinity, and sartorial ostentation meet on the body of the spiv. Osbert Lancaster, "Pocket Cartoon" for *Daily Express* (October 18, 1947). Courtesy of Express Pictures.

"Is that a brand-new number, dearie, or have you just let the hem down?"

hiding out across London, the easy availability of erroneous firearms, and the damage caused to a generation of adolescents by the familial disruptions of the war. Capitalizing on these anxieties, a rash of popular British films (memorably termed "the spiv cycle" by film historian Robert Murphy) presented cinemagoers with cautionary tales of delinquent young lads, impelled by a damaged home life to seek wealth and notoriety within London's criminal underworld.[44] In many ways, these tragic narratives—usually ending in the spiv's imprisonment or death—reworked earlier concerns about the insidious effects of American mass culture on Britain's undisciplined working-class youth, but within a climate of increased faith in the reformist potential of social science, they also made recourse to the ideas of criminal psychiatry that would become ever more prominent during the early postwar decades.

The spiv as he emerged during the late 1940s, therefore, remained a stubbornly amorphous cultural figure that resisted a straightforward attachment to any actual individuals on the streets. As Peter Scott, one of the few criminologists to use his experience with juvenile delinquents to investigate the phenomenon of postwar spivvery, wrote:

> Everyone seems to have a different notion of what a spiv might be. The more young people one studies the more one becomes uncertain as to whether there is such an entity, or whether it only arises in the mind by combination of characteristics abstracted from many young men none of whom, if standing before one, would constitute the complete article.[45]

Yet it was precisely this ineffable fluidity that allowed the spiv to do such important cultural work. For Gavin and Lowe, those "spivvy barrow boys defying the strictures of Austerity with their clothes as flashy as neon" were significant for presenting a superficial identity that was primarily inscribed across the surfaces of their bodies.[46] As they put it:

> The spiv's body lacks the interior depth, the points of attachment that are the basis of the calculation of environmental moulding. The body of the spiv is portrayed as resisting the demands of citizenship in the form of an immoral and diseased consumption.[47]

Young, working-class, and always on the make, the spiv was the obverse of the reconstruction citizen so tirelessly invoked by Abercrombie's model neighborhoods and the precincts of the South Bank. He placed his own self-interest over that of the community and ignored the constraints of a bureaucratized economy to pursue his own program of antisocial indulgence. Affronting the bourgeois virtues of restraint and sobriety, he spent money on his clothes and hairstyle, constructing his body as an urban spectacle that defied the functional sensibilities of good civic-mindedness, while—ignoring all programs of visual education—he exalted frivolity and fashion over any purposive social investment in progress and stability. Even more abhorrently, he advertised both his wares and himself on the streets of the city, thus threatening to corrode the equable social fabric by fostering selfish desires in others. The spiv's body, then, was a gaudy remnant of laissez-faire capitalism that had somehow survived into the bureaucratized age of the postwar welfare state. It was thus entirely fitting that both popular cinema and mainstream journalism should locate him within the decaying fringes of the Victorian inner city, a damaged product of a decrepit environment and precisely the type of unstable figure whom London's heroic architects were eager to obviate.

Above all, however, the spiv's real deviance lay in his refusal to accept the class position to which he was assigned. In "Citizenship and Social Class," Marshall would note how the welfarist confluence of equal civil status and stable economic hierarchies was bound to falter as the economy expanded. Firms, he projected, would soon have to offer greater rewards to key groups of workers as the needs of the labor market changed. This, in itself, would introduce new mobilities into an essentially static class system, antagonizing the ideologies of one-nation community through which stability was currently being sought. Marshall envisaged two potential outcomes: either entrenched social hierarchies would start to break down, or else "social stratification persists, but social ambition ceases to be a normal phenomenon, and becomes a deviant behaviour pattern—to use some of the jargon of sociology."[48] With his desire for personal gain and his defiant exhibitionism, the spiv encapsulated this latter dynamic and became an early figure through whom individual ambition and antisocial behavior could be ideologically equated. It was this, perhaps, that ensured his cultural prominence—a metropolitan character around whom some of the contradictions of social democracy could be articulated and (only partially) resolved. Furthermore, the spiv served an additional purpose, for his unwillingness to accept his rightful class inheritance could be firmly identified with his willful eschewal of civic metropolitan sensibilities. His clothes, movements, pleasures, and labors all rejected the prevailing model of prescribed urban citizenship toward which reformist planners were working, conflating this defiance with a wider set of didactic warnings around class, individualism, and the perils of dissent.

Importantly for us, the amorphous nature of the spiv's metropolitan criminality also extended to his libidinal desires. Against the familial paternalism of *Britain Can Make It*'s dynamic young architect, the spiv was rendered as a complexly queer figure. This was most forcefully presented in the film *The Blue Lamp*, Basil Dearden's melodramatic crime thriller produced by Ealing Studios and one of the highest-grossing films in British cinemas during 1950. Largely inspired by the recent Charlotte Street shooting and prefaced by a dedication to the "men and women of the Metropolitan Police . . . and their colleagues in the Police Service of Britain," this film collapsed a whole set of oppositions to articulate the threat posed by the spiv to London's spatial, social, and sexual orders. It is worth considering it at some length, for although its central spiv is not explicitly queer, he reveals much about exactly what was at stake in the postwar formulation of metropolitan criminality.

The Blue Lamp's hero is one Police Constable Andy Mitchell (Jimmy Hanley), a new recruit at Paddington Green Police Station, who is taken under the wing of old-timer Police Constable George Dixon (Jack Warner), himself shortly to retire after twenty-five years of service. This paternalistic relationship is extended further when Dixon and his faithful wife Em (Gladys Henson) welcome Mitchell into their home, both as a lodger and as a partial replacement for their much-mourned son, killed in action during the war. In diametric opposition to Mitchell is the young spiv Tom Riley (Dirk Bogarde) who, along with his accomplice Spud and his young runaway girlfriend Diana (Peggy Evans), carries out a series of small-scale robberies that culminates in the abortive stickup of a cinema cashier. During the ensuing scuffle, Riley shoots Dixon, who later dies in hospital. The remainder of the film follows the officers of Paddington Green Station— both uniformed and plainclothed—as they piece together the evidence and close in on Riley. It ends with a reliably Oedipal climax, in which Mitchell apprehends Riley, thus completing his initiation as a bobby and taking up the place vacated by his fallen mentor.

This foundational contrast between the young policeman Mitchell and the juvenile delinquent Riley structures the entire film, for Mitchell both expresses and embodies the dominant reconstruction order that Riley and his actions seek to undermine. Dixon's twenty-five years of service—and the quarter century that Mitchell will also surely serve—become the marker of an ongoing social stability, perpetually reenacted through the rhythm of their daily beats around Paddington Green. In a sense, Dixon and Mitchell are perfect reconstruction citizens; as nodal points for the neighborhood community, they remain content with their allotted station in life and happily enact its prescribed routines. Their proud uniforms render this civic integrity immediately legible, while, by extension, they are consistently able to read the motives and intentions of those individuals they encounter on their patch. In the final denouement, Mitchell has to borrow a mackintosh from a plainclothed colleague, but after Riley's capture, he eagerly returns to the fidelity of his uniform and its public reassurances of stability and order. Circulating around the district, Mitchell's amiable banter with those neighborhood men, women, and children he routinely encounters enacts a perfect fusion between the local rituals of civic citizenship and a more impersonal form of institutionalized law and order.

Yet, while aligning themselves fully within this design for community living, Dixon and Mitchell also become the genial agents of its ongoing regulation. Their primary concern—like that of Abercrombie and his architect colleagues—is to maintain the circulation of their fellow Londoners, safeguarding the city's flows and regulating the ordered usage of its component functional spaces. As they patrol their district, their work is seen to consist in moving on barrow boys, helping old ladies cross the road, and apprehending a car driver who ignores a pedestrian crossing. At one point, Dixon's flashlight illuminates a young couple kissing within the shadows of a shop doorway; he swiftly moves them on, returning urban space to its normative and proper practices. The main task of these bobbies, the film repeatedly insists, is to complete the prescribed circuit of their beat, phoning through to the station at each allotted hour to report back: "All correct."

Riley's criminality, of course, is constructed as the complete antithesis of all this (Figure 3). His desire to escape his working-class background and the miserable future to which he thinks this will confine him becomes manifest as an eschewal of all civic sensibilities and a willfully perverse relationship to the urban environment. This is most clearly signaled by his sartorial transgressions—his garish tie and the phony broad shoulders of his oversized jacket. Like Diana, his girl, he is easily distracted by the city's cheap entertainments, preferring the brazen thrills of the music hall and cinema to the more managed pleasures of communal leisure (such as the police station's male-voice choir, whose coordinated harmonies perfectly encapsulate the hierarchical community at the heart of reconstruction ideology). Riley's inability to inhabit his environment properly—"Act natural!" he says to Diana when they spot a copper on the street—is also rendered as a failure to comply with its normative circulations. Instead, Riley and his gang persist with their own illicit geographies, loitering in doorways, hanging out in cafés, and escaping through windows instead of using the door. When they move through the city, they run—in marked opposition to the copper's steady walk—or race through red traffic lights in a stolen motorcar. Riley's antisocial material desires, then, inherently corrupt his mode of metropolitan engagement and destructively subvert the stability of its spatial and temporal orders.

Most crucially, of course, *The Blue Lamp* extends this opposition onto the specific level of sexual desire, for it plays heavily with the contrast between its two heterosexual couples: George and Em Dixon, and Riley and Diana. While the Dixons are repeatedly shown in the domesticity of their kitchen,

Figure 3. Bobby meets spiv, the twin poles of metropolitan (dis)order, in *The Blue Lamp* (Basil Dearden, 1950).

deeply in love after many years of marriage and eager to welcome Mitchell as a surrogate son, Riley and Diana end up sharing a grotty rented room that only becomes a site for confrontation and abuse. When George is wounded, Em rushes to his bedside with flowers from their garden; yet, after George's death, Diana's mounting anxiety is met by sadism and beatings from Riley, who eventually tries to strangle her. Never offering Diana any affection, he persistently refers to her only as an object and feverishly relishes her subservience and fear. Their sole moment of erotic passion comes just after Riley has pointed a loaded pistol into her belly, a crude phallic substitute for the normal loving intercourse that is so conspicuously absent.

As a central articulation of postwar metropolitan criminality, the character of Tom Riley interwove a number of contemporary transgressions against class acquiescence, domestic propriety, urban sensibility, movement, and desire. When, shortly after *The Blue Lamp*'s release, the tabloids began to escalate their sensational coverage of "male vice" in London, they constructed its antisocial intent through exactly the same combination of failures and threats. The metropolitan "pervert" upon whom these accounts dwelled was cast, in a melodramatic update of late-Victorian "new journalism," as a merciless predator who preyed on young lads who were vulnerably astray within the wilds of the metropolis. Seeking to debase his victims by proffering money or gifts in exchange for sex, he forced them to cultivate tastes way above their station via elaborate rituals of inappropriate consumption. Like Riley in *The Blue Lamp,* the once-corrupted pervert— who slowly became indistinguishable from the agent of his downfall— rejected all imperatives of civic affiliation, pursing instead his own willful program of individual self-gain. As an inextricable mixture of the material and the erotic, these criminal desires were again seen to coalesce within an illicit urban geography. Played out once more against the emotive backdrop of a decayed Victorian city, the urban queers of tabloid scandal were not only criminalized through their obvious distance from normative family life, but also by their invidious delight in corroding boundaries of social class, and by the covert techniques they had conspiratorially developed for reading, negotiating, and moving through the metropolis.

From Criminal to Citizen: Redesigning the Metropolitan Homosexual

Yet while such articulations of antisocial queerness conflated a coterminous set of criminal behaviors, transgressive mobilities, and inappropriate selfish desires, the medical terminology employed by tabloid journalists to lend their reports an air of modernity also pointed to the direction from which they would soon be challenged. As the chorus of outraged reporters, magistrates, and politicians grew louder, a counterdiscourse fought for attention by mobilizing the authority of psychiatry and criminology to assert alternative truths about what they now positioned as the condition of "homosexuality." The mid-1950s, then, became increasingly marked by a public contest over the ontology of queer male behavior, its moral dynamics, and its precise significance as a contemporary urban problem.

As Gillian Swanson has recently shown, psychological disciplines of eugenics and social psychiatry had an escalating impact in Britain after the Second World War, as officials sought a means through which to address a cast of problematic figures who seemed dangerously out of place within the postwar urban landscape.[49] Time and again, new forms of metropolitan liberty opened up by London's expanded leisure economies—particularly those afforded to the young and working-class—became a point of visible disorder, which experts were keen to root in the psychological failings of the impoverished "broken" home. Like his sympathetic colleagues, the architect and the town planner, the social psychiatrist appeared as a conduit for a scientific modernism that offered to repair the faulty inheritance of a decrepit urban fabric. These figures represented a similar type of interventionist reform that sought to cure social ills by restoring individuals to a more integrated mode of ordered urban citizenship. Thus, like the war-damaged districts of London's Victorian slums, the interior space of the pathological psyche was also laid open, to be charted and redesigned as part of that same class-bound drive toward a lasting social cohesiveness.

Again, it is constructive to make comparisons between the "homosexual" and the spiv, for the latter's treatment at the hands of juvenile criminologists reveals much about the parallel reformulation of the metropolitan pervert and the terms through which his rehabilitation was pursued. When Peter Scott inquired into spivvery in his essay of 1954, he began by cataloging the spiv's resplendent hairstyles, his pink shirt and ox-blood creepers, and the comic-paper protruding from the pocket of his belted coat. But he swiftly asserted the fatal limitations of such superficial accounts:

> Ask a group of people what they consider to be the essential qualities of a spiv and the answers will surely include references to their dress, their work or lack of it, their characteristic activities, their language, to which *we* may add some impressions of their family life.[50]

By setting up this opposition between the ordinary general public and the first-person plural of professional science, Scott drew the battle lines over which the truth of postwar spivvery would ultimately be fought. No longer just a collection of garments, a set of practices, or a particular urban attitude, the spiv's essential locus was relocated away from the streets and into two related—but much less visible—spaces: that of the spiv's own psyche, and that of the home in which he had grown up. As Scott explained: "the factors which we regard as the essence of 'spivdom' are no more than a top dressing to character deviations which may be expressed in comparable but quite unspivish ways."[51]

On these terms, the public existence of the spiv—his actions, appearance, and manifest desires—was rooted in the same set of childhood events that were also used to explain the occurrence of male homosexuality. His "calculated loudness," a pathological desire to be seen and to be reckoned with, could usually be traced back to a substandard father—either hostile or absent—or an "over-protecting, spoiling mother" who had later spurned her son as he entered adolescence. These conditions had instilled in him profound feelings of guilt, insecurity, and a sense of inferiority, such that the spiv's language, jewelery, and acts of petty crime were forged as a suit of psychic armor that he ineffectually brandished to dispel lingering feelings of social inadequacy.

According to this logic, women became just another object employed by the spiv for his own pathological ends. As Scott noted, "nearly all spivs like to have a girl-friend but she is worn on the arm as a flower and it does not last long"; his deep insecurity and dread of exposure made him fearful of the testing grounds of sex and romance. Thus, Scott made an explicit link between spivvery and homosexuality, arguing that the two should not be understood as qualitatively different states, but as variants within a "series" of conditions—all rooted in the same failed parenting—that extended from chronic masturbators and exhibitionists to fetishists and transvestites. Patients positioned along this sliding scale all revealed similar environmental disturbances, which had arrested their ability to enter proper sexual relations. Terrified of women, they took refuge in fantasy, whether through indecent exposure (a substitute for actual contact with women), fetishism (the fetish as a substitute for a woman), transvestism (the self imagined as that woman who cannot be had), or full-blown homosexuality (using other men to confirm one's own female self-projection). On these terms, the spiv and the homosexual, united by their fear of heterosexual contact, were distinguished only by the strategies that they employed to deal with it. The spiv, in effect, lacked the homosexual's "passivity and quiet acceptance of [his] inferior, but for the moment satisfying, solution to the problem," for while standing on the precipice of homosexuality, he had somehow found the residual masculinity required to fight it off.[52] As Scott admiringly concluded: "It seems reasonable to suppose that [the spiv] has the ability to deal with things realistically and aggressively, and so avoids the self-sufficiency and the mental self-deception of the [homosexual] pervert."[53]

Yet if psychology and psychoanalytic criminology bracketed the spiv and the homosexual through their complicit narratives of psychosexual development, then the social disparity between London's juvenile delinquents and its more well-connected queers collided with these discourses to very different effect. Indelibly working-class, those positioned as spivs remained predominantly the object of such knowledge, largely unable to influence the ranks of professionals by whom their social pathology was being proclaimed. In marked contrast, a stratum of privileged queer men had, since the early twentieth century, enjoyed a selective access to volumes of Continental sexology, whose medicalized notions of the homosexual condition had proved deeply amenable to their constructions of self. Such ideas provided a workable conceptual schema through which such men could rethink their own moral culpability, away from a dominant framework that equated all forms of sex between men with sin or willful perversion. If homosexuality was rooted in a constellation of childhood factors, then, as a condition of being, it lay beyond the realms of personal responsibility. The moral agency of queer behavior now lay less in the desire itself—recodified as an anterior, if unfortunate, given—but in the degree to which the sufferer allowed those desires to become manifest within the public arenas of the city.

The postwar period thus saw an uneasy collusion between professional ranks of psychological scientists and certain groups of bourgeois queer men, who worked together to fashion an account of metropolitan homosexuality that accorded with more dominant notions of legitimate social citizenship. Generalist books such as Gordon Westwood's *Society and the Homosexual* (1952) and D. J. West's *Homosexuality* (1955) presented numerous case studies of respectable men who discovered their affliction to be in no necessary conflict with the normative values of domestic monogamy and public restraint. (Significantly, West's most well-adjusted homosexual case study was also a professional architect.)[54]At the same time, personal testimonials such as Peter Wildeblood's *Against the Law* (1955) carefully articulated a model of urban homosexuality fully in accordance with reconstruction ideologies, creating their own firm distinctions between the practices and experience of men like themselves and the unacceptable behavior of those degraded, damaged perverts whom the tabloids repeatedly misidentified as proper homosexuals.[55]

This emergent formulation was abetted by a cluster of sympathetic novels to appear throughout the mid-1950s. The protagonists of Mary Renault's *The Charioteer* (1953), Audrey Erskine Lindop's *Details of Jeremy Stretton* (1955), and James Courage's *A Way of Love* (1959)—whose respectable homosexual narrator is not only an architect but also working on a school—all aligned themselves with sanctioned codes of urban comportment, romantic fulfillment, privacy, and discretion.[56] Perhaps more important, the twin novelistic devices of first-person narration and interior monologue provided a more affective supplement to the distanced objectivity proclaimed by psychologists. As these protagonists moved around the city, guiding their readers through its various queer subcultures, they went beyond a behavioral depiction of people and places to construct a more emotional and felt form of metropolitan sensibility. Always with an eye to the goal of legal reform, such characters were largely made to feel pity and disgust at the pansies and perverts they saw plying themselves around London, as well as a profound sense of sadness and frustration at their own difficulties in finding lasting true love within such an inhospitable society.

In Rodney Garland's popular novel *The Heart in Exile* (1953), the narrator is both a psychoanalyst and a homosexual, epitomizing the kind of hopeful rapprochement between medical science and bourgeois queer lifestyles on which this polemical project was founded.[57] When, during the following year, the Wolfenden Committee embarked on its major inquiry into male homosexuality, it followed this lead by securing evidence not only from doctors, criminologists, and psychiatrists but also from several prominent homosexuals themselves. The authoritative respectability of these latter men—including Peter Wildeblood, who made liberal use of both sexology and psychoanalysis in his careful apology—was already deeply attuned with those professionalized experts who together pointed the committee toward its final recommendation: the decriminalization of private consensual sex between two men over the age of twenty-one.

Recent commentators have stressed the hegemonic nature of this reformist project and of the homosexual citizen it worked hard to design.[58] The mobilization of "objective" science concealed the deeply bourgeois cultural imperatives through which it was defining the "genuine" homosexual. In addition, by ring-fencing the limits of what these latter words could mean, other modes of queer urban experience—particularly those of the working-class quean and the laddish young workingman—became firmly reemphasized as a psychopathological social problem in urgent need of redress. Yet, for those able to align themselves with this highly selective model, a respite had now been publicly offered from the catalog of actions, movements, and situated desires that constituted earlier postwar accounts of metropolitan male vice. Such behaviors could now be interpreted as only a contingent aspect of urban queer experience, since the essential locus of homosexuality had been displaced from London's streets and public houses into the more private spaces of the sufferer's own mind. According to this logic, any lingering displays of public immorality became a variable matter of individual self-discipline with no necessary connection to one's sexual proclivity.

"Environmental Factors" and the Revenge of the Commodity

While thus reinforcing hegemonic social investments in public restraint, private discretion, and ordered civic-mindedness, the progressive impact of psychology and criminology complexified earlier attempts to combat manifest instances of unruly queer behavior. Calls to stamp out metropolitan male vice had focused on the city's streets, parks, and public toilets, but such strategies were deeply complicated by psychoanalytic etiologies in two distinctive ways. On the one hand, they confirmed an existing set of anxieties around the pernicious and lasting influence of the family home—for if substandard parenting or other environmental mishaps could permanently arrest a boy's sexual development, then the domestic environment became critical if the health of future citizens was to be properly secured.[59] Yet, at the same time, any form of sanctioned queer morality premised on discretion and restraint required a more careful supervision of even the most prosaic everyday spaces. As the Wolfenden Committee made clear, no serious attempt need be made to alter the direction of a homosexual's proclivities providing that he was sufficiently well adjusted to the norms and values of society. "As often as not," its final report urged, "it will be a matter of guiding the patient to help himself, not only by personal influence but also by helping to manipulate environmental factors."[60]

Although the planners and architects of the early reconstruction had assumed that civic sensibilities would naturally coalesce within a visibly ordered and reformed urban environment, the ideological ascendency of the psychological disciplines returned attention once more to the perpetual moral dangers that lurked silently in the shadows. On these terms, the metropolis became reinscribed as a site of instability and solicitation, in which the flickering lure of its commercial surfaces was a permanent temptation to its susceptive queer subjects. As Wolfenden understood, this involved attending on a more intricate level to the spatial orchestration of familiar quotidian rituals.

One key area in which these tensions were felt involved those situations in which a boy or young man might gain his knowledge about sex. Psychologists and doctors all heartily concurred that the ready availability of honest sexual information was vital in the fight against psychic maladjustment—a project to which socially progressive publishing houses such as Penguin Books Ltd. were eager to contribute. But at the same time, reading itself was emerging as a practice in need of more delicate spatial management, as evidenced within the postwar recentralization of the municipal branch library as both a key institution within the public provision of culture and a central site for the performance of local community life. These two endeavors were in fundamental sympathy and operated through a shared and somewhat delicate set of assumptions about how reading should be made available to London's citizens and the forms of sexual enlightenment to which it might lead. Perhaps unsurprisingly, all of this became elaborately spatialized through a developing set of prescriptive geographies that sought to manage the public presence of the book, the manner of its visual display, and therefore the terms through which it made its appeal to the browsing reader-citizen.

Yet this delicate construction was soon to be challenged by an alternative, less stable economy of everyday reading practices. As the 1950s progressed, the increased prevalence of garish mass-market paperbacks within London's newsagents and bookstalls seemed to advertise a less worthy set of textual pleasures, rooted not in the calm attainment of dispassionate knowledge but in the breathless rush of the ephemeral cheap thrill. In response, Britain's cultural gatekeepers worked hard to devalue such disruptive commercial blatancy, stigmatizing such paperbacks via a deeply heteronormative code of readerly (im)maturity. Yet such books continued to loiter provocatively within the city's busy public spaces, where they also facilitated new possibilities of queer self-understanding that were strongly antagonistic to the more sanctioned model of homosexual citizenship currently being developed elsewhere. In many ways, the challenges presented by the mass-market paperback were exactly those of the postwar spiv: an unapologetic urban showmanship and a shameless solicitation of deregulated desires. Yet the anxiety they produced was also rooted in these books' seeming ability to leave their street-corner habitat and cross over ruinously into the private sanctity of the reader's family home.

The postwar popularization of psychoanalytic frameworks had already focused a greater attention on the dangerous consequences of domestic mismanagement. Yet, paradoxically, bourgeois imperatives continued to position the home as the sole domain of legitimate sexual expression, made respectable as a site of moral training only by its privacy and impermeability to the unwarranted public gaze. Within this climate, heightened political importance became attached to another cultural arena: that of interior design. As its emphatic foregrounding at both *Britain Can Make It* and the *South Bank Exhibition* clearly testified, reforming and redesigning one's own domestic spaces was a central component within early postwar citizenship. If individuals could be directed in—and through—the basic arrangement and decoration of their rooms, then family life might be rendered more open to expert supervision without requiring an intrusive invasion by impersonal agencies of state.

Yet, paradoxically, the pedagogical importance attached to interior design during the reconstruction seems to have offered a surprising level of freedom to London's queer men. The mental abstractions and functional projections inherent to "planning" one's rooms presented a challenge to more traditional understandings of domestic space, which understood the decoration of an interior as an accumulation of bodily traces, dialectically accreted through the practices of ordinary life. The new "contemporary" style—propagated in earnest by the COID—marked a shift away from this ingrained and deeply patriarchal moral economy, toward a more cybernetic paradigm based on communication and control. Yet while this sought to make the domestic sphere more amenable as a site of instruction and order, it also promised to unshackle queer men from a more tortuous relationship to their own interiors, whereby any decorative anomaly was always ready to stand as evidence of an implied, if absent, set of routine sexual perversions. Thus, in the 1961 film *Victim*—Basil Dearden's careful articulation of the case for homosexual reform—it would be the most "contemporary" out of all the film's interiors that became the setting for a new type of mature and modern queerness that fused social responsibility with an inherent appreciation of functional design aesthetics.

During the later 1950s, these new possibilities would be further enhanced by the rise of the Do-It-Yourself (DIY) "movement," a largely self-conscious creation of industrial manufacturers who sought to reframe their products within the seductive context of enjoyable leisure, rather than one of necessity or work. In the present context, DIY is significant because, like the mass-market paperback, it revealed the destabilizing effects of the more assertive form of consumer capitalism that was developing by the end of the decade. Thus, while largely following the decorative prescriptions previously established by the COID, DIY introduced new and disruptive dynamics into the home that corroded the simple postwar formulation of domestic space as a potential site of programmed instruction. In celebrating the pleasures of the laboring body, it introduced a degree of homosocial ambiguity into the familial suburban home, while also making possible new and unexpected forms of domestic queer self-creation.

Ultimately, the arrival of the colorful mass-market paperback, and of the paint pots and wallpapers of Do-It-Yourself, demonstrated—in public and private space, respectively—a latent weakness within those strategies of spatial management on which the planners and officials of postwar reconstruction had premised their visions of a lasting social order. London's wartime architects had sought to stabilize the metropolis by reforming the citizen's structural relationship to the ordinary built environment, inserting them into cyclical routines, a spatialized patchwork of prescribed social practices, and by embedding them within an aesthetic order that necessarily fostered a more profound civic sensibility. All of this, of course, assumed the effective insertion of a layer of bureaucratic governance between the individual and the market—be it through the intervention of the Regional Planning Board (which, Abercrombie proposed, would oversee every square inch of London's redevelopment) or through the work of the COID (who would reeducate consumers' basic aesthetic tastes, teaching them to reject the shiny surfaces of superficial decoration in favour of more functional and fitting manufactured commodities).[61]

In many ways, the homosexual citizen of the mid-1950s had been fashioned according to these logics. Willfully renouncing the flickering temptations of the modern city—its cheap commercial thrills and sexualized economies—he would embrace a more controlled mode of metropolitan engagement based on rational purpose and committed participation. Yet, as early austerity turned into the affluence of the later 1950s, the irrepressible dynamics of capitalist accumulation complicated this type of normative response. Instead, a new and more expansive form of urban sensibility took root within the city, more playfully engaged with the ephemeral temporalities of the metropolitan economy, its decentered mobilities and fragmented performances. London's younger queer men were by no means unique in their ability to exploit the city's assertive commercial cultures and media opportunities. Yet amid the proliferation of images, sounds, performances, and products, a different type of queer selfhood was emerging that had far less interest in the projected coherencies and reformist agendas of popular psychoanalysis. The gaudy, sexualized images exhibited at the bookstall and the latest tips for doing up your living room were just two small elements within an expansive urban environment, out of which queer men could assemble together more viable and expressive ways of being in—and relating to—the postwar metropolis.

The Way to Go Round

These variant models, the residual tensions between them, and the various spatial formations within which these were played out are explored across this book's five chapters. In the first of these, "Reconstructing Everyday Life in the Atomic Age," I return to Abercrombie's twin plans for London, as well as the *Britain Can Make It* and *South Bank Exhibitions,* to examine in more detail the prescriptive logics around space, time, movement, and repetition that underscored the reconstruction vision of an ordered postwar metropolis. Through the careful arrangement of the city's functional zones and an attention to the construction of individual trajectories, planners and designers sought to lay the groundwork for an urban environment that would disavow the structural contradictions of midcentury capitalism and ensure a form of social stability within the decades to come. Yet crucially, these spatial structures were marked by a concerted effort to reformulate time, to use cycles of repetition to preclude the possibility of unplanned conflict and thus perpetuate a city beyond the reach of history. Thus, for all the attention to the past contained within both the London Plans and the component pavilions of the South Bank, both gestured toward a future that was deeply ahistorical.

A key object of analysis in this first chapter is the figure of the solitary atom, a recurrent motif within reconstruction texts and exhibitions, and a key device for explaining to the public the basics of nuclear physics. Yet the atom in this period also functioned as something of a map, a model for explaining—through an endemic confusion of scales—how certain structures of center and periphery, trajectory and repetition, perpetuated the stability of the basic material world. Exploring the presentation of this atom and its pedagogical centrality reveals an ideological device that was deeply in consonance with the more grounded projections of London's postwar planners. It also suggests that the basic spatial logics at the heart of reconstruction may have functioned as an ambiguous mechanism for working through the traumatic experience of life under bombardment.

If chapter 1 explores the social imperatives that became attached to the everyday performance of ordinary space and time, then the second chapter, "The Perversity of the Zigzag: The Criminality of Queer Urban Desire," examines how the urban machinations of London's queer men would soon become figured as a malignant mode of spatial criminality. It thus returns to the tabloid moral panic around metropolitan "male vice" in the early 1950s, tracing out the complex geographies by which queer male behavior was marked as a demonic social force. Ultimately, the challenges posed by such practices involved a complex imagined synthesis of deregulated consumption, disordered interclass sociality, illicit choreographies, and conspiratorial sign systems. The sexual criminality of the metropolitan pervert was thus emphatically rendered as a multifarious form of deviancy—at once economic, spatial, social, and semiotic.

Yet, while these dynamics could seemingly provoke abject panic, they also hinted at a certain tediousness within normative forms of postwar urban citizenship. To this end, the chapter also analyzes one of the most popular British films of 1951, *The Lavender Hill Mob* (Charles Crichton, 1951), starring Alec Guinness and Stanley Holloway. Now canonized as one of the great "Ealing Comedies," this film was penned by T. E. B. Clarke shortly after he finished work on *The Blue Lamp,* and in both its overall dynamics and in several key scenes, the two films have a great deal in common. Yet, freed from the conventions of realist melodrama, *The Lavender Hill Mob* could both play up the constrictions of postwar spatial citizenship and take a more obvious joy in their criminal subversion. Further, in the characterizations of its two protagonists, Holland (Guinness) and Pendlebury (Holloway)—as well as in the uncanny articulations of its central narrative—the film provided something of an essay on the model of queer criminality that would soon be configured in the courtroom and on the newsstand. That this film could go on to become one of the most enjoyed

British comedies of all time suggests a fundamental ambivalence about reconstruction spatial logics, the defiance of which the film identifies with a
queerness that is barely kept below the surface.

Chapter 3, "Trial by Photobooth: The Public Face of the Homosexual
Citizen," explores the concerted attempts made during the mid-1950s to
formulate a model of acceptable homosexuality. The nascent homosexual
citizen as codified by Westwood, Wildeblood, Wolfenden, and others was a
highly contradictory construction. Born out of a set of class-marked assumptions about how to move through and respond to the urban environment,
his claim to a valid membership of the metropolitan community was inextricably expressed through the imperatives of privacy and discretion.
Homosexual men who looked to this model were thus interpolated into a
fraught and impossible spatial structure, in which any attempt to register
a legitimate public presence simultaneously marked them out as a socially
disruptive force.

This chapter delves deeper into this contradiction by exploring the
work of the painter Francis Bacon and, in particular, his postwar engagement with the automatic photobooth. The photobooth would become a
timely and significant presence within London, taking up residence within
its major bus and Tube stations from the mid-1950s onwards. It soon established itself as a central—but always highly unstable—postwar apparatus
for the visualization of self. Its aesthetic output and universal accessibility
were deeply in tune with dominant forms of social democratic citizenship, yet it remained a situated apparatus that could also be used to subvert
such notions of sovereign subjectivity. Within this context, Bacon's own use
of the photobooth reveals the paradox inherent in presenting a legitimate
homosexual selfhood in this period—a preoccupation that also ran through
many of his canvases. Placing this work in relation to a number of other
contemporary images—including two photographs of Peter Wildeblood and
the identikit reconstructions of the "A6 murderer"—reveals how Bacon
could articulate these contradictions and announce the wider affective structures that many men must surely have negotiated as they tried to find a
place in London's public arenas.

Chapter 4, "Of Public Libraries and Paperbacks: The Sexual Geographies of Reading," turns to the issue of "environmental factors" and the
prescriptive geographies that surrounded the public life of books. By contrasting the spatial economy of London's municipal branch libraries to that
of the mass-market paperback, it reveals the complex conceptual imperatives

that librarians and policy makers invested into the act of reading itself. In particular, reading came to be understood as having its own internal structures of time, space, movement, and trajectory, all of which became mapped onto the physical relationship of the book on display to the body and mind of its prospective consumer. The irruption into London of the "gaudy" paperback challenged these constructions and led to an investment in heteronormative—and ultimately psychoanalytic—notions of both readerly and sexual development.

At the start of the 1960s, all this was played out within two separate trials to take place in London, both of which tried to establish the legitimate sexual possibilities of the metropolitan book: the failed prosecution of Penguin Books Ltd. for its planned publication of D. H. Lawrence's *Lady Chatterley's Lover* (1960); and the successful conviction of two queer lovers, John (later Joe) Orton and Kenneth Halliwell, for the theft and mutilation of books from the Islington and Hampstead branch libraries (1962). Returning to these two incidents, the chapter unravels the sexual orderings that governed the postwar visibility of books and the attendant enlightenment to which they could lead, as well as the ways in which queer men could challenge this by attending to the solicitations of the brash urban commodity.

The fifth and final chapter, "Life in the Cybernetic Bedsit: Interior Design and the Homosexual Self," looks at the postwar importance of the home and the widespread deployment of "contemporary" interior design as an indirect method of domestic social management. In particular, it relates the public design advice of the COID to the theoretical writings of the queer computer scientist Alan Turing, not only to reveal the computational logics already at work within the color schemes and contrasting textures of the contemporary style, but to suggest how these interiors—despite setting out to program a more respectable family life—incidentally created new freedoms for certain queer men. This chapter also considers the impact of Do-It-Yourself on this schema and finally finds evidence, in the vast collages pasted by Orton and Halliwell onto the walls of their Islington bedsit, of a wider corporeal expressiveness that could open up domestic space to far less manageable modes of domestic habitation.

Finally, the book concludes by surveying how, by the later 1950s, certain queer men were finding new ways of orienting themselves within the metropolitan landscape, by subverting its administrative logics and pursuing more readily its fragmented images and commodified surfaces. Turning to the queer journalist and novelist Colin MacInnes, and considering his work in relation to that of the so-called Independent Group of artists and designers, it finds evidence of an increased engagement with metropolitan consumerism, expansive urban media, and proliferating forms of popular culture. Such queer men were not alone in exploiting these emergent possibilities of urban sociality and self-creation. But their distinctive approaches to the commercial metropolis signaled both the ways in which queer urban politics would develop in Britain and the contradictions that would emerge as the ensuing decades wore on.

chapter 1

RECONSTRUCTING EVERYDAY
LIFE IN THE ATOMIC AGE

Are we to continue the old haphazard methods or are we to work to a plan
so that every new construction, road or open space fits into and builds up
gradually an ordered, more healthy and more beautiful town?

—PATRICK ABERCROMBIE and J. H. FORSHAW,
The County of London Plan, 1943

A few hours spent here will make you a better shopper, and help you later
on to build a better home and choose better clothes for your money.

Now look carefully at the Exhibition plan overleaf and note what you
are going to see.

—1d *Guide* to *Britain Can Make It* exhibition, 1946

After the blitz had devastated great swaths of London, but long before
final victory had been secured, planners, designers, and policy makers were
already presenting its inhabitants with ambitious projections of what life
would be like in the postwar metropolis. The reformist potential of modern
urban planning had become accepted by young architects and designers
between the wars, but such ideas were now loudly promoted within a new
hegemonic social vision. The public was informed of how uncoordinated
building in earlier decades had produced great disparities of wealth and
squalor within London, as well as social fragmentation and aesthetic disorder. Soon, however, the postwar city would arise from the rubble. Decent
housing, modern new schools, and safe municipal precincts would enrich
the life of all London's citizens and revitalize their sense of metropolitan
belonging. As the strength of this rhetoric testified, the built environment
had now been identified as a legitimate object of public management, as
central to the production of an optimal society as welfare, education, and
the provision of public culture.

Crucial to the gestation of this reformist orthodoxy was the figure of Patrick Abercrombie, Professor of Town Planning at University College, London, and a leading planning expert since before the First World War. His *County of London Plan* (1943), commissioned by the London County Council (LCC) and cowritten with County Architect J. H. Forshaw, provided a comprehensive scheme for repairing and revitalizing the central London area.[1] Abercrombie's sole-authored companion volume for the Ministry of Town and Country Planning, *The Greater London Plan* (1944), extended this vision out to London's suburbs and considered its relation to the wider region and beyond.[2] Both texts revolved around an ambitious program to decant over a million Londoners from the overcrowded slums to the east and south of the city, and rehouse them within eight satellite "new towns" to be built outside the Green Belt. Just as radical, however, was Abercrombie's projected reworking of the city's social texture. Victorian investments in laissez-faire economics, he argued, had left a disordered, congested, and segregated city. In its place, Abercrombie would return London to its component archaic settlements, creating a network of organic districts that would—once supported by sufficient land-use and traffic regulations—create greater social integration and community identity.

Such postwar projections assumed an inextricable confluence between social and spatial forms of order. The remolding of London was seen as a basic prerequisite not only for producing metropolitan cohesion, but for recentering the city as the vibrant capital of both a revitalized national social democracy and its associated Commonwealth. As Abercrombie made clear, London's future hinged on whether the various opportunities presented by its devastation could be seized upon and exploited, repairing in the process the decades of uncoordinated development, speculative profiteering, and general deterioration that had left it teetering on the brink of crisis even before the bombs had begun to fall. The rationale for this planning, Abercrombie insisted, was also one of brute economics. London as it stood was choked by uncoordinated flows of traffic and people; it thus needed to be made more efficient, to eliminate waste and ensure productivity. Yet he steadfastly refused to separate such considerations from the grounded experience of Londoners themselves. As with any living organism, the city's efficiency was aligned with its general health and happiness, and this could only be achieved by excising its slums, creating more parkland, and removing dirty industry from its residential areas.

Such self-conscious modernism, of course, should not obscure the deeper and more conservative dynamics contained therein. As the sociologist T. H. Marshall would have already discerned by 1949, the "total planning" of the mid-1940s sought social stability by improving the conditions of its very poorest groups, bringing them deeper into the fold of the national community while relegitimating their position at the bottom of the class structure.[3] The blueprints of planners, therefore, sought to embed a design for community living within the reformed urban environment, as a set of collective engagements and activities that would interpellate all citizens into a performance of civic participation. Reconstruction planning was thus always more than just a pragmatic desire to patch up the city and improve its efficiency. It also sought to provide a network of spaces for a form of daily life that might erase at a stroke the kind of class antagonism and political agitation that had threatened British cities during the interwar years.

During the immediate postwar period, these dynamics could be traced within the rhetoric and layouts of a number of high-profile pedagogical exhibitions. At *Britain Can Make It,* staged during 1946 in the Victoria and Albert Museum in Kensington, visitors were taught how to appreciate the functional design qualities of British manufactures as they circulated en masse around its startlingly modern displays. Organized by the newly formed Council of Industrial Design (COID)—a body under the auspices of the Board of Trade—such scenes of material abundance struck a chord amid a climate of ongoing austerity, and between May and December, almost one and a half million visitors passed through its halls.[4] Many of the display innovations used at *Britain Can Make It* were subsequently repeated as part of the *South Bank Exhibition,* the centerpiece of the 1951 Festival of Britain, which was itself visited by almost eight and a half million people between May and September. Built on a site freshly reclaimed from the river Thames, it purported to tell visitors "the story of British contributions to world civilisation through the medium of tangible things" via sixteen themed pavilions that were themselves a striking introduction to progressive modern architecture.[5] In addition, the buildings of the South Bank were connected by a network of plazas, precincts, and elevated walkways that emulated the municipal civic spaces that Abercrombie had proposed as the focal points of each remodeled neighborhood district. More than anything, the power of both the *South Bank Exhibition* and *Britain Can Make It* lay in how they combined their ideological messages of national tradition, social progress, freedom, and community with an affective experience of collective participation that spatially enacted those very same values.

These two events and the twin London plans were only the most notable elements within a much wider program of social reconstruction that sought to reconfigure the individual's relationship to the reformed built environment. At base, this refashioning hoped to instill in Londoners a grounded appreciation of their future city for its order, stability, and fitness for purpose. This, reformers hoped, would inspire a form of purposive civic sensibility, a new form of quotidian citizenship, as people enacted their affiliation to the local community through the ordinary practices of their daily lives. Yet a more coercive logic was already embedded within these new environments that worked to isolate the individual and insert him or her into a prescribed set of preprogrammed routines. Uncovering these more covert strategies is the real concern of this chapter, for while they helped to articulate a dominant form of prescriptive spatial citizenship in this period, they also established the conceptual parameters through which queer male subjectivities would be both remolded and contested during the following two decades.

As commentators have noted, reconstruction planners celebrated the picturesque tradition of the eighteenth century and sought to replicate its playfulness and visual surprise within their own spatial layouts, as a suitably indigenous answer to the impersonal abstractions of international modernism.[6] Yet this increased attention to movement and trajectory belied the deeper interest in the planned environment as a tool of social manipulation. Reconstruction planning was also the formative crucible for a cybernetic mode of urban governance in which social order, stability, and national cohesion were pursued through the fragmentation of the populace into mobile individuals and their insertion into different patterns of circulation. By discretely spatializing daily activities and ordering these within prescribed routines, planning visions tacitly worked to project a city outside of historical time in which conflict, change, and social upheaval were perpetually kept at bay by an endless repetition. Hence, these urban environments invoked a new form of spatial citizenship that was itself an important mechanism for imagining London's future security. Abercrombie's plans, *Britain Can Make It,* and the *South Bank Exhibition* came together to promulgate a similar moral imperative about how and how not to move through everyday urban space. Thus, if the London plans mapped out a set of imagined choreographies that might stabilize life in the postwar metropolis, then the two exhibitions offered London's citizens an experiential taster of how these choreographies might feel to live out.

In a very real sense, of course, Abercrombie's plans and the wider urban visions of which they were a part remained firmly in the realm of science fiction. Shortages of labor, finance, and basic raw materials meant that little was built in the aftermath of the war, and from 1951 Tory housing policy would favor deregulation and speedy cost-effective building over the more attentive social planning favored by Abercrombie.[7] Similarly, early new towns such as Stevenage and Harlow became mainly repositories for working-class newlyweds, who—severed from the kinship networks of the old inner city—often experienced social isolation and were forced to adapt to the bourgeois domestic assumptions built into the architecture of their new model homes.[8]

Yet, despite this haphazard implementation, these reconstruction programs had a massive cultural influence and effectively set the moral agenda for imaginings of British metropolitan life well into the 1950s. Arriving in public consciousness during a moment of great national insecurity and trauma, the benefits of town planning were propagated through an extensive range of popular media, including books, booklets, education packs, press articles, and exhibitions.[9] Promotional films and newsreels communicated to war-weary cinemagoers the virtues of functional zoning, variable housing, and pedestrianized precincts, while visitors to the *South Bank Exhibition* could catch a boat downstream to the Lansbury Estate at Poplar, a "live exhibition" of architecture and planning hastily erected by the LCC to showcase one of Abercrombie's model neighborhoods in action.[10]

As Frank Mort has shown, the force of such planning pedagogy lay not only in the terms of its rationalist address. It also reworked older, more emotive understandings of the decaying Victorian city as a breeding ground of social misery and moral danger.[11] Dark, high-contrast photographs of overcrowded slums were thus presented alongside airy sunlit shots of London's historic parkland, while designs for new shopping precincts were lightly drawn in pen and washed with bright colors to suggest the joyful, clean modernity of the future life therein. Such images proclaimed a new civic order that inextricably fused the aesthetic with the moral, establishing an emphatic cultural agenda that continued to shape both official discourse and the popular media. This sense of a collective moral project was reinforced via the recurrent motif of addressing the "common Londoner"—always part of a metropolitan community—through the theatrical staging of an ongoing dialogue. In *Proud City* (1945), for instance, a film made by the Crown Film Unit to explain the *County of London Plan,* Lord Latham, the leader of the LCC, looks into the camera and announces:

> What we want to know now is: what do you, the people of London, think about it? That is why we want you to think about the plan, to talk it over amongst yourselves and then to let us have your ideas about it.

From his office in County Hall, the film then cuts to a number of representative Londoners—the working-class housewife at her sink, the young boy playing cricket in the road, the lower-middle-class typist sitting at her desk—to interpolate their eager questions against Latham's assured replies. This sense of popular participation also structured the design and literature of events such as *Britain Can Make It* and the *South Bank Exhibition.* Visitors were constantly asked to interact with the displays, whether through design quizzes, imaginative identifications, or by simply pausing to appreciate the inherent qualities of such marvelous new environments.

Yet crucially, these texts and exhibitions persistently attached their presentations of civic renewal and democratic inclusion to specific logics of movement, sociality, and everyday routine, themselves cast as the necessary means for ensuring the vitality of the city. In short, Abercrombie's London plans, *Britain Can Make It,* and the *South Bank Exhibition* coalesced to demand a new mode of participatory urban citizenship—a reformed way of engaging with, understanding, and moving through the built environment—that itself provided the conceptual mechanism for projecting an image of social consensus and for resolving the contradictions of London's continuing economic disparities. Finding its ultimate validation in the figure of the atom—a ubiquitous motif within reconstruction culture and an insistent model of how structured circulations lay at the heart of the natural order—such patterns of prescribed routine came together to feed a powerful postwar fantasy of a brave new city to come, impervious to historical trauma and the kind of terrible social crises so recently endured during the blitz.

The *County of London* and *Greater London Plans*: Reprogramming London

Planning hagiographies tend to celebrate Patrick Abercrombie for his promotion of zoning principles and his ambitious schemes to remove more than a million Londoners from the overcrowded inner city.[12] Yet his major attempt to redraw the moral contours of the postwar metropolis lay in his close attention to the intricate fabric of urban communities. Early in the twentieth century, Raymond Unwin and the Garden City Association had argued that a healthy town required the integration of members drawn from all social classes, a principle that Abercrombie reworked via the U.S. planner Clarence Perry's more recent conception of the sustainable local neighborhood.[13] For Abercrombie, such interclass neighborhoods were the foundational unit of metropolitan community, an assertion that allowed him to endow his London with the nostalgic qualities of preindustrial village life, while also effecting a sly scalar confusion—endemic to the reconstruction—that figured the neighborhood as a microcosm of the integrated nation at the heart of welfare-state ideologies. Thus, the *Greater London Plan* denounced the speculative development of London's interwar suburbs for extracting young middle-class couples out of the inner city and for leaving behind impoverished communities segregated along axes of age and class. Against this, Abercrombie asserted the planner's moral authority to overrule such free-market profiteering and to reconfigure the city's demography to provide "for a greater mingling of the different groups of London's society."[14] Unchecked private building, he argued, should immediately stop, and middle-class districts were to be forcibly opened up to people from a much wider spectrum of occupations and incomes. Large gardens and private playing fields were to be appropriated for public recreation, while the Georgian squares of London's West End would remain without those railings recently removed to provide iron for the war effort.[15] Even more radically, "the so-called 'high-class' lodging houses" in the districts around the Royal Parks would also be requisitioned and converted into more modest flats, "with rentals within the reach of the normal Londoner whether in factory, office or shop."[16]

Mayfair and its environs were thus to be transformed by an influx of West End shop assistants, clerks from the City, and workers from the nearer East End factories, refashioning them in turn into more dynamic and inclusive metropolitan districts. Here, as elsewhere, Abercrombie's rhetoric assumed the existence of a willful interclass sociality that would bind all citizens within their reformed localities, a dynamic most neatly captured within the *Greater London Plan*'s eight proposed new towns, which provided an exciting opportunity to forge such communities from scratch. These were primarily devised to extract working-class families from the overcrowded squalor of their inner-city slums, and Abercrombie remained adamant that "the clergyman, the doctor, the bank manager, the factory manager, the retired person and many others" would soon move out, along with "shop-keepers and business folk," all eager to engage with the rich corporate life on offer within these new municipalities.[17]

Here, as in those central areas made more amenable by such an exodus, Abercrombie advocated the building of new communal precincts to instill in local citizens "a sense of civic pride and of healthy corporate life."[18] At the approximate geographic center of each district, these were imagined as being a mixture of municipal and commercial buildings—shops, markets, museums, churches, schools, community centers, public libraries, and post offices—that would facilitate "the closer integration of individual communities" by providing a universal focal point for the "vital elements in community life."[19] Yet the terms of this integration were never fully worked out, and Abercrombie merely asserted—somewhat simplistically—that these hubs were "points to which the inhabitants [would] automatically gravitate for their social, educational and cultural activities," an impersonal and mechanistic metaphor that elided questions of agency and difficult issues of individual will, choice, or desire.[20] Here, as elsewhere within the plans, London became cast as a dynamic system of forces that would, through its own mechanics, draw citizens in toward these neighborhood centers and the meaningful sociality they promoted and sustained.

This important tension around individual agency hints at the wider cultural assumptions contained within this influential vision of London as a thriving network of local interclass communities. Throughout his plans, Abercrombie made a persistent recourse to job titles as the marker of social difference, suggesting a hierarchical society bound by class, but one that repeatedly pointed toward soothing images of peaceful consensus rather than any real conditions of antagonism or dissent. Ultimately, this contradiction was made possible by a complex discursive mechanism buried deep within his plans for London that slyly doubled the conceptual framing of its inhabitants' existence. While occupationally stratified as a member of an economic community, Abercrombie also presented "the Londoner" as an abstract, generic unit around which new forms of spatial management could tacitly be devised. Hence, the London plans were founded on a basic modular unit: the individual's minimum "general living conditions"—defined as a fixed quantity of essential "living space" and "play space" per head of population.[21] Londoners, it was claimed, should live no more than 136 to an acre and with four acres of recreational open space per thousand people (or seven acres if the Green Belt was factored in), a requirement explicitly privileged over other industrial or military considerations.[22]

This motif of the individuated, abstract Londoner became the linchpin around which a consensual metropolitan order could be structurally devised. These determining measures of "living" and "play" space were symptomatic of a wider approach to urban space that remapped it through the quotidian activities of its residents' bodies. In part, this was an inheritance from a tradition of geotechnic regional planning rooted in Patrick Geddes's work at the turn of the century, which understood the landscape in terms of sympathetic human use.[23] Popularized via the Land Utilisation Survey of the early 1930s, this approach heavily inflected the plans' presentation of the Green Belt, a sizable ring of rural land encircling the metropolis that had, since 1938, been progressively bought up by local authorities to safeguard it from being built on. As Abercrombie and Forshaw explained, "what happens to the countryside around London is of great importance to the County, for it forms the main place of week-end recreation for walking, bicycling, picnics, etc., and for holidays of short duration." Only the Green Belt, they argued, could provide "an effective antidote to town-dwelling," for it offered a level of openness not available within the more modest urban park or parkway, while also supplying valuable fresh produce for the Londoner's table.[24] Through all of this, the intrinsic value of the Green Belt was conceived only via an explicitly functional relationship with the activities of the metropolitan citizen, such that even Abercrombie's urges toward environmental protection were made as calls to prevent its aesthetic degradation for future generations.[25] In approaching such sites through the lens of appropriate human activity, therefore, the plans could position Greater London and its inhabitants within a set of symbiotic restrictions. If their actions alone justified the creation or maintenance of these spaces, then such sites, in turn, became regulatory agents, firmly attached to a set of prescribed activities that they permitted or demanded.

Abercrombie's easy bisection of his Londoner's spatial needs into those of "living" and "play" suggests a foundational desire to remap the metropolis as just such a patchwork of disciplinary functions. By recognizing plots of land only through their presumed dominant usage, planners projected a spatial order that would actively preclude alternative practices or excessive urban behaviors. Sensing this disorder, the *County of London Plan* attacked the "veritable 'peppering' of whole [residential] districts with factories," which it viewed as "a hybrid type of development" that catastrophically intermixed the domestic and the industrial.[26] Instead, Abercrombie and Forshaw argued, such factories should be relocated within newly demarcated industrial estates, close to—but clearly separated from—all distilled areas of housing. Such zoning strategies combined the pragmatic desire to cleanse residential neighborhoods of noise, pollution, and traffic congestion with a more covert but entrenched urge to fix paid labor, domesticity, and recreational leisure within their own discrete locations, as distinct and manageable components of everyday life.

To this end, the London plans displayed a strong anxiety toward any urban spaces whose functional logic was unclear or confused. A major offender was the Children's Play Street, a 1930s innovation whereby nonresidential vehicles were forbidden from entering a side road to create a makeshift urban playground. Described by Abercrombie and Forshaw as "the worst recreation defect of the old London borough," the play street was unsatisfactory because it was "an attempt to use land for two incompatible purposes. Something properly designed for play in right relation to house and school should be provided."[27] The danger to children of slow-moving traffic could thus easily become expressed via the self-evident undesirability of two promiscuously intertwined spatial functions. This raised the specter of an unstable and improper form of play, disordered, unmanaged, and away from the normative field of adult supervision. A proper space for play was therefore needed—spatially defined and amenable to order—that would naturally coalesce as a space for proper play. As Abercrombie and Forshaw argued:

> There should be a systematic provision [of parkland, playing fields, and playgrounds] for all age groups, for strenuous exercise and retired leisure, for in school and out of school hours and the distribution must aim at the least possible walking distance.[28]

Leisure activities were not to be left to chance, but were to be already programmed into the built environment and to encompass all sectors of the urban community. As their concern here with "in school and out of school hours" suggests, this was not just a question of organizing space but of organizing time as well.

Throughout the plans, attention was paid less to the constitution of London's spaces per se than to how they would be used in practice, arranged as a contiguous sequence via the imagined routines of phantom generic Londoners. The city's transportation was to be rationalized accordingly, with road, rail, river, and air networks coordinated to regulate the flow of people between its component zones of work, home, and leisure. Roads were to be classified according to their type and speed of traffic, while the Green Belt would be fully integrated into this system through a network of landscaped parkways. This, of course, all sought to reduce congestion and improve the efficiency of London as an economic machine, but it also revealed the founding preoccupation with the movement of individuals. One of Abercrombie and Forshaw's major stated goals was to "reduc[e] the excessive amount of time and money now spent in travelling between residence and work place," later conceived within the *Greater London Plan* through the figure of an "average man," living on a suburban LCC estate, who currently traveled sixteen miles a day and spent twelve pounds a year on commuting.[29] As they declared, "the ideal situation for people to live in is within reasonable distance of their work but not in such close proximity that their living conditions are prejudiced by it," a "reasonable distance" presented less in terms of mileage than of the time their journey took.[30] This commuter was, of course, implicitly positioned as male and upper-working-class, for the plans often divided their imagined mobile Londoners along fault lines of class, age, and gender.[31] Yet, by equating their efficient metropolis with the journey of this generic commuter, Abercrombie and Forshaw developed a new level of administrative attentiveness to the individual's daily life. If each component space was ordered through its designated practice, then the motif of the Londoner's routine—further subdivided by whatever variables—arranged these activities and inserted them within a more totalized form of quotidian urban management.

Replanned London was thus ultimately founded on a certain construction of time. The radical proposal to rehouse shop assistants and factory workers within Mayfair's swanky apartment blocks was as much a strategy to reduce their journey time to the West End or docks as to reinvigorate the texture of their neighborhood communities. Temporal considerations could even take priority over zoning principles—small shopping centers for "day-to-day" need, for instance, were to be integrated into residential areas to reduce the housewife's trips to her local district precinct.[32] This attention to the wife's shopping trip, like that to her husband's twice-daily commute and the weekend jaunt they both took out into the Green Belt, revealed Abercrombie and Forshaw's investment in regular cycles of individuated spatial repetition. London's planned spaces—a totalized patch-work of ordered activities that extended over the entire surface of the city—were to be managerially effective by becoming sequestered into generic routines of work, domesticity, and authorized leisure. Aiming, albeit implicitly, toward a total organization of everyday time, the internal logics of the London plans provided an imaginative mechanism through which nondesignated activities might, quite literally, be prevented from taking place.

Abercrombie and Forshaw were particularly attentive to those interstitial portions of the day in which the disciplinary imperatives of functional zoning appeared at their weakest. The commute, as a period of neither work, domesticity, nor properly leisure, had already been identified as a site of anxiety—an unproductive time defined by no activity, and thus haunted by the specter of social instability. The weekday lunch hour was another such potentially-disruptive moment. The *County of London Plan* asserted that strips of landscaped parkland should be built between industrial estates and residential areas to provide "a valuable lunch-time recreation ground for factory workers," a measure beyond mere utility that clearly revealed an urge to manage this ambiguous hour by programming it, via its spatialization, into the ordinary weekday routine.[33] Indeed, as we shall see, both the daily commute and the weekday lunch hour would recur throughout the following decades as persistent sites for the imagining of metropolitan sexual disorder.

In a telling passage within the *Greater London Plan,* Abercrombie discusses the kinds of activities that were to be encouraged within the Green Belt. Citing the Ramblers' Association for its proper approach to spending time in the countryside, he writes: "When escapism becomes of a mass character it must be organised—otherwise it tends to defeat its own ends and leads to mutual disadvantage and untidiness."[34] This was, in itself, a typical attitude among bourgeois reformers to the problem of working-class leisure during the interwar period—a welcome extension of individual liberty, but something to be managed through collective pursuits.[35] Yet Abercrombie turned such prescriptions into the wider structuring principle of quotidian urban space. Londoners' routines as they moved across the city would likewise be a matter of both compulsion and consent. Everyday movement, by becoming inscribed within various repetitious circuits, would work toward a similar governance of social life, but one ultimately produced through voluntary consensus. If this form of complicit spatial citizenship could be rendered into the fabric of the built environment, then the daily functioning of an inclusive, yet resolutely hierarchical, social democracy would somehow be assured.

It was this, in the end, that allowed Abercrombie to propose his vision of London as a network of harmonious communities, for this careful coordination of everyday activities provided the mechanism for ordering the terms of such interclass mingling. When Abercrombie and Forshaw wrote of Londoners "automatically gravitat[ing]" to their local civic centers, this was the force to which they gestured. Each neighborhood, the plans proposed, was to center on its local primary school, whose catchment area of between six and ten thousand people would define that community's natural boundaries. A nucleus at once spatial and symbolic, this school would play "a far more important rôle in the life of the community than it does to-day," while also providing an exemplar of the kind of institutional contexts to which postwar urban sociality was here being restricted.[36]

More fundamentally, this investment in circuitous routine provided an additional, if much more abstract, vehicle through which urban cohesion might be pursued. Abercrombie argued that London still retained its foundational structure as an ancient network of villages, whose boundaries had been blurred by decades of uncoordinated development but whose importance still lay in the "strong local loyalty" its citizens felt to their own local districts. The planner's task, he believed, was to reinvigorate these archaic communities by carefully rerouting main roads around them and by marking out their edges with strips of landscaped parkland. As he and Forshaw wrote:

> The proposal is to emphasise the identity of the existing communities to increase their degree of segregation, and where necessary to reorganise them as separate and definite entities. . . . At the same time care would be taken to ensure that segregation of the communities was not taken far enough to endanger the sense of interdependence on the adjoining communities or on London as a whole.[37]

This objective reveals the profound conservatism lurking beneath the plans' apparent modernity. Abercrombie's return to these ancient municipalities produced a city that was both superficially historical and deeply ahistoric. To claim that London's component communities still remained as they always had was equally a prescription that they should stay the same forever. In this way, the traumas and upheavals of the preceding century could be quietly disavowed within a stronger assertion of continuity and tradition, cleansing the metropolis of its history of conflicts and smoothing out its existence into one long *durée*. By seeking to rebuild London outside the temporality of industrial modernity, therefore, Abercrombie planned to eviscerate history of its disruptive events.

This projection of continuity ultimately rested on those repetitious trajectories that were to be built into the fabric of the replanned city. Following their endless circulations around the metropolis, Londoners would keep historical time perpetually at bay. Their regular journeys between home, workplace, and recreational Green Belt would enact an eternal everyday that would, on its own terms, preclude the irruption of anything unforeseen. This dynamic gave the individual trajectories embedded within the London plans their insistent political imperative. As the foundational supports for both a new form of metropolitan community and a self-sustaining and stable social order, Abercrombie had devised a new morality of everyday movement in which civic participation and social responsibility became identified as a matter of following the circuits and pathways to be tacitly programmed into the fabric of the postwar city. This new figure of the abstract, mobile Londoner—the fundamental building block of urban reconstruction—would perform, through their ordinary daily living, the conditions of possibility for an imagined timeless peace.

Britain Can Make It and the *South Bank Exhibition*: Experiencing the New Urban Choreographies

Against the backdrop created by the extensive media promulgation of these ideas, *Britain Can Make It* and the *South Bank Exhibition* stood out for the way they offered Londoners a much clearer sense of just how it would feel to perform this new mode of civic participation. Within their layouts and innovative displays, they concretized those same dialectics of freedom and compulsion already articulated within popular planning discourse. Both exhibitions shared the plans' totalizing impulse and sought to project an everyday life that was similarly unified and comprehensive. *Britain Can Make It*'s "exhibition of design in everyday things" included consumer goods from all fields of British manufacturing, a complete vision of the material fabric of the visitor's life to come. Everything one needed was here on display and thus, the exhibition implied, no part of life remained outside. The *South Bank Exhibition* was similarly inclusive, offering a total survey of Britain, its "land," its "people," and its national traditions of discovery and enlightenment. While both were, of course, deeply selective in practice, such totalizing ambitions enhanced the exhibitions' cultural impact, helping to ensure their authority during an anxious time of national realignment and renewal.

Here again, these visions of the future were dependent upon the construction of a coherent, unitary, and firmly bounded space. *Britain Can Make It* was held in a closed section of the Victoria and Albert Museum in Kensington, while the *South Bank Exhibition* was built on a special site "so newly won from the river [Thames]," whose dynamic location gave the exhibition its name.[38] The inclusion of floor plans within all leaflets and guidebooks gave visitors an immediate impression of the exhibition space as a larger whole, while simultaneously encouraging them to locate themselves within it (Figures 4 and 6). Both shows reinforced this sense of spatial coherence via the meticulous coordination of all aspects of their design, weaving together everything from the most basic architecture to signposts and typography into a visually striking *Gesamtkunstwerk*.[39] As the *Architect's*

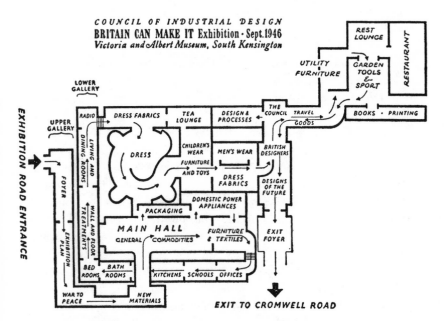

Figure 4. A prescribed trajectory through a totalized space: plan of the exhibition *Britain Can Make It,* Victoria and Albert Museum, 1946. Courtesy of Design Council/University of Brighton Design Archives.

Journal noted of the South Bank, this was "a still greater thing than architecture, a modern *background,* a twentieth century urban environment."[40]

At *Britain Can Make It,* commodities were grouped according to their function in separate rooms, such as "Domestic Power Appliances," "Travel Goods," "Garden Tools," and "Books." The *South Bank Exhibition* replicated this on a grander scale, dividing its exhibits between sixteen themed pavilions with monikers such as "Homes and Gardens," "The New Schools," and "Sport." Here was the same administrative urge that had structured Abercrombie's metropolis, the organized fragmentation of everyday life into a succession of functional zones. Both constructions also emulated the very latest in exhibition design, using a technique developed during smaller wartime Ministry of Information exhibitions of marshaling visitors along a predesignated route.[41] Built space was thus forcefully used to construct a predetermined pathway, emphatically reproduced on the ubiquitous floor plans. As in Abercrombie's replanned city, visitors were addressed through a linear succession of discrete activities, emphatically articulated within a preprogrammed order. The movement of the visitor became the central organizing principle of the whole designed environment.

After visiting *Britain Can Make It,* the industrialist John Nicholas wrote:

> I expected just another exhibition, a bewildering collection of products, laden with advertisement and set out with all those clever tricks of display with which we have become familiar. . . . Instead, and to my delight, I found myself moving through a vision, a succession of scenes each one obviously created by an artist, and all co-ordinated and controlled within a single conception.[42]

That Nicholas "found [himself] moving" shows just how these environments refused to leave movement to chance, rigorously controlling it to promote a passive experience that was also simultaneously one of collective participation. Herbert Read discerned this too when he compared *Britain Can Make It* to a "vast intestinal tract" where "traffic is peristaltic and progress inevitably in one direction," the crowd's motion encouraging involuntary movement as it propelled the visitors along their preordained pathway.[43] The exhibition's layout even included spaces explicitly signposted "You May Rest Here" to allow weary individuals a temporary respite from the perpetual collective flow.

These heavy investments in spatial regulation produced a certain anxiety over time for the exhibition's organizers. The *Guide* to *Britain Can Make*

It was particularly explicit in instructing visitors on how this should be managed:

> The Exhibition has many sections. On your first visit, look carefully at them all. If your time is limited, make up your mind in advance and stay longest in certain chosen sections. But in any case, after your first general survey, come again and concentrate specially on the things that interest you most.[44]

Tellingly, when the COID commissioned Mass-Observation to investigate the public's response to the show, it soon became preoccupied with exactly how long people were spending in each of its component displays. The resultant chart, "Percentage of Total Time in Exhibition Spent in Each Section" (Figure 5), compared the actual time visitors were taking to an established "normal walking time" determined by the comparative size of each individual section. This document is remarkable not only for its concern with monitoring visitor movement, but for its primary desire to establish a normative pattern against which those flows could be measured and appraised.

Similar devices were later deployed within the *South Bank Exhibition,* where maps of the site featured bold colored lines to indicate the route along which visitors should circulate (Figure 6). Yet, because of its much larger size, the exhibition's designers had to employ more subtle forms of control. The *Architectural Review* wrote of how, "as the visitor walks round it, with its thematic story unfolding before him, he might as well be exploring a subtly designed town"; but, like such a town, the South Bank's numerous piazzas, cafés, and other rest spots made the peristaltic marshaling of *Britain Can Make It* pragmatically impossible.[45] Hence, as the *Architectural Review* explained:

> There are many places where the town-planner needs to guide the pedestrian in one direction rather than another and prevent his feet straying where they shouldn't. Rather than rely on the solid wall or the forbidding high iron railing he can make use of many more imaginative means, generically known as "hazards," which, instead of putting a solid barrier in the pedestrian's path, *suggest* a barrier by subtle psychological means: by the use of slight changes of level, of water, of grass and of planting. The potential decorative value of these is illustrated in many parts of the exhibition.[46]

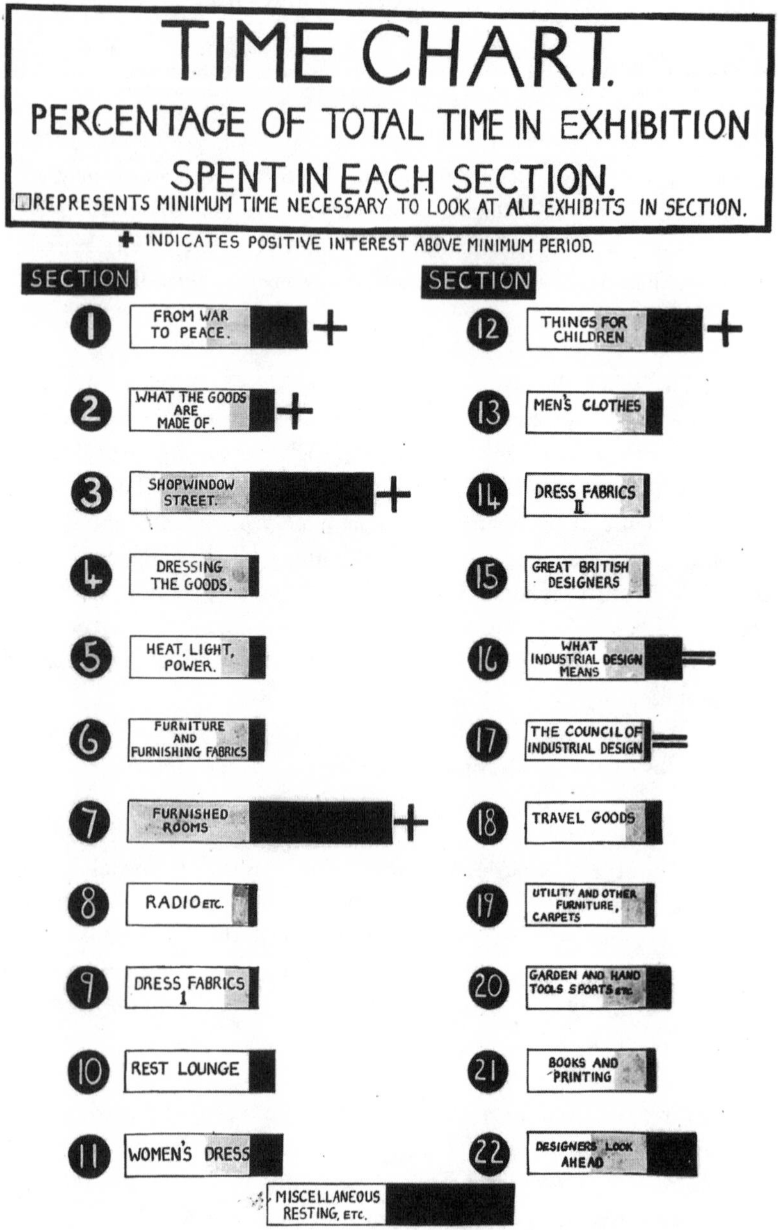

TIME CHART.

PERCENTAGE OF TOTAL TIME IN EXHIBITION SPENT IN EACH SECTION.

☐ REPRESENTS MINIMUM TIME NECESSARY TO LOOK AT **ALL** EXHIBITS IN SECTION.

✚ INDICATES POSITIVE INTEREST ABOVE MINIMUM PERIOD.

SECTION

1 FROM WAR TO PEACE. ✚

2 WHAT THE GOODS ARE MADE OF. ✚

3 SHOPWINDOW STREET. ✚

4 DRESSING THE GOODS.

5 HEAT, LIGHT, POWER.

6 FURNITURE AND FURNISHING FABRICS

7 FURNISHED ROOMS ✚

8 RADIO ETC.

9 DRESS FABRICS I

10 REST LOUNGE

11 WOMEN'S DRESS

SECTION

12 THINGS FOR CHILDREN ✚

13 MEN'S CLOTHES

14 DRESS FABRICS II

15 GREAT BRITISH DESIGNERS

16 WHAT INDUSTRIAL DESIGN MEANS

17 THE COUNCIL OF INDUSTRIAL DESIGN

18 TRAVEL GOODS

19 UTILITY AND OTHER FURNITURE, CARPETS

20 GARDEN AND HAND TOOLS SPORTS ETC

21 BOOKS AND PRINTING

22 DESIGNERS LOOK AHEAD

MISCELLANEOUS RESTING, ETC.

Figure 5. Monitoring deviations from "normal walking time": Mass-Observation, "Time Chart: Percentage of Total Time in Exhibition Spent in Each Section," 1946. Reproduced with permission of Curtis Brown Group Ltd., London, on behalf of the Mass Observation Archive. Copyright The Trustees of the Mass Observation Archive.

This terminology of guidance and suggestion captured precisely the paradox that underlay these spatial strategies. As the South Bank's "The Lion and The Unicorn" pavilion loudly proclaimed, Britain's libertarian tradition extended at least as far back as the signing of the Magna Carta; yet such freedoms were clearly in tension with the choreographies of compliance here being sketched out. "Hazards"—like the Ramblers' Association and the sequential zoning of basic urban practices—offered a partial resolution. Through the construction of a "guiding" environment, the visitor could be tacitly encouraged to move in certain ways, at certain speeds, and in certain directions. A form of spatial citizenship was again being created

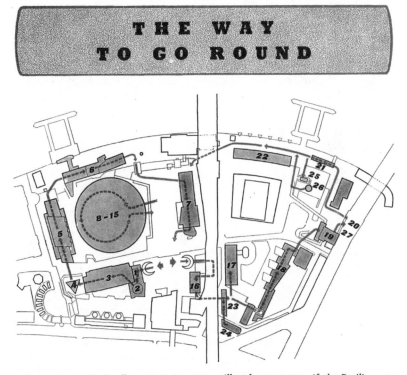

The Exhibition, which tells a continuous story, will make most sense if the Pavilions are visited in the order shown; but each Pavilion can be visited separately if so desired.

Figure 6. Narrative as a vehicle for ordering movement: "The Way to Go Round," in Ian Cox, *The South Bank Exhibition: A Guide to the Story It Tells* (London: His Majesty's Stationery Office, 1951), 4.

here, one that negotiated the fraught opposition between collective coercion and individual consent by embedding its contradictions within the reformed built environment.

This construction was fragile, however, and so the South Bank made an additional recourse to narrative as the organizing principle of its display. As the *Guide* explained:

> The Pavilions of the Exhibition are placed in a certain deliberate sequence on the ground as chapters are placed in a certain deliberate sequence in a book. And, within each Pavilion, the displays are arranged in a certain order, as paragraphs are arranged in a certain order within each chapter of a book.[47]

If, as the *Picture Post* wrote, the entire site really was "an imaginative attempt to work out our story in logical sequence from the very land itself to the homes we live in and the games we play today,"[48] then the *Guide* made clear that to ignore this trajectory was to turn away from being able to comprehend the force and dynamism of 1950s Britain:

> This is a free country; and any visitors who, from habit or inclination, feel impelled to start with the last chapter of the whole narrative and then zig-zag their way backwards to the first chapter, will be as welcome as anyone else. But such visitors may find that some of the chapters will appear mystifying and inconsequent.[49]

Following the twists of the exhibition's prescribed route, therefore, became a duty of national citizenship, by which participation in the collective flow enacted those very same values of Britishness that only such compliance would reveal. Already, however, a contradiction had appeared. Here, this imperative could only be stressed by invoking the specter of a mysterious spatial deviant, impelled by some strange proclivity to enter in at what should only have been the exit. Soon, as we shall see in the next chapter, this type of dissenting trajectory would become more firmly attached to notions of metropolitan queerness, itself repositioned as an antisocial mode of navigating through public space.

Owen Gavin and Andy Lowe have already noted the lack of dynamism within the *South Bank Exhibition*'s story of Britain. Its narrative tour, they argue, lacked any real beginning, climax, or end; instead, it worked primarily to direct visitors toward a succession of stunning vistas across the site from various unexpected viewpoints.[50] This revealed the wartime interest among young British architects in the principles of the English picturesque, for—as the *Architectural Review* had celebrated in 1944—"contrast, concealment, surprise [and] balance" were endemic to "the surface antagonisms of shape which a vital democracy is liable to go on pushing up in its architecture as a token of its own liveliness."[51] Yet, in thereby serving to order visitors' feet, the story that the exhibition told become also a strategy of social and spatial management, foreclosing unexpected or unmanageable practices through its totalized deployment.

The *South Bank Exhibition* shared with Abercrombie's London plans a similar desire to halt the flow of historical time. The exhibition's displays rehearsed what Becky Conekin has called a "trans-historical, trans-class" view of Britain, presenting a Janus-like picture of how the latest scientific advances would ensure the survival of "our" great national traditions long into the future.[52] This was, of course, already the message proclaimed by Abercrombie: that planning science would revitalize and strengthen London's archaic communities, by returning the metropolis to its timeless organic structure. Once again, the appeal to historicity worked to deny proper history; tradition and continuity became mere instruments within the projection of a social order impervious to the disruptive potential of unforeseen events. This temporality, of course, remained inseparable from the individual movement that ordered and sustained it. The layout of the South Bank, in mimicking those of Abercrombie's ideal neighborhoods, taught visitors that to move along the prescribed circuits laid out for them by the planner was already to secure Britain's future position at the center of the postwar world.

This desire to foreclose historical time was perhaps most evident in the South Bank's famous Skylon (Figure 7). A three-hundred-foot aluminium suspended structure built to celebrate the achievements of modern engineering, this soon become both the centerpiece of the exhibition and a dominant motif within Festival iconography. For the architectural critic J. M. Richards, the Skylon was "a first-rate demonstration of the romantic potentialities of twentieth-century building science, imaginatively exploited";[53] yet what these potentialities were was anything but clear.[54] J. B. Priestley described the Skylon as "a glittering riddle of a symbol, like some genie's device in the *Arabian Nights*,"[55] while an anonymous critic for the *New Statesman and Society* went even further:

No, Sir, the Skylon has no purpose. It is not functional in any way. It does not light the Festival; it burns with its own inner light. It's not even a phallic symbol or totem pole. It has no social significance; it doesn't stand for Democracy, Freedom, Progress, or the Future Happiness of Man. It doesn't stand at all; it could stand on the ground but it doesn't. It's like everything else in the Festival—a huge lively joke, a tribute only to the spirit of nonsense and creative laughter.[56]

Figure 7. "A glittering riddle of a symbol": the *South Bank Exhibition*'s Skylon, designed by Philip Powell and Hildalgo Moya. Courtesy of Design Council/ University of Brighton Design Archives.

Yet a satirical cartoon in *Punch* perhaps went some way to revealing its elusive function (Figure 8).[57] Here the Skylon had been replaced by an inverted Nelson's Column, as a Festival guard explains to a family of perplexed visitors: "Of course we shall put it back after the Festival is over." Gavin and Lowe have read this cartoon as a comment on Britain's postwar imperial crisis; the Festival's social-democratic vision was literally turning the empire on its head.[58] Yet this juxtaposition of monuments undoubtedly reveals something more. Nelson's Column—a memorial to the defeat of Napoleon at Waterloo—was rooted in a specific moment of historical conflict, itself bound up with Britain's progressive ascendancy as a major imperial power. Landseer's marble lions, gazing out to the four corners of the world, appealed less to any timeless national tradition than to the active colonial ambitions of mid-Victorian London. The Skylon, however, made no such appeal. If it did show the romantic potentialities of twentieth-century building science, it was strangely silent about what those potentials were. It referred to little beyond its own self-evident existence—less a monument *to* an event than a monument *as* an event. In diary entries, the Skylon primarily appears as a thrilling experience—something to be seen, stood under, and photographed.[59] Thus, while Nelson's Column could still ask questions about a dynamic history of imperial expansion, the Skylon merely posed the riddle of how it could stay up. As a monument to the future, it was sorely undermined by its lack of vision about the possibility of social change. Instead, it promoted a more vacuous state of passive fascination, an invitation to marvel at its cutting-edge technicity. The Skylon's appeal was one of ostentatious novelty rather than genuine newness, an emptying of the historical future in preference for a cycle of wonder and familiarity that extinguished itself within the moment of its present. Unsurprisingly, it was soon dismantled for scrap when the exhibition closed.

Emblematically, the Skylon's architects embedded a metal ring in the floor beneath the monument to mark the optimum spot on which the visitor should stand and look up. Film records show visitors patiently queuing to enter this circle and address themselves to its wonders.[60] Its apparent engagement with futuricity therefore—in common with so much of the South Bank—was tacitly directed toward managing the movement of individuals. What united those visitors standing beneath the Skylon with both the abstract figure of Abercrombie's Londoner and those earlier visitors circulating around *Britain Can Make It* was an organized compulsion carefully concealed within a dazzling display of modernity and progress. Each

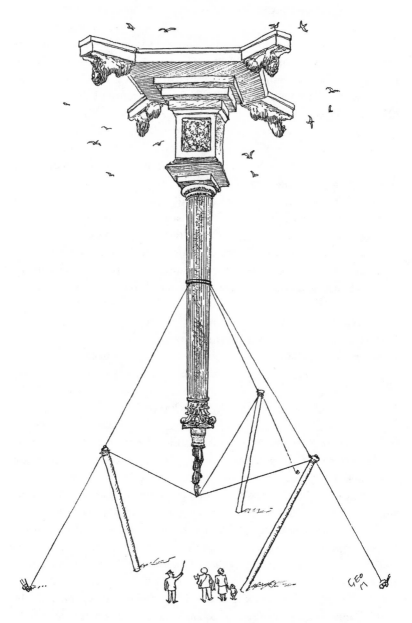

"Of course we shall put it back after the Festival is over."

Figure 8. Questioning the meaning of the South Bank's Skylon: George Morrow, "Of course we shall put it back after the Festival is over," from *Punch* 220, no. 5766 (9 May 1951): 582. Reproduced with permission of Punch Ltd., www.punch.co.uk.

gestured toward a foreclosure of history by establishing cycles of ordered movement, the blueprint for a new type of civic engagement with a reconstructed built environment. Through the careful administration of trajectories and routines, daily life had become privileged as the central vehicle for imagining a perpetually stable metropolitan order.

Such prescribed circuits were also deployed to set the parameters of the interclass sociality so central to the reconstruction vision of the renewed metropolis. This was particularly evident within the "Furnished Rooms" section of *Britain Can Make It,* twenty-four life-size interiors that displayed "things in their home setting," and a lesson in how to combine well-chosen British-made commodities to create lively and functional domestic spaces (see Figure 30). Taken together, the Furnished Rooms provided a striking prescription for the kind of inclusive community at the heart of the new town planning, while also replicating its hegemonic emphasis on the sequential arrangement of functional zones—from schoolrooms and offices at the start, through to kitchens, bathrooms, bedrooms, and living rooms. Mass-Observation's report revealed them to be popular; twice as many visitors voted the rooms "the thing that interested them most" about the exhibition, and people spent a proportionally greater amount of time looking at them than at anything else in the show.[61]

Between the wars, model interiors like these had enjoyed limited use within commercial contexts such as department store displays and at the *Daily Mail Ideal Home Exhibition,* but *Britain Can Make It* marked a watershed in their pedagogical deployment. These rooms, of course, were less about what artifacts should fill Britain's homes than about where those objects should be placed and how they should be arranged. Here commodities appeared within a set of spatial relations that visitors were invited to appraise and endorse, thus implicitly positioning them as prospective designers themselves. As one "middle-class housewife" commented: "I liked the way they were spaced out. It gave you a pretty good idea what things looked like and how a lot of things could fit into a small space."[62]

Much of the Furnished Rooms' success was due to the precise mode of their public address. As a COID press release explained:

Each room was visualised as belonging to a particular family of a certain size, the breadwinner being of a certain occupational status. Information about each family, with a sketch of imaginary members by Nicholas Bentley, is displayed on the facia of each room, and the designer's task was to work out an appropriate plan for the equipment, functioning and decoration of the room.[63]

Presented as a sequence, these rooms could act both as a metonym for a socially cohesive postwar nation and as a miniature realization of one of Abercrombie's interclass neighborhoods. Here, the living room of a middle-aged storeroom clerk and his picture-going wife stood happily beside the kitchen of a managing director, his well-traveled wife, and their daughter, now at boarding school—a democratic juxtaposition reinforced by the design sensibility that united all families within the same functional, clean, and purposive way of living. By privileging the occupation of the male bread-winner, the rooms stressed contributions to the national economy over potentially divisive disparities of income. Indeed, when the *Times* erroneously wrote that the rooms were designed for members of different "classes," coordinating designer Gordon Russell was quick to reply that, on the contrary, "a real attempt had been made to furnish them for people doing various *jobs*."[64]

By aligning themselves with these particular family groupings, visitors were encouraged to recognize their class-marked place within an imagined community at once neighborly and national. On one level, there was a manifest conservatism within this arrangement, as working-class dwellings were shown to be "improved" by the colonizing principles of bourgeois decorative taste; once again, the designed environment was inscribed with a set of prescriptions for how to live properly within the family home.[65] Yet the terms of this interclass mingling were also deeply circumscribed. This powerful image of inclusive urban community was only produced by the visitors themselves as they walked through the displays, from one room to the next. The interiors remained impenetrable to all but the viewer—the storeroom clerk may have lived side by side with the managing director, but their only link was the layout of their furniture and the sympathetic color schemes of their walls and soft furnishings. The only real cross-class relationship in evidence was the managing director's "two maids and a man-servant," which affirmed, rather than denied, the structural hierarchies of class. The Furnished Rooms, then, clearly set a limit to their own vision of social-democratic community. The domestic realm, they asserted, should remain private and nonporous, the impenetrable domain of the confident nuclear family. The message of *Britain Can Make It*, and finally also that of Abercrombie's London plans, was that interclass mingling was only to take place in those designated spaces where collective sociality could be choreographed and administered—whether in the post offices and precincts of the local neighborhood or in the exhibition halls of the Victoria and Albert Museum itself.

"Everything Is Made of Atoms": Repetition, Reassurance, and the Legacy of the Blitz

The force of these vocal investments in zoning, trajectory, movement, and repetition undoubtedly owed much to the legacy of the war and the recent experience of life under bombardment. Historians have linked the swift ascendency of town planning to the state's wartime success at social management and the propagandist pledges made to boost morale.[66] But the cultural impact of these visions—particularly in defiance of their limited implementation—suggests that they might have provided a more complicated and less rational apparatus through which to come to terms, in part at least, with recent traumatic experience.

During the blitz, German bombs killed an estimated 80,000 Londoners and destroyed or made derelict around 116,000 houses.[67] In 1942, the year after the sustained bombing raids came to an end, the Ministry of Information swiftly published *Front Line, 1940–1941: The Official Story of the Civil Defence of Britain,* a booklet central to creating what Angus Calder would later term "the myth of the blitz"—the active attempt to construct a public memory of bombardment in terms of pluck, camaraderie, and unfailing resolve.[68] *Front Line*'s emphatic narrative was that, despite the disruption and mortal peril brought on by the bombs, ordinary Londoners had courageously soldiered on with their everyday routines. As it eulogized:

> All this meant early rising for the clerks, the shop-girls, warehousemen, waitresses, and the rest—early rising after short, broken nights. But one had to look far to find any uninjured Londoner who could not say that he or she had got to work, even if sometimes a little late, every day of the blitz. Damage to their own homes did not stop them; often bereavement did not. Indeed the unchanged routine of the place of work helped them to face these things. Much that had been familiar all their lives was being torn away in the blast of the high explosive, and Londoners did not weep to see it go. But, being human, they needed the feel of something fixed and persistent. In their normal daily work they found it and gripped it hard.[69]

Front Line bought home this message by including two prominent photographs of a milkman making deliveries and a postman collecting the mail, neither one deflected from his duties by the enormous heaps of rubble through which they picked their way (Figure 9).[70] Here, the routine activities of daily life became cast as acts of bravery, as ordinary Londoners refused to allow their city to grind to a halt under the assault of German bombers. As one auxiliary fireman was quoted as saying:

> Most of us had the wind up to start with, especially with no barrage. It was all new, but we were all unwilling to show fear, however much we might feel it. You looked around and saw the rest doing their job. . . . You began to make feeble jokes to each other and gradually you got accustomed to it.[71]

Ordinary routine, therefore, became a crucial part of living through the blitz, but in a way that remained decidedly ambivalent. On the one hand, daily schedules became sharply repositioned as a matter of national duty, an ongoing heroism in the face of extraordinary conditions. Yet, at the

THE MILK COMES . . .   . . . AND THE POST GOES

Figure 9. Daily routine becomes heroic performance: "The Milk Comes . . . and the Post Goes," from Ministry of Information, *Front Line, 1940–1941: The Official Story of the Civil Defence of Britain* (London: His Majesty's Stationery Office, 1942), 57.

same time, those same routines also became an important way of coping, a refusal to show fear and a form of psychic defense against the perpetual assault of terror and grief. The well-known motto "Keep Calm and Carry On," subject of an early but aborted poster campaign in 1939, became doubly prescient; for not only was carrying on now a form of active and exhausting war work, but it had also emerged as the very precondition for the possibility of keeping calm.

The complex inheritance of these fraught dynamics remained largely unacknowledged within the vocal promulgation of postwar planning visions. However, a 1942 propaganda poster, designed by Abram Games for the Army Bureau of Current Affairs, neatly articulated the terms of this promise as well as the inherent limitations of its proffered panacea (Figure 10). Here, Tecton's newly built Finsbury Health Centre was shown glowing like a new dawn, decontextualized within a clean abstract space and pasted onto the side of a healthily pink brick wall.[72] Behind this, a malnourished boy plays with a toy boat, in a grimy ruined backyard with "disease" and "neglect"

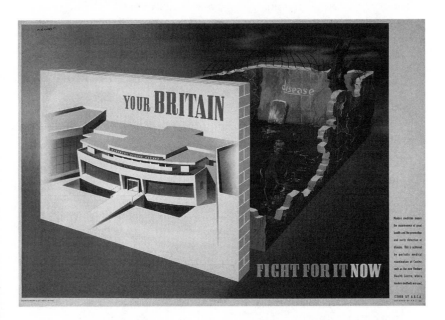

Figure 10. Social modernism promises to block out the traumas of the past: Abram Games, "Your Britain: Fight for It Now," poster designed for the Army Bureau of Current Affairs, 1942. Copyright Estate of Abram Games. Courtesy of Christie's Images Ltd.

feebly inscribed across its crumbling walls.[73] While intentionally recalling the impoverished conditions of the prewar slums, the decaying debris and the fiery night sky were also classic motifs of blitz iconography—an invocation, perhaps, of the bombed City churchyards that children so quickly colonized to create a disordered urban playground.

The promise made by this poster was clear: a bright new social future would rise up from the ashes, and one that could already be encapsulated synecdochically within certain key civic buildings. Yet here bricks and concrete took on a complex double role. Not only would modern facilities like Finsbury Health Centre create a renewed mode of everyday living, but they would also—as the brick wall itself suggests—render that future solid and impervious to the memory of the past. Wartime trauma, Games's image suggested, would be rendered literally ob-scene by such brave new constructions, sealed off impermeably and unable to penetrate into the stable environment of the postwar world. (This would also be the message of the *South Bank Exhibition*, whose pavilions were built on land reclaimed from the Thames by the dumping of rubble from London's bomb sites—the legacy of the war safely hidden beneath a smooth blank surface of freshly laid concrete.)[74]

Yet the obvious Freudian dynamics of Games's image also reveals the limitations of this fantasy. For as much as its wartime iconography still remained naggingly visible to the viewer despite its concealment behind the wall of reconstruction, the trauma of life under bombardment may also have required a more ambiguous, complex, and ongoing process of resolution in the years succeeding the war. If, during the blitz, the ordinary routines of daily existence had become a vehicle for disavowing and adapting to the terror of sustained attack, then this might also explain the continued investment in such routines within the dominant visions of a rebuilt metropolis. Those same mechanisms that had previously been required to survive enemy assault became, through their projected persistence long into peacetime, an important means through which to reassert control over ordinary daily life. The endless repetitions embedded within the plans offered a fantasy of remastery over a terrain recently made fraught by bombing, while simultaneously giving reassurances about the city's imperviousness to any future conflict.[75]

This dynamic may also explain the significance of one of the most prominent motifs of postwar reconstruction: the enlarged diagram of the solitary atom, whose structure offered exactly the same ambiguous set of cultural reassurances. That this image should recur during this period is hardly surprising. In the immediate postwar period, spurred by the recent bombings of Hiroshima and Nagasaki, concerted efforts were made to teach an uncertain British public about the science behind this strange and terrible new force. During the Festival of Britain, for instance, presentations of the atom were central to the South Bank's Dome of Discovery, to the *Exhibition of Science* (held in the Science Museum at Kensington), and to Glasgow's *Industrial Power Exhibition*. Yet the story of the atom as it was here relayed to visitors remained fundamentally ambivalent, for the fission of uranium in 1938 that had enabled the atomic bomb also promised exciting possibilities for the generation of electricity. Thus, the rhetoric surrounding the atom repeatedly contrasted two future scenarios, whereby the social benefits of nuclear energy were cautiously foregrounded against the foreboding possibility of global apocalypse. As Raymond Blackburn MP intoned over images of the mushroom cloud during a Pathé newsreel in August 1946:

Here is the true challenge of our time: whether science is to be used to destroy us or, by releasing new sources of power, lighten the daily work of every one of us . . . [A]tomic energy can bring new power and knowledge just as it can bring universal death.[76]

Such texts were keen to explain the atom's force by translating its potential effects into more readily familiar contexts. Another Pathé newsreel, for instance, drew a thick white line over an aerial photograph of London to mark the four square miles that would be "vaporized" if a bomb was dropped on Tower Bridge, the inclusion of place names such as "Shoreditch" and "Bermondsey" making frighteningly clear the scale of potential obliteration.[77] Viewers were also offered direct identifications with victims of the bomb. One film closed in on a swatch of dress fabric before cutting to a woman's back on which the blast's heat had "branded [its] pattern into her flesh." Through a hideous parody of their own quotidian environments, the realities of the atomic bomb were quite literally brought home.[78]

The Festival of Britain used similar methods to present its more cheerful accounts of life in the atomic age. Central here was the work of the Festival Pattern Group, a collaboration between the COID and various private manufacturers, who produced a range of furnishings and household objects that incorporated patterns derived from atomic crystallography. In the South Bank's Regatta Restaurant, for instance, visitors walked on carpets patterned

with the molecular structure of resorcinol, and used glass ashtrays decorated with pehtaerythritol designs. Arnold Lever even presented a dress silk
based on the structure of hemoglobin, produced in fuchsia, lemon, and
black on a background of turquoise and pink.[79] Encapsulated within this
tiny moment of both scientific and aesthetic enlightenment, a brand-new
pattern for a woman's dress became the celebrated alternative to its disavowed other: a dress pattern branded into a woman's flesh.

The sheer ubiquity of the atom across these displays suggests that it might
have been more than merely a pragmatic means to illustrate the basics of
nuclear physics. The existence of the atom bomb had clearly ushered in a
mode of daily living that was saturated by a vague and persistent sense of
unknown terror. Yet if, as during the blitz, everyday routine became mobilized as an indirect form of defensive strategy, then the atom itself, through
its mapped configurations of space, time, movement, and repetition, also
offered an implicit set of comforting messages about the foundational stability of matter and, by analogical association, the structure of postwar
everyday life.

As Simon Rycroft has noted, midcentury planning ideology was deeply
influenced by technological advances in scientific visualization. New
images produced by the microscope and telescope "revealed" how the natural world was characterized by a common set of structural forms that were
apparently replicated across all spatial scales. Planners already schooled in
the organicist principles of Patrick Geddes began to suggest that rebuilding
the built environment in adherence to these forms would create a harmonious symbiosis between mankind and nature, and ensure the optimum
functional order for society's future.[80]

Such organic formalism was clearly in evidence throughout the early
years of postwar reconstruction. At the *Exhibition of Science,* for instance,
visitors were told how the biological cell—the essential unit of all organic
life—had its own specific microgeography:

Each cell in every animal has much the same structure. At the centre of the
cell lies the round kernel or nucleus; this plays the most important part in
the life and division of the cell. The nucleus is enclosed in a thin skin or
membrane. Outside this skin, the nucleus is surrounded by a watery jelly, the
cytoplasm, which fills most of the cell. Finally, there is another skin or membrane round the cytoplasm. Food seeps into the cell through this membrane
and the waste seeps out.[81]

This structure was almost identical to that of Abercrombie's ideal neighborhood, with its civic nucleus and permeable membrane of main road or parkway. The *County of London Plan* even included a plate in which London's districts were cast as a mass of cellular blobs, floating around in an aqueous jelly of open space and with a healthy red dot to mark the nucleus of the local town hall (Figure 11). The *Exhibition of Science* extended this scalar confusion by interpellating visitors as mere cells within a more permanent civic organism:

> Cells die and new cells are born. The material of every living cell in the body must be constantly renewed; yet the whole body keeps its identity. The body is like a town; each year some people die and some are born, yet the population remains the same.[82]

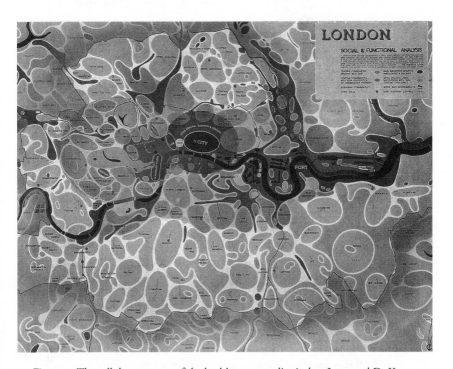

Figure 11. The cellular structure of the healthy metropolis: Arthur Long and D. K. Johnson, "London: Social and Functional Analysis," from Patrick Abercrombie and J. H. Forshaw, *The County of London Plan* (London: Macmillan, 1943), facing page 21. Courtesy of City of London, London Metropolitan Archives.

But while the cell remained the most explicit microcosmic reference point for both planning doctrine and the visual arts well into the 1950s, the forceful presentation of the atom within reconstruction displays reveals an important—if unacknowledged—shift in this kind of cultural investment.[83] To be clear, I am not claiming a causal relationship between midcentury atomic science and its contemporary planning discourse; there is little evidence, for instance, that Abercrombie conceptualized the urban environment in anything approaching atomic terms. But the mechanistic figure of the atom as here put on display offered a very specific understanding of how a certain structure of time, space, and circuitous repetition inherently underpinned the stability of the material world. That formally similar configurations had already been developed by planners and designers suggests that this atom must have functioned as a meaningful motif, unwittingly supporting and giving reassurances about the kinds of spatial organization being propagated elsewhere.

Certainly, the atom—for the Dome of Discovery, a "whole new territor[y] of beauty and order"—was bound up in similar fantasies of cross-scalar identification.[84] This happened most emphatically at the Festival's *Exhibition of Science*, which took as its founding question: "How is matter—the very substance of the world about us—built up, why does it take so many different forms and why do they behave as they do?"[85] Much of its display was devoted to explaining the structures of both the atom and the cell—the basic units of the physical and biological world, respectively—and each was again configured through the familiar and quotidian. (The concept of chemical elements, for instance, was introduced through a discussion of the atoms to be found in a fish slice.)[86] As the *Guide* reassured visitors: "The wonders of this exhibition are not larger than life; they are the fabric of modern life, and they have grown of themselves from science."[87]

This message was most forcefully presented via the prefatory approach to the main exhibition hall. Here, the visitor was guided through a sequence of five darkened rooms which, the *Guide* explained, would "take you, step by step, into the heart of matter":

Going through these rooms you seem to shrink like Alice in Wonderland, and the things round you seem to grow larger and larger. There are pencil and paper in the first room. Now you find yourself apparently shrinking, first to the size of the pencil, and then to the thickness of the paper; you see that the pencil lead slides off in layers as it writes. Another step, another thousand times smaller, and you see the structure of the graphite crystals which make up the pencil lead. And then a last step, you are ten thousand million times smaller than you began, and now you see into the atoms themselves.[88]

As the *Guide* explained: "You have now plunged headlong through these five rooms into the structure of matter"—the atom had become, literally, the fundamental structure of the visitor's architectural environment.

Of course, this carbon atom served the exhibition's narrative as the link between the chemical elements and the biological cell. Yet by manipulating space such that the individual came to "stand within an atom," it also revealed a deeper investment in this microcosmic structure.[89] This version of the atom was deeply mechanistic, but this transformed it into an important sign of lasting stability and provided some form of heuristic device for understanding how space, time, and cycles of movement could sustain a natural order as eternally secure as the building blocks of matter themselves. As the exhibition explained, the atom's permanence was rooted in the unchanging yet dynamic relationship between a heavy, stable center and a set of individuated mobile units:

> Each atom consists of a heavy nucleus at its centre, and electrons moving round it in such a way that they are more likely to turn up in some places than in others. We can picture each electron spinning a sort of cloud round the nucleus; where the cloud is thickest, there the electron is most likely to be found.[90]

This rather simplistic image, untouched by recent developments in fission or fusion, rooted material stability in a set of repetitive and predictable choreographies. It thus repeated precisely the mechanisms of projected order being inscribed within Abercrombie's plans, on the walkways of the South Bank, and in the exhibition hall at *Britain Can Make It.* The implied message, deeply resonant when communicated alongside the visions of London's planners, was that a similar system of predictable, repetitious circulations would offer the best—and most natural—structure for a coherent and stable postwar metropolis.

This presentation of the building block of matter chimed with replanned London in two important ways. First, the atom was an eternal structure, sustained by its own internal temporality. Like Abercrombie's village communities, whose archaic existence had only just been recovered by modern planning doctrine, it took the latest advances in electron microscopy to confirm the persistence of its unchanging form.[91] The atom, too, was undisturbed by the trauma of historic events; yet, at the same time, its stability was founded on the constant circulation of its individual electrons, perpetually encircling the nucleus along predictable and ordered paths. Like the programmed trajectories of a reimagined London, the atom's security was premised on a double temporality in which timeless eternality was perpetually enacted through an endless repetition of spatialized routine.

Second, the atomic structure successfully mediated between both difference and equality and between compulsion and consent. Its hierarchical model of center and periphery brought the nucleus and its myriad electrons into a formal equality that together maintained the equilibrium of the whole. Electrons were formally autonomous in their orbital movements, yet where they would travel was more or less known in advance. When the *Exhibition of Science* described these pathways as where electrons were "most likely to be found," it captured perfectly the dialectical synthesis of administered freedom at the heart of reconstruction planning—whether in Abercrombie's inscribed trajectories or amid the guiding hazards of the South Bank.

The mapping of this stable hierarchy may also have been consonant with the wider recapitalization of London after the Second World War, as the metropolis became ideologically repositioned as the radiant epicenter of a range of spheres of influence from the regional to the international.[92] Fighting to recover from its obvious devastation, London's future as a post-imperial capital had become increasingly reimagined in terms of flows and circulations, which would ensure its centrality within the postwar world. Something of this could be seen in Abercrombie's remodeling of London's road network into four concentric "orbitals," each encircling the city center at a particular and steady radius. Like electrons in their shells, motorized Londoners would circulate unhindered—at once individuated and collective, directed yet autonomous. On a regional level, this structure was replicated by the eight proposed new towns to be built beyond the Green Belt. Independent of London for both their employment and their everyday leisure needs, the centrality of the capital would still be ensured by the regular flows of goods and people that would travel between the two. Thus, argued Abercrombie, the new towns "should be sufficiently far out to deter people permanently from travelling backwards and forwards," while still "rely[ing] on London for their major amusements and important cultural activities."[93] The metropolis would also remain the primary market for decentralized industries, sustained by the constant traffic of commodities and capital facilitated by the city's reintegrated transport network.[94] As the *County of London Plan* stated, London's place in the region could be thought of as a "dense nucleus encircled by a series of more or less important closely-knit townships."[95]

The recentering of its capital even extended to embrace London's international role as it faced the uncertainties of postwar global politics. The dissolutive forces already at work within the ailing British Empire had been accelerated by the war, as indigenous nationalists exploited the paradox of Britain's principled defense of national self-determination while simultaneously denying it to many of its own colonies.[96] U.S. pressure to sign the Atlantic Charter in 1941—proclaiming "the right of all people to choose the form of Government under which they live"—produced a mounting sense of domestic unease at Britain's apparent global decline, which was further exacerbated by the granting of dominion status to India, Pakistan, and Ceylon, plus the withdrawal of troops from Greece and Palestine, in 1947. Britain's reliance on the Marshall Plan also suggested a worrying shift of power to the United States, exaggerated by the increasing encroachment of American firms into traditionally safe commodity markets.[97]

Against this backdrop, the idea of the British Commonwealth became an increasingly important vehicle for projecting a state of postimperial stability and the lasting security of British global influence. Yet importantly, the Commonwealth was not bound together by direct imperial control, but was becoming conceived—in accordance with the 1926 Balfour Declaration's definition of dominion status—as an association of "autonomous communities . . . equal in status, in no way subordinate one to another in any aspect of their domestic or external affairs, though united by a common allegiance to the Crown."[98] Although, in 1949, this condition of royal allegiance was removed, the paradox remained of a democratic association of equal and autonomous states, within which Britain still somehow retained its primacy of influence. Caught between the need for formal parity and Britain's desire to maintain supremacy, this postimperial structure resonated deeply with larger postwar tensions—both domestic and metropolitan—around communitarian order and individual liberty.

To negotiate this contradiction, London became increasingly important as both a spatial and a symbolic center. In the *County of London Plan*, Abercrombie and Forshaw argued that "it is for this new world, foreshadowed in the Atlantic Charter, that the Capital of the Commonwealth must prepare itself" and accordingly proposed that an area round Westminster Abbey and the Houses of Parliament—already "a focal point of special interest"— should be specifically redesigned "as the scene of the chief ceremonies of State and, by its historical associations, a centre for countless visitors":[99]

> The noble group of buildings around the nation's ancient shrine calls for a more tranquil setting without the distractions associated with great volumes of quick-moving and heavy traffic. It demands, too, for ceremonial occasions, a dignified and reasonably spacious environment.[100]

Explicitly positioned as "the heart of the Commonwealth," this small area would concretize London's metaphorical position as the nucleus of its postimperial world. Yet to do this would involve extracting it from the ordinary flows of the functioning metropolis, removing it from the daily circuits of normal Londoners, and reconfiguring it within the more occasioned orbits of those countless overseas visitors whose allegiance to Britain such a pilgrimage would enact. London's role as the nucleus of the Commonwealth, therefore, relied on the same kind of managed trajectories as did its position at the heart of the region and, on a more local level, the centrality of the civic center within the life of the metropolitan district.

During the immediate postwar period, then, London's international centrality was repeatedly imagined through circuitous flows of people, capital, commodities, and ideas. *Britain Can Make It,* for instance, was explicitly mooted as an attempt to attract visitors and buyers from the old colonial territories, and many of the fabrics on display featured motifs and color schemes that signified economic or kinship status within specific tribal cultures.[101] Such trade routes, institutionally supported by the maintenance of the Sterling Area, were thought vital to securing Britain's economic future in the face of U.S. competition. In a sense, then, the hermetic space of the exhibition hall can be seen as a microcosm of the Commonwealth itself, its orchestrated circulation of overseas visitors mimicking the international flow of goods and currency it also hoped to stimulate. To this end, the Festival of Britain was also heavily promoted as an attraction for foreign visitors and its displays made much of how "our" place in the Commonwealth would be premised on the global flow of ideas, discoveries, and enlightened political traditions that already circulated out of Britain via the historic English language—in print or though the "radio system which itself is part of our contribution to the welfare of mankind."[102]

When the designer Robin Day produced a poster for the Kensington *Exhibition of Science,* he fittingly placed Britain at the nucleus of a structure at once atomic and planetary (Figure 12). Fixed within a network of regular orbital flows—of goods, people, capital, and knowledge—Britain's centrality might be made to appear lasting and secure as it faced the uncertainties of the postwar world. Once again, circuits of movement and repetition offered a powerful means for imagining how historical change could be kept at bay, forestalling the kind of colonial conflict and U.S. ascendency that threatened Britain's place on the global stage. At the same time, the scalar confusion that Day could exploit allowed more everyday engagements with metropolitan space to assume a wider cultural importance, as they became conceptually linked to a wider set of anxieties about the nation, its security, and its international prestige.

All of this, then, came together to promote a dominant image of the postwar metropolis in which a new and highly administered form of everyday life promised to set the foundational conditions for a stable and peaceful social democracy. Yet, with its bomb-damaged landscapes and expansive districts of dilapidated housing, London on the ground could only appear more lacking and problematic against the bright new city projected by its planners. This foundational mismatch between image and reality would produce a number of social conflicts over the next two decades, whose implications would be felt across a range of social domains.

That queer male activity was one of these flash points is perhaps hardly surprising, for the powerful projections of the immediate postwar era had paid little attention to male same-sex desire. Reconstruction planners remained firmly focused on the needs of the nuclear family and those future citizens—still in their infancy—who would grow up to perpetuate its stable social order. That Abercrombie's neighborhoods should have centered both physically and symbolically on the local elementary school accorded with his primary desire "to produce such conditions as shall induce the young married people to remain and bring up families in what should be attractive urban surroundings."[103] Concurrent reorderings of domestic space were similarly directed at promoting the welfare of the nuclear family, with the majority of the Furnished Rooms being fictitiously inhabited by occupationally defined husbands and their recreationally defined wives. The sense of civic pride and of healthy corporate life that these reformed urban neighborhoods would instill in their citizens was not, in any meaningful way, being proffered to queer men.

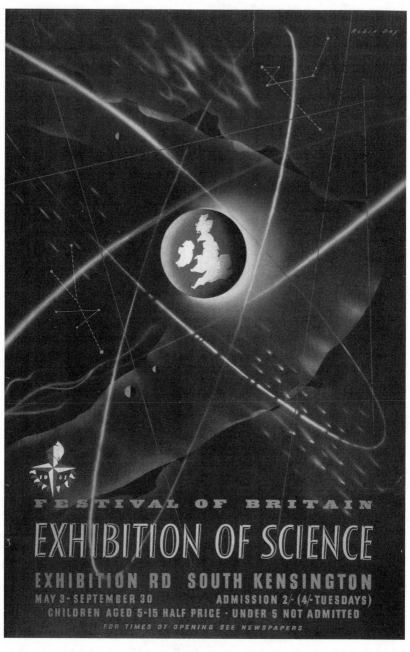

Figure 12. Britain at the nucleus of a planetary atom: Robin Day, poster for *Exhibition of Science,* Science Museum, Kensington, 1951. Courtesy of Victoria and Albert Images, Victoria and Albert Museum, London.

Yet, some intimations of nonnormative sexuality could be found lurking ambiguously on the fringes of the reconstruction project. The London plans, for instance, recognized the need to rehouse a large number of both single people and childless couples—ideally in blocks of flats of up to ten stories high, to enable the maximum number of families with children to have their own private gardens.[104] And among the cartoon families on show at *Britain Can Make It* could be found a "single man, sportsman and sports commentator at Broadcasting House," untroubling enough in his "bed-sitting room in a London apartment block." In the wider climate of early reconstruction, such marginal presentations remained largely benign. Although the war—with its perpetual blackout, forced proximities, and increased sense of living for the moment—had provided ample opportunity for queer encounters across the city and beyond, the dazzling sunlight of urban renewal obscured all such activity.[105] Attention became focused on the nascent child-citizen and the replanned playing fields and modern new schools that would ensure his or her future welfare. The unmarried man, although pushed to the fringes, had yet to become placed outside the normative imperatives of postwar spatial citizenship or beyond the inclusive metropolitan community that this would, in turn, secure.

All this would radically change a few years later, however, as the initial optimism of reconstruction planning began to run aground against the messy contingencies of life in the outmoded capital. Against the projected orderings of functional zoning, cyclical routine, and managed civic sociality, the persistence of other, less proper urban pursuits became insistently problematic. In the early 1950s, many of these anxieties would coalesce within the tabloid figure of the metropolitan "pervert," whose day-to-day engagement with the urban environment became a focal point of popular alarm and outrage. Yet, as we shall see in the next chapter, the unstable geographies, disordered sociality, and illicit choreographies that he was made to represent could still remain a persistent—if ambiguous—source of covert public pleasure.

chapter 2

THE PERVERSITY OF THE ZIGZAG: THE CRIMINALITY OF QUEER URBAN DESIRE

It seems clear that there has been a considerable increase in the number of homosexual offences since 1946. The explanation for the steep rise in 1951 and fall thereafter is that in that year a large number of provincial visitors came to London for the Festival of Britain. This is borne out by the fact that the increase took place during the exact months when the South Bank Exhibition was open.

—SIR JOHN NOTT-BOWER, Commissioner of the Metropolitan Police, in a memo to the Wolfenden Committee, 1954

When, in May 1952, the weekly tabloid *Sunday Pictorial* began a three-part series of articles titled "Evil Men," the journalist Douglas Warth felt it necessary to justify the topic of his piece within the opening paragraphs:

The natural British tendency to pass over anything unpleasant in scornful silence is providing cover for an unnatural sex vice which is getting a dangerous grip on this country . . .

I thought, at first, that this menace could best be fought by silence—a silence which Society has almost always maintained in the face of a problem which had been growing in our midst for years. But this vice can no longer be ignored. The silence, I find, is a factor which has enabled the evil to spread. Homosexuality is an unpleasant subject, but it must be faced if ever it is to be controlled.[1]

Warth's presumption of an outraged readership for whose sake the "conspiracy of silence" surrounding urban vice must now be broken was a journalistic trope with a distinguished heritage. In the 1880s and 1890s, the "new journalism" associated with radical titles like the *Pall Mall Gazette*

81

and *Truth* had similarly embarked on self-styled crusades to expose London's institutionalized networks of sexual exploitation, supposedly kept hidden by a sinister combination of vested interests and editorial discretion. In July 1885, the *Pall Mall Gazette*'s sensationalist exposé of child prostitution within the capital, "The Maiden Tribute of Modern Babylon," had provoked a massive public uproar and helped precipitate the Criminal Law Amendment Act, whose Labouchère Amendment would famously create the offense of gross indecency between men. Five years later, the sustained coverage of the Cleveland Street scandal, in which aristocrats were discovered cavorting with telegraph delivery boys in a private West End brothel, suggested further how illicit vice was entrenched just below the surface of the city. All this reached its climax, of course, during Oscar Wilde's prosecution of 1895, his acts of gross indecency with assorted young valets and grooms confirming London's image as a metropolis in which the young and vulnerable were ever at risk from the irrevocable damage of sexual debasement.[2]

Warth's three-part article was one of a cluster of similar exposés to appear in the early 1950s and followed the same contrived dialectic of conspiratorial concealment and heroic exposure. Provoked by an increasingly competitive fight for sales, populist tabloids posed as outspoken moral guardians and deployed melodramatic narratives, emotive tones, and stock characterizations of urban villainy that were all deeply reminiscent of their late-Victorian predecessors.[3] Central London—and the commercial leisure district of the West End in particular—became presented once more as a shadowy zone of danger and intrigue, in which affluent older perverts could be found mercilessly preying on naive and impressionable hard-up young lads. Warth, for instance, conjured for his readers "a man in Mayfair nicknamed 'the Duchess,' who acts as procurer for rich degenerates" and who regularly scoured the city's all-night cafés in search of vulnerable borstal boys he could willfully seduce into a life of vice and squalor.[4] Following the Cleveland Street telegraph boys or Wilde's young valets, London's guardsmen, laborers, and other urban drifters now became cast as potential victims, dangerously afloat amid the promiscuous entertainments of the decadent West End and ever on the brink of irreversible corruption.

Matt Houlbrook has shown how the renewed concern over London's male vice in this period was largely provoked by certain operational changes in the procedures of the Metropolitan Police. As the force returned to full manpower after the war, those divisions with responsibility for managing the city center stepped up their surveillance of urinals and street corners in response to a generally perceived increase in visible queer activity. The number of men that appeared before the magistrates rose exponentially— at Bow Street, from 106 in 1942 to 212 in 1947; and from 13 to 103 over the same period at Marlborough Street—which produced an attendant increase in column inches while creating the erroneous impression that London was in the grip of a new epidemic.[5] Investigative journalists, magistrates, court reporters, and alarmed members of Parliament unwittingly colluded in the ongoing presentation of a city under siege. In October 1953, the fining of the actor John Gielgud for persistent importuning in a Chelsea public toilet led even the more reticent broadsheets to begin reporting on this and other such cases. That winter, the trend reached its peak with the extensive coverage of the two "Montagu trials": first, in November, when Lord Montagu of Beaulieu and the film director Kenneth Hume were tried for offenses against two Boy Scouts; and then, two months later, when Montagu was tried again, along with journalist Peter Wildeblood and landowner Michael Pitt-Rivers, for conspiring to commit offenses with Edward McNally and John Reynolds, two young airmen they had met casually in London.

This media coverage was, of course, by no means unequivocal. More liberal publications soon began to counter such populist outrage with calls for a more enlightened understanding of "homosexuality" as a medical condition, a social tragedy that required a compassionate and psychiatric response rather than a vindictive punitive one. But the tabloids' vociferous attack on male vice, in both its careful articulation of a specific discursive structure and the emotional pull of its populist agenda, marked an important moment of wider cultural realignment. Britain's swiftly declining birthrate, an increase in the number of divorces, and the apparent wave of petty crime that was plaguing its inner cities all seemed to tally with the multiple disruptions to family life incurred during the war. Set against an urban backdrop pockmarked by bombs, ongoing shortages, and a persistent black market, the metropolitan pervert became a key figure through whom various anxieties about social, sexual, and economic disorder could be articulated and partially resolved.

Like many other postwar scandals, these vilifications of male vice reworked older late-Victorian imaginings of a seething metropolis in which decadent luxury and social deprivation were promiscuously intertwined. As Frank Mort has noted, these depictions continued to provide an effective counterpoint to those more progressive visions of urban renewal being loudly proclaimed by London's planning experts.[6] Such sensationalist accounts also made uneasy references to a set of more recent psychiatric concepts, seeking to conceal their reactionary narratives behind a veneer of scientific modernism. Yet, despite this, queer urban practices were overwhelmingly presented within the tabloid press less as the inevitable expression of some innate anterior psychology than as a culpable form of behavioral misconduct, emphatically rooted in individual moral failure. If, in the immediate postwar years, the bachelor had remained a largely benign figure, peacefully on the margins of the new urban community, then the early 1950s saw his very definite reformulation as a malignant social threat.

This sudden moral panic over male vice in London was more than a revalorization of the postwar nuclear family.[7] It also produced a diffuse set of meanings around economic exchange, social mobility, and a certain way of inhabiting the urban environment that delineated, in relief, the boundaries of normative spatial citizenship to which social renewal had become attached. Again, this had a set of clear precedents, for at successive moments of national crisis since at least the mid-nineteenth century, the press had produced alarmist reports about London's queer street cultures in an effort to reassert the acceptable boundaries of masculine behavior, dress, and public deportment.[8] Yet within a postwar climate dominated by the ordered communitarian visions of urban planners and policy makers, the sexual immorality of the queer male pervert became newly configured in terms of his distinct and complex criminal relationship to the metropolis itself. His antisocial sexual activities were inseparable from how he earned and spent his money, with whom, how, and where he socialized, and with his most basic navigations of the built urban environment.

This timely rearticulation of queer urban engagement not only ran through the affronted press coverage of the early 1950s but was also evident in less obvious and less vitriolic texts of the period. The most significant of these, which I analyze here in some depth, also happened to be one of the most popular British films of 1951: *The Lavender Hill Mob,* made by Ealing Studios and directed by Charles Crichton. Citing this film within the present context may seem perverse in itself, for *The Lavender Hill Mob* was clearly not a film "about" male vice in London. It remains, instead, a lighthearted comedy about two mild-mannered bachelors who plot to hijack a vanload of bullion, recast the stolen gold as Eiffel Tower paperweights, and then smuggle them to France to be sold on the black market. Both its farcical narrative and its gently affable humor remain far removed from the demonic accounts of "evil" queer men that were appearing contemporaneously on the newsstand. Yet, as I hope to show, the film remained preoccupied with both the new urban logics of postwar reconstruction and specifically queer and—pleasurable—ways of subverting them. *The Lavender Hill Mob* thus stands as a contemporaneous counterpoint to the tabloids' scandalized depictions of a city gripped by vice. Both were concerned with exploring the limits of a hegemonic vision of metropolitan order by articulating the terms of a queer mode of opposition; yet they did so within diametrically opposed affective registers. What could, in certain contexts, become a site of great anxiety could equally, in others, become a cause of celebration and collective glee.

To understand how *The Lavender Hill Mob* could function in this way, it is worth recalling the explanation given by Michael Balcon, the film's producer and head of Ealing Studios, for the success of his postwar comedies:

> In the immediate post-war years there was as yet no mood of cynicism; the bloodless revolution of 1945 had taken place, but I think our first desire was to get rid of as many wartime restrictions as possible and get going. The country was tired of regulations and regimentation, and there was a mild anarchy in the air. In a sense our comedies were a reflection of this mood . . . a safety valve for our more anti-social impulses.[9]

Balcon's final metaphor here, with its twin appeals to thermodynamics and the oppositional drives of desire and regulation, strongly recalls Freud's notion of displacement as developed in his *The Interpretation of Dreams* (1900).[10] For Freud, displacement described that psychic mechanism endemic to dreaming by which an unacceptable libidinal impulse finds expression by attaching itself to an alternative, seemingly unconnected idea. If Balcon's analogy holds, then these comedies—and *The Lavender Hill Mob* in particular—might covertly have enabled their contemporary audiences to indulge in a set of antisocial pleasures very different from those made manifest on the screen.

Like many of the other postwar Ealing comedies, *The Lavender Hill Mob* explored the shifting tensions between individual freedom and collective social duty.[11] The benign, victimless crime around which the film revolves allowed an ostensive celebration of anarchic transgression, but one ultimately contained by a final reassertion of authority when the thieves are caught at the end.[12] Its narrative thus effected the same reconciliation between individual autonomy and communitarian constraint that structured Abercrombie's routine trajectories and the circulations of the South Bank. Holland (Alec Guinness) and Pendlebury (Stanley Holloway) may have entertained fantasies of excessive luxury and personal wealth, but the film presents them as the two exceptions that otherwise prove the rule. Elsewhere, London is founded on consensus, contentment, and stable class hierarchies; bank clerks work dutifully for their bosses, everyone knows their place and respects policemen, and even Shorty (Alfie Bass) and Lackery (Sidney James)—the two working-class crooks recruited to complete the "mob"—remain deferent to their "Guv" throughout. Within this film, class structures remain a source of stability, order, and social harmony, rather than inspiring any conflict or dissent. And all this is played out against an urban landscape in which Wren's surviving City churches stand proud among the bomb sites, a testament to the imperviousness of Britain's timeless cultural heritage.

Yet, if this film was indeed some sort of safety valve, then the mildly anarchic action presented on the screen—in Balcon's words, "who has not wanted to raid a bank . . . as an escape to a life of ease?"—might have served to conceal, rather than announce, the deeper and much darker pleasures that it covertly entertained.[13] Charles Barr has already noted what he calls the "poverty of desire" within postwar British cinema, a necessary immolation to the ideologies of social responsibility and civic community such films worked tirelessly to promote.[14] In *The Lavender Hill Mob,* with its apparent endorsement of the reconstruction social vision, this repressed energy found something of an outlet, under the cover of its narrative of theft. If the moral projections of the immediate postwar years recast urban citizenship as affiliative participation in its designs for community living, then the film sanctioned a momentary involvement in the duplicitous joys and disreputable urban pleasures that its planners sought to erase. In doing so, it strangely conflated its thrilling endorsement of social instability and spatial disorder with an unacknowledged celebration of sexual dissent.

Thus, although this film is not "about" homosexuality, a strong connotative queerness bubbles just below the surface. Holland and Pendlebury are both middle-aged bachelors and presented as strangely sexless. Holland is meek, subservient, and has a lisp, while Pendlebury is portly, jovial, and prone to theatrical gesticulations. Importantly, the film contains no suggestion that either man has ever had any relationship with a woman. In fact, the only females in this cinematic London are the elderly gentlewomen of the Balmoral Private Hotel, the dilapidated Victorian conversion where Holland and Pendlebury board, and the pubescent public schoolgirls of

St. Christopher's in Hendon. Both enjoy a certain comic perversity—Mrs. Chalk is a connoisseur of salacious potboilers while pupil June Edwards has a "boyfriend" in the police—but neither is sexually available to our protagonists. The film's only "proper" woman is a pre-stardom Audrey Hepburn who appears briefly in the prologue. Here, in the exotic setting of a Rio café-bar, the film introduces Holland as the triumphant thief in exile as he starts to recount his story to an unspecified interlocutor. Awkward and English in these louche Latin surroundings, he distributes his spoils to a diverse local population of minor crooks and seedy ex-pats, an emphatic point of contrast to the industrious, law-abiding Londoners to which the film will shortly return. It is during this sequence that Hepburn glides into shot, exchanges some brief lines with Holland, embraces him sexlessly, and then relieves him of some cash. Referred to in both the dialogue and the credits as "Chiquita," she is literally the film's token girl, a comforting, though depthless, stamp of heterosexuality with which to frame the ensuing narrative and divert the viewer's attention from any queerer interpretations of what might be going on.

Once back in London, the real comic engine of the film is Holland and Pendlebury's outrageous parody of a heterosexual romance. From their initial encounter in the hallway of the Balmoral, via some flirtatious double entendres as they negotiate their mutual interest, to an affectionate private naming ceremony after the successful robbery, the narrative tension relies on an understanding that this pair are in it together, for better or for worse, for poorer or—hopefully—for richer. Accordingly, the film's publicity poster showed the two men joyfully clinging together, united but separate from the chaos they have caused (Figure 13). This deeply homosocial—if never quite homosexual—romance rushes in to fill the void left by its absent heterosexual counterpart, and continues through their Parisian pseudo-honeymoon right up until Pendlebury's final selfless urge to "Run, Dutch, Run!" as he succumbs to a policeman in the closing reel.

What makes *The Lavender Hill Mob* so productive to read against the more obvious tabloid renditions of metropolitan male vice is its emphatic investment in precisely those same logics of space, time, movement, and visuality that dominated the ideologies of the postwar reconstruction. On the surface, the film's London appears far removed from the plazas of the South Bank or the tidy neighborhood precincts sketched within the pages of *The County of London Plan*. Its city, in contrast, remains decayed and obsolete. Lavender Hill is a Victorian inner suburb to the south of the river

Figure 13. A riotous celebration of homosocial romance: *The Lavender Hill Mob* (Charles Crichton, 1951). Courtesy of British Film Institute.

and appears long deserted by its original inhabitants. Its converted town houses now offer only a semblance of faded imperial glamour to the elderly relics who still reside there. Holland may work as a bullion clerk for the Bank of England, but even the neoclassicism of Threadneedle Street speaks of a past glory and a confidence now faltering among the bomb sites and disused warehouses that exist alongside.

Yet despite this scenography of homely obsolescence, the film's narrative is deeply rooted in the familiar spatial and temporal strategies of postwar urban planning. To encourage identification with Holland and his crimes, the city is exaggerated as a place of stasis, routine, and mundane spatial conformity. This is made clear at the very start of the narrative. As Holland begins his flashback, the Rio club lounge dissolves into a grimy shot of commuters trudging to work across London Bridge under an overcast sky. Over the top, Holland tells of how he had "never lost sight" of his plan to rob the bank, "inaccessible as it often seemed to me when I was merely a nonentity among all those thousands who flock each morning into the City." This image, straight out of T. S. Eliot's *The Waste Land* (1922), frames central London as a zone of work that is emphatically built on routine and repetition.[15] In the following sequence, we are guided through the movements of Holland's typical day, a synecdoche for the last nineteen years of his life that necessarily invokes a stasis in which nothing will ever change. This was, of course, the same temporal strategy expounded within the pedagogical visions of a replanned London: the preclusion of social conflict through the deferral of historical time, sustained by an endless performance of preprogrammed dailiness. In addition, Holland's day presents the metropolis as an unexciting patchwork of monological spaces, ordered and activated through his own sequential trajectory. London Bridge, for instance, clearly bisects the financial space of work to the north of the Thames (already seen as the backdrop to the opening credits) and the residential suburbs to the south (including, of course, the eponymous Lavender Hill).

When, at the end of this establishing sequence, Pendlebury appears as a new arrival on the steps of the Balmoral, the stasis is broken and the events of the film can properly begin. Holland and Pendlebury's shared criminality becomes the dynamic force that will—for a while, at least—subvert the strictures of these quotidian spaces that manage their daily lives, and this motivation remains as rooted in their homosocial desire as in the theft of the bullion with which it is elided. *The Lavender Hill Mob,* therefore, elaborated the hegemonic logics of urban reconstruction only to articulate the potential challenge of queer relations to them. Yet, unlike the articles in contemporary tabloids, it could present its queer criminals as unthreatening and lovable, in total contrast to the more troubling representations of antisocial viciousness in circulation outside the cinema.[16] Here, the illicit pleasures of social transgression and urban disorder that were elsewhere being excised from the moral projection of the replanned metropolis could be legitimately, if momentarily, enjoyed. Safely contained within the auditorium, *The Lavender Hill Mob*'s audience became joyfully complicit in what was in fact a very queer mode of reading, experiencing, and negotiating the city.

The Malignant Economics of Queer Urban Desire

The central narrative of *The Lavender Hill Mob* also reveals how postwar concern over queer male behavior inextricably conflated sexual and economic anxieties. The film is preoccupied with London's position as the center of a number of dynamic flows, evidenced above all by Holland's job. As a bullion clerk for the Bank of England, he is at the nucleus of the Sterling Area that would, it was hoped, ensure Britain's continued dominance within the postwar Commonwealth. The bullion he delivers to the vaults each week is the fulcrum on which this entire circulation rests. In stealing the gold on its way to the bank, therefore, he attacks London's security as the economic hub of its postimperial world. On these terms, recasting the bullion into Eiffel Tower paperweights becomes a profane act of reverse transubstantiation. It eviscerates the gold of its transcendent use value—as that which sustains the traffic of paper money—by transforming it into just another commodity. Now in the form of holiday souvenirs, its newly degraded use value becomes irrevocably tied to the moment of its purchase—from a souvenir kiosk on top of the Eiffel Tower during a memorable vacation in Paris.

Thus *The Lavender Hill Mob* centered on a very specific crime and one that allowed the film to express a wider anxiety about the threat posed by queer men to the future health of the nation. If gold in the above diagesis is replaced with sperm—a conceptual substitution with an established history within modern Western culture—then the mob's crime becomes emphatically that of queer male sex.[17] Queer men, of course, hijack sperm on its normative journey from the refinery in the testicles to the guarded vaults of the uterus. Only upon its arrival there can it realize its transcendent use value, as that substance which produces children and thus perpetuates the entire social economy. The queer orgasm, in effect, steals this precious load, profaning it within a moment of wasteful erotic pleasure that is as fixed to the time and space of its expenditure as any holiday souvenir.

When, after the theft of the bullion, an MP in the House of Commons asks the prime minister whether "in view of rising public anxiety, [he] can assure the House that this very large sum of money is not irretrievably lost to the nation," his concern over the deterioration of Britain's gold reserves could already be understood to express a wider anxiety about the queer squandering of sperm. As Britain's birthrate continued to decline after the war, homosexual men were repeatedly positioned as external to the national community for exactly this theft of its future children. In 1953, for instance, Joseph Brayshaw would inform readers of the *Daily Herald* that there was "more than mere convention in the distaste and horror with which people view this problem. . . . *Everywhere there is bound to be a suspicion of a deviation that might threaten the future of the race.*"[18] Likewise, Warth in "Evil Men" advised that "if homosexuality were tolerated here Britain would

rapidly become decadent," and cited France as the place in which a toleration of homosexuality had produced an "alarming fall in the birthrate."[19]
That France should be the country to which Holland and Pendlebury
smuggle their paperweights only reinforced the queerness of their crime,
for within the postwar imaginary France became persistently linked with
the degenerate dangers of unchecked queer behavior. Lord Montagu's voy-
age there on hearing of his imminent arrest became reported as a clear
inference of his guilt, as had the known journey to Paris of the spies Guy
Burgess and Donald Maclean two years earlier.[20] The standard use of "the
Code Napoléon" as journalistic shorthand for the legal toleration of private sexual acts perpetuated an impression that queer male sex was inherently Continental and could not properly belong within the renewed social
democracy of postwar Britain.

Remarkably, *The Lavender Hill Mob* even endorsed this reading of its
central plotline. In the foundry, just as the first golden paperweight emerges
from its cast, Holland and Pendlebury cradle it affectionately, Holland sighs
"Our firstborn," and the two men look into each other's eyes and fondly
smile. Here, the towers are explicitly presented as the barren offspring of
a criminal male partnership, parodying the baby that a heterosexual union
would produce. With these dynamics kept just below the surface, the film
could invite its audience to relish and endorse exactly that type of illicit
queer thievery that was being concurrently vilified by a concerned and
angry press.

This wider conflation of antisocial economic and seminal appropria-
tions cast queer sex as a form of willful selfishness that put individual pleasure over the communitarian social interest that it so blatantly undermined.
As Joseph Brayshaw wrote:

> These men often claim that because their emotions are different they are not
> to be blamed if they don't control them; but this is mainly self-pity. *As with
> normal men, self-control is possible.* The greatest difficulty is that some homo-
> sexuals *do not want* to be any different.[21]

Here, the homosexual's refusal to control his own desires expanded the
terms of his social malignancy. His erotic practices not only refused the
social imperatives of heterosexual procreation, but also revealed an amorphous selfishness that would inherently destabilize the careful class hierarchies that the reconstruction sought to emphatically reaffirm. Journalists

made clear that the motivational force behind queer urban encounters was largely that of personal economic greed. As Warth told his readers:

> One of the most unpleasant aspects of a thoroughly unpleasant subject is the fact that an overwhelming proportion of the homosexual vice that has got a grip on Britain is conducted commercially. There are perverts—and these are the least offensive—who simply settle down and live a "married" life with someone of their own sex. But by far the greatest number, throughout the country, meet casually and promiscuously. Money or presents change hands.[22]

Warth's claim, though willfully distorted, had some grounding in reality. For much of the century, many of the queer encounters that took place on London's streets had indeed been mediated via some form of material exchange. In certain areas of the city, large populations of young servicemen, dockers, and migrant casual laborers had produced a masculine working-class street culture in which sex with an older, richer man was perceived as both an acceptable sexual outlet and a display of urban resourcefulness.[23] Working-class gender systems firmly identified queerness with the effeminate, painted queans more commonly found mincing around Piccadilly and Leicester Square, allowing "normal" workingmen to pursue such encounters without experiencing any particular personal anguish. Indeed, until the mid-1950s, sexological models of "homosexuality" remained largely confined to those middle-class queers with the capital or education to encounter them. Until these ideas became more widely disseminated—partly thanks to their inconsistent use by journalists like Warth and Brayshaw—workingmen could still enjoy sex with middle-class "poofs," particularly if the encounter was buffered by some form of material patronage that insulated them against charges of being "queer."

Warth thus described how "a number of Guardsmen in London" could be seen "hanging round the streets, drifting off with perverts who pick them up in serious numbers," particularly on Wednesdays and Thursdays. On Fridays (the day on which they were paid, Warth noted), they were more likely to go out with women, until they ran out of cash and returned to the streets. It was the sheer adaptability of these young men—"men whose instincts are normal but who, for money, are prepared to descend to unnatural practices"—that signaled the dangers of male perversion and its insidious, progressive creep.[24]

On the one hand, sensing the class-bound nature of these encounters, the tabloids perpetuated a binary logic in which the richer decadent "homosexual" was set against the poorer and more vulnerable "normal" man. But while this distinction tacitly invoked contemporary sexologists' division between "homosexuals" and "pseudo-homosexuals," it was heavily blurred by journalists' persistent use of the term "male perversion" to designate any form of urban queer vice. Indeed, reports undermined the basis of this originary opposition by attributing a set of internal dynamics to the queer act itself. Letting oneself be used for another man's pleasure was read as an inherent act of submission, which already revealed a dangerous lack of masculine resolve. To engage in such acts was thus to become feminized and embark on a steady progression away from proper male conduct toward amorphously queer forms of urban perversity. The original sin of material indulgence thus slowly transmuted into the illicit sexual appetite that it both precipitated and foreshadowed. According to this logic, the normal lad may have been tempted only by the prospect of cash or presents, but he could not prevent his slow transmutation into his original opposite—the homosexual pervert—as his material consumption slowly transformed into a growing enjoyment of the sex that facilitated it. This notion of "corruption," always presented as a one-way process, became the narrative engine through which these postwar accounts of London's male vice could construct their sense of social urgency.

This was clearly evident during the second Montagu trial of January 1954, where even the prosecution presented the two airmen who had turned Queen's evidence as too irrevocably debased to be treated as reliable witnesses. As the *Times* reported:

> Reynolds and McNally . . . were put forward as perverts, men of the lowest possible moral character, men who were corrupted and, apparently, accepted corruption long before they met the three accused men.[25]

Although the pair had been "under the influence of lavish hospitality from the men who were their social superiors," their consent as "willing parties" to such "unnatural offences" implied an earlier violation for which Montagu and his codefendants could not be held responsible. No longer the naive victims of predatory homosexuals, the airmen had become their own moral agents and could thus be vilified for an established appetite for both material and sexual excess. McNally's and Reynolds's culpability was firmly rooted in their original submission to self-interested temptation. This placed them clearly outside competing psychiatric understandings of "homosexuality," which Wildeblood would try to invoke both during and after the trial in an attempt to deflect attributions of blame.[26] Thus, when McNally was asked by the defense, "How long have you been a pervert?" he could logically reply: "About five years, sir."[27] It was the repetition of these indulgent practices that made them coalesce into something residual, as inappropriate economic greed transmogrified into the sexual avarice of the pervert proper. As Warth explained in "Evil Men":

> Habit is so strong in all of us and, once a callow youth becomes enmeshed in the practices of the pervert—through ignorance, curiosity, drink, blackmail or flattery—it is hard to win him back to normal life.[28]

As Houlbrook has shown, most workingmen who engaged in queer metropolitan encounters would later settle down to become husbands and fathers, as they left the bachelor culture of London's casual labor force and entered more reputable trades in established working-class neighborhoods.[29] Against this, the popular narrative of queer "corruption" was as an irreversible process that inevitably ended in ruinous perversion. Queer acts, therefore, were less troubling in themselves as discreet moments of transgression than for the centrifugal dynamics already inscribed within them. These allowed their malignancy to diffuse outwards and slowly corrode the wider social fabric. If such practices were precipitated not by anterior sexual proclivity but only by a thirst for material self-advancement, then any man in London was open to temptation, not only those young guardsmen and wayward borstal boys that the tabloids presented as most readily at risk.

The concentration of policing within London's West End ensured its lasting position as the imagined epicenter of this pervasive system.[30] With its dangerous and cosmopolitan mix of pleasure and possibility, queer activity seemed to radiate out from here as corruption and debasement spread into the suburbs and across the country more widely. Newspaper coverage of the Assize courts reinforced this notion, as magistrates exploited the issue's topicality to make vocal proclamations on the seriousness of the threat:

> Mr Justice Streatfield, at Norfolk Assizes at Norwich, said: "It is perfectly appalling that when judges go north, south, east and west in this country on

circuit they find the criminal calendars packed full of cases of indecent assault
and gross indecency between males. It is a most distressing thought . . . An
indication of moral decadence that is wholly regrettable."[31]

Mr. Justice Stable, referring at Leeds Assizes yesterday to offences between
male persons, said: "Wherever we go in England to-day, at these Assizes, this
thing is a great black blot on the national life, and it is getting bigger and bigger and bigger. Look at the percentage of these cases in this list at Leeds. This
sort of thing is very alarming."[32]

Passing sentence on a man for five offences committed with two male persons, Mr. Justice Cassels said at Hereford Assizes yesterday: "This type of
offence seems like a disease sweeping through the country. No assize court
seems to take place without a case of this kind coming before it. So far as the
law is concerned, it must be stamped out."[33]

All three of these speeches were reported in November 1953 in the wake
of Gielgud's conviction, and they clearly sketched out the dynamic geography of homosexual corruption. The circulations of the Assize magistrates,
as they left the capital and toured the provinces, traced the routes along
which queer corruption already appeared to have traveled. Emanating out
from the nucleus of the West End and invading the hinterlands of Norfolk
and Herefordshire, male perversion seemed to ripple across the country
in successive criminal waves—and at the same moment as London was
itself being ideologically repositioned as the vibrant epicenter of a dynamic
postwar nation.

The corrupted pervert at the rhetorical core of these reports owed much
to the figure of the spiv, his immediate precursor within the postwar popular media. Both characters were young, working-class, and adrift within a
metropolis whose dangerous temptations continually threatened to pull him
under. Both were also subject to their own foolish self-interest, which left
them perpetually vulnerable to exploitation and ruin. The spiv's dabbling in
the illicit black market, a willful subterfuge of the utilitarian constraints of
state-imposed rationing, spoke of an immaturity and lack of self-possession
that left him unable to manage his own criminality. As David Hughes
recalled in a eulogistic essay of 1963, spivs "never planned their opportunities, as criminals did; they merely took them, snatched and improvised,
inventing as they went along." And it was this mere flirtation with crime—

"tagg[ing] on, like sycophants, to the tail-end of rackets"—that rendered them dangerously vulnerable within the brutal milieu of the metropolitan underworld.[34] The spiv's desire to impress, outwardly signaled by his ostentatious clothing and propensity for self-aggrandizement, made him curiously feminine when set against the aggressive resolve of more hardened criminals. As the rash of "spiv films" produced in the late 1940s made clear, such personal moral failure could only result in his imprisonment or—more probably—his death.[35]

The spiv and the pervert, two intimately related media figures, provided similar cautionary tales about the dangers of transgressive metropolitan consumption. Both reveled in an antisocial desire for self-gain, caught within a narrative that demonstrated the pitfalls of excessive greed and inappropriate class mobility. In this sense, they were the complementary obverse of those reformed citizens being imagined by events like *Britain Can Make It*, recently trained to appreciate well-designed, functional, and sincere commodities and ready to share in the production of a stable, appropriate, and ordered urban environment. Within this context, such willfully inappropriate acts of consumption—particularly, but not solely, by young working-class men—could easily become recast as queer in themselves.

Reports on the Montagu trial could thus already infer a sexual perversion from the lavish treats supposedly enjoyed on the night of Lord Montagu and Reynolds's first encounter. *The People* described how Montagu had paid for Wildeblood, McNally, and Reynolds to all attend the theater, before the four of them briefly returned to Montagu's flat:

"Lord Montagu and Wildeblood went in while Reynolds and I sat in the car. They came back with a bottle of champagne and we went to Wildeblood's flat. At the flat," said McNally, "I noticed Lord Montagu go into the bedroom with Reynolds." He and Wildeblood stayed in the sitting-room and committed a serious offence.[36]

During a time of austerity, this eager proffering of theater tickets and champagne—and the ready consumption of these things by two working-class airmen—already signified the illicit sexual exchange on which they must have been premised and to which they had surely led. In his defense, Wildeblood eagerly asserted that it was merely "supper and champagne cider" that they had enjoyed at the flat, effectively a claim that no sexual misconduct had taken place.[37]

Wildeblood's relationship with NcNally became the site of an intense discursive battle over the legitimate boundaries of cross-class sociality. For the prosecution—rehearsing the rhetoric of the Wilde trials sixty years earlier—the association between these men could only have been sexually motivated, for it transgressed the normal endogamic patterns of bourgeois masculine friendship. The return of this logic in the early 1950s reveals just how troubling such interclass sociality had become to the structures of the nascent welfare state. If, as T. H. Marshall claimed, the postwar extension of social citizenship worked toward the relegitimation of basic class inequalities, then the transgression of these boundaries was already a form of antisocial deviancy.[38] As suggested within Abercrombie's carefully articulated neighborhoods and by the happily assorted tenants of *Britain Can Make It*'s Furnished Rooms, the projected social order of postwar London foreclosed the possibility of class conflict under the aegis of an inclusive and consensual urban community, in which people of all occupations would live side by side. Alternative, unruly forms of interclass mingling, away from normative sites of managed sociality and authorized civic performance, threatened to blur the economic hierarchies toward which this vision strove.

Demarcating the legitimate boundaries of interclass sociality was thus an urgent project of the postwar years, to which journalistic and juridical attention to London's "male vice" earnestly contributed. In his final summing up, the judge at the Montagu trial even admitted as much:

> Referring to the friendship between the accused men and the two airmen, his Lordship said that the jury had to consider whether they thought the fact of that admitted friendship was in itself evidence corroborating the story of McNally and Reynolds and whether it supported the submission of the prosecution that the only link between these people was the link of improper sexual practices. That was the way the prosecution had put it to the jury, and that was really the way the jury would have to consider it.[39]

Much could be inferred from the prosecutor Mr. Roberts's loaded question to Wildeblood: "What was the common link which bound you, a highly intelligent man and a beautiful writer, with Corporal McNally, who started honourably in the pits at Glasgow?"[40] Faced with this impossible question, Wildeblood invoked dominant notions of a national economic community. On first meeting McNally, the *Daily Express* reported:

"He [McNally] said he was thinking of going to the Union Jack Club to find a bed for the night, but it was rather late and he did not know whether he would get in. I said I had a sofa or couch in my flat and he was welcome to use that." Wildeblood went on: "He said there were various things that had to be done at his hospital whenever the Duke of Edinburgh went flying. I thought it might make an interesting item some time for a gossip column. So I did what I usually do when I meet someone who may be helpful. I gave him one of my cards."[41]

It was their occupations, and more specifically Wildeblood's, that had brought them together: "Part of my work is to be equally at home with all kinds of people. I should be no use as a journalist if I was not."[42]

Similarly, when Wildeblood tried to account for the presence of McNally and Reynolds at Montagu's private beach hut, he did so via conventional distinctions of labor: the airmen were there because they could help with the washing up.[43] At other times, he tried a different variation on this tactic by identifying his own class position with that of the airmen after all:

I thought I had made clear that my social position was a completely artificial thing. I have already said I was a waiter working at £5 a week after leaving Oxford and when I first became a reporter I was paid £6 a week and lived in a council house. It just happened that one of the jobs I had to do was to go about in society—but that was not my normal social status.[44]

These strategies were largely doomed to failure, of course, for by re-affirming the class boundaries of normative postwar sociality, Wildeblood inevitably highlighted the oddness of these particular friendships. Within the pages of the press and in the minds of the convicting jury, such awkward relations could only register as out of place, excessive, and thus criminally queer.[45]

The disorder of such encounters and of male vice more generally stemmed not just from the class boundaries they seemed to transgress, but from the disparate urban spaces in which they were conducted. These relationships were not taking place within the ordered sites of civic sociality that made up Marshall's "design for community living." Instead, Wildeblood and his codefendants had entertained their airmen in theaters, flats, and once at a beach hut. All of these were private or semiprivate spaces, suspiciously beyond the eyes of London's planners and municipal administrators and a world away from the clusters of community halls, public libraries, precincts, and elementary schools through which the ordering of sociality was now being sought.

Indeed, tabloid journalists worked hard to chart a specifically queer and demonic geography of the postwar metropolis. In one article from 1951, the *News of the World* reported on how three soldiers from the Household Cavalry had been court-martialed for committing improper acts, while two more were facing the additional charge of conspiring to procure others. The case in question centered on a number of parties held at a flat in Curzon Street, Mayfair, by one Arthur Birley at which the soldiers had allegedly associated with a number of "BBC officials." As Corporal Walpole, one of the alleged procurers, was quoted as saying:

> I knew Corpl. Stiles was Birley's agent and introduced young soldiers to him. I've been to the flat dozens of times with other troopers, and generally, after we had something to eat and drink, we would leave Birley with a trooper. Besides buying us clothes, cigarettes, and drinks, he would nearly always fork out a fiver.[46]

From one angle, the interaction between Birley, Walpole, and Stiles exemplified Abercrombie's utopian vision of a revitalized Mayfair, in which all classes mixed together with democratic fervor (this was also true of Warth's enigmatic "Duchess" and his quarry of ex-borstal boys). Yet these grotesque parodies of the reconstruction vision ensured that such associations would be emphatically criminalized. Men may have been happily mingling across class boundaries, but they were doing so in a disordered fashion away from the municipal centers purposely designed to promote and sustain a healthy corporate life.

While these events were taking place, however, *The Lavender Hill Mob* was inviting its audience to take a vicarious pleasure in just such spectacles of deviant interclass consumption. In a key scene after the successful casting of the Towers, Holland marks the event by giving his accomplices "a little surprise." In the next shot, the four members of the mob are shown drunkenly enjoying a lavish blowout in a private dining room at the Threadneedle Restaurant (Figure 14). In contrast to Holland and Pendlebury's ambiguous softness, their associates Shorty and Lackery are clearly presented as normal from the start and are only ever in it for the money. Yet here, freed from the wider consternation that such consumption elsewhere

provoked, the sight of two working-class men being inappropriately in-
dulged by their bourgeois bachelor patrons became a cause of triumphant
joy. The film even mimicked the *News of the World*'s contrived journalistic
exposure by offering viewers this spectacle through a half-open doorway,
replicating both the court's revelatory invasion of Montagu's apartment and
the press's sudden incursion into the private flats of Mayfair.

Much of the anxiety attached to the tableaux of Birley's private parties
was that such rituals of excess should be happening within the domestic
home, which—as the Furnished Rooms at *Britain Can Make It* had made
clear—were privileged familial spaces designed to be impermeable to any
casual semipublic interaction. Not only did this Curzon Street apartment
affront these ideals through the obvious absence of a loving wife and children but, through the parodic presence of working-class lads, it turned a
key site of moral training into a sordid lair for the active corruption of the
young. The presence therein of airmen, guardsmen, or others on the make

Figure 14. The staged revelation of illicit cross-class consumption in *The Lavender
Hill Mob.*

sullied this prescriptive zone of managed emotional citizenship with an illicit form of work. Far removed from the industrial estates through which labor could be managed, here was an illegitimate form of sexual trade that sat uneasily with those official occupations that should have bound these men into the national economic community. This, in itself, revealed the paradox of the home—one clearly apparent within such anxious exposés— by which its valorized codes of privacy and discretion left it problematically beyond the reach of the administrative gaze. Alarmingly, then, the type of queer activity that was apparently the most damaging was also the type that seemed hardest to detect.

Queer Choreographies and Spatial Transgressions

Outside of such private apartments, tabloid reports about metropolitan male vice mapped out a selection of other, more public urban spaces that festered with excessive possibilities and illicit desires. The most prominent of these was the down-at-heel café, a recurrent location within Warth's "Evil Men":

> There is a dirty café, off Shaftesbury-avenue, where dozens of the most bla-
> tant perverts meet, calling each other by girls' names openly. There is, too, a
> snack bar where they leave each other messages. It was there, last week, that
> I heard some of the most shameless of them complaining about the first
> report I made on their activities. . . . Another said that some of them had
> scrawled slogans attacking me on the walls of a place near Victoria where
> they meet—a fact I immediately checked and found correct.[47]

These cafés were always presented as just off the main thoroughfare, half concealed from the ordinary public gaze and thus in urgent need of journal-istic exposure. Yet they also provided a staple trope within wider accounts of postwar urban delinquency. In *The Blue Lamp,* for instance, they provide the main public meeting place for Riley and his gang of crooks; indeed, as Hughes recalled, the spiv was consistently shown against "a flashy, decrepit half-world of sloppy pubs and steamed-up caffs."[48]

Against those more manageable sites of sociality propagated by the drive for urban renewal, the side-street café was saturated by an unstable set of spa-tial dynamics that could easily provoke promiscuously disordered forms of behavior. The café may have served a legitimate function within the urban landscape as a place to find refreshment when out and about, but it could never quite disassociate itself from the wider dynamics of the metropolis outside. In contrast to more administered sites of eating and drinking—the domestic dining room, the South Bank's Regatta Restaurant, or the lunch-time recreation zone on the fringe of an industrial estate—the side-street café was not only concealed from view but remained open to a transient flow of diverse metropolitan types. Cheap, located in the city center, and seemingly always open, the real danger of the café was that it replicated the transient flow of strangers on the pavements outside, while encouraging its patrons to linger over their cup of tea in a state of constant distraction. Freed from the temporal constraints of any bounded lunch hour, the café immobilized its seated customers without quite extracting them from the bustle and flow of the public metropolis. Thus Warth could situate his pred-atory "Duchess" within Mayfair's all-night cafés; already a site of temporal disorder, its social danger lay in how it rendered its young lads vulnerable by trapping them within a promiscuous, distracting, and functionally am-bivalent space.

The imagined geography of male vice was inextricable from such crowded sites of ephemeral flow and transient encounter. As the *People* reported shortly after the Gielgud case: "Men of Scotland Yard's vice squad are patrolling main railway stations. Another special patrol is being carried out in London's parks and open spaces."[49] Within the spatial logics of the post-war reconstruction, such anxious sites lacked a clear functional purpose, providing only the connective tissue that linked the city's more definable zones of prescribed activity. Railway stations and other busy public spaces existed only as interstices, there but to be moved through. The presence therein of static, lingering bodies was already problematic. In a space nor-matively defined by perpetual flow, any lack of movement could already be understood as a shadowy form of criminality. In "Evil Men," therefore, Warth introduced the "steamer," a type of aging queer man who "hang[s] round Leicester-square late at night, mingling with the crowd in the gar-dens on the look-out for youths just up in London job-hunting."[50] If, at *Britain Can Make It,* those who were static had been neatly separated off from the ordered flow of circulating visitors, then the steamer promiscu-ously conflated these two modes of spatial inhabitation within a disordered state of ambiguity. Hanging around Leicester Square—milling about but never quite moving—he wrote large the more enclosed choreographies of the public toilet importuner, another deviant loiterer within a zone of tran-sience, while fixing this more firmly as an inherently illegitimate mode of inhabiting metropolitan public space.

Such dynamics were forcefully deployed during the second Montagu trial of January 1954. As the *Daily Mirror* reported:

> "The case begins in March, 1952, in Piccadilly Circus Underground," Mr Roberts went on. *"McNally is up on leave seeing what London has in store for him. He meets Wildeblood, they smile at each other, and then they get into conversation.* 'What are you doing?' asks Wildeblood. 'I am looking for a bed,' says McNally with a smile." Then, said Mr Roberts, Wildeblood and McNally went back to Wildeblood's flat in Roland-gardens, South Kensington, where, it was alleged, serious offences took place.[51]

Piccadilly Circus, with its cosmopolitan street culture and gaudy commercial illuminations, had long been imagined to be the epicenter of London's queer street culture. As the meeting point between Piccadilly, Regent Street, and Leicester Square (the latter via Coventry Street), it was already marked by its transient hordes and incessant bustle. The symbolic centering of Alfred Gilbert's *Eros,* proudly visible in the middle of the roundabout, seemed only to crown the space as a site of sexual pleasure and possibility. That Wildeblood and McNally's encounter should have occurred at Piccadilly Circus, therefore, was already amenable to forceful queer inference; but this was further exaggerated by the particular dynamics of the Tube station itself. Functionless, other than as an interstice between the pleasures (or labors) of the commercial West End and the residential areas to which its passengers were dispersed, this subterranean conduit was clearly authorized only as a space to be traveled through, at specific moments within its citizens' day. That two men should not only be lingering here amid these careful circulations, but that they should make some form of contact across its individuated flows, revealed a spatial disorder that seemed to gesture toward only one explanation. Clearly sensing this, Wildeblood tried hard to translate his presence into the more acceptable terms of functionalist logic; he had just left the theater without a coat and was sheltering from the rain.[52]

In *The Lavender Hill Mob,* when Holland and Pendlebury decide to enlist the help of two professional crooks, their first recourse is also to the London Underground. Here, within a Tube carriage, they cruise for other criminals in a metropolitan space wherein loitering is the prerequisite for its actual proper use. Packed full of unknown men promiscuously gathered in enforced proximity, such dangerous instability becomes productive for

our protagonists, because it holds their fellow passengers within a temporary stasis while providing no particular activity to direct their attention.
Like the side-street café or the Tube station ticket hall, it invites an unstable
confluence of disengagement and distraction, stillness and movement, that
opens the space up to a potential queer *détournement* by other men amenable to irregular temptations. Interstitially located between the more ad-
ministrable zones of work, home, and leisure, the Tube carriage becomes a
telling point of weakness within a city ordered through the routine orchestration of individual trajectories. This was, of course, the same anxiety
already expressed by the aim of the *County of London Plan* to reduce the time
commuters spent in transit, but here—within the context of an inoffensive
popular comedy—it could be inverted and celebrated as a pleasurable site
of disorder and dissent.

Such queer inferences could also become attached to more general temporal irregularities, as men were discovered within legitimate spaces but
outside of the prescribed periods through which they had been ordered.
Within *The Lavender Hill Mob,* this is played out within Pendlebury's
foundry, a legitimate space of production during business hours but a locus
of illicit criminality at night. In the sequence following their solicitous
Tube ride, Holland and Pendlebury are shown hiding there in the dark,
waiting for their quarry to try and break in. Shadowy, full of echoes, and
just below street level, the foundry becomes analogous to a late-night public toilet as two men loiter in patient anticipation of the arrival of accomplices. Minutes later, when a passing policeman notices the window that they
have temptingly left ajar, Pendlebury tries to recast their presence through
the logics of legitimate use. Prefiguring the excuse of the sheltering Wildeblood, he hastily explains: "Yes, thank you, officer. My partner and I are
busy stocktaking."

Such temporal deviations from the normative patterning of daily routine were crucial to the press construction of metropolitan male vice. Warth
used them to stress the deviancy of another of his stock characters: the
"skipper"—"a painted pervert who solicits men in the evening and late at
night, then goes, by day, to sleep in one of the parks."[53] Five years later, the
Wolfenden Report would show a similar logic still being employed in its
description of the detection and arrest of the unfortunate "Case IV":

The offence was discovered when it was observed by police that E., a man
known to spend a good deal of his leisure time in company with men

considerably younger than himself, was, during the evening, returning to the shop at . . . . where he was employed. He was joined by F., and the men frequently did not leave the shop until after midnight.[54]

On the basis of these temporal irregularities, F. was brought in for questioning and he subsequently confessed to committing buggery.

Alongside the enforced loitering demanded by both Tube travel and the daily commute, certain other moments of the day remained ambiguously unstable within the ordered prescriptions of urban routine. During the hearings of the Wolfenden Committee, Police Constable Butcher of the Metropolitan Police's B Division described the illicit timetable of male perversion as it seemed to coalesce within the toilets of the West End:

> We choose our own hours, and I think I can safely say that the Mayfair area is strongest in the lunch hour, when the people who work in the offices in Mayfair go for their lunch breaks. I am not exaggerating when I say that 90 per cent. of the people I have arrested in the Mayfair area are actually in their lunch break.[55]

As Abercrombie and Forshaw may already have sensed, it was the connective interstices in the working day that were most troublingly amenable to the incursion of corrosive illicit activities.

Yet if the urban dynamics of queer behavior were repeatedly attached to forms of temporal disorder, then they could also be expressed via a set of deviant movements. Set against a spatial citizenship that would adhere to the programmed circuits of the reformed environment, alternative trajectories became equally legible as a cause of suspicion, a site of danger, or an act of willful antisocial individualism. In January 1953, the *News of the World* gave this account of the trial for importuning of the Labour MP William Field:

> "He seemed to be persistently pursuing young men," said Mr Humphreys [prosecuting]. "There is curious evidence beginning on the night of Jan. 6 which I do not attempt to explain. Mr Field was seen to leave the Leicester Square convenience at 10.1 p.m., literally run along the north side of square, walk into the Standard Bar and buy a drink, and come out at 10.7 after having finished his drink. He left by the Haymarket entrance, ran down the Haymarket and along Jermyn-street and later went into the Captain's Cabin.

He stayed but one minute and came out, crossed Jermyn-street and went into the main subway, and into the convenience. The same behaviour began again. At 10.14 he left."[56]

Humphreys's contrived sense of bafflement only reveals how such convoluted West End trajectories could already stand as evidence of an implied, yet absent, form of sexual deviance. Again prefiguring Wildeblood, Field tried to recast his journey within a more acceptable set of spatial logics; he thought that a friend might be in the Captain's Cabin, and his visits to the conveniences were from a genuine need to urinate ("I think the cold affected me").[57]

Once again, this conflation of sexual with spatial deviancy was most forcibly expressed by Police Constable Butcher as he stood before the Wolfenden Committee. Two years after Field's arrest, he said:

I might just tell you a little story about this following. I had one one day and he was interested in me, and I said to the chap at work with me that if he will follow me to such lengths he will follow me to the police station, and he did. I gave him a smile, I turned and walked from Piccadilly Circus up Regent Street, Vigo Street, Old Burlington Street, and even walked him in the back door of the West End Central Police Station. I there arrested him, and he said "I thought we were going to your place", and that was true![58]

Here, it was the victim's trajectory alone that constructed his crime of importuning, an illegal queerness consisting of nothing more than an unexplainable zigzag through the streets of the metropolis.

It was thus entirely consistent that within *The Lavender Hill Mob,* the protagonist's criminal intentions should materialize through the hijacking of the van, as they force it off the main road and reroute it toward the derelict warehouse in which the gold will be unloaded. In a brief shot, reassuringly framed against an indestructible City church, the stolen van is shown "zig-zagging rapidly down a winding hill"—in the words of the scriptwriter T. E. B. Clarke (Figure 15).[59] This sudden zigzag marked the first visible eruption of Holland and Pendlebury's queer ambitions onto the surface of the city, neatly fused within an interwoven moment of social, spatial, and sexual deviation. Here again was that same strange impulse already recognized by the writer of the *Guide* to the *South Bank Exhibition*—an unexplainable habit or mysterious inclination to turn away from the ordered route inscribed upon the floor plans and to stubbornly "zig-zag their way backwards" from the end to the beginning.[60]

Such antisocial zigzags persistently recurred throughout the early postwar period. The criminality of the spiv, for instance, lay in his hijacking of commodities—always, somehow, having "fallen off a lorry"—and his convoluted redirection of them across metropolitan space. As Hughes wrote, his spoils "started at the dockside, pirouetted through a routine of Soho pubs and murky basements in Paddington, and eventually danced into the lap of an ordinary customer too long thwarted by the spastic efforts of the country to get back on her feet."[61] Within the *County of London Plan,* a similar geometry of selfishness had been charted through the figure of the antisocial car driver:

> Whenever a taxi-driver takes his private route zig-zagging across the squared plan of an office quarter, he is offending against the neighbourhood preserves:

Figure 15. The hijacked van zigzags through the bomb sites.

so also is the private motorist on his journey to the office, finding his new unfrequented route, dodging traffic lights, invading quiet suburban security: his newly discovered route is soon found by others and becomes a recognised channel until it too is congested.[62]

In all of these examples, nonprescribed and deviant trajectories were effectively collapsed into a form of self-interested desire, cast in demonized relief against a more managed spatial order.

The postwar press exploited these conflations by repeatedly equating unorthodox spatial trajectories with the antisocial individualism of the criminally queer man. Warth claimed that some London taxi drivers even allowed perverts to use their cabs for sex upon payment of a special price, thus fusing the threat of queer desire with Abercrombie's self-centered car driver zigzagging through the streets of the city.[63] In the first Montagu trial, Kenneth Hume's desire for one of the Boy Scouts was implied through his invitation to accompany him on a car ride. ("On the way back . . . , said the boy, Hume said to him: 'Do not tell the others about the drive because it may make them jealous.'")[64] This excessive journey's lack of functional purpose could only mean one thing, while concurrently, under the heading "What to Tell Your Children," the *Sunday Pictorial* constructed another version of the same queer spatial threat:

> [T]hey must be careful about ANY strange man who speaks to them, offers them sweets or car rides, or tries to take them away alone. Tell them to come straight to you if they are worried by any stranger. If they are away from home, tell them to go at once to the nearest people or the nearest house.[65]

Car rides, like sweets or gold bullion or a brief exchange of words in an Underground ticket hall, tempted vulnerable young citizens into selfish indulgences and produced a dangerous disorder at once spatial and sexual. The only fitting response to such solicitous distractions was to return at once to the sanctity of the familial home, in as straight a line and as short a time as possible.

Semiotic Deception and Queer Conspiracies

The inherent instability of spaces like the Tube station and the side-street café—and the ease with which they could precipitate illicit queer encounters—brought with it a specific anxiety around how such sites might be read by those individuals who traversed them. During the second Montagu trial, the press became fascinated by Wildeblood's initial contact with McNally, not only for his apparent loitering but for the way this immobility could so quickly lead to an alleged pickup. As the *Daily Mirror*'s headline boldly proclaimed: "It All Started 'When Two Men Met and Smiled.'" The ambiguous and uncertain meaning of this smile—and the ways it could be understood by another man across a crowded ticket hall—became an anxious focal point that appeared to disrupt the wider postwar effort to manage the semiotic possibilities of metropolitan public space.

As Gavin and Lowe have explored, the renewal programs of the early reconstruction worked toward the inculcation of a certain urban sensibility that would regulate the inhabitants' perceptual relationship to their everyday built environment. Supported by a plethora of postwar visual education initiatives, the brave new urban landscape was thought to be inherently legible for its values of honest integrity and fitness for purpose, which would soon become appreciated by the citizen through ordinary daily contact. Against the showy extravagance of Victorian civic architecture or the distracting bedazzlement of commercial display, the sober virtues of the reformed metropolis would produce a more purposive sense of belonging within those who routinely moved through it. As its social-democratic values became more clearly understood, the citizens themselves would be reformed and more consciously aware of their ongoing contribution to the sustenance of the urban community.[66] Visitors to *Britain Can Make It*, therefore, were instructed on how to appraise the things they saw for those meritorious design qualities that made them a suitable presence within the moral landscape of the postwar home. The discerning eye, they were taught, should judge any artifact according to three crucial criteria: its functionality, its basic attractiveness, and its semiotic truth. As the *Guide* instructed, a key question to ask was:

> Is it genuine or is it a sham? (i.e., are the materials good and soundly put together? Does it look like what it is, or is it pretending to be something else?)[67]

This foundational criterion of semiotic fidelity was to be applied to both urban buildings and manufactured commodities, but it was also extended to encompass other metropolitan bodies.[68] This could already be seen within the more standardized menswear sanctioned by the wartime Utility scheme, whose sober and "classless" styles would later inform the garments on display at *Britain Can Make It* and on the racks of new chain stores such as Burton's. The promotion of these generic two-piece suits emulated the more universal ideal of inclusive national citizenship into which their wearers were elsewhere being interpellated.[69] During the reconstruction, therefore, self-presentation became similarly a duty of affiliative citizenship, as the surfaces of one's body assumed their place within the general visual order of the functional urban landscape.

Against this background, the figure of the spiv had stood out sharply in the late 1940s. In newspaper cartoons, feature films, and concerned social commentaries, he was persistently presented through his loud clothes, his bold snazzy tie, and the excessive cut of his oversized suit. Such attire not only spoke of shameless overindulgence at a time of great austerity, but it was also in itself a form of semiotic deception. "The first rule of spivvery," recalled Hughes, was "pretending to be something other than he was."[70] Because his clothes were deployed primarily to impress, his body became reduced to a set of duplicitous surfaces that concealed, though never quite successfully, the inadequacies and self-interest that lurked beneath.

Although the body of the metropolitan pervert was equally ambiguous, this was opened up to a far more complex set of meanings. If the spiv's sartorial pretentions announced his fundamental inauthenticity, then the pervert was seen to persist in a much more invidious and convoluted style of semiotic infidelity. In "Evil Men," Warth drew attention to those mincing "pansies" who "most people know . . . [and] regard as freaks and rarities,"[71] but he crucially distinguished these from other, more dangerous queers who were far more threatening to the hegemonic social order. As he went on: "Few of them look obviously effeminate—that is why people, so often, remain in ignorance of their danger." Like spivs, these queers were shams and pretending to be something other than they were; but unlike either the spiv or the mincing pansy, their fakery was undetectable to even the most discerning of eyes—no matter how closely they had paid attention to the pamphlets at *Britain Can Make It*.

This semiotic duplicity was most heavily exploited by *The Lavender Hill Mob* and formed a major source of its comedy. Its cinematic London was earnestly filled with the felicitous uniforms of policemen, schoolgirls, and besuited City gents, all providing clear sartorial signals by which the film's characters—and, by extension, the cinema audience—could swiftly appraise each other and navigate their city. Yet the narrative consistently exploited the simplicity of such perceptual structures. Through Holland in particular, viewers gained a license to subvert the sanctioned visual codes for reading metropolitan space, just as they were being reinforced within wider public culture. Holland may wear a suit and bowler hat, but his covert desires make him unique among the generic commuters with whom he trudges over London Bridge. On the Council of Industrial Design's terms, he is a sham—he does not look like what he is, he is pretending to be something else. Yet in a city built upon a semiotics of civic integrity, this suit and hat make his criminality illegible and neither his employers nor any uniformed policeman can see beneath its conventions. Tellingly, Holland first thinks of cruising for criminals in the carriages of the Underground when he catches his bowler in a mousetrap, for it is this hat—as the faithful marker of the honest City gent—that conceals his deviancy as he circulates around the capital.

At the top of the Eiffel Tower, the precise turning point in the film's plot, this semiotic duplicity comedically collapses as the pair begin their pursuit of the erroneously sold paperweights. Running at speed down the Tower's spiral staircase, Holland's hat flies off and Pendlebury discards his overcoat, two crucial synecdoches of their uniform disguises. Suddenly liberated from the pressures of conformity, the pair experience a moment of blatant queer *jouissance,* laughing uncontrollably as they spin around the staircase, completely unable to halt their descent. At the bottom of the Tower, they come spinning out into a frenzied collision that even implicates the camera in its chaotic instability (Figure 16). Yet, suddenly trapped without their urban uniforms, the pair's unorthodox trajectories are problematically exposed. They fail to board a train to Calais and are forced to take a private taxi instead. Then, on arrival at the dockside, they fail to board the ferry due to their complete inability to master the circulations of the ticket office. Instead, they zigzag desperately from window to window in a hopeless display of spatial incompetence. At the start of this sequence, the pair even attempt to enter the ticket office through its exit—a further revelation of their sodomitic intent. Only upon their return to London, with overcoat and hat both firmly back in place, can they once more rise above suspicion and reinsert themselves unnoticed into the city's everyday routines. In the closing moments of the film, it is entirely consistent that Holland should escape from the police by placing his bowler hat back on his head and resuming his place among the ranks of unremarkable commuters filing into Bank Underground Station to begin their journey home.

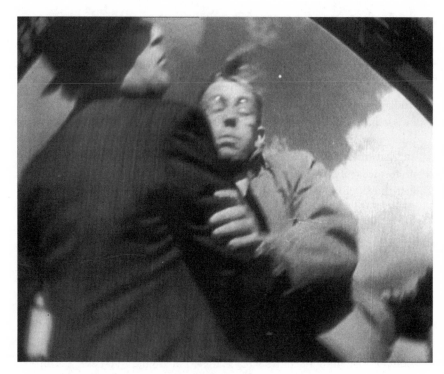

Figure 16. Queer *jouissance* under the Eiffel Tower.

This was also the fear attached to the metropolitan pervert—that he could operate invisibly within the city's normative circulations and thus spread his corruption without being detected. This essential invisibility meant that queer social encounters were figured as relying on their own, unknowable system of secret significations. Again, Warth formulated this most succinctly:

> Homosexuals have their own private language, constantly changing as some of their expressions go into common usage. They recognise each other by the phrases they use. Make-up, which they sometimes wear, is "slap". Putting on women's clothes is "dragging up". A man whom they recognise as unsympathetic to them, and likely to mock and scoff at their mincing ways, is a "send up". Anyone strutting and posturing as they do is "very camp".[72]

The Lavender Hill Mob likewise exploited this notion of a deviant secret language. In their Tube carriage, Holland and Pendlebury attempt to lure conspirators by enacting a staged conversation about a broken safe in which staff wages will be left vulnerable overnight. To the honest model citizens who live within this London, such a conversation can only ever be about fixing a broken safe, and only those individuals already attuned to the existence of excessive possibilities can hear within it an illicit invitation to do wrong. Yet the audience, of course, is fully cognizant that this is all a ruse, and thus can thrill at its own sudden privy access to a secret urban semiotics.

Throughout the early 1950s, press reports persistently returned to this Masonic rendering of a queer epistemology. Accounts of the second Montagu trial dwelled on McNally's statement that "Homosexuals have a language of their own. If you happen to let a word slip out homosexuals will know."[73] Later in the trial, the *Daily Mirror* reported this exchange:

> McNally said that he had never spoken to Reynolds about his "vices," but Reynolds knew that he was a homosexual. Mr Fearnley-Whittingstall: Neither of you told the other he was a pervert?—We just knew. McNally said later, "Our guesses were right," and Mr Fearnley-Whittingstall asked: "Do you say that on the strength of a guess you told Lord Montagu that Reynolds was 'a queer'?" McNally: Yes.[74]

This recourse to "just knowing" constructed homosexuals as a covert community, premised on and sustained by their selective access to this concealed and secret knowledge. Since any understanding of this semiotic system could now stand as proof of one's own criminal desire, perverts necessarily appeared as a conspiracy, distinct from other members of the metropolitan population. As the prosecution suggested during the trial:

> "Everything has been hurled at McNally—every shell, every stone, every insult. Why? What has been his crime?
> *"You may think it has been to tell the truth. You may think that his crime has been to let down the side and give the game away."*[75]

As Warth had suggested only three years earlier: "Homosexuals support each other. Influential ones will often go to extreme limits to compromise anyone who pries into their secret affairs."[76]

This notion of a freemasonry, mediated and sustained by its own semiotic codes, caused important tensions around the policing of male vice, for this now required access to an illicit mode of reading both the city and other men that respectable citizens simply should not have. In a sense, to be able to detect queer behavior was already to be implicated in that which was being detected.[77] In December 1953, the *Sunday Pictorial* reported on a new cleanup drive being launched by Scotland Yard in which "specially-picked squads of plain-clothes men" would begin new operations to combat queer activity across the West End. According to the paper, one hundred policemen "of slight build and smart appearance" would shortly be chosen, to replace the uniformed bobbies who had previously been responsible for dealing with male vice.[78] Historical inaccuracies aside, this report worked hard to distinguish between the uniformed policeman on his repetitious beat and the newfound figure of the plainclothes policeman, more ambiguously free to move around the city.[79] Within the popular discourses of postwar polic- ing, the latter became the pervert's necessary counterpoint because he risked a similar disparity between appearance and motive that legitimated his access to the illicit codes of queer communication. The fictitious ignorance of the uniformed bobby could thus be preserved and the faithful legibility of reconstruction space invested in once more. Within *The Lavender Hill Mob,* therefore, ordinary policemen are never allowed to suspect Holland and Pendlebury's concealed criminality; only the film's plainclothes detec- tive can entertain the possibility that there might be rather more to them than initially meets the eye.

During the proceedings of the Wolfenden Committee, plainclothes policemen became the focal point for a strong anxiety about the permissi- ble limits of metropolitan policing. Although they were recognized as being absolutely necessary for eradicating queer activity—"in the detection of [these] offences . . . ," the final report confirmed, "a police officer legiti- mately resorts to a degree of subterfuge in the course of his duty"—con- cerns were expressed that such methods might slip over into deliberate provocation.[80] The committee's tortuous efforts to reinscribe the boundary between respectable detective and agent provocateur reveals how this drive to prevent illicit queer practices was inherently imbricated with the very thing that it was trying to eradicate. Something of this had already been intimated during the *Britain Can Make It* exhibition of 1946. When Mass- Observation was commissioned by the COID to gauge reactions to the displays, it advised its staff to create a secret "sign system" to signal to pho- tographers which individuals they were following and those on whom they were eavesdropping.[81] Thus, while the commodities on show were being celebrated for their virtues of visual truth, Mass-Observation's observers were forced to become shams—in total opposition to the values of the exhibition that they were trying to monitor. Like the "new" plainclothes policeman of the Met's "anti-vice drive," the policing of reconstruction space was deeply problematic and threatened to expose the contradictions on which the whole edifice rested.

Sensing these contradictions, the tabloid reports of the early 1950s worked hard to construct queer activity in London as an entirely separate system of metropolitan (anti)sociality. Against the careful civic order proposed most succinctly by Abercrombie's plans or articulated within the layout of the *South Bank Exhibition,* London's queers were endowed with their own deeply corrosive design for community living. This both opposed and parodied the type of hegemonic urban citizenship through which social renewal was elsewhere being imagined. Their collective networks of self-interest and deceit, figured most of all through the secret urban language that only they understood, became the discursive foundation on which journalists and others could construct a form of malignant anticitizenship poised to insidiously undermine the corporate unity of the postwar community.

Against the uncertain legacies of imperial decline and wartime disruption, and in the midst of heavy cultural investments in the child as future citizen, queer men appeared as an obvious point of social disorder and a legitimate object of wider moral outrage. But beyond this, the particular dynamics of metropolitan queer activity as they were emotively reworked supplied an obverse to the sanctioned mode of urban engagement through which social stability was more widely being envisaged. Queer sociality, flagrantly transgressing multiple boundaries of class and age, undermined those very hierarchies on which welfare-state ideologies had become founded. Like the spiv, whose cultural mantle he inherited, the working-class pervert threatened to destablize the economic disparities that universal social citizenship covertly sought to legitimize. Thus, just as a raft of new planning and welfare legislation sought to bind the economy toward the needs of this social order, the pervert revealed the existence of a thrillingly free market and its attendant opportunities for individual social mobility. Mocking the more manageable interclass minglings of the plaza or the precinct, these orgies of deregulated consumption promiscuously ruptured the sanctity of domestic space, while always existing just beyond the limits of municipal control.

The real threat of male vice, then, lay in how it imperceptibly overlaid the cartography of ordinary urban space while seeming to exceed its methods of quotidian spatial management. Queer men and their activities appeared as an undetectable presence within the metropolis, spreading their malignancy through little more than a candid smile, a casual loiter, or a craftily inscribed zigzag across the surface of the city. Against the virtuous legibility of the functional built environment, London was shown to still operate—for some—as an array of flickering surfaces and transient possibilities that made its future stability seem less certain and secure.

It was this sense of a threatened order that gave the moral outrages of the early 1950s their force and sense of urgency. Yet they soon encountered their own limitations, because their dynamic narrative of centrifugal corruption could never quite sustain its own journalistic momentum. The Masonic rendering of a metropolitan queer society in which all members were united by their antisocial intent sat unhappily alongside what was, in reality, a diverse set of men, riven by differences of class, mobility, identity, and privilege. In this sense, the cross-class community of London's queer anticitizens was as much a fiction as its discursive counterpart: the metropolitan local community whom they jeopardized and parodied.

As the 1950s progressed, the shouts of the tabloids became progressively eclipsed by an alternative set of more sober public voices. Broadsheet journalists, medical professionals, and a stratum of largely middle-class queer men came together in what can best be thought of as a counterdiscursive project in the battle to define the truth of queer London. Turning to the formulations of sexology and criminal psychiatry, they presented an account of "homosexuality" not as a behavioral set of urban practices, movements, and secret signs, but as an internal psychological disposition grounded mainly in the events of a boy's early childhood. This cluster of apologists, themselves deeply invested in preserving the extant class privileges of postwar society, repeated many of the attacks on metropolitan queer practices that the tabloids had made familiar. But crucially, they remolded these to formulate an alternative model of homosexual citizenship, largely in concordance with the wider imperatives of urban and social renewal. The next chapter, therefore, examines the terms through which this respectable form of urban homosexuality was constructed and reveals its complex, often tortuous relationship with the wider moral imperatives of everyday time and space.

chapter 3

TRIAL BY PHOTOBOOTH: THE PUBLIC FACE OF THE HOMOSEXUAL CITIZEN

I've always wanted and never succeeded in painting the smile.

—FRANCIS BACON, in interview with David Sylvester, 1966

The Photomat always turns you into a criminal type, wanted by the police.

—ROLAND BARTHES, *Camera Lucida,* 1980

In 1952, Gordon Westwood (a pseudonym of the sociologist Michael Scho-field) published his book *Society and the Homosexual,* an "attempt to eval-uate the social implications of homosexuality" for a general nontechnical readership. Deploying a similar rhetoric to Douglas Warth's contempora-neous series of "Evil Men" articles, Westwood also presented his work as an urgent attempt to end the "conspiracy of silence on all sides" that con-tinued to disavow the prevalence of male homosexuality in Britain.[1] Yet as much as he mimicked the journalist's structure of contrived revelation, his text was primarily directed against Warth's type of populist reportage. Westwood shared with Warth and his colleagues a founding desire to address queer male practices and fix them in relation to the emergent ideologies of the postwar social order. But if the tabloids colluded in an entirely demonic account of London's queer cultures, then Westwood's project was firmly one of reconciliation—in part, in least. The conjunction in his title concealed an important dynamic. The commonsense opposition between "society" and "the homosexual"—endemic to populist thinking on the subject—was a misguided notion built on outmoded ignorance and received opinion. Instead, Westwood argued, the modern dynamism of postwar Britain, with its founding principles of equality and diversity, demanded that the re-sponsible law-abiding homosexual citizen should become an inevitable—if

still not much more than tolerable—member of the imagined metropolitan community.

Society and the Homosexual was a formative text that helped to set the
template for how reformers throughout the 1950s would seek to integrate
queer male desire into the normative social frameworks of postwar reconstruction. Sympathetic novels such as Rodney Garland's *The Heart in Exile*
(1953) and Audrey Erskine Lindop's *Details of Jeremy Stretton* (1955), confessional testimonials such as Peter Wildeblood's *Against the Law* (1955), and
editorial opinion pieces in the broadsheets and liberal press all coalesced to
oppose the vilified queer geographies of tabloid and courtroom scandal,
promoting a cultural climate of greater social tolerance that would, it was
hoped, open the way to legislative reform.[2] This was ultimately a bourgeois
project whose recurrent polemics stood in close relation to those mid-1940s
rhetorics of urban renewal whose dynamics they fundamentally emulated.[3]
Both homosexual reformists and town planners invested in a set of scientific discourses that had originally emerged in the late nineteenth century
and become increasingly professionalized in Britain between the two world
wars.[4] Both movements also mobilized the authoritative figure of the expert
and framed the forceful promotion of their ideas as the progressive enlightenment of an ignorant, if well-meaning, general public. In addition, they
both projected a consensual, happy, and peaceful postwar society in which
the latest modern science would finally dislodge the obsolescent remnants
of the Victorian past, under the cover of which they covertly installed a
hegemonic set of bourgeois assumptions about civic sociality, domestic
respectability, and appropriate urban conduct.

As Gavin and Lowe have so astutely observed, the urban designers who
came to prominence during the reconstruction understood the planned
environment as an active means to reorder the values and sensibilities of
the inhabitants who dwelled there. In this sense, social order and civic participation would be assured by the manner in which citizens responded to
their ordinary surroundings, expressing this in turn through their routine
daily practices.[5] Advocates for homosexual reform adhered to this logic and
worked hard to endow their nascent political subject with both a similar
sensibility and a normative mode of engaging with the city. The key tools
in this construction were the overlapping professional discourses of psychology, psychiatry, and medical criminology, which were used to carve out a
space of psychic interiority within the homosexual that in turn transformed
the moral significance of queer urban behavior.[6] Homosexual practices,

according to this model, were no longer the accreted residue of habitual self-indulgences, the sorry result of repeated capitulation to deadly metropolitan temptation. Instead, they became the unfortunate manifestation of a defective psychological condition, largely determined by a child's environment before he reached the age of five.

This discursive shift had significant political consequences, for if a man's sexual proclivities were seen to be decided before he was old enough to be held responsible, then current blanket calls for a punitive response to queer activity became increasingly untenable. Rooted in an anterior psychological state rather than existing simply as a set of immoral behaviors, "homosexuality" became ontologically distanced from those metropolitan practices that were now being cast as only its variable expression. How a man dealt with his homosexuality—the ways in which he allowed it to become manifest—suddenly became important. Although this didn't challenge the dominant coding of pubic queer behavior as immoral and disruptive, it did suggest the possibility of an alternative mode of queer living. At the rhetorical center of *Society and the Homosexual,* therefore, could be found a figure, newly endowed with psychological depth, who was an utter misnomer within the more behaviorist logic of tabloid reportage: "the socially conscious homosexual, anxious to play his part in the world."[7]

In what this part actually consisted still required some negotiation, yet the psychological etiologies through which it was conceived allowed the imagined cartographies of homosexuality to be suddenly redrawn. If London's West End had largely been presented as an unstable crucible of opportune temptation, inculcating queerness through its very existence, then Westwood et alia displaced attention onto the childhood home and schoolyard as the real locations where homosexuality was instilled. Through this, the queer man could be formatively extricated from the center of the metropolis. The link between the city and male homosexuality became contingent rather than necessary, allowing the drafting of a new queer spatial sensibility that accorded with more normative modes of inhabiting, understanding, and moving through urban space. Within this new thinking, public queer activity remained immoral, antisocial, and essentially corrosive, but—for the first time—a conscientious homosexual was being publicly imagined who turned away from such behavior and sought his place within the egalitarian diversity of the postwar community. While this infused his own urban engagements with a richer and more complex moral economy, it also diffused the responsibility for queer behavior outwards from the homosexual himself

to encompass his parents, his educators, and those designers of his childhood everyday environment in which the seeds of his condition were now
seen to be sown.

The emergent homosexual citizen of the mid-1950s, however, also revealed a set of deeper tensions and contradictions within the dominant logics of the reconstruction in whose image he was being fashioned. This was
most clearly evident in the workings of the Wolfenden Committee—more
formally, the Home Office Departmental Committee on Homosexuality
and Prostitution—established in 1954 to consider, in part, "the law and
practice relating to homosexual offences and the treatment of persons con-
victed of such offences by the courts."[8] *Homosexual* was not at this time
a word to be found in statute, but the committee's framing terminology
already impelled it toward an understanding of queer activity as the result of
a psychological condition, rather than as a set of manifest criminal behaviors. This was further reinforced by its deference to those same professional
experts who had already found a platform within the pages of Westwood's
book. As is well known, the committee's main recommendation in its final
report of September 1957 was for the decriminalization of private homosexual acts between two consenting males over the age of twenty-one. This
measure, despite taking a further twelve years to finally become law, effectively set the agenda for public homosexual reformism for at least the ensuing decade.

As the Wolfenden Report reasoned:

> Unless a deliberate attempt is to be made by society, acting through the
> agency of the law, to equate the sphere of crime with that of sin, there must
> remain a realm of private morality and immorality which is, in brief and
> crude terms, not the law's business.[9]

Figured in decidedly spatial terms, the spheres of crime and sin stood
here for public and domestic space, respectively, a normative division that
echoed the functional logic of postwar urban planning. In accordance with
bourgeois notions of propriety, the sexual and emotional life of the homosexual citizen was to be safely concealed behind closed doors, relegitimating
public space as the proper sanctioned domain of work, leisure, and certain
forms of administered sociality. Yet, in spatially codifying this notion of
the private sphere, the Wolfenden Committee formalized a latent contradiction within its own construction of homosexual citizenship. For the first

time, official public discourse had acknowledged queer men as having some legitimate right to membership of the urban community. Yet, paradoxically, this act of recognition required that all homosexual expression be placed outside of that community in the concealed spaces of the private home. How, then, was this nascent homosexual citizen to inhabit the public realm—to which he was now being admitted, but only on the condition that he was simultaneously refused? How exactly might the public face of this necessarily nonpublic form of homosexuality be recognized?

This chapter pursues these questions by exploring two sets of images produced by the queer painter Francis Bacon at either end of the 1950s, both of which came to play a major part in constructing the artist's public persona. One of these is a collection of photobooth portraits that Bacon took of himself at some unknown time between the mid-1950s and the end of the 1960s, and which came to prominence via their inclusion in art critic David Sylvester's book *Interviews with Francis Bacon,* first published in 1975. Celebrated by its cover blurb as "a unique statement" about "his aims as a painter, the ways in which he works, and about his life," this self-consciously revelatory publication included only three actual images of the artist: two *Self-Portraits* from 1972 and 1973 (reproduced on the cover and frontispiece, respectively); and a monochrome plate showing a selection of the photobooth images (Figure 17) inserted halfway through the second interview.

There is a certain robust logic in using photobooth self-portraits to illustrate an artist's "unique statement" about his own life and work, but the privileging of these images within Sylvester's interviews is interesting on at least two counts. First, although Bacon seems to have used such strips as source material for his painted self-portraits from around 1967, they resonate uncannily with another set of images produced more than a decade earlier, toward the beginning of his career as a painter.[10] In November 1949, Bacon received his first commercial one-man show at the Hanover Gallery in Mayfair, as part of which he exhibited a series of canvases titled *Heads I–VI.* Each of these portraits showed the malformed head and shoulders of an anonymous male figure that, in retrospect, appears to make an explicit reference to photobooth imagery. Each head is held before the spectator's gaze in a shallow, depthless space that, in five of the six paintings, is marked off at the back by a drab gray-blue curtain. The almost monochrome pallet and the numerical sequencing of the works only reinforce this impression, while *Head VI* (Figure 18) is even enclosed within a geometric cage-like structure that now appears to mimic the familiar architecture of the photobooth

Figure 17. The unstable disclosures of the photobooth portrait: "Plate 40: Photographs of Bacon taken by himself in automatic booths," from David Sylvester, *Interviews with Francis Bacon* (London and New York: Thames and Hudson, 1975), 42. Copyright The Estate of Francis Bacon. All rights reserved. Design and Artists Copyright Society 2008.

Figure 18. Francis Bacon, *Head VI,* 1949. Oil on canvas, 93 × 77 cm. Arts Council Collection, Southbank Centre, London. Copyright The Estate of Francis Bacon. All rights reserved. Design and Artists Copyright Society 2008.

Figure 19. Francis Bacon, *Head II,* 1949. Oil on canvas, 80 × 63.6 cm. Ulster Museum, Belfast. Copyright The Estate of Francis Bacon. All rights reserved. Design and Artists Copyright Society 2008. Photograph reproduced courtesy of the Trustees of National Museums Northern Ireland.

itself. *Head II* (Figure 19) is the most suggestive of all. Here the head has collapsed into an ill-defined blob from which the upper part of an animal's jaw seems to be emerging, but the figure's body still addresses the viewer in the conventional manner. Further, the canvas is edged on three sides by a frame of black paint that directly foreshadows the irregular borders that the photobooth would give Bacon's own image a decade or so later.

To be clear, I am not claiming that *Heads I–VI* were in any way influenced by the apparatus of the photobooth or the images it produced. Before the mid-1950s, such machines were most likely to be encountered as an amusing novelty at a seaside resort, a world away from Bacon's well-connected metropolitan milieu. Yet these early canvases, in their generic equivalence and unadorned presentation of the anonymous male head, reveal him to be already concerned with a set of representational structures that resonated with postwar investments in the expansion of social citizenship. A decade or so later, this interest would find renewed expression through his own engagement with the photobooth, by that time an important and increasingly familiar presence within the ordinary urban landscape and one that aggravated many of the emergent tensions around the postwar presentation of the individuated self.

In 1955, the first photobooth was installed on the London Underground network, in the booking office of Baker Street Station (Figure 20). Over the next few years, similar machines would appear across all major Tube, railway, and bus stations and in many other sites in which a dense flow of people made them commercially viable. During the 1950s, then, entering an automatic booth and posing for one's pictures became an increasingly unremarkable experience, but one whose sheer familiarity—coupled with the plain format of its resultant portraits—served to mask the complex negotiations around self-presentation that were played out within its cramped interior; for the photobooth offered two competing aesthetic structures, both of which pointed to the production of differently inflected images of self. On the one hand, its automated mechanism, its cheapness and accessibility, and the formal simplicity of the pictures it produced were all deeply in sympathy with the participatory ethos and social inclusivity of welfare-state citizenship. Yet, as we shall see, its apparatus also allowed the deployment of an alternative, more challenging set of tactics. At the hands of an increasingly affluent and oppositional urban youth, the photobooth could be used to resist the dominant frameworks of social-democratic citizenship by producing a set of images that fragmented the self, undermining more unitary

Figure 20. Automatic photobooth in Baker Street Underground Station, 1955.
Copyright Transport for London. Collection of London Transport Museum.

notions of the coherent individual. Thus, the postwar photobooth and its imagery became an ambiguous site of contestation over the meanings of the self, its public visualization, and its implied relationship to the wider urban community.

Located within Sylvester's *Interviews,* Bacon's photobooth portraits—taken by Bacon, from Bacon's own collection—take on an intimate, even autobiographical tone that enhances the book's general sense of candid revelation. But this, I suggest, is the result not only of his distinctive appearance in these photographs, but of the wider role of the photobooth within the developing visual economies of postwar London. Here, Bacon's strips take on a crucial ambiguity as he shifts his body around the booth's interior in a seeming state of distraction and discomfort. This, I propose, has much to do with his sexual identity and reveals a great deal about the limited and paradoxical structures through which the homosexual self could be visually expressed within the public arenas of the postwar decades.

The photobooth strips presented within the *Interviews,* like his exhibition of *Heads I–IV* twenty-six years earlier, formed part of Bacon's ongoing search for recognition as an important and credible fine artist—yet one who was also avowedly queer. As Simon Ofield has shown, these two subject positions were generally considered antagonistic within the cultural climate of postwar London—particularly given Bacon's interwar work as a successful interior designer—and debates about whether his work was serious art or merely superficial decoration continued well into the 1950s.[11] Sylvester's *Interviews* and his show at the Hanover Gallery provided two crucial forums in which Bacon wrestled with his own public presentation of self and its potential reception by both the art world and the wider public.

Some of this complexity was caught within Sylvester's accompanying text, where Bacon's sexuality finds a firm if oblique acknowledgment at the beginning of "Interview 3." During a discussion about how he came to be a painter, Bacon mentions (among other things) his rejection from the army, the influence Eric Hall had on his early life—although who Eric Hall was is never made clear—and his time spent as a furniture designer in the late 1920s. He also mentions his terrible shyness as an adolescent, describing himself as "a late starter in everything."[12] Inquiring into his early obsession with Velázsquez's portrait of *Pope Innocent X,* Sylvester asks whether this may have been rooted in his relationship with his father (the pope being *il Papa* in Italian). The interview progresses:

DS: And what were your feelings towards him?

FB: Well, I disliked him, but I was sexually attracted to him when I was young. When I first sensed it, I hardly knew it was sexual. It was only later, through the grooms and the people in the stables I had affairs with, that I realized that it was a sexual thing towards my father.[13]

Within this exchange the dialogue changes register, from that between a critic and an artist to that between a psychoanalyst and his patient. Bacon inserts himself into an inverted Oedipal narrative and a personal history of same-sex cross-class encounters, both of which confirm to the readers what they probably thought they knew anyway: the fact that Bacon is a queer. Suggestive details from earlier in the interview—Bacon's rejection from the army "through asthma and everything else," the ill-defined presence of Eric Hall, his generally arrested development—suddenly open up to a revised reading, as evidence of a queerness that has now been confirmed. Importantly, Sylvester doesn't pursue the issue of Bacon's sexuality and the conversation swiftly moves on to a discussion of his screaming popes. But the fact has nevertheless been signaled that, yes, the reader was right in his or her suspicions; he is, indeed, one of those.

There is, I want to argue, a complicity between this textual presentation of Bacon's homosexuality and the book's prominent foregrounding of these photobooth portraits; for, unusually among its illustrations, these strips are not explicitly referenced in the text. Rather, they hang mysteriously above it, perhaps linked to the discussion about his use of photography, but never quite anchored to anything definite. They do, however, encapsulate a particular set of tensions around the public presentation of male homosexuality. And while this structure is most succinctly articulated via the inclusion of these photobooth strips, it was also endemic to Bacon's most basic portraits of the anonymous male head—all of which highlight a more general contradiction experienced by many queer men in London at this time. Bacon's own adventures on the streets of Kensington and Soho were far removed from the kind of reformist sensibilities through which the homosexual citizen was concurrently being sketched, but he still sought to create a similar public legitimacy around his own queer self.[14] If, as he told a reporter from *Time* magazine in 1949, the *Heads* series was "just an attempt to make a certain type of feeling visual. . . . Painting is the pattern of one's own nervous system being projected on canvas," then these early paintings and their photobooth successors both enunciate, in remarkably similar ways, the semantic paradoxes and affective complexities of trying to face the public realm as a valid, but also visible, homosexual man.[15]

Designing the Homosexual Citizen

As Westwood had already established by 1952, the conflict over the public acceptability of male homosexuality would be framed as one between a dynamic postwar society informed by modern science and those archaic, outmoded institutions that continued to frustrate its progress. As he explained to his readers:

> The new medical and psychological discoveries of the last fifty years have changed our social needs, but the sex code has remained as before, producing a continual disparity between our lives and our rules.[16]

That the 1885 Criminal Law Amendment Act could still govern the lives of homosexual men in the early 1950s revealed, for Westwood, the regressive obsolescence of a legislative system "built up bit by bit through the centuries, often to meet situations that no longer exist or have now widely changed" (84). As with Britain's war-damaged cities, the decaying rubble of the nineteenth century must now be cleared from the statute books in the name of social reform. "Medicine," he argued, "is a dynamic science"; the psychiatrist or doctor—much like the town planner—"must be prepared to throw over long-held convictions and adopt new ideas and new methods" (ibid.).

This project of renewal also set itself in opposition to those outmoded strands of populist opinion that were likewise relics from an earlier era. Westwood attacked both "the Victorian aftermath of timidity and evasiveness" that shied away from any sober discussion of homosexuality and the vitriol with which the tabloids persistently misread the phenomenon as an abhorrent moral evil (21–22). Modern psychology, he explained, now understood that many apparently normal men disguised what were in fact unconscious homosexual urges "by means of a special defence mechanism called 'projection'" (105). By thus transforming the most aggressive opponents of homosexuality into those most likely to be afflicted, the expert psychologist could undermine their authority and effectively trump all competing accounts of urban corruption, here transforming the most aggressive opponents of homosexuality into those most likely to be its sufferers.

In their place, Westwood asserted a conglomerate of loosely psychoanalytic etiologies, whose historical origins in the late nineteenth century remained

unacknowledged within his own assertions of scientific modernity. Homosexuality, he advised, was generally instilled by an unloving or overbearing
mother, an absent or hostile father, an excessively feminine environment,
or an overly forceful propulsion into masculine pursuits. All of these could
damage a boy's psychic development in the first years of his childhood,
although segregation from girls in adolescence—a typical feature, Westwood noted, of Victorian public schools—or a protected ignorance regard-
ing sexual matters could also have deleterious effects. Via this extensive
catalog of early determinants, Westwood could effectively deactivate the
twin narrative engines of metropolitan "male vice": seduction and corruption. That first queer encounter was no longer understood as a damaging
initiation into a life of perversion, for any youth without prior homosexual proclivities would not enjoy the experience and was unlikely to repeat
it given appropriate access to girls. Any boy who relished it, however,
would already be suffering from a condition whose existence had long been
decided elsewhere. In Westwood's terms, such acts were merely "the final
stage in what would be the inevitable result" (45).

This framework made the moral significance of public queer activity
much more complex. No longer equated with immorality per se, such behavior was now seen to express some anterior and covert psychic urge over
which the perpetrator had only a limited control. Thus, while a responsible
homosexual could now be sketched out who actively resisted the public
expression of his desires, it was "the continual persecution and unrelent-
ing scorn of society" that so often caused his moral resolve to crumble. As
Westwood reasoned:

> When [the homosexual] realizes that he is doomed to become either the butt
> of the people around him, or else for ever hide his emotional life away from
> them, in time he will begin to despise the moral laws of this society that has
> so unreasonably put him in the social pillory. He gets the idea that either
> society will break him or he must break from society. (114)

Here, the reformist logic was clear. Involvement in illicit public queer
activity had been recast as primarily a neurotic reaction, produced in the
individual by society's archaic refusal to provide him with a workable moral
code to live by. The active agent of urban corruption had thus been displaced from the predatory older pervert haunting the city's cafés and train
stations to the ignorant and misguided general public who caused the young

homosexual to seek solace in these sites. This didn't change the demonic status of London's queer subcultures, but their distance from the normative sensibilities of urban reconstruction was now viewed differently through the prism of expert psychology. In *Society and the Homosexual,* therefore, the practicing metropolitan queer—so dangerously ill at ease within an intolerant society—was pathologized through a litany of imposed character flaws, which again brought him close to the postwar spiv: an ostentatious wardrobe, a paranoid blaming of others for his own failings, an inability to accept authority, and a violent sadism toward the women he tried (and failed) to love (114–15, 144–45).

The root of queer public disorder, then, lay not in any essential immorality within homosexuality itself, but in the social intolerance that denied it a sanctioned outlet for its emotional and sexual energy. "[W]hichever course he takes," Westwood wrote, "he will still be left with an inner conflict which eats up his energy and saps his vitality" (143). This argument, of course, involved a clear presumption of an original will to do good, a yearning by the homosexual to take that very place within the urban community that society still refused to grant him. In a neat reversal of tabloid moral logic, Westwood even suggested that those men most likely to be charged with gross indecency were the least antisocial of all homosexuals; it was their self-imposed exile from London's criminal subcultures that made them more susceptible to arrest during their sporadic moments of weakness (165).

In the space to be cleared by this demolition of archaic legislation and outmoded social attitudes, reformers could design a homosexual citizen eager to take his place as a productive and contributory member of the postwar national family. As Westwood argued:

> Although the advantages are outweighed by the disadvantages, it does seem that the homosexual sometimes possesses attributes that can be of value to society as a whole. A contrary sexual impulse is bound to change a man's personality, but the change is not always for the worse. (153)

On these terms, the time that any homosexual must spend musing over his potential contributions to society could leave him with a fuller and more developed personality, while freedom from the responsibilities of fatherhood might spur him to excel in creative or other pursuits. Britain, Westwood argued—using the same rhetoric deployed at the previous year's *South Bank Exhibition*—was "a nation . . . renowned for our tolerance and our ability

to recognise individual differences," a country enriched by the "bewildering array of beliefs, crusades and modes of living" coexistent within its borders (173). In a social democracy founded on such traditions of diversity
and equality, the public acceptance of the reformed homosexual was more
than just a question of consistency; it was an innate expression of "our"
basic national character.

Above all, this emergent homosexual citizen was forcefully aligned with
the spatial codes and environmental sensibilities so fundamental to reconstruction thinking. "To the well-adjusted man," Westwood reasoned,
"homosexuality is but one phase of his personality just as heterosexuality is
but one phase of the personality of a normal man"—a problematic bifurcation that nevertheless enabled his integration within the functionalist spatial
logics that underlay the projected reordering of urban life (131). Unsurprisingly, that "one phase" in which the adjusted homosexual acknowledged
his desire was mapped both spatially and temporally onto the time he spent
in private within the confines of his home. Such psychic topographies thus
constructed a sociospatial imperative. Homosexual desire, in and of itself,
had no need to seep out into those other domains of a man's life, such as
his workplace, the sites in which he socialized, or the more general connective interstices that linked these spaces together.

Westwood's loaded presentation of his well-adjusted man, then, had
already codified a spatial framework for homosexual citizenship that would
run through to the Wolfenden Report and beyond. Homosexual practices
performed in public space were—just like their heterosexual counterparts—
an offense against public decency, which could already be dealt with under
existing legislation. If they were carried out in private, where they posed
no threat to public civility, then they were only the expression of an incul-
pable psychology and ought to be left alone. "Society," Westwood concluded, "is entitled to protect itself against acts of public indecency but it
is not entitled to 'punish' psychological disorders" (170). Yet, ultimately,
this distinction was only made plausible by its original postulation of an
invisible psychic interiority that could be prescriptively mapped onto the
inside of the home.

Outside of this realm, public queer activity remained a sign of psychic
maladjustment and a symptom of a lack of purposive self-management.
Thus, Westwood took great pains to distinguish his privatized homosexual from the "two classes of perversion which the layman is apt to confuse
with true homosexuality": the "infanto-homosexual," a psychic regressive

attracted only to little boys; and the "pseudo-homosexual" of "sub-normal intelligence," who—out of ignorance, fear, captivity, or debasement—used men in a substitute for heterosexual intercourse (23). Thus, Westwood insisted,

> the *genuine* homosexual turns towards adults of his own sex as naturally as a normal man is sexually attracted by a woman as a potential mate and he is no more attracted to a young boy than a heterosexual is attracted to a young girl. (24; my emphasis)

In addition, he claimed, true homosexuals preferred mainly mutual masturbation over the acts of sodomy favored by pseudos—a curious endorsement of the former's natural leanings toward normative forms of companionate relations (113). Westwood's ring-fencing of the "genuine homosexual" entirely contradicted his simultaneous endorsement of Kinsey's sexual continuum, which placed most men on a variable sliding scale between total heterosexuality and complete homosexuality.[17] Yet the persistent recurrence of this trope within polemical texts of the 1950s and 1960s reveals its fundamental role in staking out the psychospatial structure of a viable homosexual citizenship. All this, of course, required a willful misunderstanding of London's existent queer culture and the complex sexual practices of many of its "normal" workingmen.[18] Instead, the economic patronage that typically mediated these encounters enabled them to be recast within reformist discourse as mere prostitution, outside the norms of companionate love and so equally beyond the experience of the true homosexual. Westwood's sensational depictions of such workingmen were more suited to the metropolitan journalism of the late nineteenth century than to a dispassionate tome of popular science:

> They are often completely depraved and are prepared to perform any perversion if it will increase their reward. . . . They despise the people who pay for the lease of their bodies and do not enjoy sexual relations outside their professional activities any more than a road-sweeper would enjoy sweeping the road without payment.[19]

This imagined urban underclass of fallen male perverts was already familiar from the pages of the popular tabloids, yet the latter's moral dynamics were here exactly reversed. In a clear reference to the Arthur Birley case discussed in the preceding chapter, Westwood criticized a magistrate's charge that a forty-three-year-old bachelor had "corrupted" the young guards-man whom he had been caught entertaining in his flat. Instead, Westwood argued, the soldier was the true moral culprit, for he had cynically exploited a man "suffering from a mental disorder," driven to "pay[ing] for some meagre sexual satisfaction in his own private room."[20] The bachelor's failed attempts to limit his sexual expression to the confines of his apartment testified to his exemplary morality. It was the forceful intrusion of a young and ambiguous working-class body that profaned this private sanctity, dis-rupting it with his insistent demands for cash.

Beyond the domestic realm, London's queer subcultures had to be reem-phasized as a site of ongoing immaturity and perversion. Anticipating many queer novels of the decade, *Society and the Homosexual* offered its readers a panoramic tour through a range of metropolitan queer spaces, each figured with its own degraded moral economy, but each more acceptable and healthy than the last.[21] At the lowest level was what Westwood termed "the street-corner," his dismissive synecdoche for a promiscuous street culture in which male prostitutes, blackmailers, and habitual criminals mingled with those misguided "genuine" homosexuals without the means or insider knowledge to access the city's more propitious queer spaces. Already disor-dered by its lack of spatial specificity, "the street-corner" became the locus for a dissolute form of criminal antisociality, at once diverse and inclusive. It thus parodied the projected civic centers of the planned urban neighbor-hood, promoting no localized performance of national affiliation but brief disordered relationships built on exploitation, duplicity, and disappoint-ment. As Westwood made plain: "homosexuals at other levels look down upon this heterogeneous group and they will never try to find a partner at this level; most of them are as repulsed by the sight as normal people and earnestly desire to have no connection with them."[22]

At the second spatial level, London's queer public houses were more favorably presented as a semiprivate surrogate in which those homosexuals without access to their own private space could go to "feel at home" (129). While the pub thus gestured toward domestic respectability, its failure to achieve this goal made it an unsatisfactory site for social investment. For Westwood, then, it was simply too public; the intrusive presence of other queer men meant that pub-bound relationships were never long-lasting, for stealthy rivals were always waiting to move in and destroy the loving cou-ple, with a view to carrying off one of the partners for themselves.

Against the undesirable domains of street corner and pub, Westwood's third level of metropolitan queer society—the exclusive men's club—was deemed as inherently more attractive to the proper homosexual:

> In the exclusive clubs he is more likely to find someone *at his own cultured level* and he will meet people who have met and partially solved the *same problems that he has had to face.* These people are good-mannered, polite and have some respect for the ethics and other moral laws of society, but beneath the façade of contentment he will not find many homosexuals who are inwardly at peace with themselves. (140; my emphasis)

Here the class interests that motivated Westwood's apparently dispassionate sociology rang out loud and clear. Finally among people at his own cultured level, the true homosexual could approximate the prescriptive codes of bourgeois respectability. "Little or no public love-making will be seen in these clubs," Westwood wrote, "not so much because there is a law against it but simply because it is regarded as bad manners in the same way as love-making between heterosexuals in public places is considered to be bad form" (131). Far more lasting and institutionalized than the seasonal queer bar or the transient "street-corner," the exclusive club took on a strangely double role. On the one hand, it came closest to the kind of managed space of mannered sociality through which community participation was being reordered in the city outside. Yet, at the same time, its concealment from the ordinary public gaze gave it an impregnability that emulated the discretion of the bourgeois home. Populated by men who inherently respected companionate relationships, Westwood noted how "affairs tend to last longer in this group although few of them are permanent" (132). In his exclusive club, then, the homosexual citizen could almost—though, importantly, not quite—find a form of self-fulfillment in the mature love of a lifelong partner. From here, it was only a small conceptual leap to a logical resolution: the confinement of homosexual expression properly to the home and his attendant sanctioned admittance to the wider participatory spaces of the reformed metropolis.

This cartography of respectable homosexuality would recur within reformist polemics throughout the 1950s and dominated the agenda of legislative campaign groups such as the Homosexual Law Reform Society (HLRS) formed in 1958.[23] Once empowered by greater legal and social tolerance, this logic ran, homosexuals would finally extract themselves from the

parodic sociality of London's queer underworld and participate within the
ordered everyday life of the postwar capital. Yet this bourgeois prescription
for urban assimilation concealed an important contradiction. For if such citizenship was premised on the confinement of all homosexual expression to
the private domestic sphere, then how was the homosexual—*as* a homosexual—to take his place as a recognized part of the postwar urban community?

This ambiguity came sharply into focus during the meetings of the
Wolfenden Committee when members were forced to negotiate between
competing understandings of how a man's homosexuality might register its
visibility within the public realm. One model was provided by members
of the Metropolitan Police who gave extensive written and oral evidence
detailing their methods of detection. On December 7, 1954, Commander
Robertson of A Division described at length how his men identified persistent importuners in his district's public toilets:

> It requires great concentration and attention to detail to get the evidence that
> is necessary here to justify the station officer accepting the charge. . . . These
> policemen are always in pairs . . . but they keep observation on the suspect
> in turns, therefore if one policeman keeps a man under observation for five
> minutes, he goes outside and he makes notes, either in his pocket book or on
> some paper, and during the time he is doing that the other man is watching
> him, and so it goes on, for a period of half-an-hour, 35 or 40 minutes. The
> methods adopted by the suspect vary, but generally they follow the same pat-
> tern; they stand next to a young, likely person whom they think they may get
> some encouragement from, and they look up into his face and smile at him,
> they look down at his person, and if there is any reaction, they may be lucky
> in striking someone who is of the same mind as themselves, they go some-
> where else to complete whatever they intend to do. But generally they are
> rebuffed, no notice is taken of the advances, and they look around and they
> will change the stall and they go to someone else with whom they think they
> will have some better success. They even leave the lavatory and go back again,
> or perhaps go to another lavatory altogether and start some actions there.
> That goes on, as I say, for half-an-hour or 40 minutes, and then the two offi-
> cers make up their minds to arrest him. They tell him what they have seen,
> the time they have watched him, and that they are going to arrest him for
> persistent importuning.[24]

As Robertson made clear, the criminality of the persistent importuner
did not reside in any actual same-sex contact but was produced instead

through a particular choreography within and around the space of the toilet. The illicit intentions that defined his crime became manifest merely as a catalog of standings next-to, changings of stalls, and leavings and enterings—all transformed into "evidence" as notations in a pocket book.

Later that afternoon, Police Constable Darlington of B Division fleshed out the details of Robertson's account:

> These people come in. . . . They stand there and there are three or four or more and you are all standing there, and it is deathly quiet. There is no sound of anybody urinating at all. . . . You see these men, they start to look about them, and give each other the glad eye. They nod their head, they sometimes speak and reach out and touch one another, and practically everyone you see will be masturbating himself. . . . They are in there for two or three minutes and some of them are cunning. Some go in for three or four minutes and will not do a thing, they just stand there, and you cannot tell what they are doing, but the majority of them do it quite openly.[25]

As Leslie Moran has argued, such operations worked to fix the body of the man under surveillance and turn its surfaces and gestures into a "set of decipherable signs."[26] For the officers of the Met, then, the importuner's homosexual desire was rendered visible as a collection of citations previously known to be queer, a lexicon of movements (standing still for too long, changing stalls), bodily gestures (reaching out, nodding the head), or facial expressions loaded with excessive meaning (the glad eye, the leering smile).

Matt Houlbrook has found such citational logics to have been a staple component of policing methods in the first half of the twentieth century. Officers charged with clearing behavioral disorder from the capital's streets focused on the body of the working-class Dilly Boy whose clothes, cosmetics, posture, and deportment became legible markers of his sexual trangressions.[27] Such queer tropes could also extend to include particular possessions. Between the wars, for instance, a suspect's guilt as a persistent importuner would often be "proved" by a powder puff or lipstick discovered in his pocket.[28] Yet, as a letter to the HLRS suggests, such logics remained operational well into the 1950s. During a police raid on the flat of two queer lovers, officers removed a litany of objects they had found in the bedroom—a tin of talcum powder, a jar of Nivea cream, a piece of toweling, several commercial physique magazines, and two pairs of briefs. On the basis of these, both men were brought in for questioning.[29] Once again, queer desire was made visible before the law as an aggregate collection of known citations, in this case, a list of ordinary commodities that became transformed into the prosthetic extensions of their owners' criminal bodies.

As the Wolfenden inquiry progressed, it turned from the evidence of magistrates and policemen to that of medical professionals and of homosexual men themselves. Here they were presented with an alternative conception of homosexuality's visible significance. Central to this construction was the testimony of Peter Wildeblood, recently released from prison after his conviction in the Montagu case and one of three self-identified homosexuals to come before the committee. Wildeblood testified in May 1955; later that year he would publish a book-length version of his argument as *Against the Law*, which reached a wide audience when reprinted as a Penguin paperback in 1957. Commentators have already analyzed Wildeblood's intervention as an attempt to maneuver the committee toward a politically efficacious understanding of the homosexual self.[30] Inevitably, he repeated much of the rhetoric and topological schemata already set out by Westwood. It was the present antiquated law, he argued, not the desires of homosexuals themselves, that made life:

> extremely difficult, almost impossible, for a very large number of men . . . who in all other respects are perfectly good citizens. There is no doubt about it, once you fall foul of the law in one respect it is very difficult to behave as a proper citizen in other respects as well.[31]

Through these remarks, Wildeblood was offering the committee a by now familiar choice: it could either endorse a notion of homosexual citizenship that allowed queer men to align themselves with the sociospatial order, or else it would perpetuate a set of metropolitan behaviors that placed even the most respectable homosexual in a reluctant state of opposition.

As Chris Waters has explored, the homosexual citizen offered up by Wildeblood was a familiar composite of Freudian psychology, interwar criminology, and older sexological models of gender inversion.[32] Together, these allowed him to craft a homosexual ontology rooted in psychic narratives and personal biography. As he told the committee:

> From all the people I have talked to, it seems to me that homosexuality begins at a very early age indeed. Most people seem to remember being attracted to

their own sex at six or seven, and that rather leads me to suppose that it is almost inevitable really. I think perhaps in some borderline cases you can turn them the right way, but the ones who are going to be homosexuals will become homosexuals.[33]

Here homosexuality was made to shift registers from a catalog of behaviors, movements, and prosthetic commodities to an interior psychological state that could only be properly known through speech and personal testament. Through this, the terms of homosexuality's public visibility was similarly renegotiated. Wildeblood reworked Westwood's distinction between infanto-, pseudo-, and genuine homosexuals to construct his own spatial typology of metropolitan queers. His preferred differentiation was between "glandular" inverts (who regarded themselves as women), pederasts (who were attracted to young boys), and homosexuals—of which he was one— "within the strict meaning of the word: that is to say, being attracted to men like themselves."[34] The first two groups, he suggested, were inherently tied to specific locales within the old Victorian city—the West End, the "family" public houses of the East End, or its antiquated prisons—but they also remained marked by their visible deviancy. Wildeblood claimed abhorrence, for instance, at how inverts within Wormwood Scrubs could smuggle in cosmetics and at the "extraordinary amount of licence" with which warders allowed them to paint their queerness upon their faces.[35]

Against this, Wildeblood's true homosexuals transcended localization. They could inhabit ordinary urban space because their homosexuality registered at the level of internal psychology and was therefore invisible to people around them. In *Against the Law,* he wrote:

Everyone has seen the pathetically flamboyant pansy with the flapping wrists, the common butt of music-hall jokes and public-house stories. Most of us are not like that. We do our best to look like everyone else, and we usually succeed. That is why nobody realises how many of us there are. I know many hundreds of homosexuals and not more than half a dozen would be recognised by a stranger for what they are. If anything they dress more soberly and behave more conventionally in public than the "normal" men I know; they have to, if they are to avoid suspicion.[36]

This basic public invisibility of the genuine homosexual became, of course, the foundation on which the Wolfenden Committee erected its final proposal for the partial decriminalization of sex between men. By progressing from an ontology of queerness inadequately propped up by legible signs and criminal citations to a homosexual essence built on narrative, biography, and interior psychology, it could extend the rule of law to this new type of man. As its final report argued:

> Many heterosexual acts are not criminal if committed in private but are punishable if committed in circumstances which outrage public decency, and we should expect the same criteria to apply to homosexual acts. . . . It will be for the courts to decide, in cases of doubt, whether or not public decency has been outraged, and we cannot see that there would be any greater difficulty about establishing this in the case of homosexual acts than there is at present in the case of heterosexual acts.[37]

Such self-conscious liberalism, of course, concealed its fatal paradox. Although the implied set of outrageous heterosexual acts were surely only those approaching displays of explicit sex, almost any visible manifestation of queer subjectivity could be understood as an outrage to normal public decency. In short, the homosexual citizen had been rendered an acceptable public presence via the very sexuality which, at the same time, he was forbidden to express. How, then, was this nascent homosexual citizen to register this presence within the imagined public community of postwar London?

Imaging the Self: The Ambiguities of the Photobooth

The work of Francis Bacon reveals a determined contemporary engagement with precisely this question. From the exhibition of his *Heads* in 1949, through his obsession with the automatic photobooth in particular, to the inclusion of these latter images within Sylvester's *Interviews,* he persistently wrestled with formats and apparatuses through which the visual meanings of the quotidian self were more generally being negotiated within postwar metropolitan society. To understand the place of the photobooth within the image economies of postwar London—and how Bacon's deployment of it came to articulate the paradoxes inherent to visualizing the homosexual citizen—it is necessary to look back at the emergence of the machine and trace two genealogies of representation that uneasily coincided within its apparently straightforward portraits.

When the first wave of "Photomatons" appeared in the major cities of North America and Europe in the mid-1920s, they were initially marketed as a thrilling entertainment for downtown shoppers.[38] The first British machine was installed within the basement of Selfridge's department store on Oxford Street in 1928, where the experience of being photographed by a machine—in eight different poses and for only a shilling—was sold as an initiation into a little piece of urban modernity, as fast-paced, exciting, and technologically advanced as the West End itself. The Photomaton's output reworked the *carte-de-visite* format of the mid-nineteenth century, but made it at once more metropolitan and democratically accessible to a wider sector of the public.[39] Stripped of the stuffy pseudo-domestic settings of conventional studio portraiture, the machine's speed and location invoked a more modern range of visual media. The early Photomaton, embedded within sites of commercial mediation and spectacular display, condensed its surroundings into a brief experience of commodified glamour, soliciting its users to address the camera in the style of a fashion model or film star. On these terms, the Photomaton was marked as an apparatus of theatrical performance that offered its patrons a momentary identification with the more reified star systems to which their poses gestured.

Marketed primarily as an experience, the Photomaton's pictures took on a souvenir quality that tied them firmly to the time and place of their original production. This, coupled with their diminutive size, made them eminently suitable as a portable technology of personal remembrance, kept hidden within the purse or wallet and with an affective value that only seemed to increase with the aging of the sitter or the outmoding of his or her costume. Although initially promoted for use by the individual, two (or more) people could always squeeze into its tight pictorial frame, producing a moment of physical intimacy that was forever memorialized within the final image. As photobooths developed over the following decades, their increasingly enclosed architecture exploited this effect, as the transient privacy afforded by the curtains protected the sitter(s) from external gazes for at least the few seconds that it took to be photographed. Thus, although the photobooth remained a highly impersonal apparatus dependent on its location within busy urban space, the resulting portraits could paradoxically be understood to reveal the individual at his or her most private, intimate, and emotionally exposed.

Yet the photobooth portrait also made reference to another set of representational logics very different from those of the fashion model or movie star. From its inception, the financial viability of the Photomaton was premised on the speed of its turnover and the mechanical automation that reduced the need for labor. This, in turn, produced a visual uniformity within the resultant imagery, whose decorative embellishments became reduced to a blank backdrop or curtain against which the sitters positioned themselves. In moving away from the pseudo-domestic props and settings of *carte-de-visite* photography, and toward a more depersonalized and abstract space, the photobooth resonated with another mode of Victorian photography that had developed alongside—and in opposition to—bourgeois society portraiture. During the second half of the nineteenth century, an increasingly mobile and urbanized population had impelled the development of various bureaucratic disciplines that used photography to locate—both epistemologically and spatially—specific types of problematic individual. These new regimes, from criminology to anthropology, shared a particular way of fixing the body in front of the camera, rendering it an amenable object of knowledge and administration. As John Tagg describes it, "the bodies . . . [were] taken one by one: isolated in a shallow, contained space; turned full face and subjected to an unreturnable gaze." In addition, Tagg notes, the disciplinary camera sought to purify the field of vision in which the individual was placed, creating "a clear space, a healthy space, a space of unobstructed lines of sight, open to vision and supervision."[40] The Photomaton of the 1920s, bereft of the ornamentation and domestic settings of more fanciful studio portraiture, unwittingly inherited these dynamics. It isolated its patron within a similarly shallow space that was equally sustained by clear sight lines and diffused full lighting. In so doing, it inevitably opened up the photobooth portrait to another set of meanings and ways of being read.

It is instructive, therefore, to consider the Photomaton portrait alongside the modern passport photograph, with which it was roughly contemporary. The 1914 British Nationality and Status of Aliens Act codified the British passport in its modern form and for the first time integrated an affixed photograph of the bearer into the physical design of the document—a development that can perhaps best be conceptualized as an extension of the Bertillonage system of criminal identification, first developed in France by Alphonse Bertillon during the 1880s. Bertillon's innovation was to produce a card for each apprehended suspect, on which were recorded eleven anthropometric measurements alongside two affixed photographs, in full face and in profile. Lodged within an indexed filing system, these cards allowed the authorities to quickly ascertain whether any newly arrested criminal had ever been detained before.[41] The modern passport, which also required certain anthropometric details of its bearer, extended this visual logic from the domain of suspected criminals to all national citizens who wished to cross state borders. In so doing, the standardized format of its full-face photograph enshrined a new formal aesthetic of citizenship that became more and more familiar as the number of passport holders increased. The passport photograph hereby took on a performative role that determined, in effect, what a citizen looked like. Its tight pictorial framing and abstract iconography soon became established as the dominant aesthetic framework for envisaging the citizen's face, and a semiotic structure with which the photobooth portrait inevitably resonated.

The logic that structured the passport photograph, like that of the Bertillonage system that it both quoted and extended, was premised on the irrefutable individuality of the person in the image. This liberal notion of a sovereign uniqueness was embedded within its front-facing pose, its clear pictorial space, its diffused full lighting, and its unobstructed sight lines. That these aesthetic conventions should be simultaneously disseminated by the emergent Photomaton reveals how the photobooth portrait—itself unattached to any formal state technologies in Britain until 1966—could already be understood to capture the subject's unique individuality, less as a private person with his or her own history and emotional life, but in a more formal sense as an individuated national subject.[42]

The architecture of the photobooth lent support to this construction. Concerned to establish a moment of privacy within a necessarily bustling space, the design of the booth came to recall the camera obscura of the seventeenth century. As Jonathan Crary has noted, the pinhole through which light rays entered the camera obscura produced a visual projection of the world whose clear objectivity seemed guaranteed by the dispassionate mechanics of the apparatus itself. Once inside, spectators found themselves positioned as what Crary terms a "sovereign free individual," able to contemplate and know the external world on the basis of their temporary extraction from it.[43] The modern photobooth, through its degraded evocation of this structure, offered its patrons a similar fantasy of sovereign knowledge. Located within the transient flows of a railway terminus or Tube station, the booth removed its users into a sudden interior and presented them with an image whose truth value seemed similarly guaranteed by its mechanical impartiality. This image, of course, was not a projection of the external world but a representation of their own face, reflected back to them in the glass panel as they addressed themselves to the lens. By mimicking the architecture of the camera obscura, therefore, the photobooth invited individuals to invest their self-image with a specific metaphysics. What they saw within the reflection of their face—and later reproduced on a strip of printed photographs—was a visualization of their own free sovereignty and ontological security as a unique individual.

The photobooth, then, offered the metropolitan populace a new process of individuation, not just by expanding the number of people who sat for their portrait, but by implicating them (both pictorially and architecturally) within a visual articulation of their own individual sovereignty—an approximate confirmation of their abstract citizenship. The photobooth portrait can thus be thought of as an incarnation of the mass ornament, explored by Siegfried Kracauer in an essay first published just five months before the Photomaton arrived in London.[44] According to Kracauer, industrial urban culture had arrived at a new visual aesthetic based on the largest arrangement of identical units. For him, this phenomenon was exemplified by the Tiller Girls, the popular female dance troupe whose coordinated routines and replicated costumes reflected back, he believed, a stylized incarnation of the audience's status as regimented workers within the Fordist apparatus. His most useful observation was that the mass ornament could only be seen from a position external to it; each Tiller Girl—positioned within the row just like a worker on a production line—still perceived herself as a unique individual and not as being just another instance in a generic replication. The Photomaton, it would seem, worked in a strikingly similar way. While it offered a visual valorization of sovereignty to anyone with a shilling and a few minutes to spare, its populist appeal tacitly interpellated its patrons into a mass community of similar users. Its portraits offered a reassuring image of unique individual sovereignty, but via a mechanical apparatus that necessarily interpolated the sitter into a mass aesthetic form.

A constitutive ambiguity, therefore, attached to the dual and overlapping frameworks through which photobooth portraits were available to be read. Although their formal abstraction pointed toward a quasi-official representation of a sovereign citizen, it could also present a more expressive image of a private person, caught in a pose at a particular time and place. Its output was equally amenable to bureaucratic processes of formal identification or to private rituals of personal memorabilia. The aesthetic meanings assumed by such portraits were largely determined by how the patron managed his or her body. Freed from the guidance of a directing photographer, its mechanism granted an unusual degree of autonomy to its subjects; the individual could address the lens in whichever way he or she felt appropriate, transforming at a stroke the status, meanings, and aesthetic uses of the portraits that resulted. The bureaucratic regimes of the late nineteenth century, of course, had demanded that their subject address the camera without smiling or frowning. Emphatic facial expressions, in all their transient variability, were understood as a form of disguise that obscured the unique contours of the individual face and prevented the reproduction of its singular ontology. Such expressions, however, were endemic to the souvenir portrait of the private individual, for they marked the moment as one of joy and thus justified its memorialization. These unstable and vacillatory modes of address impacted heavily on the status of the photobooth portrait and the meanings of the self it made available. The formal aesthetics of authenticity could always be challenged by a more playful and dispersed mode of self-visualization, enacted through little more than an expressive smile or a comedic frown.

Returning now to postwar London, the significance of the photobooth becomes suddenly apparent. Progressively establishing itself as an unremarkable urban presence, its cheapness, accessibility, and formal aesthetic gestures were strongly consonant with a social ideology that embraced all individuals within an inclusive national community. Via the photobooth, increased numbers of people encountered an image of themselves that confirmed their formal uniqueness, but through an aesthetic appeal to a founding categorical sameness. At the same time, the machine's automation aligned this experience with the kind of participatory rituals through which urban consensus was more generally being sought. Imaging oneself as an authentic citizen involved a process of strategic self-management, a specific submission in the way one arranged one's face in response to the lens. Yet, at the same time, because the machine announced itself as a democratic apparatus easily accessible to all, it offered an implicit identification with a larger community of users, all bound together through their generic self-portraits. Entering a booth and using it properly, then, became a small—if always indirect—act of affiliation to the wider social whole, one of T. H. Marshall's "new common experiences" and a localized performance of national citizenship.[45]

At the same time, however, the swift proliferation of booths throughout London pointed to deeper social transformations that were already calling such ideologies into dispute. By the mid-1950s, changing patterns of education and employment were providing young people with a greater mobility and disposable income, which in turn found expression in emergent urban subcultures based on music, fashion, and commercialized leisure. Inexpensive, autonomous, and already located within sites of urban display, the photobooth fed into these developments by supplying a tool for experimental self-fashioning that emulated, in a somewhat limited fashion, the more glamorous image systems of an expanding mass media. Alongside its more proper usage, therefore, the booth could also become an enclosure in which one could playfully try out multiple presentations of self, as fleeting and inconsequential as the apparatus itself. Its aesthetic instability allowed it to become a rehearsal space for a diverse set of performances eminently suited to an increasingly mediated and fragmented city.

These possibilities would finally become evident within the Beatles' film *A Hard Day's Night* (Richard Lester, 1964), which celebrated many of the city's new performative dynamics. While a photobooth appears briefly during the opening credits—where it provides the band with a momentary refuge from a horde of rampaging fans—its aesthetics were also taken up within Robert Freeman's famous poster for the film (Figure 21). Here, thirty-one black-and-white photographs of John, George, Paul, and Ringo (and one of their costar Wilfrid Brambell) appear at first glance like eight strips of photobooth portraits arranged side by side.[46] Each band member is presented a number of times, framed in identical tight squares against a plain gray background, and all exploit this multiple format to address the camera through a series of alternating facial expressions, head turns, and hand gestures. Rowena Agajanian has noted how, within this image, the four band members' identical mop-tops and sweaters create an impression of interchangeability that supported the fraternal communality played out within the film.[47] Yet this derived less from the similarity of their hairstyles and clothing than from the theatrical face-pulling that this both supported and reinforced. This simultaneous presentation of multiple portaits, clearly borrowed from the photobooth strip, works to subvert the expressionless pose that—since Bertillon at least—had proclaimed the irreplaceable uniqueness of the sovereign individual. By exploding this image across a protean mass of comedic citations, this liberal ontology becomes dissolved and the four individual band members could become reconfigured as the media abstraction that was "The Beatles." By 1964, as Agajanian notes, the British press had already recast the band as a quartet of affectionate stereotypes—John the witty one, George the quiet one, and so on—which the film's slight

characterization happily endorsed.[48] By turning the photobooth's inherent
liberty against those conventions of citizenship that it could also support,
the poster enabled these four individuals to be newly envisaged as a b(r)and.

The sense of modernity expressed by Freeman's poster owed much to
its implied urbanity, a theme explored further in Lester's next feature, *The
Knack and How to Get It* (1965), starring Rita Tushingham, Michael Craw-
ford, and Ray Brooks. This film also featured a photobooth near the beginning, but here its dynamics were examined in greater detail. The film's
female protagonist, Nancy (Tushingham), arrives at Victoria Coach Station
from an unnamed northern town, where her first excited action is to enter
the station's photobooth. In a shot-countershot relay that oscillates between
the camera's gaze at Nancy and Nancy's gaze back at her own reflection, she
adopts a succession of four different poses—a nervous, full-faced smile, a
three-quarter turn to the camera, a pose with her hands behind her head,
and a pose pulling her cap down. While Nancy waits outside the booth for
her pictures to be printed, a young blonde woman steps up in high heels

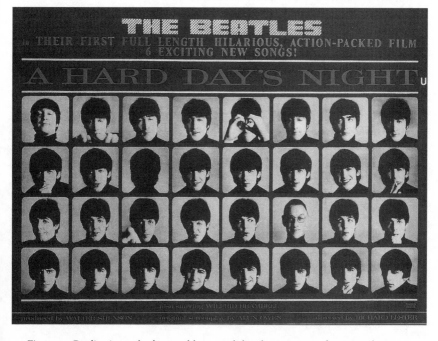

Figure 21. Replication as both resemblance and dissolution: poster for *A Hard Day's
Night* (Richard Lester, 1964).

and a raincoat, closely pursued by an older man in a mackintosh and bowler hat. The woman hurries into the booth, but when the man goes to follow, she pushes him back and defensively draws the curtain. Somewhat taken aback, Nancy watches as the woman's hand emerges to drop various items of clothing into the man's waiting hands. He makes frequent eye contact with Nancy but—although embarrassed—makes no real attempt to conceal what is going on. Having seen the woman discard her underwear, the film cuts to a floor-level shot of her calves and feet—the only part of her still visible from outside the booth—as she performs a succession of glamour-model poses inside (Figure 22). The man returns her clothes and she emerges from the booth fully attired. When, shortly afterwards, Nancy's photographs are expelled from the machine, the man rushes in to collect them. He realizes his mistake just as Nancy is viewing the second strip to emerge. They awkwardly swap photographs and hurry off in opposite directions.

This fast-paced sequence lasts less than ninety seconds, but it goes some way to articulating the specifically urban dynamics of the postwar photobooth. For Nancy, producing a strip of self-portraits marks her rite

Figure 22. Sexual performance in the metropolitan photobooth: *The Knack and How to Get It* (Richard Lester, 1965).

of passage into London. It confirms her ability to manage her own identity and to insert herself within those image systems that have formed her understanding of the capital (on the coach, she is shown reading an article about London's romantic nightlife in *Honey* magazine). Again, this scene is emblematic of the wider film, in which the characters are complicit with the camera and knowingly treat London as a film set against which to perform their various urban fantasies. Nancy's succession of poses embraces this performativity, swiftly progressing from an orthodox assertion of selfhood (the conventional muted smile) to exaggerated theatrical posturing (her hands behind her head as if on a fashion shoot). Throughout *The Knack*, the sound track is overlaid with disembodied vox populi that provide a disapproving chorus on the action taking place. While Nancy is in the booth, a woman's voice intones: "If you ask me, they're a new brand of person altogether with their image they give"; a recognition, perhaps, of Nancy's challenge to more essentialist postwar modes of photographic portraiture and her embrace of a more dispersed set of composite self-images.

Yet this key sequence also announced the illicit possibilities presented by the insertion of a semiprivate booth into a set of bustling urban spaces defined by transience, anonymity, and material exchange. The exact terms of the older man's relationship to the blonde woman is left unclear, although presumably he has just picked her up during one of the myriad encounters such spaces can promote. Her refusal to allow him into the booth reinforces this reading; private intimacy has been replaced by the estrangements of the pornographic image, and physical contact parodically reduced to the insertion of coins into a slot. In this scene, then, the booth's architecture serves to concentrate the casual eroticism already available within such public spaces, while never quite managing to keep it concealed. The viewer peeks underneath the three-quarter-length curtain in a covert act of voyeurism, which reaches its delayed climax when the strip of portraits shoots back out—all exposed—into the public realm. The modern photobooth, this short sequence suggests, already contained its own dialectic of concealment and revelation. As an apparatus, it both facilitated and exposed the erotic dynamics that promiscuously circulated around those metropolitan spaces in which alone it could be found.

Facing the Homosexual Citizen

It is tempting to see something similar within Bacon's own photobooth portraits as re-presented by Sylvester, but here the inference of urban eroticism is decidedly marked as queer. The public spatial dynamics already endemic to accounts of male vice seem to emphatically spill over into these images, particularly invoking the context of Wildeblood's first encounter with McNally on the subterranean concourse of Piccadilly Circus Underground Station. Indeed, always installed within those same bustling interstices of transience and flow, the booth's mechanism inherently required a certain amount of hanging around from its users, as they waited for their portraits to be processed and printed. Thus, both the geographies and the choreographies of the photobooth patron were closely aligned to those of those of the loiterer, a correlation that may or may not have been felt by queer men at this time, but that certainly adds resonance to the strips in Bacon's *Interviews*. Now, located in a site of potential queer contact, his turned-up collar becomes a gesture of concealment. Pulling himself in and out of focus between each shot, he seems to want to escape into the vignetted corners of the image, the camera lens coming to stand for a wider network of public scrutiny from which the enclosed booth should rightly have offered some momentary respite. Caught inside a space of participatory citizenship, Bacon cannot settle down. Yet the inclusion of so many strips on the page suggests his compulsion to keep returning to the machine, if only to hang around outside for just another few minutes.

Here, then, the photobooth appears as a Catholic confessional—an enclosed yet problematically public space of private self-scrutiny. Like the interviews themselves, with their suggestion of an overheard conversation between friends, these images seem to promise a secret access to Bacon at once more personal than his publicity photographs or those painted *Self-Portraits* produced for public exhibition. The strips' crumpled grubbiness and their casual arrangement, plonked across the page, only increases this suggestion of candid intimacy. Although salvaged from the floor of his studio, they look as if they might have come from under Bacon's bed, a testament perhaps to some onanistic ritual that makes their sudden discovery within the book feel like an act of voyeuristic complicity.

Within a culture already familiar with the photobooth portrait as a sentimental keepsake, these homosexual overtones were readily available. As Simon Ofield has noted, postwar British queer novels often relied on the discovery of a mysterious photograph as their central narrative conceit.[49] At the start of *The Heart in Exile*, for instance, Anthony Page finds a photograph of an unknown man in the flat of his dead ex-lover, and in Stuart Lauder's *Winger's Landfall* (1962), an image of a dead youth is discovered in the locker of an older man.[50] Each of these pictures becomes an episte-mological riddle, such that the mystery of what its presence there reveals drives the narrative for the rest of the novel. The affective economies of the photobooth portrait thus turn the staged discovery of Bacon's strips within Sylvester's *Interviews* into a similarly posed—if never quite answered—question. His unease as he shifts around the booth—turning his head first this way, then that; now leaning forward, now leaning back—suggests a physical discomfort, as if caught in a space in which he cannot settle down. He persistently refuses to return the camera's gaze and, perhaps more important, he seems distinctly lonely. Trapped within an apparatus in which friends and lovers laughingly enact their intimacy, Bacon's strips become marked by the absence of another body, either within the pictorial frame itself or as the portraits' implied recipient. Dirty and uncared for, they are the neglected possessions of a clearly single man—which may also explain the strange in-clusion of the larger photograph in the bottom left-hand corner that seems more like a destroyed snapshot, bitterly ripped to disavow the existence of a now ex-lover.

Yet, if the presentation of these strips in 1975 retroactively endowed Bacon's life in this period with a complex set of queer resonances, then it is their relation to his earlier work that reveals most about the limited possibil-ities of homosexual self-presentation during the early postwar decades. If the photobooth strips do indeed mark a continuation of Bacon's engagement with the public presentation of his own queer self—a preoccupation, I argue, that also ran through the *Heads* series painted for his major London debut—then these two sets of images go some way to articulating the internal para-doxes inscribed within the fashioning of a legitimate homosexuality.

As we have seen, the postwar formulation of the respectable homosexual involved remapping his lifeworld in accordance with the normative spa-tial logics of urban reconstruction. Adhering to bourgeois codes of privacy and discretion, his emotional and sexual life would remain confined to the domestic sphere, which would, in turn, sanction his public recognition in accordance with dominant notions of decency and comportment. This bifurcation was, of course, made possible by a new assertion of psycholog-ical depth that presented homosexuality as a concealed internal state. Pop-ular equations between queerness and behavioral indecency could thus be challenged, allowing reformists like Westwood and Wildeblood to make their counterclaim that proper homosexuals rarely manifested their desires within the public spaces of the city.

Yet despite the Wolfenden Committee's endorsement of this model, it left behind a set of unresolved tensions around the visibility of such homosexual citizenship within the public realm. This was already present within an earlier exchange between Wildeblood and the committee, when the former was interrogated about how it had felt to have his homosexuality made forcibly public during the course of his trial:

> CANON DEMANT: Was part of your feeling better adjusted due to the fact that [your homosexuality] had come out in the open?
>
> A: Yes, I found it a tremendous help towards that. The worst thing about being a homosexual in this country at the moment is the fact that you have to wear a mask all the time, conceal it from the people you work with and the majority of your friends, and your parents.
>
> MR. ADAIR: If it was removed, do you think that would disappear?
>
> A. Yes, I think it would.
>
> Q. And there would not be such a feeling in the public mind as to insist on the mask remaining?
>
> A. There again I can only give my own feelings about it and I am certainly very much happier now that I do not have any need to conceal.[51]

On the final page of *Against the Law*, Wildeblood would return to this metaphor of the discarded mask, as he described the profoundly liberating effects of his enforced confessional:

> I was able, at last, to move out of a false position and take up a true one. There was no further need for pretence; I could discard the mask which had been such a burden to me all my life.[52]

This metaphorical alignment between his public visibility as a homosexual and the discarding of a mask, however, reveals a great deal about the aims and limitations of Wildeblood's discourse and its proffered model of homosexual citizenship. On the one hand, this mask was clearly that of enforced heterosexual passing, of not being able to publicly reveal his true homosexual face. Here, then, was an implicit valorization of the normative aesthetics of sovereign individuality in accordance with the more sanctioned incarnations of the photobooth portrait. Presenting to the public his homosexual face marked, for Wildeblood, a moment of personal triumph, allowing him to visibly take his place as a queer individual within an enlightened social community.

Yet, in demanding the recognition of this *true* homosexual face, Wilde-blood also turned his oppressive mask into that comprised of known criminal citations, as constructed by the operations of the Metropolitan Police and refracted through the tabloids—that false composite of painted lips, glad eyes, and leering smiles by which queer men had hitherto been dragged into the public gaze. Thus the mask that Wildeblood had managed to prise off was really an elision of two, and herein lay the problem; for, away from these false images of queer criminality and heterosexual passing, it failed to establish exactly how the true face of the homosexual could be publicly envisaged at all.

This paradox was already being played out within two contrasting photographs of Wildeblood to be published during this period. At the height of his trial in March 1954, the *Daily Mirror* printed a photograph of him in eveningwear that had been retouched to make it look like he was wearing lipstick (Figure 23).[53] While his costume already resonated with popular stereotypes of the upper-class homosexual, it was the citation of those darkened lips within this image that confirmed Wildeblood's face as being that of a definite queer.[54] As a journalistic ruse, this had a clear historical precedent; coverage of Oscar Wilde's trial had similarly dwelled on the playwright's fleshy, sensual mouth and the "cynical smile" and "weak open mouth" of the procurer Alfred Taylor.[55] The dark ink that the *Mirror* painted onto Wildeblood's lips did much the same work, betraying a clear anxiety that his deviance was simply not fixable enough across the surfaces of his otherwise conventional body. Echoing the smile that he had previously directed at McNally across Piccadilly Circus Tube Station—which may or may not have signified his criminal intent—Wildeblood's lips once again became the terrain of a visual ambiguity, recrossing the line between normative discretion and the public iteration of a knowable queerness.

A year later, Wildeblood wrote of his trial:

When the searchlights of the law were turned on to my life, only a part of it was illuminated. . . . It will be my task, therefore, to turn on more lights, revealing, in place of the blurred and shadowy figure of the newspaper photographs, a man differing from other men only in one respect.[56]

The fully illuminated Wildeblood finally appeared in a small black-and-white photograph on the back cover of the Penguin edition of *Against the Law* (Figure 24). As an image of a notorious offender trying to repackage

Figure 23. The visible iteration of queer criminality: Peter Wildeblood apparently wearing lipstick in "Wildeblood speaks of 'My lonely moments,'" *Daily Mirror*, March 19, 1954, 6.

himself as a serious moral authority, this picture inevitably carried a heavy semantic burden. Wildeblood's chin rests on his clenched fist in a determined pose of gravitas—already too reminiscent of Rodin's *The Thinker*, perhaps—while his heavy brow and stony stare exaggerate the torment of the unjustly afflicted man. Yet, aside from its suggestions of forced theatricality, the photograph suffered from a structural weakness that it could never properly overcome. Here, at last, is Peter Wildeblood—author of *Against the Law*—whose legitimate public sovereignty was inextricable from his constitutive homosexuality. As the climactic visualization of the man without the mask, it clearly appeals to the same normative aesthetics of citizenship as the more proper photobooth portraits it in no small way resembles. Yet this image remained blighted by the inadequacies of Wildeblood's own discourse, for he could provide no interpretative structure through which it could be viewed.

Here was a true face of a genuine homosexual, but one, the text tells us, that is entirely indistinguishable from the heterosexuals who surround him. Yet, having discarded this mask of heterosexual passing, the viewer is left with no indication of where in this image such sexual difference can be located. Unable to be read in any other way, the photograph inevitably regresses toward the only mode of reading that was presently available. Wildeblood's homosexuality crumbles back into an aggregate of understood queer iterations—the staring eyes, just a little too desperate; the theatrical fist disavowing its own limpness; the mysterious name of Lotte Meitner-Graf who may or may not signify a connection to the queer excesses of interwar Germany.[57] This was, it would seem, the only means by which Wildeblood's essential homosexuality could possibly be visualized. Thus, as much as he laid claim to the expressionless composure of the sovereign portrait, his face was perpetually being pulled apart into a dispersed composite of significant details, centrifugally dissolving under that hermeneutics of detection that alone could render his homosexuality legible.

It is striking that half a decade before Peter Wildeblood first submitted his evidence to the Wolfenden Committee, reviewers of Bacon's show at the Hanover Gallery used precisely the same language to describe to their readers his anonymous male *Heads*. The rhetoric most commonly deployed was that these figures seemed to be dissolving under the weight of the paint, decomposing before the viewer into an unstable composite of discrete and disconnected features. Wyndham Lewis in *The Listener*, for instance, wrote of "the shouting creatures in glass cases, these dissolving ganglia the size of a small fist in which one can always discern the shouting mouth, the wild distended eye"; and over the following decades, such tropes would come to dominate criticism of Bacon's work.[58] Thus, John Russell's highly successful monograph of 1971 would also locate these *Heads* as revealing "the disintegration of the social being which takes place when one is alone in a room which has no looking-glass," in which "we may well feel . . . that the accepted hierarchy of our features is collapsing, and that we are by turns all teeth, all eye, all ear, all nose."[59]

It is tempting to relate the canvases that provoked this critical discourse to Bacon's own lived experience and his habitual forays through the restaurants and drinking clubs of Soho. Alistair O'Neill has already drawn attention to the cross-pollination between the artist's use of theatrically applied makeup and the chromatic smears of paint through which his portraits took shape.[60] To this extent, Bacon's own highly cultivated appearance as a slovenly queer bohemian exploited those same visible citations—those painted lips and glad eyes—that so affronted the sensibilities of London's homosexual reformists.

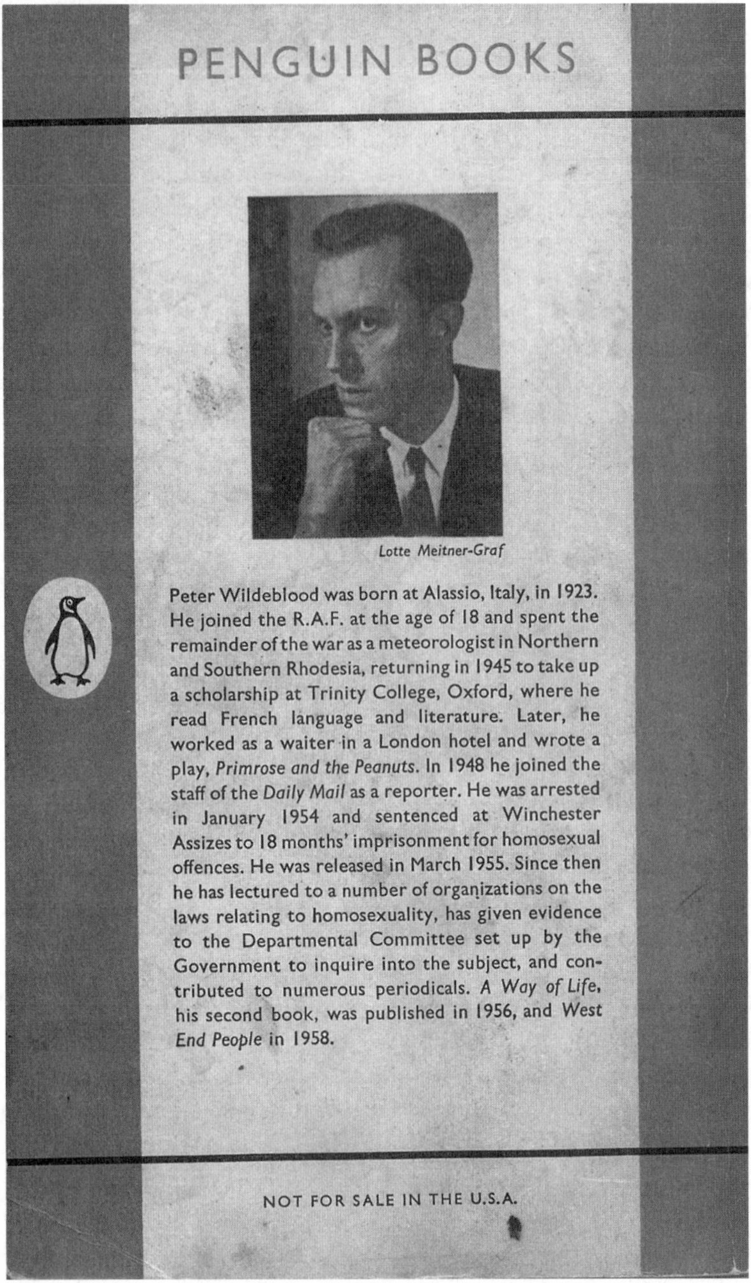

PENGUIN BOOKS

Lotte Meitner-Graf

Peter Wildeblood was born at Alassio, Italy, in 1923. He joined the R.A.F. at the age of 18 and spent the remainder of the war as a meteorologist in Northern and Southern Rhodesia, returning in 1945 to take up a scholarship at Trinity College, Oxford, where he read French language and literature. Later, he worked as a waiter in a London hotel and wrote a play, *Primrose and the Peanuts*. In 1948 he joined the staff of the *Daily Mail* as a reporter. He was arrested in January 1954 and sentenced at Winchester Assizes to 18 months' imprisonment for homosexual offences. He was released in March 1955. Since then he has lectured to a number of organizations on the laws relating to homosexuality, has given evidence to the Departmental Committee set up by the Government to inquire into the subject, and contributed to numerous periodicals. *A Way of Life*, his second book, was published in 1956, and *West End People* in 1958.

NOT FOR SALE IN THE U.S.A.

Figure 24. A sovereign portrait of a homosexual citizen: back cover of Peter Wildeblood, *Against the Law* (Harmondsworth: Penguin Books, 1957).

Yet when he strayed beyond the familiar stomping grounds of Soho and Fitzrovia and entered the more critical public environment of Mayfair's Hanover Gallery, his sense of queer embodiment became decidedly less assured. *Heads I–VI* can be read as a reflection of this and an early articulation of a larger paradox around the public presentation of a legitimate homosexuality that united—despite their metropolitan polarity—Bacon's form of queer bohemianism with the more conciliatory construction of the homosexual citizen. As suggested by Wildeblood's own collapse when he left the verbal terrain of personal biography and entered the visual arena of the everyday media, homosexuality could either remain invisible or else would necessarily dissolve back into the glad eyes, flapping wrists, and other prostheses of criminal queer citation. The public visualization of homosexual men, despite an ongoing project to reformulate its structure, could not resist its own dissolution into the stigmatized tropes that still marked queer visibility during the postwar years. The very condition of an authentic homosexuality premised on its normative restriction to the private and domestic was its inevitable fragmentation when it sought to assert a legitimate presence within the public life of the city.

Yet if homosexual citizenship remained visually inarticulable, then the dominant logics of queer iteration gave queer men a compensatory protection in their everyday encounters with more hostile social forces. When Sir John Nott-Bower, Commissioner of the Metropolitan Police, appeared before the Wolfenden Committee in December 1954, he was questioned about an earlier raid on a pub in Soho's Rupert Street in which, he had claimed, "there were 137 customers in the bar of which 91 were known homosexuals."[61] One unrecorded member of the committee was keen to know exactly what Nott-Bower meant by the words "known homosexuals," and here the commissioner became rather flustered:

> Possibly that was not very well expressed. "Known homosexuals" I suppose really should mean people who had convictions, but it does not mean that; it really means in much more general terms that 91 of those people were regarded by police as homosexual, from either their previous convictions or their appearance or their behaviour at the time.[62]

The Met's Prosecuting Solicitor, R. E. T. Birch, quickly interjected that the homosexuality of these men had been "perfectly obvious from paint and powder and made-up eyebrows and waved hair, and calling each other girls' names, and so forth," as well as from some observable kissing, some fondling of body parts, and a certain amount of sitting on each other's knees. Yet he too was forced to concede that this catalog of sartorial and behavioral tropes still did not equate to the claim that their homosexuality was in any way "known." Instead, he admitted the clearly circular maneuver by which, during such raids, an observing officer would stand at the door with the pub's licensee, who would state as each patron left: "This is a man I know is homosexual."[63]

With this in mind, if Bacon's *Heads* and agonized photobooth portraits articulated the contradictions that marked the public face of the legitimate homosexual, then so too, perhaps, did another set of images to emerge from the same historical moment: the Identi-kit pictures of the "A6 murderer" that were disseminated throughout London in the late summer of 1961. On the evening of August 23 of that year, Michael Gregsten and his lover Valerie Storie were sitting in a Morris Minor in a Buckinghamshire cornfield when they were ambushed by a neatly dressed young man brandishing a revolver. For most of the night, the gunman forced Gregsten to drive aimlessly around northwest London, before making him stop in a lay-by just off the A6 arterial road. There he shot and killed Gregsten, raped and shot Storie—who was paralyzed but survived—and drove off by himself in the stolen car.

The "A6 Murder," as it soon became known, was the case that brought the Identi-kit device into public consciousness, for it had only reached London from the United States earlier that spring. As the *Times* explained to its readers:

> The Identi-kit . . . consists of more than 500 facial features drawn on transparent slips. As the witness describes all the possible features of the subject he can recall, an officer trained in this work places corresponding slips one on top of the other until a complete facial picture has been built up.[64]

Here, then, was a new technique for envisaging the face of an antisocial criminal that was entirely comprised of iterated features, carefully combined into some form of ensemble. Yet, as a technology of detection, the newly imported Identi-kit proved immediately problematic. While experts worked diligently with Storie and a number of other witnesses to try to fix the face of the murderer, none of the resulting pictures looked very much like each other. As a consequence, it was decided to circulate two images among the public rather than to risk falsely amalgamating them into one (Figure 25). This disparity prompted the *Spectator* to cast doubt on the basic suitability of the Identi-kit as a viable method of detection:

> [W]hether the man the police want to see is found or not, a number of men who have no knowledge of the killing will be looked at askance by their neighbours and perhaps will be subjected to the unpleasant experience of police questioning—if not of even more serious unpleasantness.[65]

Figure 25. The elusive search for the composite criminal: policeman showing two Identi-kit images of the "A6 murderer" to a passerby, Kennington Lane, August 31, 1961. Photograph by Davies. Courtesy of Hulton Archive/Getty Images.

The A6 murderer, then, like Bacon's *Heads* or the photographed author of *Against the Law*, seemed to elude figuration, always dissolving back into the composite citations of his own criminality and becoming ever more indistinct through the hermeneutics of suspicion.

When, in January 1962, James Hanratty was finally put on trial for the murder, the proceedings were dominated by debates over the lack of similarity between his face and either of the two Identi-kit images. The setting of his eyes, the color of his hair, and whether he held his right eyebrow higher than his left all became matters of great significance, particularly given the discrepancy between the two portraits and also between the Identi-kit composites and the subsequent testaments of witnesses in court. As Paul Foot argued ten years later in his plea for a public inquiry into the case:

> Hanratty had a box-like square face. Both the Identikit faces were oval. His hair was not slicked back as in the first identity picture, nor brushed back as in the second. It fell forward at the front and could not be brushed back because of a "widow's peak" on his forehead. His eyes were not dark. They were light blue.[66]

Following Hanratty's execution in April 1962, doubts lingered over the fairness of his trial and the key role that visual identification had played in determining his guilt. Commentators complained that too little attention had been paid to the question of motive, especially given the sexual nature of the offense; indeed, Hanratty's combined history of mental instability and petty crime had not been made available to either his judge or jurors. In a 1963 Penguin Special on the case, Louis Blom-Cooper used Hanratty's psychiatric prison records to depict him as an ill-at-ease metropolitan delinquent, following the familiar contours of the pathologized spiv. Hanratty, he wrote, was an immature bragger whose sartorial exactness and career of minor housebreaking were desperate compensations for a defective personality and a regressive psychology:

> The total picture of Hanratty . . . was of a man whose emotions and outlook were characteristic of an unintelligent schoolboy with little capacity for close relationships, particularly with women. He would almost certainly have been classified as an inadequate psychopath.[67]

For Blom-Cooper, then, it was the trial's refusal to proceed beyond the visual logics of criminal identification and into the verbal terrain of criminal psychiatry that marked the fatal limitations of the postwar British justice system. The instability and dispute that surrounded Hanratty's conviction dramatized the limits of a visual economy of criminal guilt that was rooted in a system of legible citations. Like the men found drinking in their Rupert Street pub, his criminality could never be properly "known" without recourse to some supplementary narrative—be that the psychobiography favored by Blom-Cooper or the DNA testing that would finally confirm Hanratty's guilt in 2002.[68]

During the 1950s, homosexual men were offered a similarly unstable mode of inhabiting the public realm, which oscillated uneasily between the visual authenticity of the sovereign citizen and the citational assemblage of the antisocial criminal. Never quite able to assert the legitimacy initially promised by Wildeblood's narrative of self, they were equally impervious to any determinate fixing as authentically criminal beings. Public space, therefore, was a forum in which respectable homosexuality remained necessarily invisible, where any attempt to assert itself could only dissolve back into the tired clichés of illegal queer mannerisms, physiognomic peculiarities, items of clothing, and commodities. As Bacon's images reveal, this particular form of metropolitan homosexuality was inherently caught up within its own dynamic paradox, a perpetual and deeply unstable oscillation between two opposing poles of coherence and disintegration.

chapter 4

OF PUBLIC LIBRARIES AND PAPERBACKS: THE SEXUAL GEOGRAPHIES OF READING

She looked. There were books about Bolshevist Russia, books of travel, a volume about the atom and the electron, another about the composition of the earth's core, and the causes of earthquakes: then a few novels: then three books on India.

So! He was a reader after all.

—D. H. LAWRENCE, *Lady Chatterley's Lover,* published by Penguin Books Ltd., 1960

In the evening we watched an interview: Noël Coward talked with Patrick Garland. . . . It was disgraceful: but there was one delightful moment when Coward said that in his youth he read a lot: "I was a regular visitor to the Battersea Public Lavatory—I mean—Library . . . Oh dear! Quite a Freudian slip there, I'm afraid . . ."

—KENNETH WILLIAMS's diary, Sunday December 7, 1969

As the 1950s progressed, the reformist blueprint for the respectable homosexual gained an increased cultural currency within Britain. Promulgated across a range of forums, from therapeutic communities to the more "enlightened" popular media, it brought with it a significant shift in prescriptive calls concerning how, where, and by whom male same-sex desire should be managed. Early in the decade, tabloid reports and judicial proclamations had demanded the eradication of London's "male vice," an approach that positioned queer desire as a set of manifest urban behaviors and social practices. Yet the formulation of a model of homosexual citizenship, supported by psychiatric and criminological expertise, increasingly popularized an understanding of homosexuality as an interior psychological condition that was primarily rooted in childhood environmental influences. The effect of this was to subtly reconfigure the dynamics of moral culpability that had run through earlier accounts of metropolitan queer life. Queer expression and illegal urban practices were now being approached as only one possible manifestation of a man's homosexuality. Such behavior remained criminally offensive, as those bourgeois ideologies of discretion and restraint that had enabled the crafting of a respectable homosexuality continued to cast such public encounters as deviant and despicable. But the ascribable blame that accompanied these activities had become increasingly mediated by deeper accounts of psychic immaturity and intemperance, rather than being more simply equated with willful antisocial intent. At fault in such behavior was an individual lack of purposiveness in the homosexual himself, an inability to manage those anterior proclivities that should have more rightly remained circumscribed within the twin private realms of his psyche and his home.

This subtle shift had important implications for how metropolitan queerness could most effectively be administered and it complicated more simplistic calls for a sharper punitive response. Through media figures like Peter Wildeblood (the brave confessional author of *Against the Law*) and Dr. Anthony Page (the protagonist of Rodney Garland's reformist novel *The Heart in Exile*), a respectable type of homosexual had been revealed, capable of exercising his own moral agency and acting in accordance with larger social imperatives. Such men, these texts suggested, had been able to repudiate London's queer underworld and see it for the zone of tastelessness, immaturity, and emotional disappointment it undoubtedly was. Endowed with an empowering and purposive environmental sensibility, they sought only to take up their integral place within the projected corporate life of a renewed and modern city.

Of course, not all queer men related to this model of homosexuality or subscribed to its fraudulently universal values of domestic companionship and public discretion. Yet this notion of respectable homosexuality provided a persuasive ideal toward which, bourgeois reformers hoped, all queer men could be quietly maneuvered in the wider interests of civic order and social harmony. While the new homosexual was thus provided with a psychic depth and the apparent liberty of his own moral conscience, such endorsements were covertly tempered by a more coercive understanding that it was the duty of public agencies to point him in the right direction and enable him to make only those everyday choices that the wider social body required. In part, this involved a more intensive policing of public sexual disorder, itself more firmly placed outside the boundaries of civic acceptability. But it also entailed a policy shift from primarily penal sanctions toward the kind of psychiatric treatment that might help offenders—and potential offenders—to gain a more enlightened hold on their own affliction. As the Wolfenden report made clear, the metropolis with its incessant profusion of distracting temptations had already diffused the site of this endeavor. To be effective, such work had to spill out of the confines of the clinic and become a more scattered and multiagency project:

> It is important to remember that "treatment" need not necessarily, or even often, imply any active steps to be taken by a physician or by a psychiatrist. Often it will be desirable that various methods of treatment should be applied simultaneously, bringing into service a combination of many helpers. . . . As often as not, it will be a matter of guiding the patient to help himself, not only by personal influence but also by helping to manipulate environmental factors. And in this work there is a place for the clergyman, the psychiatric social worker, the probation officer and, it may be added, the adjusted homosexual, as well as for the doctor.[1]

This investment in the decentered manipulation of environmental factors repeated that same set of impulses already vocalized within the town planning and design rhetorics that had dominated the early reconstruction. Once again, the careful administration of everyday spatial contexts would, it was assumed, promote an internal sensibility that might guide the individual toward order, self-management, and social contribution through the daily practices of his ordinary life. But the explicit foregrounding of male homosexuality as both an active social problem and a dangerously unstable reaction to the metropolis meant that such environmental manipulations had to be both detailed and attentive. In addition, the loosely psychoanalytic narratives out of which such homosexuality had been constructed raised the potential stakes even further. Not only must the lifeworld of the adult homosexual be perpetually managed to help him regulate his own engagements with the city, but the social environments of the young—both the infant and the adolescent—had also to be administered, in order to prevent the inculcation of homosexuality in the first place.

One key area of focus involved those situations in which both men and boys gained knowledge about sex. In particular, how, where, and under what conditions a youth came to understand his body and the meaning of his desires became the focus of a great deal of anxiety. In his preface to Gordon

Westwood's *Society and the Homosexual,* therefore, the psychoanalyst Edward Glover opened with an emphatically spatial imperative:

> Books purporting to inform the public on the psychology of sex fall naturally into two categories: those few which should find a conspicuous place on the family bookshelves, to be consulted when occasion demands by old and young alike, and the great majority which should be consigned forthwith to the waste-paper basket.[2]

Poorly written volumes, Glover was suggesting, were worse than useless; they were a damaging presence within the family home that threatened to undermine its function as a site of personal development and emotional education. Westwood's own book, of course, was properly grounded in the latest expert knowledge, an "attempt to give a balanced outline of the problem" to the ordinary householder regardless of gender, education, class, or libidinal proclivity. As Westwood himself made clear, the availability of plain, accurate, and sober information was not only important for the homosexual, as the necessary prerequisite for his ability to manage his metropolitan impulses, but it was also an essential resource for those who must support him. Further, it also provided the best insurance against an inquisitive boy developing a warped and unnatural attitude to sex that might prevent him from progressing on to heterosexual maturity.[3]

From at least the late eighteenth century, the ordinary act of reading has been a central element within the production of the modern self. Novels, in particular, aided the phenomenological process of individuation, as the reading consciousness withdrew from its external environment and into a psychic interiority carved out by internal monologue and private contemplation.[4] Within this history, the modern homosexual has been equally inextricable from experiences of reading and their attendant moments of personal enlightenment. Oral histories of the early twentieth century, for instance, often hinge on a volume of Plato or Edward Carpenter casually discovered in Father's study that provides a new conceptual language through which to articulate a nascent queer identity.[5] Such experiences were always dependent on class and education, yet the active public provision of culture in the postwar period, coupled with the widespread dissemination of popular sexology, expanded the domain in which such ideas might then be encountered. Books, of course, have always had their own complex historical geographies as ambiguous urban commodities inherently linked to the covert pleasures of the psyche. They remain characterized by an uneasy oscillation between the public and the private, and the personal and the social—a tension clearly evident within Glover's attempt to firmly demarcate the boundary between the family bookshelf and the wastepaper basket. In the postwar period, when legitimate sexual expression was being increasingly pushed back behind closed doors, the public life of London's books became a heightened cause for concern, as various cultural agencies tried to administer both public access to certain forms of printed knowledge and exactly what that knowledge might mean when brought into consciousness by the private individual.

This chapter, then, explores the tensions that surrounded the selling, display, and general visibility of books in postwar London and how this became refracted through a set of implicit moral imperatives surrounding the legitimate possibilities of both textual and sexual pleasure. In particular, it examines two rival economies of the book that developed during this period, each rooted within its own dynamic system of space and time that sought to order the book's meaning and the ways in which it might be enjoyed. These two economies—that of the municipal library book and the mass-market paperback, respectively—were mutually antagonistic and, by the end of the 1950s, had become actively opposed. This produced a moment of crisis that would be played out and partially resolved in two courtroom dramas of the early 1960s: the unsuccessful prosecution in October 1960 of Penguin Books Ltd. for its proposed publication of D. H. Lawrence's *Lady Chatterley's Lover,* and the less well known—if more successful—trial of two roommates, Kenneth Halliwell and John Orton, at Old Street Magistrates Court in May 1962 for the theft and mutilation of a large number of books from the Hampstead and Islington public libraries. If John Orton had not soon become "Joe," the celebrated author of the hit plays *Entertaining Mr Sloane* (1964) and *Loot* (1965), this latter episode might well have sunk without trace. But although the trials clearly dealt with highly dissimilar incidents, they both revealed a common set of established sexual anxieties that was already attached to books, the manner of their urban visibility, and the attendant modes of reading implied by their display. The careful speeches of Penguin's apologists and the outrageous defacements of Orton and Halliwell both demonstrated—in their very different ways—how the public lives of books during the 1950s and early 1960s were ordered via a normative sexual system, which sought to administer how they were read, the textual pleasures that could be derived from them, and the uses of such literacy for the enlightened sexual self.

To explore this further, one needs to consider how books were presented within that space most amenable to municipal control: the interior of the local branch library. The British public library system was considerably reinvigorated after the war as the number of books issued to borrowers rose from 247 million in 1937 to 397 million in 1959.[6] In part, this reflected both state policies toward the provision of public culture and a demographic expansion of those middle classes who used the libraries most. In any case, by the end of the 1950s, public libraries had become firmly established within the book industry as a major targeted market for any newly published titles.[7] A reified space of ordered distribution in which readers borrowed—rather than bought—only the books on offer, the public branch library coincided with the wider postwar drive to bureaucratize consumption. By inserting a layer of bourgeois taste management between manufacturer and customer, it sought stability and social order via the training of demand. In Abercrombie and Forshaw's *County of London Plan,* therefore, public libraries had already been identified as a key institution within those clusters of community buildings "to which the inhabitants [would] automatically gravitate for their social, educational and cultural activities."[8] Administered by ranks of professional librarians, the reading practices of London's citizens could be guided not only in terms of what books were made available, but—via an attention to their visual display—through the suggestions these books made about the manner in which they wanted to be taken home and enjoyed.

Outside the walls of the public branch library, however, the unfettered dynamics of capital accumulation had begun to mount an increasingly visible attack on such bureaucratic strategies. As the 1950s progressed, colorful and coarsely jacketed mass-market paperbacks became an increasingly common fixture within London's newsagents and railway-station kiosks. The blatant visibility of such books mounted a fundamental challenge to the type of tasteful consumption authorized within the municipal lending library. These cheap and cheerful paperbacks—or so it would seem—hailed their readers with a sudden promise of salacious desire, rather than through any mannered invitation to dispassionate knowledge. They also lurked promiscuously amid the bustling rhythms of everyday urban life, rather than within the reified tranquillity of the public reading room. In many ways, therefore, the mass-market paperback marked the uncomfortable return of the library's repressed—a blatant celebration of the book's status as a commodity and its inherent involvement in the repetitious rhythms of transient metropolitan consumerism.

As will be explored in this chapter, guardians of the library and others within Britain's cultural establishment deployed a sophisticated rhetoric to defend proper reading against the promiscuous distractions of the urban paperback. This was dependent upon wider notions of sexual maturity and emotional development, partly inherited from interwar and wartime critiques of mass commercial entertainments like the cinema and the dance hall, but also given weight by the postwar investment in psychological and psychoanalytic expertise.[9] Against the sanctioned enlightenment more plainly offered by the authoritative public library book, the mass-market paperback became implicated in an arrested and degraded form of sexually coded pleasure. But—as Orton and Halliwell's library book defacements suggest—such frameworks conflicted violently with the more intimate relationships such paperbacks were offering to many queer men during this period. Complex negotiations around reading, looking at, and even moving one's body in relation to books became a site of active contestation that had important implications for the meaning of the queer self and for attendant formulations of metropolitan queer desire.

Revisiting the Postwar Public Library

As its explicit centering by Abercrombie suggests, the postwar public branch library was conceived as an important civic institution, not only within wider strategies of cultural provision, but as a site in which the local performance of daily life coalesced with national ideologies of consensual affiliation. After the defeat of European fascism and against the uncertain backdrop of a developing Cold War, an accessible network of well-stocked public libraries was celebrated as an important buffer against totalitarianism—a vital organ of democracy, which exemplified Britain's essential historic traditions of individual liberty and social empowerment. In 1950, the centenary of the Public Libraries Act allowed leading librarians to reaffirm these principles by celebrating their early-nineteenth-century predecessors.[10] Early public libraries, originally framed as an accessible duplication of the British Museum's library in Bloomsbury, had been rooted in a greater ideological principle that W. A. Munford (writing in 1955) would term "the public library idea": "the general accessibility of recorded fact, opinion and experience."[11] Postwar historians stressed how London's public library network had always striven to provide a point of open access to this universal archive, making all human knowledge equally available to every metropolitan citizen. As Lionel McColvin, then City Librarian of Westminster and Honorary Secretary of the Library Association, celebrated in 1950:

> We should tell our enquirers also that in this country we have, with a success due partly to our own philosophy of librarianship and partly to the nature of the British outlook, kept our libraries free from any kind of bias or ulterior motive. We have succeeded in maintaining the library as a free opportunity and thus hospitable to all varieties of creed and opinion. This characteristic—this full intellectual freedom—has, indeed, inspired both the good and the bad libraries. The bad libraries have, surely, been less able to further the ideal but they have never consciously denied it.[12]

During postwar reconstruction, such ideologies were reinscribed within London's public libraries through a range of different initiatives. In 1946, the Metropolitan Joint Fiction Reserve was created, whereby each of the city's twenty-nine boroughs was allocated a section of the alphabet and made responsible for creating a special collection of fiction by authors whose name fell within that range. In 1948, a similar initiative was adopted for works of nonfiction—each borough being allocated a set of specialist subjects—as well as for fiction in foreign languages. (Islington's libraries, for instance, hoarded fiction by authors between GRI and HOY, nonfiction between 530 and 549 on the Dewey system, and fiction published in Dutch).[13] Alongside this, the city's interlibrary loan system was strengthened and the provisional wartime measure whereby Londoners could use their ticket to borrow books from any of the city's component branches was extended indefinitely.

The early postwar years, therefore, were marked by a strong reinvestment in the idea of the public library as a collective amenity that provided every metropolitan citizen with access to a universal archive of culture and information. These values were considered largely endemic to the structure of the network itself, for each of London's boroughs was responsible for organizing and maintaining its own set of libraries and thus for ensuring its responsiveness to the local district that it served. Within each borough there was—in the words of James D. Stewart, former Borough Librarian of Bermondsey—"a central library surrounded by satellite branch libraries," a subatomic structure that mirrored Abercrombie's notion of a patchwork of

interdependent but distinctive municipalities, each one reflecting and reinforcing the character of its local populace.[14] As Stewart continued:

> I have seen large library systems in operation in this and in other countries,
> and I am convinced that the ordinary resident in Metropolitan London,
> including the man living on the outskirts as well as the man living at the
> centre, has at his immediate disposal a far better library service, for ordinary
> purposes, than exists anywhere else. Further, my experience in other capaci-
> ties of large centralised organisations has convinced me that local control
> results in greater attention being given to specific local needs, and provides
> much greater opportunities for personal initiative and experiment.[15]

Although Britain's provincial cities relied on a single central library with
only minor branch provision in the outer suburbs, the atomic layout of the
metropolitan system apparently ensured that every Londoner had access
to both a decent central library for occasional use and smaller local branch
libraries for more minor, everyday needs. Imaginatively embedded within
weekly cycles of routine—an administrative effect of the books' regulatory
due-back dates—a visit to the library was easily figured as a ritual of urban
citizenship. As a new common experience of everyday life, to borrow the
formulation of the sociologist T. H. Marshall, it transformed a local act of
civic participation into a wider performance of the timeless British values
of liberty, democracy, and enlightenment.

   In a 1967 lecture, Michel Foucault would speak of how the nineteenth-
century European library was imagined to "constitut[e] a place of all times
that is itself outside time and protected from its erosion."[16] By explicitly
presenting their institutions via notions of the universal archive and the
general accessibility of recorded fact, opinion, and experience, London's
postwar librarians gestured toward a similar spatialization of eternal tradition. Supported by the metropolitan network to which it was a portal, the
knowledge contained within the branch library became protected and secure,
confirmed by its basic presence on the shelves as a sanctioned part of the
Enlightenment tradition. Like Abercrombie's celebration of London's archaic
villages or the Britain exhibited within the pavilions of the South Bank, the
library sought to achieve a certain timelessness, a way of stabilizing knowledge and the meanings of its history by fixing it in space and submitting it
to the logic of endless repetition. All three of these important postwar constructions, then, shared the same desire to suspend the course of historical

time, to foreclose social conflict or the irruption of the unforeseen through the regulated performance of quotidian routine. Within London's public libraries, its apologists hoped, knowledge would become secure and unassailable, a permanent support for a stable social order and the democratic traditions that were reenacted by each visit.

This double temporality pursued by the public library—both a timeless repository beyond the everyday and an integral part of the citizen's routine—gave it a conceptual topography that resonated with certain psychoanalytic understandings of the human mind. Earlier in the century, Freud had described the human psyche in very similar terms, as a bounded archive of all hitherto perception and experience, which existed outside of linear time while simultaneously informing the basic operations of everyday consciousness.[17] In a sense, then, London's public libraries were being figured as just this kind of collective metropolitan memory. A safeguarded cache of all human knowledge, it would routinely insinuate itself into ordinary daily lives when one of its books was taken from the shelf, opened up, and read.

In 1934, Lord Stamp had clearly articulated this schema in an address to the Annual Assembly of University College, London:

> You will be mentally more powerful if you know *where* to find knowledge instantly than if you stuff your head with facts. . . . The man who knows his way about a library is more effective today than the man who knows twenty of the books by heart. General-knowledge papers are good, but, if it were practicable, I would hand the candidates the question paper, and set them loose in a large general library, and see who could find his way around that world of knowledge most effectively in a given period of time. . . . To know where personal storage of facts should end, and personal knowledge about where facts are stored should begin, and how to allot your time between the two courses, is the first beginning of management of mind.[18]

Stamp's concept of "management of mind" explicitly linked the library's spatial layout to a certain ordering of cognitive processes, as the two became identified and conceptually overlaid. Clearly, there existed a correct way to use the library and to retrieve the information required to support an informed and purposive mode of everyday living. Once again, spatial formations were seen as instrumental in orchestrating a responsible and mature urban sensibility. Rationality of thought became inherently bound up with the ordered layout of the library, both as a concrete space and as an imagined point of access to its larger collective archive.

Yet such analogies would soon reveal the fraudulence within the library's pretense at democratic universalism, for in psychoanalytic topography the memory's timeless repository was also the domain of the unruly unconscious. According to this structure, any material trying to enter the conscious mind was systematically policed by what Freud termed "the preconscious," which fiercely guarded the limits of what could and couldn't be known. Certain dangerous experiences were thus prevented from impinging on ordinary perception and remained perpetually inaccessible within the uncharted regions of the mind.[19]

Refuting this kind of epistemological gatekeeping, apologists for London's postwar libraries congratulated themselves on their democratic inclusivity. Their readers, they claimed, enjoyed easy access to everything without qualification. Yet such beliefs involved an implicit set of assumptions about how the material they provided would eventually be read and the mental uses to which it could be put. This, in itself, created a point of tension in relation to both their proclaimed adherence to founding archival principles and their celebrated responsiveness to local neighborhood demand. The bourgeois cultural agenda built into the library system could not easily be acknowledged, because it contravened its structuring universalism. Yet librarians routinely made decisions about which books should or shouldn't be stocked on their shelves, effectively sanctioning only those versions of "universal" human experience, fact, and opinion considered worthy of retention within their hallowed walls. As already seen at the *South Bank Exhibition,* the spatialization of a universal history required an active—if always disavowed—policing of what such history was allowed to include. As a locus for both the ritual performance of citizenship and the inculcation of good mental management, the terms of the library's provision were heavily circumscribed through basic everyday purchasing decisions. Unacceptable material that conflicted with its pedagogical project was routinely cast back—unrecognized—into the uncharted terrain of the metropolis outside.

This central disavowal at the heart of library discourse was made even more protracted by the necessary permeability of its walls. While selective purchasing could delimit the material that a reader might encounter when visiting the library, the fact that its books were bought primarily to be borrowed introduced a certain instability concerning the various ways in which they might be enjoyed. The weekly visit to change one's library books may

have insinuated its improving provision into borrowers' everyday lives, but
it also took its lending stock beyond the limits of institutional control. As
Harold Laski had told the Library Association Conference in 1935, "every
home in this country into which there is not a constant flow of books represents a failure of the public library system."[20] But although this extended
the sphere of the librarians' influence, it also undermined their ability to
supervise the act of reading itself. A constant flow of library books into the
home might exert a guiding influence on the practices of its conscientious
borrowers, but it also rendered those books amenable to other, more dangerous and metropolitan forms of deregulated textual pleasure, and in a
space far beyond the librarians' formal reach.

The Challenge of Ephemera

During the 1950s, tensions between responsive local provision and wider
cultural gatekeeping, and between domestic instruction and potential misuse, were played out within the *Library Association Record*—the professional
journal of British librarians—in a debate over how far libraries should meet
borrowers' requests to stock more light or "ephemeral" literature on their
shelves. As a performative locus of British citizenship, the library's status
as an organ of democracy would clearly be compromised if its staff were
seen to explicitly regulate the type of books it made available to its users.
As professional facilitators, they clearly had no authority to prescribe what
the public should read. Yet, on the other hand, such ephemeral novels were
clearly too lightweight and trivial to be accorded valuable shelf space within
such an important civic institution. The very term "ephemeral literature"
betrayed an awareness of how these books were embedded within repetitious cycles of mass production—a challenge, therefore, to the eternal timelessness to which its own archive pertained. Such inferior forms of reading
were clearly at home only among the transitory distractions of commercial
metropolitan life.

Ultimately, this dilemma was resolved via a general presumption that the
limited value of such ephemera was inherently obvious and that readers
would soon tire of these novels' flimsy pleasures and move on to something
more classic. Charles A. Elliott, Deputy Borough Librarian of Shoreditch
Public Libraries, expressed this neatly in 1951:

> [It] is not the librarian's function to dictate reading standards, nor should he
> try to improve people. But he *should* give them the opportunity to improve

themselves; he has a duty to serve as the link between book and reader, to make the best available for those who want it and for those who would want it if they knew its benefits.[21]

According to this rhetoric, the proper function of such ephemeral literature was to serve as a kind of training material—the first step on a developmental journey toward more appropriate modes of reading. On these grounds, it could be admitted into the library, for it maintained the latter's claims to universal provision while allowing it to mark such novels as inherently inferior and less desirable to read. Elliott's move here—entirely typical within postwar library discourse—was to displace regulatory agency away from librarians and onto the act of reading itself. Deploying a clearly Aristotelian logic, it was internal to the nature of reading, as a cultural practice with its own structural dynamics, to start from an early enjoyment of such trivial material and move toward a more mature appreciation of worthy classic texts. Conceptually, therefore, the act of reading was understood as directional, progressing in an obvious line from the transient pleasures of immature ephemera to the deeper enjoyment of more timeless works.

As the 1950s progressed, such debates became more pronounced as mass-market paperbacks gained greater visibility across the metropolis. British publishers such as Fontana and the New English Library, as well as imported American imprints like Bantam and Signet, rose to sudden prominence by embracing the modern retail principles of mass production and rapid sale, and by developing alternative distribution networks such as newsagents, smaller bookstalls, and general chain stores. These new outlets introduced paperback books into an expanded range of urban public spaces, yet the rapid turnover of stock on which they were premised was deeply antagonistic to the bureaucratized consumption that sustained the public branch library. In the kiosks and newsagents of postwar London, paperbacks could never aspire to be eternal objects of timeless knowledge, for they were always premised on a quick and repeated sale—to be bought, enjoyed for a while, and then swiftly forgotten in favor of the next one.

Paperbacks, however, were cheap and by the end of the decade many public libraries were buying multiple copies of certain titles in favor of the more expensive hardback editions and increasing their longevity by encasing them within transparent plastic jackets. The incorporation of these paperbacks into the library was itself made easier by their staff's strong preference for those editions published by Penguin Books Ltd., a firm whose celebrated mission to provide great works of literature for the price of a pack of ten cigarettes was clearly aligned with the former's attempts to insinuate proper knowledge into the daily lives of its borrowers.[22] Yet what made Penguin paperbacks so suitable for the interior of the public library was less their textual merit than the tasteful front covers within which they were packaged—a point of obvious contrast to the colorful pictorial jackets of their more "commercial" cousins. In 1959, Hans Schmoller, Penguin's chief typographer, gave a lecture in Manchester in which he celebrated the value of his firm's tasteful designs:

> "Just how perfect these proportions [of the Penguin] are was brought home to me once again this morning when I spent some hours in the John Rylands library with its unique collection of books printed by Aldus Manutius in Venice 460 years ago". Not only the format of the Aldine books (whose pro-portions, remarked Mr Schmoller, were precisely those of the Penguin) but the consistent treatment of every detail of typography were reminiscent of the discipline employed by the publishers at Harmondsworth.[23]

By slyly identifying his own Penguins' covers with those of the Aldines already in the John Rylands, Schmoller could justify the presence of the former within Britain's postwar public libraries. They gestured toward the same eternal timelessness; their covers spoke faithfully about the important human knowledge held within. A Penguin cover was unequivocal, promis-ing nothing but the dispassionate, intellectual assimilation of the text inside. Schmoller underscored this point further by giving a dismissive account of Penguin's "brief excursion into the deceptive field of mass appeal":

> Under the guidance of Abram Games, Penguin issued a group of books with pictorial covers different from anything the British paperback market had seen before. "The effect on sales was small or non-existent, while at the same time it became apparent that we were losing a lot of good will, and equally apparent that we were throwing away one of our greatest assets—namely the ability of everybody to see from a great distance that over there is a *Penguin*."[24]

The potential reader's ability to tell a Penguin from afar, and to read its cover as a sign of internal textual quality, gave the book a complex imagined geography and implicated it within a particular set of spatial relationships. Here, in the "great distance" between the reader and the Penguin "over there," Schmoller spatialized Elliott's metaphorical trajectory from immature, ephemeral pleasures to proper timeless reading. One did not rush impulsively toward a Penguin paperback. Instead, one walked soberly toward it—across the floor of the library or the reputable bookshop—along a measured line that literalized one's steady progress toward an orderly management of mind.

In contrast, the pictorial paperback undermined this sanctioned geography, as detailed within a contemporaneous report on why Berkshire County Library had refused to display them on its shelves:

> Readers in Berkshire who have seen these plastic jackets in use by other libraries are asking why their own county library scorns to use them. Mr V Jennings, in his annual report, replies that "it is extremely doubtful if there is any virtue in preserving the gaudy and often coarse illustrations with which so many of these jackets seem to be decorated. They are put out," he says, "as a bait for a certain section of the public and to display them on library shelves to attract readers smacks of the blatant publicity of the fairground." Mr Jennings continues: "There is no getting away from the fact that a certain section of the public will choose a library book because of its lurid cover. . . . It is impossible to see how the important functions of a library can be promoted by putting on a show of alluring and tawdry jackets."[25]

In contrast to Penguin's dispassionate covers, these gaudy paperbacks became bait that tempted the unwitting reader with the insincere promises of the seductive commodity. These alluring, tawdry jackets shamelessly advertised the easy availability of their inferior textual pleasures. They not only threatened to seduce readers from their literal path as they walked purposively through the library, but they also disrupted their metaphorical path from trashy popular fiction towards proper literate knowledge. Here again, inferior modes of reading and spatial deviation had become conceptually collapsed, such that—for Jennings at least—the library became a fairground, a space located by Foucault as the exact inverse of the eternal, timeless library and "linked, rather, to time in its most futile, most transitory and precarious aspect, and in the form of the festival."[26] Such tawdry jackets contaminated the library's archive with commercial repetition, profaning its managed tranquillity by opening it up to a set of ephemeral thrills that mapped the dynamics of the fairground onto the more prosaic flows and rhythms of London's newsagents and railways stations.

Both Schmoller and Jennings, then, implicitly endorsed the same values of visual fidelity that also structured dominant postwar engagements with the reformed urban environment. Echoing the rhetorics of *Britain Can Make It,* the sober covers of those Penguin paperbacks were clearly fit for purpose; they not only proclaimed the eternal worth of the text within, but in so doing, they helped construct a wider urban sensibility that responded to the spatial environment as a source of order and consensus. In contrast, the tawdry jacket of the "fairground" paperback was a distracting exercise in decorative excess, promising salacious and exaggerated pleasures that the inside of the book could never hope to fulfill. Like the exaggerated cut of the spiv's suit jacket or the loud colors of his snazzy tie, the alluring covers of these mass-market commodities combined semiotic excess with a debased form of consumption. Their public visibility was an insistent invitation to indulge in amorphously perverse textual pleasures, a malignant and unstable metropolitan presence.

On one level, it would perhaps be more accurate to chastise the restrained tones of the Penguin for being—on *Britain Can Make It*'s terms—the more pretentious sham. Like the pack of cigarettes that they explicitly sought to emulate, Penguin paperbacks were equally rooted in a fast turnover and repeated purchase. Thus, while their covers laid claim to the eternal and the timeless, the conditions of their production and distribution similarly implicated them within routine cycles of display and consumption. Yet any such charge could largely be disavowed by affirming an imagined geographic boundary between the eternal Penguin and its ephemeral "commercial" cousin. Penguin books were classic, sober, and true; they belonged in the library's archive and would secure their own passage into the sanctioned domains of the citizen's home and reading consciousness. Other more gaudy paperbacks belonged in none of these spaces. In a discussion of 1960, the publisher Desmond Flower detailed this "vast and dangerous business" of paperback retail, describing how "[o]n the New York subway alone 2,000 paper-backs are sold every day of the year," while "[i]n airports where there is 24-hour traffic slot machines are used." As the epitome of this trend, he pointed to Britain's first automated machine for books, just recently installed in Liverpool Street Station.[27] Such paperbacks, then, clearly belonged within the subway, airport, and busy railway terminus, because these spaces were already saturated with the same temporality of ephemerality and repetition. Their primitive textual pleasures resonated with the transient bustle of metropolitan life, while at the same time they contributed to the instability of these spaces, loitering there in their alluring jackets to seduce the vulnerable reader with the wayward promise of a steamy cheap encounter.

This linking of ephemeral literature with the ambiguous sociality of crowded public space had a clear historical precedent. In the mid-nineteenth century, the arrival of the railway ushered in a new experience of smooth, eventless travel and encouraged, in turn, the development of cheaper, portable volumes specifically designed to be read on the train.[28] W. H. Smith & Son opened its first railway bookstall at Euston Station in 1848 and "railway reading" soon became a site of anxiety around the increased accessibility of potentially damaging reading material, particularly for women, the working classes, and the young.[29] In *The Uses of Literacy*—Richard Hoggart's defense of proper reading, published as a Penguin in 1958—he updated this connection between the transient promiscuity of the railway station and the solicitous possibilities of the ephemeral novel:

> The "blood-and-guts" sex-novelettes can be bought not only from the "magazine shops" but from some railway-bookstalls. They are usually in a corner, all together, lying beneath the cards of aspirin and the styptic pencils. . . . The regular presence of the sex-books indicates, I suppose, that railway-reading can be a release-valve for people who would "not be seen going into" one of the "magazine-shops", and would hardly take this kind of book into the house. But boundaries move so quickly that within the last five or six years many ordinary stations have begun to stock this sort of paper-back; they are ceasing to be even slightly furtive reading.[30]

Here "railway-reading" became both a site of concern about the intrusion of market dynamics into everyday life and a release valve for expressing that anxiety. The promiscuous space of the train station could be easily opposed to the normative sanctuary of the private home, marking the latter—just like the public library—as a hermetic domain in which reading practices needed urgently to be kept good and proper. Only by fixing the textual pleasures of the gaudy paperback as ephemeral, transitory, and essentially metropolitan could their repetitive purchase and ersatz enjoyments be opposed to more purposive forms of literary enlightenment.

Lady Chatterley's Lover: Reinscribing the Straight and Narrow

Toward the end of the 1950s, then, the municipal provision of proper reading material and the challenges posed to it by the commodity paperback had produced two imagined geographies of the book, each marked out within public rhetoric through its own cartography and rhythms of consumption. The institutional branch library, as a point of local access to the universal archive, was rendered via an emphatic set of linear teleologies. The routine weekly visits of its projected citizen-borrower were not mere repetitions but a slow and steady progression toward purposive cultural enlightenment, always faithfully signposted by the sober book jackets on display and the measured movements of that reader as he or she negotiated the shelves. In opposition to this stood the unstable public presence of the mass-market paperback, promiscuously available within bustling urban spaces, where its gaudy, salacious covers might tempt unwary readers into a rushed and disappointing purchase. Here, alas, was reading only as repetition, lacking any internal development and implicated in an ambiguous set of pleasures that threatened the sanctity of both the reader's mind and the family home should these insidious commodities find their way into either.

Then, in 1960, Penguin announced plans to publish a paperback edition of D. H. Lawrence's *Lady Chatterley's Lover* and the implicit sexual inferences already in play were pushed firmly into the spotlight. The delicate spatial logics that had somehow sustained the postwar construction of appropriate reading practices were thrown into a state of crisis and Penguin was charged with obscenity by the Crown Prosecution Service. During the ensuing trial, both the claims of the prosecution and the (ultimately successful) counterclaims of the witnesses for the defense colluded to unequivocally affirm the deeply heteronormative structures through which reading, knowledge, and the public life of books had progressively become coded.

It was not so much the text of *Lady Chatterley* that caused the problem, for the trial took as axiomatic that far dirtier works were freely available on the bookstalls of the Charing Cross Road; rather, it was the orange-and-white cover within which it was due to appear (Figure 26). The recent 1959 Obscene Publications Act had reaffirmed obscenity as the tendency "to deprave and corrupt persons who are likely, having regard to all relevant circumstances, to read, see or hear the matter contained and embodied in it," a qualification that made obscenity ultimately a contextual offense, rather than a strictly textual one. According to this logic, the salacious paperbacks of the Charing Cross Road were not obscene because they stayed within the prescribed domain of the seductive ephemeral paperback—"works which

Figure 26. Obscenity masquerading as a literary classic? Front cover of D. H. Lawrence, *Lady Chatterley's Lover* (Harmondsworth: Penguin Books, 1960).

we have all seen and can see on bookstalls," in the words of the defense.[31] Pornography was located and clearly visible as such. Thus, according to the assumptions of all those present, it was not the type of reading material to be enjoyed by any citizens currently seated in the courtroom. The Penguin *Chatterley,* on the other hand, played an obscene game of masquerade. Under its pretentious Aldine cover, it threatened to leave the Charing Cross Road and go freely about the city, not only proliferating across its news-agents and railway-station kiosks but—wearing the mask of a classic work of literature—claiming a place on the shelves of London's public libraries and the ordered private homes of its respectable borrowers. The charge of the prosecution, therefore, invoked the familiar moral economy of postwar graphic design: this Penguin cover was dangerous because it lied.

According to C. H. Rolph's transcripts of the trial, public libraries were mentioned only once during the proceedings. Concern was much more focused on the book's wider presence amid the fabric of everyday life.[32] Accordingly, the judge asked the jury to assess the potential effects of the novel by imagining factory girls reading it during their lunch hour, a request that was seized upon by the press and which clearly echoed the concerns of both Patrick Abercrombie and PC Darlington about this unstable intersti-tial portion of the working day.[33] The morning after the book was finally published, newspapers reported excitedly on which shops in London were putting it on open display and the various degrees of embarrassment or bravado with which "ordinary" members of the public had been observed asking for copies. "The odd thing," wrote a reporter for the *Guardian,* who clearly sensed the lingering excesses still attached to its cover, "was that nobody seemed to be reading the book in cafés or on buses or Under-ground trains."[34]

Be this as it may, the trial soon encountered the same set of tensions around reading, knowledge, and their accompanying potential pleasures that public librarians had spent the previous decade also trying to negotiate. The first dilemma concerned how the jury was to fulfill its official role as twelve synecdochic representatives of the British general public. This, the judge insisted, required them to read *Lady Chatterley* as any normal person would—"just as though you had bought it at a bookstall and you were read-ing it in the ordinary way as a whole."[35] But the assumptions and disavowals that helped sustain the public library as a "universal" space of highly managed knowledge also threatened to corrupt the hallowed space of the courtroom. To let the jury return to the spaces of their daily lives risked contaminating

their proper reading of the book and opening it up to alternative textual pleasures:

> "'I think the Jury should read the book here", the Judge decided. "I am very
> sorry, members of the Jury. I don't want to condemn you to any kind of dis-
> comfort, but if you were to take this book home you might have distractions.
> One knows perfectly well in one's home things do happen unexpectedly. There
> are distractions. You are trying and carrying out a very onerous duty, and I
> think it would be much better if you were to read this book in your room".[36]

This was the same fear of distractions that had caused Jennings to deny
gaudy paperbacks admittance to his library—that some unstable bait might
cause readers to deviate from their straight path through the book and, by
association, toward a dispassionate knowledge of its contents. For both jury
members and library borrowers, performing their duty as British citizens
meant ceasing to live as ordinary people. To know a book meant to read it
properly, to respond to it only through the objective operations of the intel-
lect, untouched by any unrecognizable quotidian desires.

Rachel Bowlby has explored how, during the trial, anxiety at *Lady Chatterley's* textual pleasures was expressed through a veiled identification between
the book's implied audience and the protagonists of the novel. Connie and
Mellors's dual transgression of class and gender boundaries were problematic precisely because the cheap Penguin edition was affordable to the same
combination of women and working-class men. In addition, Bowlby notes,
the trial persistently equated the book's linguistic filthiness (its use of four-
letter words) with its apparent sexual filthiness (Connie's unfeminine, anti-
familial sexual appetite).[37] But these twin slippages ran even deeper and
came to structure the trial's most basic imaginings of the appropriate moral
geography of reading and its pleasures.

During a lengthy address, the prosecution stressed how the offensive-
ness of Connie and Mellors's many sexual encounters—and also, therefore,
of Lawrence's detailed depiction of them—lay in their varied distribution
across both space and time:

> There are, I think, described in all thirteen [episodes of sexual intercourse]
> throughout the course of this book. . . . You may think that this book, if its
> descriptions had been confined to the first occasion on which sexual inter-
> course is described, would be a very much better book than it is. But twelve

of them certainly are described in detail leaving nothing to the imagination. The curtain is never drawn. One follows them not only into the bedroom but into bed and one remains with them there. . . . . Members of the Jury, that is not strictly accurate, because the only variations, in effect, between all thirteen occasions are the time and the *locus in quo,* the place where it happened. So one does not follow them into the bed and remain with them in bed; one starts in my lady's boudoir, in her husband's house, one goes to the floor of a hut in the forest with a blanket laid down as a bed; we see them do it again in the undergrowth in the forest amongst the shrubbery, and not only in the undergrowth in the forest, in the pouring rain, both of them stark naked and dripping with raindrops. One sees them in the keeper's cottage, first in the evening on the hearth rug and then we have to wait until dawn to see them do it again in bed. And finally, members of the Jury, we move the site to Bloomsbury and we have it all over again in the attic in a Bloomsbury boarding-house. And that is the variation—the time and place that it all happened.[38]

These thirteen sex acts coerced the reader into a series of repeated encounters with graphic eroticism, forcing them by implication into an inappropriate mode of textual pleasure more suited to the reader of ephemeral paperbacks. In addition, because these sexual episodes escaped from the confines of the bedroom—already violated by Lawrence's firm refusal to draw the curtain—and became promiscuously dispersed across a wider range of spaces, they mapped the sites of Connie's libidinal excessive as exactly those in which the Penguin *Chatterley* might be similarly misenjoyed.

In response, the defense reframed those thirteen scenes not as gratuitous repetitions but as necessary steps on a teleological journey, thus invoking exactly the same logic as might justify the book's wider presence within the managed space of the municipal library:

Mr Griffith-Jones has suggested that here is a book which contains thirteen descriptions of intercourse and that the only variation is the time and place. I would suggest that when you read this book you will find the exact opposite of that. You will find that the early promiscuous affairs are all of them highly unsatisfactory. But Constance does fall in love and the book ends with her and Mellors being about to marry. The physical relations between her and the man, so far from being a repetition, are a slow, steady development and a development which could not be shown unless it was shown, as I suggest it is, with honesty and fairness. (31)

The novel's repeated descriptions of illicit sex acts, like the pleasures of the ephemeral novel they so troublingly mirrored, were firmly directed toward a proper destination. The ordered space of the marital bedroom had been cited as the legitimating end point of Connie and Mellors's developing propriety, and thus had also been established as the location in which Lawrence's now literary novel could be properly read after all.

This same conflict occurred during the trial's second elision between sexuality and semantics. The prosecution's charge was again one of gratuitous repetition:

> The book abounds in bawdy conversation. . . . The word "fuck" or "fucking" occurs no less than thirty times. I have added them up, but I do not guarantee that I have added them all up. "Cunt" fourteen times; "balls" thirteen times; "shit" and "arse" six times apiece; "cock" four times; "piss" three times, and so on. (20)

In response, Richard Hoggart could only defend the novel through a highly spatialized account of semantic impropriety. When asked his views on the "use of these four-letter words in the mouth of Mellors," he replied:

> They seem to me totally characteristic of many people, and I would like to say not only working-class people, because that would be wrong. . . . Fifty yards from this Court this morning I heard a man say "fuck" three times as he passed me. He was speaking to himself and he said "fuck it, fuck it, fuck it" as he went past. If you have worked on a building site, as I have, you will find they recur over and over again. The man I heard this morning and the men on building sites use the words as words of contempt, and one of the things Lawrence found most worrying was that the word for this important relationship had become a word of vile abuse . . . it has become simply derision, and in this sense he wanted to re-establish the meaning of it, the proper use of it. (98)

It was the contexts in which these words were used, rather than the words themselves, that made them improper and obscene, further underscored here by the gratuitous repetition of a "fuck it, fuck it, fuck it." Once again, the defense responded with a teleological account that legitimated both the presence of these words within the book and, by implication, the presence of the book within the various spaces in which it might soon be read. As Helen Gardner explained:

I would like to begin by saying that I don't think any words are brutal and disgusting in themselves. They are brutal and disgusting if they are used in a brutal and disgusting sense or a brutal and disgusting context. I think that by the very fact that this word is used so frequently in the book, with every subsequent use the original shock is diminished, and I would say by the end Lawrence has gone very far within the context of this book to redeem this word from low and vulgar associations, and to make one feel it is the only word the character in the book could use. If one attempts to find any substitute I think it is impossible. By the time one reads the last page, Mellors' letter, this word has taken on great depth of meaning, has become related to natural processes, and is wholly justified in the context of this book. I don't mean I think Lawrence was able to redeem the word in usage. I am talking about its usage within the book itself. (60)

This apparent repetition, then, was in fact a progression, with each additional "fuck" removing a layer of semantic misuse until the reader was left with a pure kernel of originary meaning. When this semantic redemption was unambiguously identified with the "natural processes" of heterosexual intercourse, the way had been cleared for *Lady Chatterley* to be judged not obscene and Penguin Books Ltd. acquitted.[39]

Through these machinations, the visual sobriety of *Lady Chatterley*'s Aldine cover was properly reestablished. Neither the novel's language nor its sexual episodes facilitated ephemeral and repetitious reading pleasures. Both, rather, were part of the same straight road to knowledge and enlightenment—a path soon to be replicated by the reader's relationship to the novel when dispassionately observed upon the library shelf. The trial's triumph was to successfully preserve the delicate structures of its three privileged heterotopias—the public courtroom, the public library, and the private bedroom—by effectively fusing the ideals through which each of them was ordered: judicial truth, proper reading practices, and heterosexual procreation.

The *Chatterley* trial and the wider reordering of textual pleasure to which its debates pertained were interesting for their unacknowledged debt to the psychoanalytic schemata that were influencing contemporary sexual thinking. One major channel through which these were disseminated was the cluster of sexological paperbacks that Pelican—Penguin's nonfiction imprint—published in the postwar decades. The conceptual tone of these volumes had already been in set in 1940, when Kenneth Walker informed readers of his *The Physiology of Sex and Its Social Implications* that "the word 'deviation' has now replaced 'perversion' in scientific literature, since the latter term was used at a time when all sexual anomalies were regarded as deliberate sins."[40] This new concept of "sexual deviation," clearly indebted to Freudian psychology, recoded sexual behavior within a teleological structure. Human sexuality became a quest; the individual progressed through a series of developmental stages, aided or hindered by familial and social environments, as he or she searched for a satisfactory object of sexual love. From the earliest autoeroticism, the normal child would move through a period of intense sexual friendships with members of his or her own sex before finally achieving companionate heterosexual fulfillment. As Walker confided in another coauthored volume: "If the 'I' eventually succeeds in meeting its 'Thou' hunger is at last transmuted into love."[41]

Of course, the heterosexual nature of this final destination was never in doubt. And while proclaiming a historical and anthropological awareness about the prevalence of same-sex relations in other societies, their rejection of crude biological determinism was superseded by a vaguer, though still heteronormative, social humanism. As Anthony Storr argued in *Sexual Deviation* (1964):

> Although it may be impossible to define normality in sexual behaviour even within the confines of a single society, there do exist other standards in terms of which it is possible to make comparative appraisals. One such standard is that of emotional maturity, a concept which is found under various guises in the writings of every psychodynamic school. It is a standard to which no human being ever attains and is therefore an ideal at which to aim rather than an actual achievement. . . . As displayed in the sexual sphere, maturity may be defined as the ability to form a stable relationship with the opposite sex which is both physically and emotionally satisfying, and in which sexual intercourse forms the main, though not the only, mode of expression of love.[42]

Writers were at pains to stress that this road to sexual maturity was by no means straightforward, such that by at least the 1950s, volumes of popular sexology were presenting masturbation, adolescent homosexuality, and even encounters with female prostitutes as more or less normal stages on a young man's journey toward heterosexual monogamy. Yet these transitional phases remained dogged by a persistent anxiety that for some boys these might not turn out to be phases at all—that some external factor might intervene to keep the adolescent stuck in a regressive state of sexual development. As Walker and Fletcher put it: "The pilgrim's progress may be halted at any stage of the journey by inhibitions stemming from the environment."[43]

These books, like Westwood's *Society and the Homosexual*, consistently invoked a litany of environmental factors that might cause a youth to get stuck in the homosexual phase of development—an overclingy mother who discouraged independence, an absent or aggressive father who failed as a role model, excessive boyhood teasing for some physical weakness, or strict taboos around normal intercourse that instilled a terror of heterosexual congress. Yet common to all was a perception of homosexuality not as an active attraction to men, but as a regressive substitute for a thwarted original desire for women. As D. J. West concluded in his book *Homosexuality:* "homosexual adaptation occurs when heterosexual adaptation proves too difficult."[44] Thus, while such expert knowledge could happily contribute toward the fashioning of a new homosexual citizen, disconnected from sin and seemingly able to form a lasting relationship, readers were left in no doubt that such behavior remained only a damaged parody of the heterosexual normality that still evaded him. Indeed, West argued that the "halfway refuge" of homosexuality was evident from the innate immaturity of the homosexual sex act itself:

> Since normal copulation between persons of the same sex is impossible, homosexuals depend for reaching climax (orgasm) on methods of mutual stimulation that normal couples would regard as mere incidental indulgences leading up to intercourse. Kissing, fondling, close bodily contact, and mutual masturbation are the chief forms of homosexual love-making.[45]

These popular volumes were deeply consonant with those conceptual teleologies through which *Lady Chatterley* would finally become established as a nonobscene work. The novel's early sex scenes and Lawrence's liberal use of four-letter words were likewise reinterpreted as mere phases of the protagonists' journey toward true sexual maturity, a destination finally reached in the closing pages of the book. The importance of the *Chatterley* trial lay in how it mapped this progression onto the developing maturity of the readers, as they accompanied Connie and Mellors on their quest. By fixing the novel's propriety through its spatial conclusion in the marital bedroom, the courtroom implicitly equated the improper enjoyment of ephemeral paperbacks with a form of readerly immaturity at once intellectual and sexual. If the sober orange-and-white cover of the Penguin *Chatterley* was a truthful sign of the timeless knowledge within, then the tawdry jackets of less reputable paperbacks became aligned with the indulgent mothers and hostile fathers of Pelican sexologies—a damaging environmental influence that threatened the individual's progression to his socially and sexually desirable goal. The retarded pleasures of ephemeral novels and the spatial allure of their promiscuous display were both collapsed into a wayward, nonnormative, and immature sexuality, in a complex interweaving of textual, spatial, and sexual deviancy. Thus, by the end of the 1950s, the urban mass-market paperback—with its visual solicitations and regressive reading practices—had come to be thoroughly queered.

Queer Deviations

Yet even as the *Chatterley* trial was endorsing the heteronormative logics of proper reading practices, a queerer set of geographies were developing elsewhere within London. In the late 1950s and early 1960s, an increasing number of both fictional and nonfictional paperbacks proclaiming an interest in male homosexuality became insistently visible within the metropolitan landscape. At one end of the spectrum were the Pelican sexologies that firmly aligned themselves with those hegemonic orderings of textual, spatial, and sexual propriety already propagated by branch librarians and *Lady Chatterley*'s apologists. Thus Walker and Fletcher opened their Pelican *Sex and Society* (1955) in an entirely typical fashion:

> This is not a book for experts. The medical information it contains is familiar to medical men and the psychologist is likely to dismiss as elementary what it has to say on the subject of mental and emotional phenomena. It is a book written for the ordinary intelligent reader and, more especially, for the younger intelligent reader interested, for various reasons, in the sexual problems and dilemmas of our times. The authors' object has been to provide such readers with material for thought rather than with ready-made solutions, in the hope that they will be able to reach their own conclusion concerning these problems and dilemmas.[46]

Like Elliott's public librarian, these authors did not seek to dictate opinion to ordinary readers, but to encourage them to develop those managed practices of thought that would enable them to follow the road to truth themselves.

Once again, all this was anchored within the books' front covers, which, for the Pelicans, were a blue-and-white reworking of the generic Penguin format. The sober austerity of D. J. West's *Homosexuality*, published as a Pelican in 1960, was never of course in doubt (Figure 27). As the jacket proclaimed, this was "a frank and practical approach to the social and medical aspects of male homosexuality," free from any hint of sensationalism, let alone any shadow of extraneous eroticism. This mode of dispassionate address allowed these Pelicans to locate themselves within their own calls for a clear and controlled program of sex education, yet it also allowed them to interpellate their readers into a national community of normative sexuality. Hence the framing "Editorial Preface" to Storr's *Sexual Deviation:*

> [T]he Pelicans in this series ["Studies in Social Pathology"] will not, I believe, pander to morbid curiosity. Their authors will be concerned to show how these things come about, and in so doing they will make it easier for us to look levelly at the deviants in our midst, deploring their actions but not totally rejecting the individuals themselves. As the title of the series implies all these are conditions in whose aetiology social factors play a major part. There, but for the grace of God, go we.[47]

Because attainment of this proper knowledge had already been implicitly aligned with heterosexual maturity, the readers of such truths could not but be envisaged as outside the ranks of those sexual deviants about whom these books were concerned.

Alongside these Pelicans, a number of novels about homosexuality appeared during the 1950s and early 1960s, published by a range of different paperback houses and of varying degrees of literary merit. Both sets of texts were largely united in their political motivations, seeking to present a sensitive and informed account of homosexuality as an unfortunate—and not always antisocial—affliction that required a compassionate psychiatric response. In practice, this meant that there was little to differentiate between the tropes, themes, and narrative rhetoric found in more scientific works and those of generic light fiction. The central figure of the conscientious homosexual remained burdened by the ostracism of an ignorant society and the vicious instability of the metropolitan milieu to which such hostility had confined him—a situation that offered him sporadic flickers

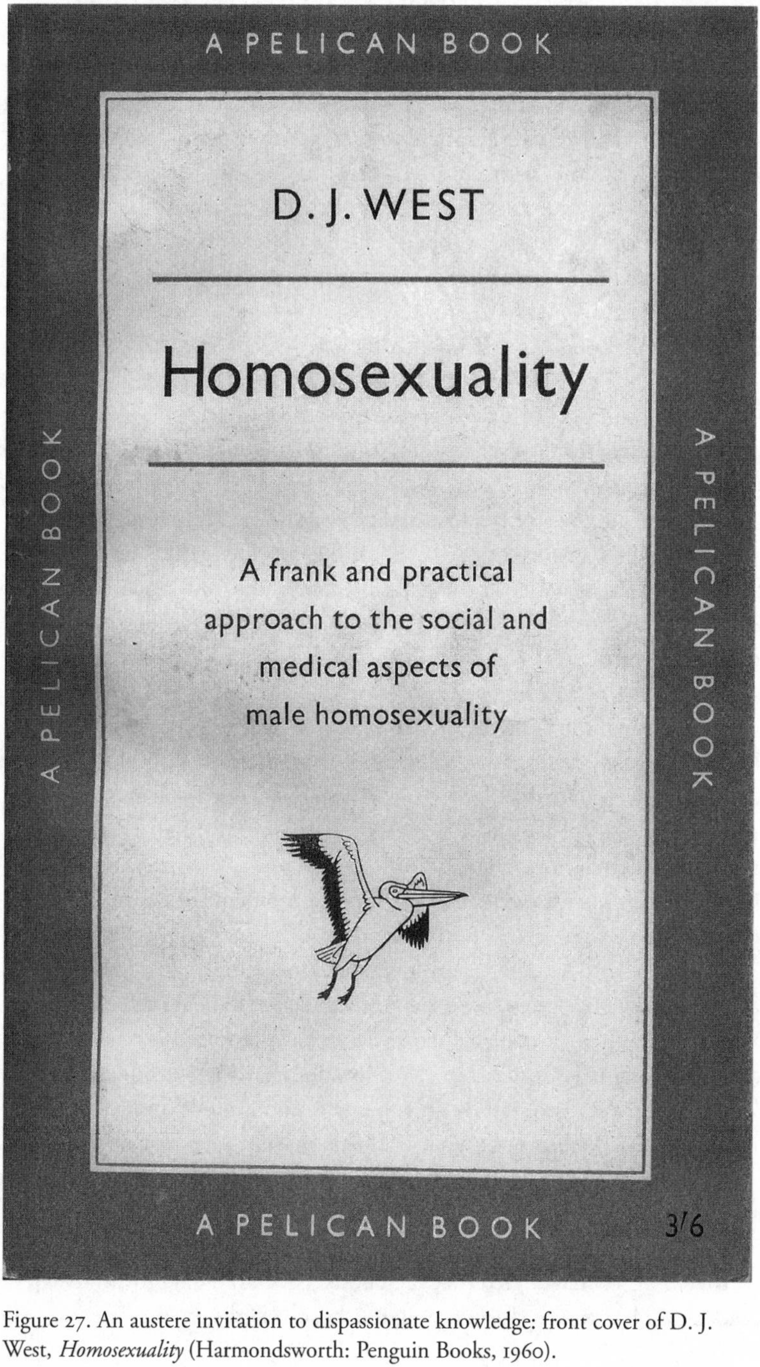
A PELICAN BOOK
D. J. WEST
Homosexuality
A frank and practical approach to the social and medical aspects of male homosexuality
A PELICAN BOOK
A PELICAN BOOK
A PELICAN BOOK
3/6

Figure 27. An austere invitation to dispassionate knowledge: front cover of D. J. West, *Homosexuality* (Harmondsworth: Penguin Books, 1960).

of companionate domestic happiness, but that extinguished these all too soon amid its endemic betrayals, its ongoing loneliness, and its residual self-hatred.[48] Thus, a dispassionate work of science such as West's *Homosexuality* could contain both emotive "case studies" and exotic descriptions of what he termed "a vast underworld of sexual deviants." Indeed, before concluding on "the frustration and tragedy inherent in this mode of life," West endorsed this casual crossover between science and literature by citing Rodney Garland's novel *The Heart in Exile* (1953) as a prime source of information about London's queer subcultures.[49]

Yet, despite this degree of intertextuality, West's *Homosexuality* and Garland's *The Heart in Exile* were clearly positioned as polar opposites by their respective front covers. In 1961, Four Square published the first British paperback edition of Garland's novel, proclaiming it on the front as "a disturbingly frank novel of homosexuality in London" (Figure 28). Frankness had also been a quality of West's book the previous year, but against the blue-and-white austerity of the Pelican edition, the Four Square cover reveled in its bold use of color and its sketchy iconography. Like other mass-market paperbacks of the 1950s and 1960s, it clearly advertised itself by suggesting the potent set of pleasures on offer inside. While *Homosexuality* would be frank and "practical," *The Heart in Exile* was frank and "disturbing," a promise of affective thrills rather than useful technical knowledge. Its side-lit image of two well-built—and weirdly identical—handsome young men, and the quiet power of that large masculine hand grasping his partner's well-filled T-shirt, addressed the reader not as a citizen, but through his or her complicity with the foreshadowed moments of desire and disturbance that consuming this book would reveal. As Susan Stryker notes, the need to appeal to a mass audience required such covers to address a wider audience than queer men alone; hence they tended to be far less explicit than their lesbian-themed equivalents, which generally found it easier to reach a heterosexual male readership.[50] Yet for all this, the Four Square *Heart in Exile* clearly advertised itself as an ephemeral commodity, one that endorsed the queerness of those momentary thrills on which its appeal depended. Through its cover, it was able to offer those queer men who encountered it an alternative mode of libidinal enlightenment, inextricably rooted in those bustling urban spaces in which it habitually loitered.

Richard Dyer has argued that such book jackets offered prospective queer readers a subjective position ambiguously split between identification and desire:

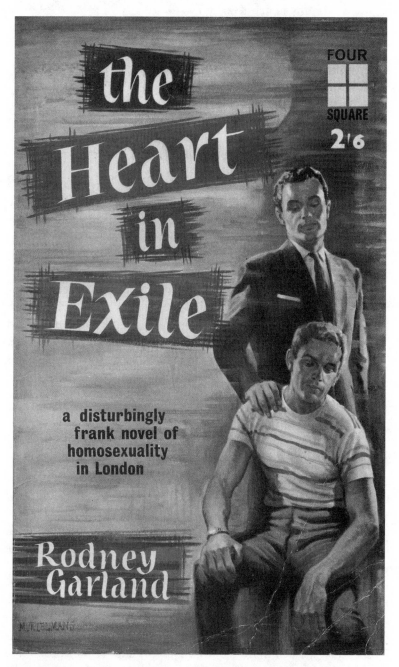

the
Heart
in
Exile

a disturbingly
frank novel of
homosexuality
in London

Rodney
Garland

Figure 28. The solicitous urban paperback advertises its thrills: front cover of
Rodney Garland, *The Heart in Exile* (London: Four Square, 1961).

[A]s much as the image may be trumpeted as being about others, it is available to be taken as being about oneself, and as much as it is about a terrible, miserable way of being it also sets it up as an erotically desirable one.[51]

These designs, then, solicited a mixture of desire-for and desire-to-be, which fused an invitation to consume the book with a promise of involvement in the sexual encounters foreshadowed on the front. Once again the pleasures of the text, the spatial relationship of one's body to its cover, and an "immature" form of sexual gratification were complexly interwoven in a sudden moment of threefold deviation. Here, firmly embedded within the ordinary spaces of metropolitan life, was a queer mode of responsive self-knowledge very different from that supposedly facilitated within the library walls—a matter not of private contemplation but of unstable public advertisement. Garland's novel existed to be looked at, to be cruised and picked up within its natural urban habitat. The act of reading thus became proffered as a protosexual act, the consumption of the novel collapsed onto both a projected identification with the men on the cover and an anticipated involvement in the queer consummations billed as about to take place inside. On the revolving bookstand of the London newsagent, such paperbacks exploded at a stroke the pretensions of the library's universal archive and put forcibly into action an alternative, much queerer economy of sexual enlightenment already dependent on its own metropolitan choreographies and rhythms of enjoyment.

In practice, of course, West's *Homosexuality* may have worked in much the same way. It might have demanded to be read only properly by that citizen-reader inferred by its cover, but potential readers must surely have felt the ambiguous excess that any visible interest in such a book would hold. It was precisely this gap between the sanctioned mode of proper engagement with such books and these books' inability to remain within those limits that Orton and Halliwell exploited so successfully when they stole volumes from the Islington and Hampstead branch libraries, defaced their covers, and smuggled them back onto the library shelves for some unsuspecting browser to discover. The pair's antics, therefore, can be read as an articulate destabilization of the heteronormative logics through which reading had been ordered within postwar London, and one cunningly targeted at precisely that space in which they were most prescriptively attached to the rituals of social citizenship. The duo's defacements both declared and celebrated an alternative, defiantly queer geography of reading, insinuating the destabilizing pull of the city's mass-market paperbacks into the most managed site of its discursive disavowal.

In his report on the incident for the *Library Association Record*, Alexander Connell, the Librarian-in-Charge of Islington Central Lending Library, divided the damage done by Orton and Halliwell into three distinct categories. First, the pair had typed false blurbs onto the inside leaves of certain dust jackets. Initially, these books would seem perfectly orthodox to potential readers, for "it was not until one had read the complete blurb that what the judge termed 'amusing or mildly obscene' wording made its impact."[52] Second, they pasted bits from other illustrations onto existing dust jackets to create surreal or iconoclastic collages, which confronted the readers when they took them off the shelf. Third, they defaced various illustrative plates located inside the books or added an incongruous or shocking caption to them. These would only be discovered by readers if they spent time flicking through the book at the library shelf, or else during the course of normal reading if they had taken the volume home.

Importantly, many of Orton and Halliwell's collages presented images of the male body as an explicit object of erotic spectacle. For instance, the cover of William K. Zinsser's *Seen Any Good Films Lately?* was reworked so that the original illustration's lone male viewer seated in an empty cinema auditorium was now made to look at the bodies of a male ballet dancer and a seminaked man wearing a blindfold (Figure 29). In another book, an illustrative plate of the actress Sybil Thorndike in her starring role as Nurse Edith Cavell was altered so that her gaze now fell on the affixed genitalia of a classical male sculpture. This imagery—and the pair's attention to the book's displayed surfaces rather than to its internal text—colluded with the layout of the branch libraries themselves to bring to public attention, in the most dramatic way possible, those immature choreographies of sexual and textual desire so sternly denied by this municipal institution.

It might be supposed that the managed consumption of any library book was organized around three contiguous stages. First the reader saw the book's spine on the shelf, filed according to the author's surname or its place within the Dewey classification system. On this basis, the interested reader would examine the front and back cover of the book and maybe peruse the blurb on the inside flyleaf. Finally, and on the basis of this information, the reader might decide to borrow the book and safely take it home to read in more comfortable surroundings. Each moment within this process hinged on a point of semiotic fidelity: the spine and cover had to truthfully

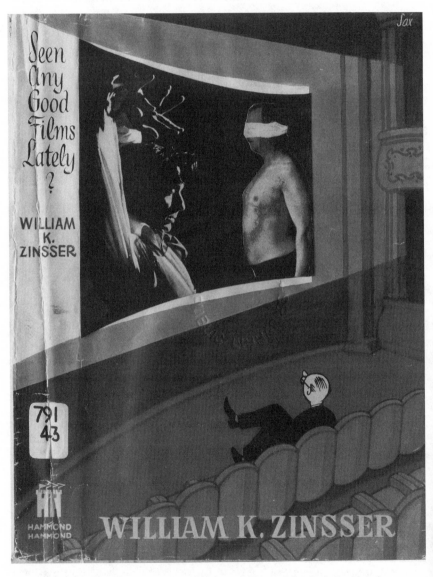

Figure 29. Deviation irrupts in the public branch library: John (Joe) Orton and
Kenneth Halliwell, defaced front cover of William K. Zinsser, *Seen Any Good Films
Lately?* (London: Hammond Hammond, 1960). Courtesy of Islington Local History
Centre. Used by permission of The Random House Group Ltd.

enunciate the value of the text inside, thus also working to announce the uses to which it might be put in the more private spaces of the borrower's home and psyche.

Orton and Halliwell's cunning defacements usually disrupted this process at the second stage, producing a moment of sudden shock that immediately foreclosed the possibility of any dispassionate intellectual encounter between the reader and the book. Within the administered spaces of the Islington and Hampstead branch libraries, the prospective borrower experienced an intense and unexpected affective reaction to the jacket, which mimicked the one more commonly occurring between the queer man and the gaudy paperback outside the library's walls. The unsuspecting victim was thus thrown suddenly into a regressive and immature mode of reading as the dynamics of the library were neatly inverted. Indeed, many of the covers provided their own metacommentary—the reader found himself or herself staring not only at a sexualized male body but at an image that explicitly foregrounded such spectatorship. Illicit desire and textual immaturity were made shockingly obvious. Orton and Halliwell's defacements, then, subverted those interwoven assumptions about knowledge, truth, and heterosexuality that underscored the hegemonic construction of the citizen-reader and in the most hallowed space of its managed operation.

The final revelation of these scandalous collages was that the municipal libraries of Islington and Hampstead were far closer to the train stations and newsagents of the repudiated metropolis than to the tranquil reading room of the British Museum to which they had historically laid claim; for the pretensions of the municipal library as a site of national citizenship could never have been borne out within such prosaic spatial structures. The same transient flows and ephemeral repetitions were surely in evidence—albeit in a more muted form—as readers came and went, often in a state of distraction, while negotiating the shelves and each other. The inadmissible intrusion of such ordinary urban practices, with all their unstable systems of pleasure and signification, meant that the postwar public branch library was already marked as a site of internalized discipline. Browsing the shelves became a self-policed performance, as the books that one was seen to select became a public disclosure of one's own private reading pleasures and—by extension— of the private conduct that went on in one's home. The library was saturated with an open secret, to borrow D. A. Miller's formulation, as an awareness of both nonorthodox reading pleasures and nonheterodox sexual pleasures merged into a covert set of knowledges that one couldn't be seen to know.[53]

To this extent, the experiences of ordinary Londoners within the city's public libraries replicated the type of interplay between discipline and desire that queer men surely experienced more generally within everyday metropolitan space. The relationship between readers, the covers on display, and their attendant—if necessarily disavowed—illicit possibilities mimicked the wider negotiations that characterized queer life outside the library's walls. Orton and Halliwell keenly exploited this and forced their victims into an unwittingly queer situation that defied the sober scripts of civic participation. This was clearly present within one of their most famous defacements: the false blurb typed on the inside flyleaf of Dorothy L. Sayers's detective novel *Clouds of Witness:*

> When little Betty Macdree says that she has been interfered with, her mother at first laughs. It is only something that the kiddy had picked up off television. But when sorting through the laundry Mrs Macdree discovers that a new pair of knickers are missing, she thinks again. On being questioned, Betty bursts into tears. Mrs Macdree takes her to the police station and to everyone's surprise the little girl identifies P.C. Brenda Coolidge as her attacker. Brenda, a new recruit, denies the charge. A search is made of the Women's Police Barracks. What is found there is a seven inch phallus and a pair of knickers of the kind used by Betty. All looks black for kindly P.C. Coolidge . . . What can she do? This is one of the most enthralling stories ever written by Miss Sayers.
>
> It is the only one in which the murder weapon is concealed, not for reasons of fear but for reasons of decency!
>
> READ THIS BEHIND CLOSED DOORS. And have a good shit while you are reading![54]

Any person at the library shelf respectably perusing this blurb was suddenly thrown into a set of deviant queer reading practices. Through its command to be read behind closed doors, the book announced its unsuitability to be properly read in the civic space of the library, while implicating the reader in an assumed set of private improprieties that already crossed over into their own homes. Further, this revelation was here linked to the toilet ("And have a good shit while you are reading!") while it positioned the victim within a structure of surveillance akin to that experienced by queer men most acutely—or perhaps most paradigmatically—in the public toilet or cottage. At the same time, the blurb linked the act of reading not only to a repeated bodily function, but to a specifically anal one—again, making a cross-identification between deviant textual pleasures and a narrative of arrested development familiar from popular sexology.

When Halliwell and Orton appeared at the Old Street Magistrates Court in 1962, it was on these terms that they were tried. Simon Shepherd has noted how the courtroom could admit no mention of the sexual nonconformity implied by their shared bedsit, deflecting it instead into "descriptions of childishness, bohemians, people without proper jobs . . . [and] failures."[55] In a climate informed by psychoanalytic etiologies, these tropes already had clear homosexual resonances, but they also appealed to a discursive genealogy of failed masculinity and immature behavior that extended at least as far back as the postwar spiv. Here, then, were those same normative teleologies that had featured so heavily in the *Lady Chatterley* trial two years earlier. The pair's attack on the spatial framework of proper reading practices, with its interwoven hierarchies of pleasure and knowledge, could only register within the sanctity of the courtroom by conflating, once again, notions of textual and sexual immaturity. In both areas, these two men had disastrously failed to achieve the desirable mode of civic responsibility.

Of course, Orton and Halliwell's pranks were just as dependent on the dominant structures of postwar reading as the more official formulations against which they were tried. Their playful attack had its own limitations; for they could only appropriate an existing relationship among textual, sexual, and spatial deviation and momentarily invert it to create a tiny space of freedom. But their work also hints at a new form of mastery, an ability to manipulate the alluring surfaces of the metropolitan commodity and deploy them for their own special ends. Less remembered among the pair's defacements are a number of Arden editions of Shakespeare's plays. These volumes—originally published in austere plain covers, not dissimilar in style to those produced by Penguin—were given evocative new jackets that sought to visualize the tone of the drama inside. These deeply respectful collages did not set out to shock the browsing reader but to communicate, with sincerity, the value of the text—an endorsement of Shakespeare's genius, against the middle-brow pretensions of both Zinsser and Sayers. Yet both types of intervention were sensitive to the affective potential of such pictorial book jackets and their ability to solicit a passionate response in the viewer.

It is this engagement with the urban commodity—a welcoming acceptance of ephemeral self-advertisement and the uses of its appeal—that marks

Orton and Halliwell in opposition to those more sanctioned modes of metropolitan engagement that dominated programs of postwar social renewal. Against Wildeblood's and Westwood's proffered model of homosexual citizenship, here was a nascent queer outlook more at home within deregulated systems of mediated consumption and the new possibilities they continued to present. The tawdry allure of the gaudy paperback was an early solicitation of such queer men, a recognition of their status as consumers, rather than citizens, and a challenge to the bureaucratic management of consumption so strategic to the hegemonic social order. New experiences of queer self-creation were thus becoming available to many men and in precisely those public spaces that had most vexed reconstruction planners. By engaging with and appropriating these commercial techniques of self-promotion and appeal, Orton and Halliwell had found a way—if only momentarily—to challenge the claustrophobia of an inhospitable program of municipal civic life.

chapter 5

LIFE IN THE CYBERNETIC BEDSIT:
INTERIOR DESIGN AND THE
HOMOSEXUAL SELF

"Oh! My dear fellow," Hubert laughed. "I'd forgotten how little the room must be to your taste. . . . No Murillo shepherd-boys or Michelangelo heads to make you feel lovin' and good. No little Greco-Roman indeterminates to bolster the itchin' palm up with a bit of culture. . . . Just man in his proper place among a lot of bigger things that serve their purpose."

— ANGUS WILSON, *Hemlock and After,* 1952

WIFE: "Oh dear!"
HUSBAND: "Modern."
WIFE: "It *is* modern, isn't it?"

— middle-aged couple of artisan class, before "Bed-sitting Room in a London Apartment Block," *Britain Can Make It* exhibition, 1946

During the early postwar era, the private home emerged as one of the most contested sites in the concerted drive for social reconstruction and renewal. Planners, policy makers, and other public experts paid particular attention to domestic space, now presented as a formative space of national citizenship and an important battleground in the attempt to secure social order and psychological stability. Against the decrepit slums, the rundown Victorian town houses, and residential bomb sites that scarred London's metropolitan landscape—surely a fertile breeding ground of delinquency and petty crime—the reform of the home and the life that took place there seemed an urgent and foundational element within the striving toward a modern and more prosperous social-democratic nation.

As the 1950s progressed, the imagined significance of the domestic home also became more complex owing to the various reformulations through which male same-sex desire was being recoded. As we have seen, the Wolf-enden Committee and other apologists for the homosexual citizen endorsed dominant notions of companionate privacy, public discretion, and libidi-nal restraint. Hence, domestic space was increasingly presented as the sole legitimate domain of queer expression, its validity premised on its imper-meability to the "'decent" public gaze. This already tallied with the every-day experience of many of London's middle-class queer men, who—thanks to the legal requirement for search warrants, a police focus on combating mainly public disorder, and their ability to afford secure accommodation—had remained largely impervious to domestic intrusion.[1] To this extent, liberal endorsements of the right to queer privacy tallied with the wider postwar valorization of companionate domesticity and helped move the respectable queer home further toward the moral—if not yet legal—limits of state interference and surveillance.

Meanwhile, as was explored in chapter 3, the loosely Freudian psychology that had helped to fashion this respectable homosexual citizen focused addi-tional attention on the potential perils of the family home, since domestic life had now been cast as the primary determinant in the production of sex-ual health. Concerns over homosexuality, therefore, not only were attached to the domiciles of actual queer men—a potential site of corruption, but also a tool in the promotion of companionate fulfillment—but extended out-wards to encompass any home that might contain children. If, as experts argued, a boy's sexual proclivities were largely determined by his familial environment—mainly before the age of five, but also through the latency period and into adolescence—then domestic space and the activities that took place there required careful and continual management if homosexual-ity was to be prevented from ever taking root in the vulnerable infant psyche. In *Society and the Homosexual,* Gordon Westwood argued forcefully that "[i]t is now an established fact that the patterns set in the home will influence the whole of the later life of the child, including the sexual life," and found "a large number of homosexuals [to] come from maladjusted parents and bro-ken homes."[2] Of course, this argument was not particularly new; it had been repeatedly used by interwar social psychiatrists to express a professionalized range of bourgeois fears about the disorder and decrepitude of working-class homes.[3] But during the reconstruction, a systematic response to the malfunctional home seemed alarmingly urgent, exacerbated by both the domestic disruption caused by the war and the ubiquitous planning visions that made London's blitz-scarred slums seem more malignant in relief.

Yet this imperative also contained a paradox. To promote the reordering of domestic home life as a necessary requirement of postwar citizenship was simultaneously to endorse those bourgeois ideologies of privacy and discretion that closed the private home to the prying eyes of the state. Thus, while the legislative reforms of the nascent welfare state overwhelmingly focused on the reformation of domestic family life, they had to stop short of actually entering the home or rendering it open to the kind of explicit interference that would undermine the same respectability they were seeking to instill.

This social context brought a new significance to interior design within postwar London, as a useful means by which ordinary private life could be made amenable to indirect forms of public social management. The centrality of the Furnished Rooms to the *Britain Can Make It* exhibition in 1946 clearly testified to this. Their striking presentation as a sequence of discrete familial spaces demonstrated how, in contrast to the future precincts and playing fields of London's postwar neighborhoods, the planner's jurisdiction stopped abruptly at the front door. Instead, this space belonged to the citizen, who now had to take up the mantle of good design himself or herself. These Furnished Rooms, then, presented the visitors with a challenge; only by appreciating expert design principles and systematically applying them to their own domestic setups could a stable and modern family life be secured. These model interiors—in which the commodities on show were always subordinate to their arrangement within a healthy, functional, and seamless environment—were one of the most essential parts of its pedagogical project.

This chapter is about the cultural imperatives that became attached to interior design after the Second World War and how its founding principles provided ordinary Londoners with a set of rules that sought to manage their domestic lives and administer the activities that might take place at home. At root, this involved a new way of thinking about the moral significance of furnishing and decoration, as heavily propagated by the COID across the wealth of public exhibitions, advice booklets, and model interiors it produced during the early postwar years. As part of the wider drive to bureaucratize consumption and rein in the excesses of free-market capitalism, the COID's style of "contemporary" interior design was remarkable for the way it could be expressed as a set of direct instructions. As I explore in this chapter, this marked a definite—if unwitting—engagement with new models of social management and subjective control that were being simultaneously worked out by Britain's computer scientists. After the war, then, the domestic interior soon emerged as a space that could be programmed—initially by design experts, but also by any private citizen who closely adhered to their advice. Produced in such a way, the model contemporary interior became reconceived as a space of discipline—a technology, perhaps, that would produce only those social practices already built into the particular decorative schemata of the latest modern style.

Ultimately, these new design principles sought to render the familial home amenable to an indirect form of quotidian management, but in doing so they mounted a fundamental challenge to earlier understandings of how interior decoration and the arrangement of furniture should operate as a force for moral stability. While firmly addressing themselves to the child-raising couple, the often unfamiliar style of the COID's model interiors affronted more traditional notions of the home as an important ground for emotional training and sexual responsibility. Instead, this contemporary style employed new paradigms of communication and control, involving a form of bodily abstraction that disrupted popular, more organic, and patriarchal conceptions of how domestic space affected the lives of its inhabitants. Although employed as a means to strengthen the family by reordering its ordinary domestic practices, the contemporary interior created new freedoms for queer men, providing them with an alternative way of relating to their interiors that bypassed more traditional understandings of the home as the site of familial reproduction. Thus, the COID's drive to promote a reformed and more modern domestic sensibility unexpectedly freed homosexuals—or at least those who could afford it—from ingrained and heteronormative approaches to furniture and decoration.

Further, when these same design principles became taken up by the nascent Do-It-Yourself industry in the later 1950s, the queer male home could become further valorized as an important site of self-making, as corporeal engagements with contemporary interior decoration opened the way to a richer and more expressive form of domestic (self-)production.

Interior Design and Sexual (Im)morality

At the COID's *Britain Can Make It* exhibition, the tensions caused by its reformist approach to interior design were already clearly in evidence. While the fictional families attached to each of its showcased Furnished Rooms were conspicuous in their diversity, they included one "single man, sportsman and sports commentator at Broadcasting House" whose "bed-sitting room in a London apartment block" was open to inspection. Along with the female journalist (whose bedsit was on display next door) and the woman dietician (whose small kitchenette visitors had already seen), he was one of the very few among *Britain Can Make It*'s model citizens to live outside of a procreative family unit.

The bedsit itself firmly adhered to the contemporary style being propagated throughout the exhibition (Figure 30). Its furniture included a splay-legged sideboard made of brick-painted aluminum and with sycamore panels on the drawers, a large wing-backed chair in a rough check material, and a divan that could be used as both a settee and a bed. Its walls were covered with two complementary wallpapers—of plum stripes on yellow and of yellow stripes on plum—and lighting was provided by a trough discreetly running along the side of the divan. Following the principles of functional good taste, the commentator's ornaments were reduced to a pot plant, a couple of mugs, and several shelves of books on various sporting activities.

Figure 30. A model domicile for a single man: "A Bed-sitting Room in a London Apartment Block," *Britain Can Make It,* Victoria and Albert Museum, 1946. Courtesy of Design Council/University of Brighton Design Archives.

The visiting public's reaction to this room can be gleaned from the report on the exhibition that the COID commissioned from Mass-Observation:

> This was one of the *least* popular furnished rooms; a number of people passed it by without making any comment at all, and in general there were fewer remarks and less interest than in most of the other furnished rooms. For most people this was a room which must have less direct reference to their own lives. . . . Not a single person was overheard making a remark that had any direct reference to their own home.[4]

The remoteness of the bachelor's bedsit and the life that he lived there ensured that most visitors who did pass comment displayed an interest in individual items of "non-essential" furniture: the wireless set, the divan, the bookshelves, or the settee under the window. As M-O continued:

> Several liked the colour scheme because it was bright and gay, but more condemned it as dazzling, or unsuitable for a man. Colour was the chief point made by those who disliked the room.[5]

As one anonymous fifty-year-old artisan was overhead to remark: "the colour scheme is completely wrong for a man to wake up and see."

Less than five years after this bedsit was dismantled and amid mounting tabloid panic about "male vice" in London, the apartment of another bachelor with connections to the BBC would come scandalously to public attention. As discussed in chapter 2, Arthur Birley's private flat in Mayfair became the imagined site for lavish orgies of consumption that seduced vulnerable young guardsmen into ruinous lives of debauchery and perversion— yet all this would seem a world away from that of the COID's sportsman. Nicholas Bentley's accompanying sketch (Figure 31) showed him to be a bespectacled, pipe-smoking man whose casual attire revealed few intimations of overt fastidiousness or aggrandized display. If this bachelor was indeed homosexual, then, freed from any traces of malignant decadence, he adhered perfectly to more normative codes of privacy and discretion. His potential queerness was certainly not registered by any visitors to the Victoria and Albert Museum in 1946.

What, then, was wrong with this broadcaster's plum-and-primrose walls? The artisan's claim that it was "completely wrong" for a man to wake up to such coordinated colors invoked a long-standing set of assumptions about

Figure 31. A benign bachelor on the fringes of the reformed urban community: Nicholas Bentley, "Single man, sportsman and sports commentator at Broadcasting House." Cartoon for the Furnished Rooms section at *Britain Can Make It,* 1946. Courtesy of Design Council/University of Brighton Design Archives.

the relationship between interior decoration and the moral bodily practices of the inhabitants who dwelled there. Seven years later, more light
would be shed on this connection when Mass-Observation undertook a
much larger survey of "ordinary" people's attitudes to contemporary interior design. In 1953, the Design and Industries Association (DIA) mounted
an exhibition titled *Register Your Choice* in the subterranean ticket hall of
Charing Cross Underground Station. This display showed visitors two settings of the same living room, each of which had been furnished to the
same overall cost. Room "L" was furnished in what the DIA felt to be the
conventional suburban style: plain painted walls with a scrolling frieze at
the top; heavy, dark wood furniture; ostentatiously "decorative" light fittings
and ornaments; and a well stuffed, monumental three-piece suite (Figure
32a). In contrast, Room "R" was furnished according to what was now
becoming established as the "contemporary" style: a combination of plain
and patterned walls; lightweight unit furniture in unadorned pale woods;
plainer light fittings and fewer, bolder ornaments; and splayed-leg arm-
chairs in a selection of bright colors (Figure 32b).

When passing travelers did register their choice, the DIA was delighted
to find that room "R" was the more popular by approximately three votes
to two. However, Mass-Observation's subsequent report found a strong
division along lines of class, with only middle-class voters claiming to pre-
fer the more contemporary setting.[6] M-O's report remains valuable because
it went beyond the DIA's binary system of choice and used those same
methods of exit questionnaires and overheard comments that it had previously deployed at *Britain Can Make It.* Thus M-O reported that although
"L" and "R" were both clearly presented as family living rooms, the latter
had produced a reaction of "shock" in many viewers, typically followed by
the expression of "a very strong dislike."[7] This M-O put down to its sheer
novelty and, in particular, its use of unfamiliar bright colors, but the recorded comments reveal a much more ingrained and fundamental objection.
Many of those questioned couched their dislike of room "R" in strongly
moral language. For instance, a thirty-nine-year-old professional surveyor
complained:

> In family life you want something substantial to build on, and children could
> get the right ideas about the one on the left; there is a tendency towards
> flippancy in the right-hand room, that is not the right background for
> children.[8]

a

b

Figure 32. The outmoded versus the "contemporary" living room: (a) Room "L" and (b) Room "R." *Register Your Choice,* Charing Cross Underground Station, 1953. Courtesy of Geffrye Museum, London.

These comments were echoed by the wife of a dental surgeon, who commented on room "L":

> This is definitely a family room, and I think that's something we should emphasise—morally we want to encourage family rooms. Come to think of it, "R" is very much for a rather immoral type of person—well, it's out to impress, it's not sincere.[9]

Like the sportsman's plum-and-primrose wallpaper six years earlier, there was something "completely wrong" with this contemporary interior that had everything to do with its assault on the gendered patterns of normal family life.

Interestingly, this dislike of room "R" in 1953 was consonant with the charges concurrently being levied by the tabloids at the demonized figure of the metropolitan queer pervert. This contemporary living room was an active threat that would corrupt children and turn them into deviants. It was flippant and insubstantial, mocking the family whose terrain it had invaded. Its gaudy furniture—prefiguring, perhaps, the vulgarity of the mass-market paperback—seemed to revel in its own ephemeral frivolity. Like the fanciful young spiv, this room was out to impress, undercutting the moral sensibilities of the conventional living room by introducing its own selfish motives of individual advancement. Contemporary interior design was thus here being positioned as an urban violation of familial stability—insincere and a sham, it concealed its real antisocial purpose.

On one level, this queering of room "R" was perhaps unsurprising. Shown against the more conventional arrangement of room "L," its ostentatious modernity resonated with a long and popular tradition of reading fashionable domestic interiors as an important signifier of deviant masculinity. In the mid-nineteenth century, the Design Reform movement had attacked modish Victorian decoration on similar charges of falsity, expense, and lack of functionality—qualities that John Ruskin claimed undermined the "manliness" of respectable moral life.[10] Throughout the 1870s and 1880s, George du Maurier's cartoons in *Punch* similarly satirized the narcissistic perversity of Aesthetic decors, their fetishized objects and exquisite decoration seeming to reflect back the unhealthy corruption of the individuals who dwelled here.[11] This view reached its crescendo during the trials of Oscar Wilde, when Alfred Taylor's rooms at 13 Little College Street were castigated in the press for their opulent, Orientalist furnishings, their artificial perfumes, and the sumptuous curtains that kept daylight at bay. Against the relative austerity, open lightness, and semipublic sociability of normal bourgeois drawing rooms, such lavish decoration could not but stand in for the immoral, decadent practices that they both announced and facilitated.[12]

This popular link between "fashionable" interiors and sexual malpractice continued well into the twentieth century. During the 1920s, Vogue's promotion of what Christopher Reed has termed the "amusing" style—a celebration of transience, whimsy, and the thrillingly novel—rejected once again the austere regulations of prewar culture and presented domestic space as a theatrical backdrop against which shifting forms of multiple selfhood could be dramatized and explored. Such was the impact of this coverage, Reed suggests, that it provoked the British design establishment of the early 1930s to seek solace in Corbusian values of masculine rationality, as it sought to rid itself of the feminized frivolities of the ephemeral interior.[13]

In many ways, the contemporary style of the COID inherited the mantle of this interwar reaction. Its muted modernism defiantly rejected the flippant excesses of Victorian opulence and the androgynous whimsy associated with the Bright Young Things. Ultimately descended from Ruskinian design reform, it set out instead to promote functional, hygienic, but—above all—livable interiors that would instill in its inhabitants purposiveness and order. Yet, for a working-class audience, in particular, this modernist style had inherited those very tendencies toward showiness, flippancy, and anti-familialism that it had, paradoxically, set out to overthrow. As the response to *Register Your Choice* demonstrated, a specter of malignant queerness haunted these forceful promotions of modern interior design and the wider attempt to present such reform as a component duty of postwar social citizenship. This was not merely an aesthetic objection—that modern furniture *looked* effeminate, showy, and insincere—but a moral claim about the relationship of that furniture to its implied owner. According to this logic, a living room had a discernible material effect on those who dwelled there, a result of its status as an active force and as a residual accretion of those everyday practices that had caused it to take shape. Room "R," then, was not only an agent of corruption that would seduce children from the normative rituals of family life; it was already tainted by the immoral practices of its unknown occupants whose everyday habits had produced it in the first place.

Mass-Observation's respondents were here invoking what Jean Baudrillard—writing in France in the mid-1960s—would later identify as the traditional "moral unity" of the domestic interior. Postwar interior design,

Baudrillard claimed, had produced a fundamental shift in the way domestic space was organized in relation to the people who used it, as new paradigms replaced older understandings of the productive role of furniture and decoration. Prewar interiors had traditionally been felt to have a kind of "presence," a symbolic resonance that both produced, and was produced by, a certain lived experience of the home.[14] Such furniture, Baudrillard suggested, was characterized by its permanence and monumentality, arranged almost theistically to facilitate the rituals of orthodox daily life. It was a solid reflection of the patriarchal structures of the family that it served, while at the same time it embodied those relationships as an organic extension of the bodies that dwelled there.[15] Ultimately, argued Baudrillard, the traditional interior was understood as a form of material reification, an organic ossification of certain domestic practices that embedded daily life within a complex structure of affect and experiential depth.

This, then, was the moral unity that many viewers found in room "L" with its heavy and immobile three-piece suite, its formally laid-out dining table, and the hanging mirror that confidently reflected the whole arrangement back onto itself. By extension, it was precisely this moral unity that was lacking in room "R." Its contemporary furniture and decor were clearly not the exoskeletal projections of a patriarchal family, while—to those visitors who affirmed the existence of such residual relationships—this lack became construed as an active testament to the immoral, unstable, and thus potentially queer domestic practices through which it must have taken form.

Queer novels of the 1950s frequently exploited the continued currency of the traditional moral economy of furniture and design, as a useful device for highlighting the domestic propriety of their respectable "homosexual" protagonists. In particular, by comparing the design of contrasting interiors, authors could announce the legitimacy (or illegitimacy) of different modes of queer life via the various traces these indelibly left on the rooms in which they were lived. In Rodney Garland's *The Heart in Exile* (1953), for instance, the central plot concerns the quest of Dr. Anthony Page, a homosexual psychiatrist, to unravel the mysterious suicide of Julian, his former lover. Page's first recourse is to Julian's Kensington flat in a converted Edwardian terrace just behind Harrods. Like both the sportsman's room at *Britain Can Make It* and room "R" at *Register Your Choice,* this was another room whose occupant's body was both conspicuously absent and strangely present as a set of marks embedded within the decor. Garland described the interior at length:

The first thing I noticed was the white Edwardian rococo mantelpiece with Ann Hewitt's [Julian's fiancée's] photograph in a brown tooled-leather frame. It was obvious that the room had been tidied up. The divan bed, in which Julian had been found dead by the charwoman, was made, and the red metal waste-paper basket with the hunting scene on it was empty. But there was already a little dust on the writing desk.

The walls were shiny and light green and quite bare except for two Cecil Aldin reproductions and a crayon drawing of Julian in Army uniform. If it had not been in his room I wouldn't have recognised it as Julian, except perhaps for his eyes. The room gave a masculine impression in negative good taste, extremely English and genteel, without the very slightest suggestion of Julian's emotional life. . . .

Nor did the books give the slightest indication of Julian's real personality. The top row consisted almost entirely of law books, the *Oxford Dictionary* and a volume called *With Silent Friends*. On the second row there were practically all of the books of G. M. Trevelyan, the second volume of the Greville diary, a few books by Maurois and Arthur Bryant, *Cassell's French Dictionary*, the history of the Coldstream Guards. The fact that he had the one-volume Havelock Ellis and Walker's *Physiology of Sex* in the Penguin Edition, was completely meaningless; practically everybody above a certain level has read them.[16]

Page's gaze here is both that of a professional psychiatrist and that of an amateur detective, two discursive positions that—like traditionalist viewers at *Register Your Choice*—reconstructed an absent truth by stitching together a patchwork of visible traces. Among the various components of Julian's interior can be found none of the well-known prosthetics of queer criminality that might have constructed his deviancy in a more juridical context—no tins of talcum paper, jars of Nivea cream, or pairs of briefs here. Instead, the tension arises from the room's obvious duplicity; its assertion of an austere masculinity is marked by something missing, an unknown irregularity that has seemingly been tidied up. The layer of dust now conceals all earlier traces of bodily activity and Julian's corpse has been freshly removed from the newly made bed. Yet the novel still forces this interior to betray Julian's queer desires through its contrived presentation of an obvious clue:

Then I noticed for the first time that there was a cigarette box beside the photograph. It was almost fascinating in its vulgarity. It was of shiny metal, cheap, shoddy and with a jazzy design, the kind of thing one might win at a fun-fair. Nothing could have been more out of place in this conservative reticent room with its Cecil Aldins, its country suits, its Harrow and Guards ties. It seemed obvious that someone had given it to Julian and that he had kept it for emotional reasons. There was a shilling piece inside it.[17]

Ephemeral, cheap, and as at home at the funfair as one of Mr. Jennings's tawdry paperbacks, the jazzy design of the cigarette box breaks the hastily imposed moral economy of the room. By rupturing its austere presence, it functions as an inescapable signifier of its absent occupant's excessive desires. Within seconds, Page has found a photograph of a working-class man—taken "somewhere, I imagined, in the Charing Cross Road"—hidden behind the framed picture of Julian's fiancée.[18] The need for its concealment, of course, betrayed the impossibility of such an image being incorporated into a domestic interior without becoming an agent of domestic corruption—just as the presence of that jazzy cigarette box had become moments earlier.[19]

In a similar vein, Mary Renault's *The Charioteer* (1953) included a scene in which the protagonist, Laurie, goes with his old school friend, Ralph, to the latter's rented room in a large mid-Victorian town house. The novel is set during the war and as the pair enter in darkness, Ralph goes straight to the window to fix the blackout:

> From the doorway, Laurie caught an indefinable, strangely familiar and nostalgic smell of shabbiness and simplicity. It was the combination of these two things, so often divorced, that stirred the memory, as much by what was absent as what was there: a positive kind of cleanness which lacked the institutional sour undertaste, a smell of scrubbed wood and beeswax and books. . . . Laurie came over, feeling his way along a table. . . . A curtain, made of some harsh stuff, brushed his hand. He was scarcely aware of it, or of what he was looking at. In a flash of recognition, he had identified the smell of the room. It was like school; not like the corridors and classrooms, which smelled of gritty boards and pencil shavings and ink and boys, but like the Head Prefect's study [where Laurie and Ralph had met]. . . . His perceptions, to everything else so dull, were full of this special feeling of the room, and, growing out of it, an intense awareness of Ralph standing close and silent beside him, not in serge and braid but in gray flannel; it seemed to him that he could even feel the cloth again. It all took him suddenly and with bewildering force . . .[20]

Laurie and Ralph end up together at the end of the book and emulate the kind of restrained, respectable, and companionate relationship that aligned *The Charioteer* with the larger postwar project for homosexual reform. In this scene, accordingly, their interaction remains limited and proper, as Ralph skillfully tends to Laurie's damaged knee. Ralph's room is here clearly marked by a traditional moral unity; its books, its cleanliness, and its austerely functional curtain material all serve as almost ritualistic mediations between the two men. Through Laurie's experience of smell, in particular, the interior registers at a bodily level to reinforce and reveal the moral order produced by its habitual way of life. Several pages on, Renault favorably invokes "the absence of all loose ornament, the mantelpiece firmly packed with books . . . [and] the wood and brass polished as a seaman, not a landlady, does it."[21] Far more obvious than in the room of Julian's suicide, the organized routines of Ralph's domestic labor become the vehicle through which his proper—if still homosexual—masculinity is secured, both proven and reinforced by the shining metal and wood that it dialectically reproduces.

In the novel, Ralph's room is contrasted vividly to that of Bunny, Ralph's present boyfriend, who also lodges in the same house:

> It was hard to believe one was in the same building. The room had been, one could say, interior-decorated. There was a single picture, which was vorticist of a kind and had patently been chosen to match the colour scheme. A large number of glossy magazines were strewn about; but such books as could be seen looked as if people had left them behind and never missed them. The furniture was very low, with that overstated louginess which rarely turns out to be physically comfortable. It was all very bright and sleek, and had the look of being kept under dust-sheets except when open to the public.[22]

Above all, Bunny's room is marked by its insincerity and flashiness. Like room "R" at *Register Your Choice*, all ritualistic authenticity has been sacrificed for the sake of showy visual effect. His room is marked by its resistance to any moral labor; while Ralph's masculinity is confirmed by his polishing, Bunny appears to use dust sheets. The magazines, we are told, remind Laurie of a dentist's waiting room, marking Bunny's room as a space of loitering, inactivity, and ephemeral transience. Renault continues:

> A leisured view of the room yielded so many awful little superfluities, so many whimsies and naughty-naughties, tassels and bits of chrome, that one

recalled one's gaze shamefaced as if one had exposed the straits of the poor. Laurie remembered the room upstairs. . . . As tactfully as he could, he said, "I expect he likes to feel as unnautical as possible when he isn't at sea." "Bunny isn't a sailor."[23]

On one level, the charge is simply that Bunny's room is too effeminate; its whimsical excesses mimic the classic Victorian feminization of the decorated home, or the queerness of the amusing style of the flippant 1920s. Yet the logic of these passages runs deeper. The absence of moral unity in this room—precluded by both the lack of any relation to a laboring masculine body and its careful composition as a showy piece of spectacle—already signifies Bunny's own immoral practices. When, while driving Laurie home later that evening, Bunny stops the car and makes an unsubtle pass at him, the reader finds that it comes as no surprise.

Within both of these scenes, traditional moral understandings of interior decoration remained efficaciously at work. Yet they also revealed the limitations built into the pedagogical design programs of the postwar reconstruction. Although the COID and its cohorts sought to promote a modern, clean, and functional style of interior design that would facilitate and instill a set of ordered domestic practices, this rubbed up against more traditional patriarchal understandings of domestic space and risked being read as something of a call to queerness. Older perceptual frameworks allowed the rooms of Bunny and Julian to become cast as scenes of crimes in which traces of queer behavior had become indelibly inscribed within their surface decoration. Their living spaces, then, were always readily available to stand as a testament to their occupants' erotic deviancy, in that any unusual feature or object was patiently waiting to be read both as an accretion of perversity and as an active agent in its further perpetuation. Yet, as we have seen, at the same time the Wolfenden Report and its attendant discourses were paradoxically positioning domestic space as the sole legitimate realm of homosexual expression. Queer men were seemingly caught in a complex and ineluctable double bind, as their interiors oscillated unstably between the sanctioned and the deviant, the respectable and the perverse.

Toward the Cybernetic Living Room

One partial way out of this dilemma had, however, already been articulated by the model rooms on show at *Britain Can Make It*. For the contemporary style promoted by the COID contained a new way of thinking about the relationship of furniture and decoration to the everyday practices of the individuals who lived there, which fundamentally opposed more populist notions of the interior's moral economy. Thus, while living room "R" at *Register Your Choice* could easily be read as a site of frivolous and antisocial practices, it could also be approached—on its own terms—through an alternative set of frameworks, far more amenable to the lives of queer men. Embedded within those room settings at *Britain Can Make It* was a major challenge to older, more traditional understandings of the body's engagement with its domestic interior. Intimations of this could be found in visitors' reactions to the exhibition, where many seemed unsettled by the precise absence of material bodily traces within the rooms on show.

This lack becomes obvious if the "bed-sitting room in a London apartment block" as it was eventually displayed is compared to its designer's original sketch for the room (Figure 33). Two things are conspicuously missing from the final exhibit: the numerous sports trophies displayed on

Figure 33. T. A. L. Belton, plan for "A Bed-sitting Room in a London Apartment Block," *Britain Can Make It,* 1946. Courtesy of Design Council/University of Brighton Design Archives.

the book case (replaced by yet more books) and the sizable arrangement of cut flowers (now transformed into a rather dowdy pot plant). There may, of course, have been solid pragmatic reasons for these changes—cost, perhaps, or a difficulty in getting hold of supplies in the immediate aftermath of the war. Yet it is tempting to make a deeper reading, for both the trophies and the flowers reveal a set of material practices that threatened the basic design economy of the room's decoration. Those trophies—particularly the ones showing an athlete in exertion—would have revealed the sportsman's investment in his own physicality, as both an expressive entity and as an object of spectacular pleasure. The ostentatious extravagance of the cut flowers would also have intimated his spiv-like spending habits and an unproductive willingness to squander money for the sake of ephemeral show. Certainly, no such accusation could be levied at the final pot plant, whose austerity and permanence was obvious to all.

In *Furnishing to Fit Your Family*, the booklet that accompanied the Furnished Rooms, the COID's anonymous author described the bachelor's bedsit thus:

> With such a definite colour scheme and so much bold pattern already in the room, more decoration in the form of pictures would have been superfluous. But we may be sure that some sports trophies will soon appear on the top of the book shelves. They will not only be decorative in themselves, but add the final personal touch in a room already pleasantly full of character.[24]

The curious deferment of this "personal touch" to a time perpetually in the future suggests that it simply could not be included within the eternal present of the bedsit's decorative schema. These traces of its occupant's material body were beyond the terms of the decor itself. On the one hand, it is tempting to read these absences as a semiotic caution, for both the classicism of the trophies and the exquisite cut flowers could easily have appeared as signifiers of queerness. At the time of the exhibition, mainstream cinema frequently exploited such prosthetic objects to connote the unspoken homosexuality of selected queer characters.[25] But such a reading would obscure a more pertinent possibility—that the flowers and trophies could not be admitted less for their queer connotations than because they spoke of a relationship between the occupant's body and the design of their interior that the Furnished Rooms could not, at their most basic level, allow.

Advice booklets from the postwar period displayed a similar urge to cleanse interior spaces of those bodily traces that would configure them as sites of ritual or meaning. Thus, readers of *New Home* were warned against indulging "the sentimental affection people feel for things simply because they are familiar, or because, rightly or wrongly, they are regarded as being beautiful and worth all the trouble they cause."[26] The reformed interiors of the postwar city were to be free from such affective associations between occupant and setting, particularly the "familiarity" of inherited furniture. Although it was recognized that most people would have to make do with pieces handed down by their parents, the imperative was clearly to replace such items as soon as that became feasible or to erase their accumulated history through modifications or painting. As another COID booklet explained, "the ideal might be to make a bonfire of it":

Mental spring-cleaning is the first move towards successful furnishing. We must clear our minds of a clutter of ideas about interior decoration that are not our own; they have come to us from the past and, put into practice today, they would suit neither the habits nor the fashion of our own time.[27]

The rationale for this erasure of both history and sentiment was the unsuitability of these things for organizing the habitual activities of postwar daily life. Through mobilizing this principle, such advice manuals and exhibitions were formulating a new mode of living in domestic space. As *New Home* stressed:

The perfect home should certainly be pleasant to look at; but, much more important, it should be, in general plan and in detail, convenient and comfortable for all the people who live in it and properly equipped for their activities—housework, hobbies, social life and rest.[28]

By marginalizing all traces of history or inherited ritual, contemporary interior design reconfigured the prescribed function of domestic decoration. No longer the accreted residue of certain moral daily practices, the newly eviscerated postwar living room was positioned instead as an abstract space in which specific practices could be effectively predetermined. As part of the wider recourse to spatial planning that characterized reconstruction London, designed interiors became an imagined apparatus that would produce a controllable set of defined activities. As Margaret Llewellyn advised, "design is something which affects each one of us and which *decides* the way we live."[29] In effect, interior space was becoming bureaucratized, no longer the organic exoskeleton of a moral material body, but a programmed domain that could direct its inhabitants to routinely perform a set of pre-decided tasks.

This point was underscored in *Furnishing to Fit the Family:*

> By good arrangement alone, a room can be divided into eating or sitting halves, work or leisure sections. Simple alterations, such as building partitions, sliding doors and hatches will often make the job easier. Before you start on the actual business of furnishing it is important to think hard about the way your family wants to live—what your normal needs are from day to day and the means you have at your disposal for satisfying them. Then consider what sort of background is best suited to those needs.[30]

This spatialization of prescribed activities clearly governed the sportsman's bedsit at *Britain Can Make It.* Divided neatly into a "work" section at the front and a "leisure" section nearer the window—placed there, apparently, due to long hours spent in the windowless studios of Broadcasting House—fitted cupboards were used to screen the divan and thus provide a private area for sleeping. The large wing-backed armchair was deliberately turned away from the table to enable the bachelor to escape his work and relax, while the placing of the shelves allowed him to make reference to his sports books without needing to move too far from his table.[31] This air of flexibility and the economical and functional use of space—the table was designed for both work and meals, the divan was both a seat and a bed, the bedsit itself was both a bedroom and a sitting room—only worked to disguise the more totalizing prescriptions already built into it, which would manage his activities and stabilize his routine.[32]

As defiantly planned spaces, therefore, such contemporary settings introduced a layer of abstraction between the material body and the interior itself. These domestic settings were produced not through the organic accretion of immanent practices, but through the intellectual workings of the mind, which sought to control—through prior design—the operations that the body could subsequently perform there. As Alan Jarvis told potential homemakers: "The importance of wise planning before taking action and spending money, cannot be stressed too much. Planning can be the foundation of future comfort and happiness, or the reverse."[33] Citizens were advised to create a plan of their room on paper (at a scale of three feet to one inch) or, better still, to make a three-dimensional model out of an old cardboard box. Matchboxes could be used to represent double beds or wardrobes and matchsticks could stand in as standard lamps. Colored paper could be affixed to try out color schemes for curtains and walls, and toy soldiers borrowed to test how much room there was for people to move about.[34] *Good Housekeeping* even advised homemakers to draw "traffic lanes" on their floor plans "to make sure there is no bottle-neck or unnecessary circling."[35]

This attempt to program all future domestic practices penetrated further than just the physical arrangement of space and furniture. It also encompassed the decoration of the walls and the style of the accompanying soft furnishings. Baudrillard would later note how, having been removed from its symbolic place within a unified moral whole, each piece of contemporary furniture was now being presented in terms of a discrete functional relationship with its individual user; "[a] bed is a bed, a chair is a chair, and there is no relationship between them so long as each serves only the function it is supposed to serve."[36] As such, the postwar interior existed only as a disconnected aggregate of separate components, brought into a syntagmatic relationship via that succession of activities that it sought to arrange into a seamless and stable routine. As Baudrillard argued:

> Traditional good taste, which decided what was beautiful on the basis of secret affinities, no longer has any part here. . . . [T]oday objects do not respond to one another, they communicate—they have no individual presence but merely, at best, an overall coherence attained by virtue of their simplification as components of a code and the way their relationships are calculated.[37]

For Baudrillard, the contemporary interiors of 1960s France had become a language system, understood by the body not on a level of affect or material experience, but as a set of semiotic instructions.

This new paradigm was already at work within the model interiors of postwar Britain. Home dwellers were advised to approach their rooms as a coordinated ensemble of elements—not to privilege any single item of furniture or decoration, but to pay attention to the relationships between them. This shift of emphasis gave a new political importance to the idea of the color scheme. As Veronica Nisbet advised in her "Shopping Guide to Light and Colour":

All of us know houses or rooms where everything seems "just right", and others where the effect is quite wrong. Very often, if you think about the difference, it can be traced to the right and wrong use of colours and patterns. Wrong, where a room with little light has dark walls and woodwork, with no relieving touch of colour—wrong, where too many colours and patterns give a feeling of overcrowding and muddle. And the contrast, where the successful use of colour and pattern gives balance and charm.[38]

Here, then, was the new moral economy of the postwar interior—no longer related to the ritualistic experience of material practice, but to the internal coherence of its decorative schema. It was the combination of colors and patterns that now made a room "right" or "wrong," envisioned as components within a totalized environment:

A room done in different shades of the same colour is not a "colour scheme". All successful colour schemes are based on the use of contrast. A yellow cushion used to highlight a mid-blue sofa covering, or red piping on a dark grey chair, are examples of effective colour contrasts. The important thing to remember is that equal quantities of contrasting colours must not be used; a bright yellow settee, beside a wing chair in bright blue, all on a red carpet, is too startling. A better effect is obtained if both pieces of furniture are covered in blue, with yellow piping to set it off. The red of the carpet is then a pleasant and effective contrast.[39]

On these terms, the correctness of an interior was now a matter of grammar. It depended on whether—like a linguistic sentence—its various component elements had been syntagmatically arranged in an appropriate and coherent fashion. This, of course, involved a sensorial shift in how a room was evaluated, as the more haptic entreaties of traditional interiors became obsolescent in the face of an appraisal rooted primarily in vision. This was evident at *Register Your Choice;* Mass-Observation found that those who preferred modern setting "R" to traditional room "L" were typically using aesthetic criteria, while those who preferred "L" to "R" cited comfort as their main concern. Yet, the latter group were already outmoded, for such corporeal engagements were being perceptibly cleansed from the instructional logics within this new type of design.

This shift toward a morality of aesthetics meant that "good" interior design could now be transcribed as a set of technical instructions, turning the citizen-decorator into what Baudrillard would later call "an active engineer of atmosphere."[40] Nisbet thus gave her readers a firm set of rules to follow:

Not too many colours in one room;
Not too many bright colours in one room;
Not too much of a single colour in a room;
Not too much pattern in one room;
Not too may different kinds of pattern in one room.[41]

Such instructions were often indebted to the latest scientific expertise. Margaret Llewellyn borrowed heavily from color psychology, claiming, for instance, that "[i]t has been found that children can work and concentrate better in a gaily painted schoolroom than in one with stone coloured or 'useful green' tiled walls."[42] In another of her booklets for the COID, she taught readers that primary and secondary colors were importantly distinct and how different hues, tones, and intensities could be used to create relationships of warmth and coolness or effects of advancing and receding. She also included a useful color wheel so that readers could experiment with these relationships for themselves.[43] Within this wheel, any historic or symbolic associations traditionally attached to individual colors had been finally removed. A color's significance now lay purely in its informational relationship to those around it and the overall atmosphere such combined messages produced.[44] Interior design, then, had become not just a matter of arranging one's furniture in an efficient, functional, and disciplinary pattern, but of creating a totalized decorative schema that strictly adhered to a set of prescribed rules.

It is enlightening to consider this kind of decorative command system in relation to that being deployed contemporaneously within the developing discipline of computer science. In 1937, the queer mathematician Alan Turing had articulated the basic conceptual model for the digital computer and, by the autumn of 1949, scientists at Manchester University had built a fully operational stored-program machine known as the "Mark 1."[45] In February 1951, Ferranti launched a commercial version of this machine and at that summer's *Exhibition of Science* (part of the Festival of Britain, discussed in chapter 1), curious visitors could challenge its humbler sibling to a round of the logic game "Nim."[46] The conceptual innovation that underpinned these digital computers was Turing's foundational remodeling of human computations as a series of interactions between three structural components: the "executive unit" (which performed the tasks); the "control" section (which provided the rules and coordinated the activities of the executive unit); and the memory "store" (in which the other two parts recorded information for future operations).[47] By formulating this structure, Turing was able to develop his idea of the "universal machine"—a mechanical device able to perform all human operations by reducing it to a set of digital computations.

Jon Agar has drawn attention to the close correlation between this basic operational model and the wider structures already adopted by modern business corporations and government departments. Both of these, he points out, had been premised on a similar divide between a decision-making executive and a lower rank of clerks, workers, or civil servants habitually restricted to implementing instructions from above.[48] That the computer should have developed alongside the welfare state—with its bureaucratic attention to the minutiae of everyday life—is thus entirely consistent. Yet Turing's model also reveals how such innovations involved a fundamental rethinking of human subjectivity, for since the universal machine was premised on a certain understanding of human computations, it also repositioned humans as mere computers made of flesh.

In 1950 Turing wrote: "The human computer is supposed to be following fixed rules; he has no authority to deviate from them in any detail."[49] As his spatial metaphor suggests—echoing Abercrombie's model citizens endlessly moving along their predictable orbital paths—the computer's reconceptualization of human activity resonated with the visions of reconstruction planners, suggesting a tacit move toward the cyberneticization of everyday life that linked Abercrombie's London to the COID's interiors and their common investment in spatial mechanisms of order and stability. Like the planned city itself, the computational subject was conceptualized outside of historical time in a Laplacian state from which the unforeseen or unpredictable event had been entirely banished.[50] As Turing made clear, the executive unit would endlessly repeat its predictable task, thus keeping the system stable through the enactment of perpetual routine. Thus, the universal machine, emerging within that same historical moment of social reconstruction, provided a perfect metaphor for a complicit, contented, and manageable citizen.

The contemporary interiors of the COID, designed by a process of mental planning and similarly abstracted from the experiential body, made similar gestures toward this computational remodeling of human activity.

Not only did these new interiors mimic computer programs in seeking to determine which ordered activities their inhabitant would repeat, but their very construction was meant to be managed through a cybernetic process of operational instruction. In *New Home,* for instance, readers were told to follow a seven-stage process when deciding whether or not to buy a particular piece of furniture for their house:

1. Can I do without it?
   (Keep asking this question until the period of shortage is over.)
2. Is it worth the money?
3. Will it do the job it is meant for?
4. Is it pleasing to look at and to handle?
5. Is it the right size—neither too large nor too small?
6. Is the material of which it is made simply and rightly used?
   (For instance, if made of heavy metal, is it plain and substantial? If glass, is it light and clear?)
7. Is it honestly made to withstand wear and tear?[51]

This was, of course, already the language of computer programming: a sequential set of operations to which the executive unit could respond with one of two possible binary answers—yes or no, 1 or 0. Only if this chain of command produced seven successive yeses would the purchase take place. The model occupants of the postwar interior, through both their daily domestic activities and the initial replanning of their own home, were being firmly interpellated into a clear computational logic. The corporeal body, with all its messy excesses and symbolic rituals, was put into parentheses and the creation of interior space became recast as purely a matter of mental decisions and intellectual choices. Everything hinged on the abstract tasks of designing, choosing, and ultimately buying; and while the hands could provide data about whether a particular object was pleasing to handle, this was always subordinated to a set of mental operations that could be performed either correctly or incorrectly. What mattered now was that nothing should disrupt the coherent semiotics of the postwar interior. No other commands should be given to the citizen apart from those already inscribed within this new type of programmable space.

Ironically, postwar interior design manuals often repeated their late-nineteenth-century predecessors by presenting interior decoration as an expression of one's own individuality. Nisbet thus finished:

Finally, after all these "do's" and "don'ts", one last word of advice. Furnishing should be fun. So do not be afraid of experimenting with colours, patterns and lighting, and do trust and develop your own taste.[52]

A common device within such booklets was to include a sparse line drawing of a room that the reader could color according to his or her own preferences.[53] *New Home* proclaimed:

> The exact colours you use and the means you choose to carry out your scheme—paint, paper or distemper—depend on you, and there are no rules to follow. It is, in fact, very important that in these matters you should stand by your own personal choice, since it is you—*not* your friends and advisers, and *not* the decorator's men—who must live with the results.[54]

Yet this stress on personality served mainly as an alibi for the removal of expression in which it colluded. Personality was reduced to a matter of choosing from the selection of well-designed chairs on offer or combining any of the complementary colors that the programmed rules allowed. On one level, this was as unchallenging and superficial as the inclusion of a random number generator within the basic workings of a computer program.

This basic tension was already clearly evident in a press release issued about the Furnished Rooms at *Britain Can Make It:*

> The designer was instructed to make his choice, so far as practicable, from articles chosen by the Selection Committee dealing with each commodity group—wallpaper, carpets, etc. . . . Each room must not only fit the circumstances of the family for which it is designed, but—as is the case with the successful furnishing of rooms in any ordinary home—must be governed by the general idea in the designer's mind and must show his individual "handwriting". The designers were, therefore, allowed freedom to find out articles or patterns which appealed to them as appropriate and to put them forward, alongside those submitted on manufacturers' own initiative, for the consideration of the Commodity Selection Committees. By this means the designers' own initiative was reconciled with the over-riding authority of the Commodity Selection Committees.[55]

The limitations within this setup were obvious, however. Mass-Observation found the decor of the rooms to be generally repetitive, particularly through their "monotonous use of colours."[56] The bureaucratic hierarchy between Selection Committee and designer had prevented the latter from deviating too far from the cybernetic instructions by which the design was deemed appropriate. The "handwriting" of the designer, an interesting metaphor of the expressive body, appeared troublingly absent to many visitors from the more sterile domains that resulted.

Imitation Games

Yet this movement away from the organic material body and toward a more abstract space of command and control paradoxically opened up new potential freedoms for homosexual men. Remarkably, an intimation of this came through in a 1950 essay by Turing called "Computing Machinery and Intelligence," which betrayed an anxious—if oblique and unintentional—engagement with that same tortuous relationship between the expressive queer body and its decorative traces that would soon be exploited by *The Heart in Exile* and *The Charioteer*. Published in the philosophy and psychology journal *Mind*, "Computing Machinery and Intelligence" was Turing's attempt to address the conundrum of whether machines might be capable of intelligent thought. He did this by reformulating the question as an empirically verifiable experiment; yet the test he offered contained a convoluted negotiation around the computational subject, the gendered body, and the relationship of both to interior space. It is worth quoting Turing's proposal in full:

> The new form of the problem can be described in terms of a game which we call the "imitation game". It is played with three people, a man (A), a woman (B), and an interrogator (C) who may be of either sex. The interrogator stays in a room apart from the other two. The object of the game for the interrogator is to determine which of the other two is the man and which is the woman. He knows them by labels X and Y, and at the end of the game he says either "X is A and Y is B" or "X is B and Y is A". The interrogator is allowed to put questions to A and B thus:
>
> C: Will X please tell me the length of his or her hair?
>
> Now suppose X is actually A, then A must answer. It is A's object in the game to try and cause C to make the wrong identification. His answer might therefore be:
>
> "My hair is shingled, and the longest strands are about nine inches long."

In order that tones of voice may not help the interrogator the answers should be written, or better still, typewritten. The ideal arrangement is to have a teleprinter communicating between the two rooms. Alternatively the question and answers can be repeated by an intermediary. The object of the game for the third player (B) is to help the interrogator. The best strategy for her is probably to give truthful answers. She can add such things as "I am the woman, don't listen to him!" to her answers, but it will avail nothing as the man can make similar remarks.

We now ask the question, "What will happen when a machine takes the part of A in this game?" Will the interrogator decide wrongly as often when the game is played between a man and a woman? These questions replace our original, "Can machines think?"[57]

Turing structured the imitation game so as to suspend the humanist prejudice that whereas human beings are sentient, electronic machines are obviously not; for only on those terms could the possibility of an intelligent machine be properly evaluated. Instead, the game appealed to the epistemological limits of inference—we only know that people are intelligent because they act and speak as if they are, and if this is how we "know" human intelligence, then it must also be how we would "know" intelligent machines if such things were to exist. Yet Turing framed this possibility through a bizarre scene of gender cross-identification. Amid a lingering, if somewhat archaic, understanding of homosexuality as a form of gender inversion, the figure of an interrogator authoritatively pronouncing the truth of whether the man in question was "really" male or female recalled a number of familiar juridical and medical scenarios.[58] It also, perhaps, echoed the position of certain queer men trying to assess the proclivities of a potential pickup. Turing's ploy was to neatly invert this scenario. The pronouncement of the man as "really" a woman served here to prove the man's intelligence, thus revealing true sentience to exist on a level of mental activity separate and distinct from its gendered material body. Tyler Curtain has pointed out the massive disparity here; unlike the man in the game, Turing's woman is condemned to speak only the truth of her body and is intelligent only to the extent that she is identified as corporeally female after all.[59] But Turing was clearly backing his man—like the machine he brought in to replace him—and thus it was through this unstable and strangely queer figure that the radical possibility of a disembodied, purely operational intelligence was ultimately sanctioned.

As Turing wrote: "The new problem has the advantage of drawing a fairly sharp line between the physical and the intellectual capacities of a man."[60] By suggesting that machines may think as well as men do, the corporeality of both was put into parenthesis and no longer presented as a relevant factor. If, as Turing argued, "[w]e do not wish to penalise the machine for its inability to shine in beauty competitions," then it was nonsensical for the human subject to be similarly approached through the terms of its gendered embodiment.[61] Within the setup of the imitation game, this was enforced via the physical separation of the interrogator from both the man and the woman, who are kept together in a separate room. This room acts as a sanctuary; the bodily presence of its inhabitants is erased and their practices leave no mark. Voice and even handwriting are reduced to the impersonal outputs of a mechanical teleprinter. Like the Furnished Rooms at *Britain Can Make It*, this was not an interior on which a signature could be inscribed. Turing's interrogation room becomes a sterile space, as cleansed of bodily traces as Julian's room in *The Heart in Exile*.

Thus Alan Turing's new understanding of the sentient human subject, sketched through a depiction of a new type of interior, was deeply in tune with the cybernetic logics already expressed within the design pedagogy of the COID. Through a clever scene of gender misidentification, he unwittingly showed how new interiors in the contemporary style could erase at a blow the complex criminality so dominantly inscribed into the fabric of queer men's living rooms. At *Britain Can Make It*, contrary to the outmoded perspectives of overheard visitors, the sports commentator's bedsit could not—on its own terms—be read as that of a queer, for such queerness lay at an expressive level that couldn't be acknowledged within the semiotic system through which it was created. Those same logics of programmed operation and cybernetic communication that aimed toward an interior space of discipline and control offered a measure of freedom—in theory at least—from those traditional moral economies of interior decoration that they hoped to supersede.

Something similar to this was suggested more forthrightly within the feature film *Victim*, released in 1961. A successful thriller firmly rooted in the postwar tradition of the British "social problem" film, its melodramatic plot (revolving around a case of queer blackmail) was carefully tethered to a considered presentation of respectable homosexuality and an eventual advocacy of legislative reform.[62] (In its director and star, it also reunited Basil Dearden and Dirk Bogarde, who had previously worked together on

The Blue Lamp [1950], as discussed in this book's Introduction.) *Victim,* like many homosexual novels of the period, takes the viewer on a carefully articulated tour through the sites of queer London, but much of its drama and reformist appeal was constructed through its juxtaposition of contrasting domestic interiors and the various possibilities of criminality or virtue that these could be made to imply. Importantly, as the film progresses, earlier, more traditional understandings of the significance of decor become complicated and the film's overall message of homosexual reform is emphatically bound to an endorsement of the COID's cybernetic design logics.

Early on in the film, Jack "Boy" Barrett (Peter McEnery), the working-class "homosexual" whose suicide will provide its main dramatic impetus, asks his queer friend Eddy to enter his bedroom and remove a mysterious and incriminating parcel from the bottom of his wardrobe. Eddy and Boy lodge with their landlady in a dilapidated Georgian terrace and as the camera scans Boy's room it reveals an austere and somewhat ramshackle interior unmarked by any signs of ostentatious queer flippancy. Boy, though, has been fraudulently stealing money from his employer, and this single parcel—containing a scrapbook of clippings about the barrister Melville Farr (Bogarde)—stands as evidence of that homosexual desire for which he is being blackmailed. Like the jazzy cigarette box found on Julian's shelf, this is the sole prosthetic object through which his sexual desires can be discerned. Soon, the plainclothes detective Bridie will complain that he has been unable to find anything of note while searching Boy's room: "Nothing worth a penny, Sir; clean, tidy, very bare." Here, then, is an interior whose kempt austerity conforms to the traditional moral economy of working-class masculinity, and Boy's homosexuality cannot be detected in the absence of the scrapbook that is its sole material trace. Following Bridie, the viewer is invited to sympathize with Boy's misguided crime precisely because his room testifies to no immoral sexual practices.

Later in the film, the viewer enters the room of the improbably named Sandy Youth (Derren Nesbitt), one of the two conspirators whose extortion racket precipitated Boy's earlier suicide. Sandy is shown sitting in a plain but contemporary lounge chair, listening to classical music on his gramophone, against a modish wallpaper that is only slightly compromised by the interwar fireplace that it surrounds. Yet, as he gets up to leave the room, the camera pans across to a freestanding punchball, which he whacks aggressively before exiting. Rather than follow him out, the camera continues its pan and comes to rest on a framed photograph of Michelangelo's *David,* which fills the frame as the shot dissolves (Figure 34). Sandy's character is never really developed, but already the objects in his room have constructed for the viewer the terms of his criminality. Although not explicitly homosexual, the punchball and the *David* reveal a psychopathological investment in his own physique that, within the context of the film's release, suggested insecurity, narcissism, and a sexual maladjustment that might explain his vindictiveness against the very homosexuality he is trying to escape. Sandy's forceful punch, a reference to both his antisocial violence and the bodybuilding through which he seeks to secure his troubled masculinity, is an expressive bodily practice that marks this interior—and Sandy's presence within it—as criminal, excessive, and potentially queer.

Yet if the depiction of Boy's and Sandy's rooms follows the more traditional postwar constructions of the expressive queer interior, then the film elsewhere challenges these logics in surprising and emphatic ways. The most striking room in the entire film belongs to Paul Mandrake (Peter Copley), an industrial photographer and old acquaintance of Farr's, who lives in a

Figure 34. *David* as a decorative trace of repressed homosexuality in *Victim* (Basil Dearden, 1961).

converted mews flat that also serves as his studio. Farr pays him a visit and, once inside, is told not only of Mandrake's homosexuality but that of another of his associates, Lord Fullbrook (Anthony Nicholls), a philanthropic and well-respected industrialist. Set against Boy's room and Farr's own home, Mandrake's flat is startlingly modern. As an open-plan conversion dramatically decorated in the contemporary style, its furnishings and decoration show an affinity with the type of ordered rooms heavily propagated by the COID. The walls are covered with a combination of contrasting textures (wood veneer, stone effect, and a plain wall painted in a presumably vibrant shade), the lounge chairs are lightweight with coordinated cushions, and the select pieces of well-placed glassware are both bold and unfussy. All this is offset by some tasteful floor rugs, an unostentatious cheese plant, and a couple of pieces of modern abstract art (Figure 35). Notably, the walls also feature a few examples of Mandrake's own work, including a small collage of commercial photographs whose artistry is evident—a selection of breads, two female models with a penny farthing, and an advertisement photograph of a woman using an electric food mixer.

Figure 35. Homosexual reformism in the "contemporary" interior in *Victim*.

Mandrake, Fullbrook, and the actor Calloway (Dennis Price)—also in the room when Farr arrives—are three close friends who clearly recall the well-to-do trio of Peter Wildeblood, Lord Montagu, and Michael Pitt-Rivers, whose trial had caused such a sensation in 1954. They also become the film's most prominent voices within its chorus of advocates for legal reform. Utterly discreet, Farr has had no intimation of Fullbrook's or Mandrake's sexual proclivities and this flat is clearly one of the few private spaces in which their restrained desires are (legitimately) expressed. Calloway announces that although he is "a born odd-man-out," he has "never corrupted the normal," a position echoed by Fullbrook in his appeal to Farr—and, therefore, the audience—that "of course we agree that youth should be protected. But that does not mean that consenting males should be pilloried by an antiquated law."

Within the film, therefore, Mandrake and his associates are promoted as the kind of respectable well-adjusted homosexuals whose innate discretion and self-awareness would make them viable members of a modern post-war social community. Although they plead with Farr to let them pay off the blackmailers, this is presented as a rational response to an impossible situation, forced on them by an unjust society badly in need of reformation. As part of this appeal, Mandrake's interior is presented not as a show-room of insincere flippancies or as the residue of any immoral practices, but rather through the informed principles of design expertise that endorse the polemics they are given to speak. Here, then, modish decoration comes to signify an embrace of scientific modernity and escapes any charges of corruption and excess. When, toward the end of the film, we return to Farr's home—the site of an unsatisfactory reconciliation with his long-suffering wife Laura—their antique furniture, fussy figurines, and the housekeeper on whom they archaically rely seem as outdated as the oppressive legal system that has both paid for such spoils and misguided the couple into a compromised marriage. Against this interior and its Victorian inheritances, Mandrake's contemporary mews flat promises a glimpse of a better, healthier, and more conciliatory future.

Doing It Themselves

In the second half of the 1950s, the tentative freedoms offered to queer men by the principles of contemporary interior design seem to have become richer and more expressive. Certainly, this was suggested by the emergence of Do-It-Yourself (DIY) as a specific leisure activity during this period. *The*

Practical Householder, a monthly magazine that gave advice on furniture
making and general home maintenance, went on sale from October 1955,
to be followed just over a year later by its rival publication, *Do It Yourself.*
By 1957, the former was claiming a monthly readership of 2,300,000 and
confidently speaking of the "Do-It-Yourself Movement" as a self-conscious
collective subculture.[63] Of course, people doing their own construction work
and decoration was by no means new. Make-do and mend had been promoted as a key moral duty of wartime citizenship, and the ensuing shortage
of both materials and labor, plus the continued hardships of working-class
life, ensured its continuation well into the postwar period. Yet, while the
COID's pamphlets and booklets often demonstrated how old and inherited
furniture could be easily renovated into more modern and functional pieces,
this was framed as making a virtue out of a necessity and the preference was
invariably to buy new—but always well-designed—contemporary replace-
ments.[64] The innovation of DIY lay in its self-assertion as a legitimate, pleasurable, and productive leisure activity in its own right.

On the whole, DIY magazines adhered to the modish vision of interior
design being propagated by the COID and thus appeared as largely an extension of its project. Articles taught how to make splay-legged coffee
tables and other pieces in the contemporary style and praised the durability
of new plastic tabletops. The twin values of function and flexibility remained basic throughout. In particular, such magazines were enthusiastic
about the need for color schemes and made similar deferrals to the scientific principles of color psychology.[65] By the end of the decade, paint manufacturers were even producing their own version of Margaret Llewellyn's
color chart, such as ICI's "Dulux Colour Comparator" and Brolac's "Color-
vogue Selector."

Yet this apparent confluence masked the deeper, more structural opposition between DIY and the COID. The articles in *The Practical Householder*
and *Do It Yourself* were generally restricted to giving basic technical advice
on how to accomplish specific tasks and projects. As commercial publications, they relied heavily on advertising revenue and left it to manufacturers
to articulate—in both images and copy—the pleasures, values, and profits
of such pursuits. The magazines even celebrated these adverts as a source of
important technical information. As one editorial announced:

> We consider the advertisements in this journal are of great interest to our
> readers and we have been unable to trace any advertisement which was "not

convincing", rather unhappy words to have used. Many of our readers in their letters to us express appreciation of our advertisement pages and of their interesting qualities. From our own knowledge of the industry, we know that advertisers do their utmost to make their advertisements interesting and factual and free from misleading copy.[66]

The imparting of technical expertise was thus elided with the solicitation of consumer desire in a move that reversed the official project to create a more controlled and controllable interior design. As a touring COID exhibition had already made clear, the moral duty of the citizen-consumer was to perpetuate a chain of command in which the informed purchaser became a communicating vessel for the state administration of industry:

> You must tell the sales assistant *why*, when you take it or leave it. Then, if she is interested in her job, she'll tell the buyer. When the traveller from the factory comes, she will tell him. And he can tell the production manager who, working with his designer, will be in a better position to give you what you really want. You can start the ball rolling when you next go shopping. But you will never get what you like unless you know what you like and say so.[67]

A customer correctly instructed in the technical art of shopping would keep capitalism within the reins of public bureaucracy, thus ensuring the strategic coherence of the furnished rooms that resulted. Yet the adverts in *Do It Yourself* upset this communicative flow and relinquished to commercial manufacturers the very authority that the COID wished to claim for itself. Rooted less in the abstract intelligence of the authoritative planner than in the promiscuous temptations of the coveted commodity, they rendered the key loci of domestic citizenship amenable to other, more unstable possibilities.

Advertisements and editorials tirelessly promoted DIY as a fun and fulfilling weekend activity—claims that were only true in part. On the one hand, many must have experienced its projects as a continuation of work, particularly those for whom it was more of a necessity than a hobby. Yet, as Arthur Marwick has noted in relation to make-do and mend, DIY could also be enjoyed as a partial return to preindustrial artisanship, particularly given its promotion as a self-conscious collective movement that in some way invoked the self-fulfillment and creativity more associated with the mid-nineteenth-century Arts and Crafts guilds.[68] Thus, while the COID's official advice focused on the intellectual moment of choosing a product, the DIY magazines disrupted this and used rawer commodities—tins of paint, laminate tabletops, and rolls of wallpaper—in an appeal to expressive labor. Despite the similarity in its end result, the abstractions of the designed interior were threatened by the return of its own repressed—the experiential material body of its active occupant. The programmed operations by which its model citizens had become easily analogous to borrowed toy soldiers were increasingly compromised by a new valorization of expended energy and self-creation.

Importantly, the return of this dynamic created new possibilities for the gendering of domesticity that collided with more traditional notions of domestic propriety. Postwar advice booklets on how to furnish a room had, with varying degrees of explicitness, positioned their readers as a newly wed couple, eager to create a home of their own and with an obvious eye to one day having children.[69] The imagery associated with DIY overwhelmingly followed suit; time and again, advertisements showed modern young couples joyfully confiding about the ease and fun with which they just laid a floor covering or repapered a bedroom. A useful device for showing just how simple a manufacturer's products were to use—apparently, even a woman could do it—consumer desires were firmly aligned with companionate domestic ideologies. As an advertisement for Brolac paints suggested, it was DIY that made a house a home through a form of active teamwork that embodied and expressed what good marriage was all about (Figure 36).[70] Through this dialectical process, the joint labor of the couple created a material foundation for their future relationship, their newly painted walls both confirming and reproducing their security as a loving couple.

Accordingly, the imagery around DIY followed the hegemonic model of companionate marriage that situated the husband and wife as two equitable partners whose complementary competencies made them such an effective team.[71] Following this neat division of labor, men were shown doing the more physical tasks such as sawing wood and plumbing, while their wives preferred to paint and work with soft furnishings.[72] Yet, at the same time, this gendered division fused with the inherent corporeality of DIY to produce a troublingly queer excess. Self-consciously promoted as a collective "movement," DIY gestured toward two single-sexed communities. If men and women were impelled toward different types of projects, then each enjoyed a homosocial bond in tension with their more orthodox relationship

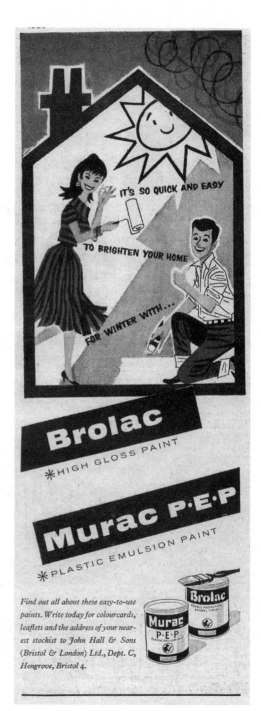

Figure 36. The companionate young couple do it themselves: advertisement for Brolac and Murac P•E•P paint, 1957.

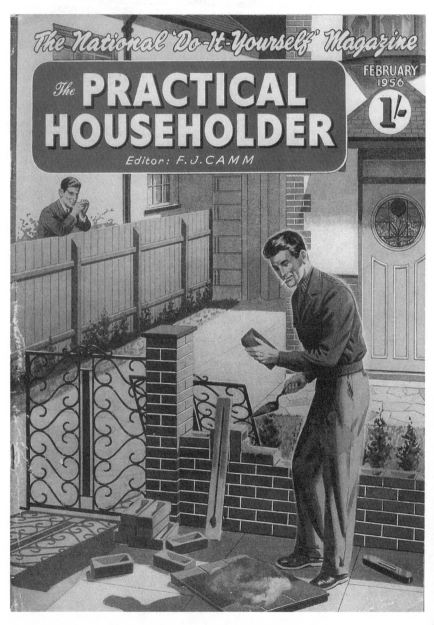

Figure 37. The homosocial delights of the laboring male body: front cover of *The Practical Householder* 2, no. 3 (February 1956).

to their spouse. Thus, in February 1956, the front cover of *The Practical Householder* (Figure 37) showed a man busy building the garden wall of his suburban home, clearly unaware that he is being watched by his male neighbor over the fence. The neighbor's gaze is, of course, legitimated by the man's wall building and the techniques and satisfactions inherent to DIY, but here the man's body becomes an object of homosocial visual pleasure that is both aroused and normalized by his spectacular exertions.

This ambiguity broke through in other places too. One striking example was in the banner heading for *The Practical Householder*'s column "Passing It On" (Figure 38), which encouraged contributors to write in and share their DIY tips with the rest of the readership. On both sides of the title, a

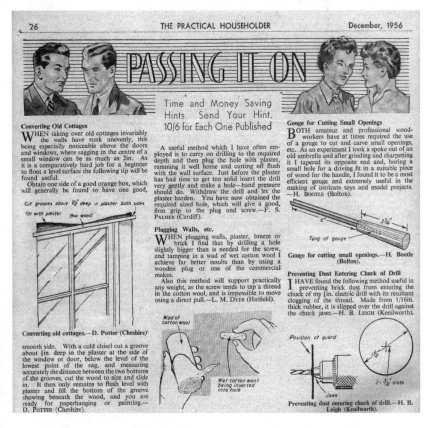

Figure 38. A secret knowledge for those in the club: "Passing It On" banner, *The Practical Householder* (December 1956).

pair of men and a pair of women were shown in close conversation wearing the nondescript uniforms of urban office life, but clearly exchanging the kind of conspiratorial secret knowledge that had previously characterized the antisocial bonds of London's queer perverts. Their direct glances and physical proximity were far more intimate than those images of energetic married couples prancing about with paintbrushes and floor tiles that filled the rest of the magazine. Here, then, was a celebration of covert semiotics and homosociality that inserted a little bit of metropolitan deviance into the more suburban terrain of Do-It-Yourself.

This was also the case with a particular advertisement for Asbestolux board that appeared in DIY magazines in late 1958 (Figure 39).[73] Under the caption "It started on the 8.14 . . . ," Bill—a self-confessed no-hoper at DIY—chats to an anonymous acquaintance on the morning train to work. The latter invites him into his house to watch him build a new Asbestolux surround for his fireplace, a process that sparks Bill's interest and turns him into "a real Do-It-Yourself man now." Here DIY activities became the premise for a growing friendship between two men that goes beyond the kind of casual acquaintanceships more appropriate for the atomized routines of daily suburban life. Bill even lingers around his new friend's home while his wife is out, watching the latter at work and even collaborating in a little bit of sawing. Returning to the train carriage for another journey into town, Bill has now been utterly corrupted. We can be sure that his new interest will soon cause him to redo his own home and he'll be equally keen to convert more men to his cause.

This advert, therefore, unwittingly echoed many of the tropes used earlier in the decade to construct a metropolitan geography of queer criminality. The commuting train is once again made a formative site of homosocial instability, partially recalling both Wildeblood and McNally's encounter at Piccadilly Circus and Holland and Pendlebury's cruising on the Tube. By no means as troubling with its intraclass dynamics and the clearly defined scope of this friendship between men—this is, after all, only a bit of DIY!—the advert still hints at new possibilities being made available by developing forms of consumer desire, the forceful return of the expressive male body, and the insinuation of both into the volatile moments of interstitial urban space.

Away from such suburban contexts, DIY's repositioning of the decorated interior as an active expression of the material body provided London's queer men with a means through which to search for a more conducive

Figure 39. Bill is recruited to the cause: advertisement for Asbestolux fire-safe board, 1958.

domestic setting. From 1959, when Kenneth Halliwell and John Orton moved into their bed-sitting room in Noel Road, Islington, the pair created a number of large murals across the walls of their room using many of the plates that they would steal from public library books over the next three years (Figure 40). The very existence of these collages and the haphazard way in which they were presumably built up clearly suggests an ongoing project that developed organically, as the pair decided where and how to assemble the next set of images. Their lengthy construction thus marks collage making as a firm and lasting component of their domestic life together.

Matt Cook has noted the masculine austerity that characterized this bedsit, as well as Orton and Halliwell's eagerness for it to remain untainted by more obvious signifiers of effeminate homosexuality. Yet he also notes how this room functioned as a sanctuary, marking their distance from the more visible queer circuits of the commercial West End that the pair generally eschewed. For Cook, the murals were a site in which these two dynamics came together, as Orton and Halliwell engaged in a form of specifically queer bricolage, actively seeking to fashion for themselves an inhabitable domestic terrain:

> [The collage] combined those putative markers of queer sensibility—Greek statuary and Renaissance art—but it crucially presented them prosaically. The men did not have a miniature replica statue of a Greek athlete or a carefully positioned and framed reproduction of a Michelangelo.[74]

It was this construction of an environment—a total, seamless background against which to live—that resisted the claustrophobic demands of postwar heteronormativity. Yet, at the same time, they succeeded in producing a thoroughly queer interior that resisted its own dissolution back into an aggregate of significant objects or images of the type that characterized Bunny's decor in *The Charioteer* or Sandy Youth's room in *Victim*.

Collage making was a staple of creative home decoration in the late 1950s, but Orton and Halliwell reworked it within the terms of their own situation. Unlike the cybernetic color schemes of more conventional contemporary interiors, these murals foregrounded the traces they bore of the pair's ongoing bodily practices as they labored to produce their own domestic environment. By working on the collages, they produced a physical expression of their affective love, while investing back into their decor a new

Figure 40. Metropolitan queer homemaking: John (Joe) Orton and Kenneth Halliwell, mural on the wall of their bedsit, Noel Road, Islington, ca. 1959–62. Courtesy of Islington Local History Centre.

and creative form of traditional moral unity. Thus, authorized by the promotion of Do-It-Yourself as a form of self-creation for loving young couples, but reworking to their own ends the more abstract principles of contemporary interior design, Orton and Halliwell found a way to affirm their partnership within a defiantly queer mode of companionate domesticity.

Such constructions, of course, remained highly volatile. In the flurry of press attention that followed the success of his play *Loot,* much coverage was given to "Joe" Orton's protestations that his newfound wealth would not change his austere way of life. The Islington bedsit featured heavily here as a symbol of his authentic working-class roots and a symbol of that thing which he would not be giving up. Newspaper articles presented the room and its murals as an expression of Orton's own wit and creativity. As Jane Gaskell told readers of the *Daily Sketch:*

> The bed-sitting-room is partly papered with immense collages of pictures cut out from magazines. These stretch up over the ceiling; a touch of fantasy in the clean, neat room which is not stark because its main colour is egg-yolky and happy.
>
> There is a rack full of LPs—jazz and Elvis; a huge television; and a telephone, the only changes Orton's rather big new money has made to the flat he's lived in since 1959.[75]

Missing here is any mention of Halliwell as Orton's lover, roommate, and coproducer of the collages. The creativity of the decor could only be celebrated in public if it was forcefully reinterpreted through the more heteronormative conventions of Do-It-Yourself.

All this was to change nine months later, however, when Halliwell murdered Orton before taking his own life. Now the *Sketch* refashioned the flat as a site of murderous perversion; Orton was killed by his euphemistic "friend," "at the bed sittingroom the two writers had shared for eight years." This reconfiguration changed the meanings of the collages too, for now "[t]he walls of their third floor flat in Noel-road, Islington, were pasted with nude photographs cut from newspapers, magazines and books."[76] No longer the creative use of old magazines, these collages became read as the untoward desecration of proper books. Orton's touch of fantasy had become the mark of his perversion, turning the private expression of their loving relationship into public proof of their joint criminality. Tellingly, this same article also reverted to marking their deviance through a cited list of significant commodities: "Both men were wearing pyjamas . . . [and] police found two men's wigs nearby." Ultimately, then, for all its importance as a domestic space in which the pair had fashioned their own queer environment, the Noel Road bedsit became yet another domestic crime scene, reinscribed as a set of traces left by the bodies of its now absent— and murderously queer—inhabitants.

conclusion

CITY OF ANY DREAM

It is not possible to produce a set of rules purporting to describe what a man should do in every conceivable set of circumstances. One might for instance have a rule that one is to stop when one sees a red traffic light, and to go if one sees a green one, but what if by some fault both appear together? One may perhaps decide that it is safest to stop. But some further difficulty may well arise from this decision later. To attempt to provide rules of conduct to cover every eventuality, even those arising from traffic lights, appears to be impossible.

—ALAN TURING, "Computing Machinery and Intelligence," 1951

If the collages pasted on Orton and Halliwell's bedsit walls were largely enabled by the cultural prominence of Do-It-Yourself in the later 1950s, then it is equally interesting that for Jane Gaskell writing for the *Daily Sketch* in 1966, its component images should be naturally presented as having been cut out from magazines. In 1962—the year of the pair's imprisonment— the *Sunday Times* would issue its first color supplement, announcing a new type of weekly lifestyle magazine that would serve to disseminate the latest trends in metropolitan culture and consumption to an increasingly affluent national readership. That the Noel Road murals could be framed so easily through these publications, apparently both providing the source material for Joe's youthful creativity and mimicking the kind of modish interiors on show within their pages, adds another layer of meaning to these collages and to the library book defacements with which they were aligned. In fashioning their own domestic environment out of the canonical images from the history of art—literally tearing them from the pages of London's public archive—Orton and Halliwell had engaged in a process of decontextualization and chic appropriation very much in accordance with those transient modes of consumption celebrated within the new Sunday supplements.

To this end, it is enlightening to compare the duo's efforts with another domestic collage that had been produced in London only three years beforehand. *Just what is it that makes today's homes so different, so appealing?* was an image created by the artist Richard Hamilton for use both in the catalog and as a publicity poster for the *This Is Tomorrow* exhibition, held at the Whitechapel Gallery in August 1956 (Figure 41).[1] Often misread as a satire on consumerism or else as a simple wish list after postwar austerity, Hamilton's collage marked his sustained attempt to grapple with the consequences of an expanding popular media and the attendant visual economy of mass-market advertising. Gathering together a profusion of commercial imagery and forcing it into a new disjointed unity, the collage sought to impel the viewer toward an evolved perceptual apparatus more suited to the overloaded visual environment of late-1950s Britain.[2] Hamilton's image, then, was a form of visual assault, conceived as a provocative aid for successfully navigating the semantic prolificacy that was coming to characterize the modern urban world.

Of course, in choosing to make a living room the subject of his collage, Hamilton also revealed how the expanded mass media of a consumerist economy was challenging the very possibility of impermeable private space. Here, the domestic realm had been invaded not only by new types of commodity (the tin of ham, the vacuum cleaner) but by incessant flows of information transmitted via a plethora of modern media technologies. The newspaper, tape recorder, television, comic, and telephone now rendered this interior profoundly porous, bringing in a cacophony of sounds, words, and images from the outside world. Suggested in particular by the nighttime cinema, its bright lights and signage imposing through the uncurtained window, Hamilton's living room is no longer a refuge from the seething metropolis—a private domain of sentimental training and managed domestic citizenship—for it is now engaged in a series of ongoing dialogues with the city's commercial entertainments and its insistent flickering surfaces.

All this, of course, had also rendered domestic space an ambiguous site of sexual instability. Hamilton's interior is no longer a suitable domicile for those confident nuclear families that had once inhabited the Furnished Rooms at *Britain Can Make It*. Instead, we find a near-naked bodybuilder (in fact Irwin "Zabo" Koszewski, cut out from the physique magazine *Tomorrow's Man*) and a provocative female pinup.[3] Now irrevocably infiltrated by the dynamics of consumerism, the contemporary home has become the setting for a much queerer—and profoundly urban—mode of domestic

Figure 41. The unstable porosity of the mediated home: poster by Richard Hamilton for *This Is Tomorrow,* Whitechapel Art Gallery, 1956. Courtesy of Whitechapel Archive.

performance. It is this, then, that links Hamilton's collage to that other interior soon to be assembled out of a different collection of found photographic images. Orton and Halliwell's bedsit—a tessellation of library plates that included a good many Classical and Renaissance male nudes—spoke of a similarly skilled orientation to their urban environment, an open sensitivity to its available image economies, and a developing competence at collecting and combining this material to produce a workable setting for their own domestic life together.

Hamilton himself was one of a cluster of young artists, designers, architects, and critics who met regularly between 1952 and 1955 at the newly opened Institute of Contemporary Arts (ICA) on Dover Street, Mayfair. Now remembered as the Independent Group, this loose band of associates organized regular lectures and seminars to explore the impact of the latest scientific technologies and forms of popular culture on the remaking of urban experience and across the visual arts.[4] The group's agenda was by no means queer, but I cite them here because—as Hamilton's collage suggests— their work revealed a youthful engagement with the expanding terrains of metropolitan popular culture that resonated with the more disparate and elusive practices of many of the city's queer men. It thus provides us with a useful reference point for thinking through exactly what was at stake within contemporary queer responses to the developing affluence of late-1950s London.

Central to the Independent Group's approach was its attention to the dynamic network of cultural forces, forms of mediation, and commercial pleasures that was refashioning the capital into a shifting, if ultimately incoherent, landscape of multiple opportunities. As already implied by *Just what is it . . . ?*, much of the group's most interesting work sought to articulate a new mode of environmental perception, which would enable the individual to forge a more sovereign relationship with these fragmented metropolitan systems of meaning and pleasure. At the ICA in 1953, for instance, Nigel Henderson, Eduardo Paolozzi, and Alison and Peter Smithson mounted an exhibition titled *Parallel of Life and Art*, comprised of more than a hundred monochrome images taken from a diverse range of sources, including scientific diagrams, newspaper photographs, microscopic images, anthropological artifacts, and contemporary abstract paintings. All of these had been rephotographed in the same deliberately grainy style, the resultant prints mounted on bits of cardboard and hung from the walls and ceiling to create a consciously overwhelming and disjointed effect (Figure 42).[5]

Parallel of Life and Art, like both the *South Bank Exhibition* only two years earlier and *Britain Can Make It* in 1946, was a tightly controlled holistic space that sought to reconfigure the viewer's relationship to it, structurally reordering his or her environmental engagement in preparation for a return to the city outside. But in contrast to the planned surprises, managed trajectories, and visual education programs embedded within those more mainstream shows, here was a space that was deliberately disorientating. The visitors were simply abandoned, left alone to posit any correlation between the images around them, while selecting their own successive viewpoints—always partial and forever incomplete.

Figure 42. Reorientation to an environment of visual overload: *Parallel of Life and Art*, Institute of Contemporary Arts, 1953. Copyright Tate, London 2008.

A more explicit formulation of this conceptual approach was provided by the critic Lawrence Alloway (another central member of the Independent Group in the mid-1950s) in a short article published in 1959. More than anything, this staked out the emergent challenges that the commercial metropolis had come to pose to the dominant spatial strategies of postwar social reconstruction. As Alloway argued, it was now hopeless to believe that a city and its people might be lastingly reformed via a principled program of managed rebuilding; the modern city was already a fluid set of forces, communication networks, and unplanned activities, to which the architect had a duty to respond without trying to enforce restrictions. As he put it: "Architects can never get and keep control of all the factors in a city which exist in the dimensions of patched-up, expendable, and developing forms."[6] This, then, was a barbed attack on the established orthodoxy—most clearly still attached to Patrick Abercrombie—that trusted urban planning to secure a projected form of stable social order. For Alloway, such disciplinary programs could only work to foreclose the variant possibilities of what modern urban living might productively become:

> The mass arts contribute to the real environment of cities in an important way. It is absurd to print a photograph of Piccadilly Circus and caption it "ARCHITECTURAL SQUALOR" as Ernö Goldfinger and E. J. Carter did in an old Penguin book on the County of London Plan. In fact, the lights of the Circus are the best night-sight in London, though inferior to American displays.[7]

By thus defending the gaudy surfaces of the commodified city, Alloway was reasserting those very qualities of ephemeral display that still worried London's cultural guardians and which had cast the spiv as such a problematic figure only a decade earlier. Yet here, the instability of the mercantile metropolis was cast not as a threatening source of antisocial or psychopathological individualism, but as a force that might open the city up to a more mature form of democracy and difference. In one sense, Alloway was clearly repeating earlier investments in the urban picturesque and the democratic values it expressed through its effects of contrast and surprise. Yet, unlike the meticulous layouts of the Festival's South Bank, this was not tied to any drive to manage the trajectories or order the sensibilities of those marshaled through it. Instead, it was the contingent fluidity of the unplannable metropolis that made it such a productive crucible for a lived dynamic pluralism. Here, amid this kaleidoscopic landscape awash with brightly colored packaging and "LP environment[s]," Alloway sensed the emergence of a new "multiplicity of roles"—he particularly cited the independent young office woman—through which disparate groups were already forging meaningful, profound, and more autonomous modes of everyday urban life.[8]

If something of this could already be traced within Orton and Halliwell's own selective engagements with their metropolitan environment, then its potential for queer men was most consistently explored within the work of novelist and journalist Colin MacInnes. Most celebrated today for his trio of "London novels"—*City of Spades* (1957), *Absolute Beginners* (1959), and *Mr Love and Justice* (1960)—MacInnes was not particularly connected to members of the Independent Group, but he shared a contemporaneous impulse to interrogate the emergent terrains of postwar popular culture and the metropolitan lifestyles these were helping to facilitate. In his regular essays for the journals *Encounter* and *Twentieth Century*, he took pointed issue with such New Left writers as Richard Hoggart who sniffily dismissed manufactured pop music and the cultural investments of the youngsters who loved it.[9] For MacInnes, jazz clubs, coffee bars, and transient teenage fashions were not symptoms of an incapacitated and "Americanized" youth or a disastrous rejection of more traditional forms of "authentic" British working-class culture. Instead, they spoke of a more open and international outlook, a challenge to more redundant forms of cultural nationalism, which dissolved inherited barriers of class and ethnicity and loosened the strictures of outmoded sexual mores. MacInnes's own investments here were complex and ambiguous; his biographer Tony Gould makes a contentious connection between his sexual and social interest in London's new young African and Caribbean immigrants, his sporadic alcoholism, and his profound unease with his own homosexuality.[10] Yet MacInnes's writings on urban youth culture clearly articulate a developing form of queer sensibility that was finely attuned to the shifting metropolitan landscapes of the later 1950s.

Perhaps the most considered formulation of this—although, ironically, the least explicitly queer—can be found in a text MacInnes wrote to accompany *London—City of Any Dream* (1962), a large book of photographs by the Czech photographer Erwin Fieger. In this essay, MacInnes took advantage of Fieger's distinctive style and subject matter to present something of a manifesto for a new mode of metropolitan perception that held exciting potentials for reconfiguring the urban self. Fieger was an early advocate of color art photography and made pioneering usage of the telephoto lens, a method which he claimed "proved to be immensely useful for my particular method of working, since it made it possible to isolate the significant details from the midst of a bewildering profusion."[11] Fieger thus presents his London as an assembled collection of fragments; grainy, incomplete, and usually obscured by some object in the foreground—a passerby or a branch, perhaps—whose out-of-focus presence allows only a section of the image to become properly intelligible.

For MacInnes, it was precisely this disjointed partiality that made Fieger's collection such an acute articulation of the postwar metropolis and of the ungovernable experience of the urban individual. Here, London's dynamic ungraspability, its confusion of scales, and its unpredictable configurations leave it permanently open to alternative experiences and pluralist perspectives. As MacInnes wrote about the experience of standing in Trafalgar Square: "we find ourselves in a higgledy-piggledy out of which *each spectator* must try to create *his own* visual image."[12] Clearly consonant with Alloway, then, the only suitable response when confronted with such an incoherent and fragmented environment was to forge one's own orientation toward it. On these terms, Fieger's composite view of London became less valuable in itself—his Victorian pubs, Ascot race meetings, and visits to the Albert Memorial seem firmly the perspective of a foreign tourist—than for the way it celebrated its own partiality, announcing a more disparate mode of autonomous engagement with the deregulated surfaces of the city.

To this extent, MacInnes commended Fieger for his strong use of color, his rejection of naturalism, and his obvious foregrounding of mediated form. It is this paradox—the "authentic coloured image in its own right"—that enabled his photographs to announce their status not as some neutral window on the city, but as an active component within its perpetual reconstruction.[13] Fieger's pursuit of the most fleetingly trivial moments of urban life—"his creating harmonies out of the reflected hues on the banal door of a London taxi"—allowed a new perception to emerge, at once incomplete and inconclusive, that sustained an ongoing negotiation between the mobile individual and the irrepressible dynamism of the contemporary metropolis.[14]

All this mounted a fundamental challenge to those official frameworks of urban engagement so foundational to agents of social reconstruction; for it ascribed value to those same distracting and solicitous metropolitan surfaces which, it was feared, might encourage postwar citizens to deviate from their purposive pathway and their consensual performance of ordered civic life. The terms of this affront could clearly be seen in one particular photograph from Fieger's book, "Policeman at Piccadilly Circus" (Figure 43). Here, a uniformed bobby stands silhouetted against the technicolor haze of neon advertisements or, perhaps, the lights of a passing bus. But he has moved during the exposure; his helmet now casts a shadow to the right of his head, while the artificial illuminations seep in from the left. Here, then, the sanctioned integrity of reconstruction semiotics has already broken down. Unlike those confident bobbies of *The Blue Lamp* and *The Lavender Hill Mob* a decade or so earlier, his ordered uniform has emphatically been compromised, contaminated by the very metropolis it seeks to patrol. Rendered indistinct within the graininess of the image, the quotidian dynamics of the commercial West End now literally overwhelm him. Instead, he becomes decentered and marginalized, as Fieger's gaze—partial, mobile, and above all autonomous—casts him as just another element within a panoramic urban spectacle.

To be clear, I am not claiming that Fieger's photographs present a specifically queer mode of negotiating the city. But—and here they accord with the work of the Independent Group—they do articulate a developing mode of metropolitan perception which, in opposing the official ideologies of social reconstruction, also offered certain queer men a pragmatic tool for renegotiating their own relationship to their city. Indeed, it may be precisely this sense of variance—its adaptability to the experience of a range of social actors—that made this mode of urban engagement such a vital force of cultural change as London entered the 1960s.

This certainly seems to be MacInnes's suggestion in *Absolute Beginners,* his fictional homage to teenage life in late-1950s London. The novel is narrated by an unnamed protagonist, a working-class heterosexual teenager who has fled his claustrophobic Pimlico home life and now fends for himself as a photographer by producing soft pornography and doing the occasional fashion shoot. But the novel also contains a young homosexual character, marginal to the narrative, around whom MacInnes structures a set of interesting ambiguities. Known only as The Fabulous Hoplite—a moniker like so many in the book that signals an aptitude for metropolitan self-creation—he functions as something of a hybrid figure. On the one hand, he reveals many of those traits commonly demonized by reformist novelists to distance their respectable protagonists from London's lamentable queer subcultures. Young and attractive ("very handsome in an elfin, adolescent sort of style"), he exploits his campy good looks and razor-sharp wit to gain

Figure 43. Overwhelmed by the flickers of the commercial metropolis: Erwin Fieger, "Policeman at Piccadilly Circus," from Erwin Fieger and Colin MacInnes, *London—City of Any Dream* (London and New York: Thames and Hudson, 1962), 36.

access to a network of private homosexual parties, forging financially bene-
ficial social connections with richer and more established queer men.[15] Yet
Hoplite is no Bunny (the scrofulous quean in Mary Renault's *The Charioteer*). Instead, his success at "get[ting] around on the Knightsbridge-
Chelsea circuit in quite an important way" becomes a marker of his social
mobility and his resourceful skill at navigating the city.[16] Thus, even as
he takes advantage of London's homosexual networks, MacInnes has him
lament over their endogamic insularity. As he explains to the narrator:

> With the law as it is, being a poof is a full-time occupation for so many
> of the dear old queens. They're positively dedicated creatures. They feel so
> naughty in the dreary little clubs and service flatlets.[17]

Although this may echo the familiar charge of homosexual reformers,
here it becomes a plea not to engage in public restraint and companionate
monogamy, but to take full advantage of the divergent opportunities available within such a solvent and dynamic metropolis. Thus, Hoplite's queerness firmly faces outwards; dressed in the casual separates of the fashionable
new boutiques, he embraces the city and its media opportunities, eventually becoming a minor celebrity through his successful appearance on a
television magazine show. Ultimately, he is very much of his own urban
creation—and if he remains shackled to the social networks of an older
queer subculture, he also looks out to a more expansive engagement with
the urban possibilities of late-1950s youth culture.

The novel insists that such liberties are dependent on a lack of social and
spatial regulation. Hoplite and the narrator each rent a furnished room in
the same Notting Hill town house; but here, the dilapidated fringe of the
Victorian inner city, with its transient population of parentless youngsters,
is far from being the breeding ground for dissolute delinquency (the familiar charge of London's postwar planners and reformers). Instead, such areas
are shown to promote a disjointed form of communal sociality that largely
remains respectful of difference and alternative ways of life. Living in the
same lodging house as the narrator and Hoplite, we find Mr Cool, an enigmatic mixed-race teenager, and Big Jill, a butch lesbian "ponce" in her early
twenties. Together these characters offer each other an irregular form of
pastoral support, while remaining mindful of each other's self-cultivations
and divergent sexual practices. What enables this—aside from their domestic proximity—is their shared investment in London's popular youth cultures

and the mediated style systems that these are shown to sustain. By engaging with their city in this way, the characters attain a new subjective independence, supported by a tolerant internationalism that looks beyond more parochial notions of an English national community to create tentative—but inescapably metropolitan—connections across boundaries of class, gender, race, and sexuality.

Throughout the novel, the narrator refers to Notting Hill as his "London Napoli" and makes clear that it is only the planners' neglect of this district that facilitates such networks of self-fashioning and sociality; "however horrible the area is," he proclaims, "you're *free* there!"[18] While the novel is aware of this structure's fragility—it climaxes with the previous year's race riots, when white working-class residents mounted a series of attacks on local black immigrants—the conspicuous diversity of MacInnes's assembly still points to a radically expanded form of urban community and one decidedly removed from those managed, hierarchical neighborhoods projected by Abercrombie and the Furnished Rooms at *Britain Can Make It*.

Placed within the dynamic urban landscape that MacInnes hoped to capture in his novel, many of London's queer men were clearly developing new ways to negotiate the mediated city, reconfiguring its objects and images to creatively forge more amenable quotidian environments. By selecting, appropriating, and recombining the cultural resources around them, a form of metropolitan habitation was emerging that stood in marked opposition to those narratives of willful perversion and discreet assimilation through which queer men were otherwise being addressed. It seems telling, then, that Lawrence Alloway, writing in 1962, should locate Francis Bacon as the first British fine artist to have engaged with the postwar urban mediascape, finding in his annexation of photographic imagery a direct precursor to the Independent Group's own concerns and working methods.[19] In Bacon's earlier canvases, he argued, one could trace the embryonic emergence of a new "pop" sensibility, a sustained encounter with the city and its images that ran through the work of Alloway's own peers and on to the new crop of self-proclaimed "pop artists."

Thus, it proves interesting that Simon Ofield has recently described Bacon's work as belonging to a wider style of queer postwar cultural production that he relates to the motif of the "scrapbook." Pointing to the cluttered chaos of the artist's Kensington studio, Ofield draws parallels with both "Boy" Barrett's anthology of press clippings in *Victim* and the cutout pictures so conspicuously removed from archival copies of 1950s physique magazines. On these terms, Bacon's disordered stacks of books, torn magazine pages, and piles of crumpled photographs become themselves a kind of scrapbook, a pertinent resource through which he sought to navigate his metropolitan environment and create his own particular form of queer urban sense.[20]

Bacon moved into his Reece Mews studio in the autumn of 1961, just as Orton and Halliwell were completing their own domestic scrapbook on the other side of London. Yet, for all their dissimilarities—Bacon's upper-middle-class background versus Orton's upbringing on a Leicester council estate; the gentility of Kensington against the run-down terraces of Islington; the self-conscious filth of the studio floor against the mannered refinement of the bedsit murals—both of these interiors reveal the emergence of a larger sensibility, a new mode of orienting one's queer self in relation to the fragmented images of the postwar city. The surfaces and solicitations of the modern metropolis had become just so much raw material to be collected and combined within divergent processes of creative self-location.

To this end, a litany of commodities once removed by the police from the bedroom of two unknown queer lovers—a tin of talcum powder, a jar of Nivea cream, a piece of toweling, several commercial physique magazines, and two pairs of briefs—may stand as more than just an aggregate of criminal queer citations. It might equally testify to an active and ongoing form of composite self-creation and one emphatically opposed to the stable interiority and environmental adjustments on which sanctioned homosexual respectability was becoming based. Together, these objects now speak of an emergent type of queer assemblage, contingently cobbled together from the city's consumer products, its ephemeral media, and its situated possibilities of fashionable display. Such dynamics clearly hark back to earlier historical moments—the interwar quean's use of portable cosmetics, perhaps, or even the promenades of Fanny and Stella in the 1860s—but they remained inextricably rooted in the expanding consumer economies of 1950s London. Thus, just as the Wolfenden Committee was sketching out its blueprint for a model of homosexual citizenship—a coherent subjectivity that turned away from the distractions of the city, to pursue a discreet life of companionate monogamy and corporate sociability—alternative and less manageable forms of queer life were also taking shape, vitally dependent on the incessant and accelerated tempos of the contemporary commercial metropolis.

But while they remained decidedly ambivalent toward bourgeois agendas for legal reform, such disparate queer engagements with the city had yet to coalesce into anything like a recognizable politics. Thus, whereas in 1959 *Absolute Beginners* ends with its narrator realizing the need to look beyond mere fun and take action against racial prejudice and inequality, The Fabulous Hoplite is granted no such epiphany. Instead, he remains torn between the expansive worlds of the metropolitan teenager and the more inward-looking circuits of homosexual society in which he retains an important stake. It would take until the end of the 1960s for a more definable activism to emerge from the performative potentials of the metropolitan environment and the semiotic possibilities of its mediated cultures. By then, just as consumerism had become more entrenched in the city's quotidian landscape, enchantment with its novel opportunities had been superseded by a countercultural critique that stressed its systematic role in the structural oppression of queers.

The Gay Liberation Front (GLF) was founded in London in the autumn of 1970 and within its politics one can certainly trace the inheritance of this earlier reorientation to the city. Rejecting the hegemonic assimilationism of welfare-state ideology (as recently endorsed by the 1967 Sexual Offences Act), liberationists remained deeply committed to the expansive internationalism of metropolitan culture and pursued active coalitions with Black Power groups and feminists. Above all, though, it was their investment in the "zap"—a shocking and subversive public intervention orchestrated to expose the homophobia of social institutions—that revealed the GLF's profound understanding of media imagery and the theatrical possibilities of ordinary urban space. As Jeffrey Weeks recalls:

> Gay liberationists, men and women, held hands in public, kissed each other in Underground trains or on the streets, encouraged their comrades to come "out of the closets", danced together at straight discos, demonstrated together, zapped public meetings, held openly homosexual dances and events.[21]

Thus, when in 1971 Pan Books published Dr. David Reuben's homophobic psychology book *Everything You Always Wanted to Know about Sex—but Were Afraid to Ask,* members of the GLF infiltrated W. H. Smith, demolishing publicity displays and inserting bogus pages that purported to offer a full refund to anyone unhappy with their purchase.[22] On one level, this was, of course, a more conscious articulation of that same quotidian queer politics that Orton and Halliwell had expressed within their own book defacements almost exactly a decade earlier. It is thus tempting to position this earlier moment as part of the complex prehistory to such radical engagements, the beginnings of an aptitude for reworking and recombining the materials of the built environment that would fuse with more international forms of gay liberation and run on to the queer activism of the late 1980s and 1990s.

The late 1950s, however, also saw the emergence of an awkward and residual paradox that has similarly come to haunt the contemporary politics of metropolitan queer life; for, by turning to the resources made available within its commercial landscapes, London's queer men were developing a productive mode of self-making intimately rooted in consumerist practices and modes of urban display. From the early 1990s, this inherited contradiction would become increasingly apparent in the area around Old Compton Street in Soho. In a political climate characterized by the vicious prohibitions of Clause 28 and homophobic reactions to AIDS, the concerted promotion of this district as the vibrant epicenter of a new gay London became an important strategy of political assertion—the indelible scoring of homosexual lifestyles into the visible topography of the city. At its most pertinent, to move between the "Continental-style" cafés and plate-glassed bars of newly branded Gay Soho was to enact a quotidian performance of protest and subcultural solidarity. Yet this tactical investment in metropolitan consumerism rendered such practices dangerously complicit with the dynamics of neoliberal capital.[23] Thus, the spatial consolidation to which it aspired already set limits to what this strategy could achieve. If today this queer presence has proved less troubling to municipal elites, then the stabilization of its often insular gay lifestyles—affluent, youthful, residually male, and predominantly white—has provoked mounting consternation from more radical queer commentators. Yet despite their concerns—or, perhaps, even because of them—the dialectic of this paradox appears to remain in motion, for away from the visibility of central London, particularly in more outlying districts to the south and the east, many of the capital's queer men seem intent on recapturing a more expansive and unsettled engagement with their urban terrain. Perhaps, at their best, the contingencies thrown up by the dynamic metropolis might still provide the material for new, diverse, and at present unforeseeable ways of living with others in the city.

ACKNOWLEDGMENTS

As with many first books, this one has taken a while, so perhaps it's best if I proceed chronologically. First, then, a big thank you to Adrian Rifkin for screening *The Lavender Hill Mob* as part of his M.A. module "Cities and Film" in 1995. From a small epiphany half an hour later (over a plate of chips and cheese in Leeds University's Student Union), all else has ultimately followed.

I owe a considerable debt to my Ph.D. supervisors at the University of Sussex: Simon Rycroft, Andy Medhurst, and Jon May. Their support, expertise, and readiness to allow me to pursue my hunches allowed this project to take the shape it has. I must also thank a group of remarkable scholars with whom I was fortunate enough to study at Sussex, including Thomas Austin, Matt Bennett, Clare Birchall, Kay Dickinson, Ewan Kirkland, Suzy Gordon, Paul Myerscough, and Bryony Randall. Their careful combination of interdisciplinary irreverence and intellectual rigor provided an excellent laboratory in which to test out and develop the ideas in this book. From this period, I am particularly grateful to four people—Caroline Bassett, Iman Hamam, Michael Lawrence, and Meredith Miller—who not only got me through some wobbly moments but whose astute insights can be found scattered liberally throughout these pages.

My Ph.D. was generously funded by the Arts and Humanities Research Council. I am also grateful to the staff at the following archives: British Library Newspapers, the Geffrye Museum, the London Transport Museum, the Mass Observation Archive at the University of Sussex, the National Archives, and the Victoria and Albert Museum's Archive of Art and Design. Lesley Whitworth and Catherine Moriarty at the University of Brighton's Design Archives were especially good fun and unfailingly generous with both their expertise and their material.

I am grateful to my colleagues in what was the School of Cultural Studies and is now the Department of Media, Culture, and Drama at the University of the West of England, Bristol. Not only have they succeeded in creating a stimulating research environment, but their wizardry with rather limited resources enabled me to have more leave for this project than perhaps I rightly deserved. In particular, Michelle Henning, Ben Highmore, and Gillian Swanson deepened both my knowledge of and fascination with the intricacies of British modernity and provided welcome reassurance that the most productive research seminars usually take place over a nice long lunch with a decent bottle of wine.

Alan Sinfield, David Pinder, Michael Moon, John David Rhodes, and two anonymous readers for the University of Minnesota Press read this manuscript at different points in its gestation and offered insightful, challenging, and highly productive comments. Jason Weidemann, my editor at Minnesota, has been exemplary; his unstinting enthusiasm for this project from the moment it landed on his desk made this book immeasurably easier to write. Thanks, too, to David Thorstad for his attentive copyediting, and to Denise Carlson for her excellent index.

Finally, *danke vielmals* to James Freeman, my technical adviser and long-suffering valet, for putting up with all the madness.

NOTES

Introduction

1. See Chris Waters, "Havelock Ellis, Sigmund Freud and the State: Discourses of Homosexual Identity in Interwar Britain," in Lucy Bland and Laura Doan, eds., *Sexology in Culture: Labelling Bodies and Desires* (London: Polity Press, 1998), 165-79.

2. Peter Wildeblood, *Memorandum to the Departmental Committee on Homosexual Offences and Prostitution* (1954) (The National Archives [TNA]: Public Records Office [PRO] /HO/345/8/CHP/51), 8.

3. Chris Waters, "Disorders of the Mind, Disorders of the Body Social: Peter Wildeblood and the Making of the Modern Homosexual," in Becky Conekin, Frank Mort, and Chris Waters, eds., *Moments in Modernity: Reconstructing Britain, 1945–1964* (London: Rivers Oram, 1999), 134–51.

4. See Jane Rendell, *The Pursuit of Pleasure: Gender, Space, and Architecture in Regency London* (London: Athlone, 2002); Christopher Breward, *Fashioning London: Clothing and the Modern Metropolis* (Oxford: Berg, 2004), 21–96; Hermoine Hobhouse, *A History of Regent Street* (London: Macdonald and Jane's, 1975); Erika Rappaport, *Shopping for Pleasure: Women in the Making of London's West End* (Princeton, N.J.: Princeton University Press, 2001); Mica Nava, "Modernity's Disavowal: Women, the City and the Department Store," in Mica Nava and Alan O'Shea, eds., *Modern Times: Reflections on a Century of English Modernity* (London: Routledge, 1996), 38–76; Judith R. Walkowitz, "Going Public: Shopping, Street Harassment, and Streetwalking in Late Victorian London," *Representations* no. 62 (1998): 1–30.

5. Jerry White, *London in the Twentieth Century: A City and Its People* (London: Viking, 2001), 7-12 and 20–21; Gavin Weightman and Steve Humphries, *The Making of Modern London, 1914–1939* (London: Sidgwick and Jackson, 1984), 31–34.

6. See Elizabeth Wilson, *The Sphinx and the City: Urban Life, the Control of Disorder, and Women* (Berkeley and London: University of California Press, 1992), 26–46; Gill Davies, "Foreign Bodies: Images of the London Working Class at the End of the Nineteenth Century," *Literature and History* 14, no. 1 (1988): 64–80; Jeffrey Richards, "Introduction," to James Greenwood, *The Seven Curses of London* (Oxford: Basil Blackwell, 1981), v–xxi.

7. See G. R. Searle, *The Quest for National Efficiency: A Study in British Politics and Political Thought, 1899–1914* (Oxford: Basil Blackwell, 1971); J. Harris, *Private Lives, Public Spirit: Britain, 1870–1914* (Harmondsworth: Penguin, 1994).

8. Elizabeth Darling, *Re-forming Britain: Narratives of Modernity before Reconstruction* (London and New York: Routledge, 2007), 51–52, 109–10; Weightman and Humphries, *The Making of Modern London, 1914–1939,* 156–59.

9. Darling, *Re-forming Britain.*

10. Weightman and Humphries, *The Making of Modern London, 1914–1939,* 58–69, 111–16. See also Alan A. Jackson, *Semi-detached London: Suburban Development, Life, and Transport, 1900–39,* rev. ed. (Didcot: Wild Swan, 1991); and Paul Oliver, Ian Davis, and Ian Bentley, *Dunroamin: The Suburban Semi and Its Enemies* (London: Pimlico, 1981).

11. White, *London in the Twentieth Century,* 26.

12. For contemporary alarm at the growth of British cities, see Clough Williams-Ellis, *England and the Octopus* (London: Geoffrey Bles, 1928), and the essays collected in Clough Williams-Ellis, ed., *Britain and the Beast* (London: J. M. Dent and Sons, 1937). Many of the contributors to the latter anthology would go on to become influential figures in the postwar drive for urban renewal.

13. Frank Mort, "Scandalous Events: Metropolitan Culture and Moral Change in Post-Second World War London," *Representations* no. 93 (2006): 106–37.

14. Mica Nava, "Wider Horizons and Modern Desire: The Contradictions of America and Racial Difference in London, 1935-45," *New Formations* no. 37 (1999): esp. 76-83.

15. John Carey, *The Intellectuals and the Masses* (London: Faber, 1992); Keith Williams, *British Writers and the Media, 1930–45* (Basingstoke: Macmillan, 1996), 70–94; Gillian Swanson, *Drunk with the Glitter: Space, Consumption, and Sexual Instability in Modern Urban Culture* (London and New York: Routledge, 2007), esp. 54–72; Sally Alexander, "Becoming a Woman in London in the 1920s and 30s," in Morag Shiach, ed., *Feminism and Cultural Studies* (Oxford: Oxford University Press, 1999), 200–227; Matt Houlbrook, "'The Man with the Powder Puff' in Interwar London," *Historical Journal* 50, no. 1 (2007): esp. 154–59 and 166–70.

16. Houlbrook, "'The Man with the Powder Puff,'" 159–62.

17. Matt Houlbrook, *Queer London: Perils and Pleasures in the Sexual Metropolis, 1918–1957* (Chicago: University of Chicago Press, 2005), 139–66.

18. See Morris B. Kaplan, *Sodom on the Thames: Sex, Love, and Scandal in Wilde Times* (Ithaca, N.Y., and London: Cornell University Press, 2005), 19–101; Matt Cook, *London and the Culture of Homosexuality, 1885–1914* (Cambridge and New York: Cambridge University Press, 2003), 14–18; H. G. Cocks, *Nameless Offences: Homosexual Desire in the Nineteenth Century,* (London: I. B. Taurus, 2003), 105–12; Charles Upchurch, "Forgetting the Unthinkable: Cross-dressers and British Society in the Case of the Queen vs. Boulton and Others," *Gender and History* 12, no. 1 (2000): 127–57.

19. This book makes a set of axiomatic assumptions about the foundational plurality of forms of queer life, their material intractability from specific locations at

certain moments, and their complex formative intersection with other cultural vectors of class, education, gender, ethnicity, and nationality. As historians have long established, "homosexuals" or "gay men" are not a transhistorical constant; more important, at no synchronic moment do queer men ever approximate such a misleadingly unified or coherent grouping. Rather, at any historical juncture and in any particular location, there always exists a multiplicity of categories, definitions, and ways of being queer that collude or collide with each other in various dynamic ways. How a man understands or manages his desires, fashions a sense of self, or forges a social network will depend on his wider subjective positioning, his access to different social and economic resources, and the knowledges, beliefs, and cultural formations available to him. In any period, therefore, we should expect to find what Matt Cook terms a "controlled plurality" of queer formations (*London and the Culture of Homosexuality,* 5), which overlap, reinforce, refute, or antagonize each other in different material spaces or in different discursive sites. To follow David Halperin, "there is no such thing as a history of male homosexuality. At least, there is no such thing as a singular or unitary history of male homosexuality" (*How to Do the History of Sexuality* [Chicago: University of Chicago Press, 2004], 109). This book, therefore, is no simple history of male homosexuality in postwar London, although—somewhat confusingly—it does trace the notion of "homosexuality" as a specific formation to come to prominence during this period. But remaining class-marked, exclusionary, and limited in its appeal, "homosexuality" was not the only way that queer men could understand themselves or organize their lives in postwar London. In this book, accordingly, I have tried to reserve the word *homosexual* to refer to this specific formation, derived from sexology and containing implicit moral imperatives about appropriate urban conduct. In contrast, *queer* is used more generally, sometimes to refer to all men who desire or have sex with other men, and sometimes to refer more pointedly to those men who remained outside or in opposition to the emergent model of "homosexuality." This dichotomy is not clear-cut, however. London in the early postwar decades was marked by the progressive entry of the word *homosexual* into popular consciousness; thus, as much as it came to occlude other formations of queer male behavior and desire, it also lost something of its therapeutic rigor and became more generally applied. This semantic dissipation is reflected in the later chapters of this book, where I occasionally use *homosexual* in a more expansive sense in accordance with its wider application at the time.

20. Houlbrook, *Queer London,* 167–94.

21. On the wider dynamics of such "new journalism," see Gary Weber, "Henry Labouchère, *Truth* and the New Journalism of Late Victorian Britain," *Victorian Periodicals Review* 26, no. 1 (1993): 36–43; Cook, *London and the Culture of Homosexuality,* 49–50; Cocks, *Nameless Offences,* 136–54; Judith R. Walkowitz, *City of Dreadful Delight: Narratives of Sexual Danger in Late-Victorian London* (London: Virago, 1992), 81–134, 191–228.

22. Cook, *London and the Culture of Homosexuality,* 50–63. On the Cleveland Street scandal, see Cocks, *Nameless Offences,* 144–53; Kaplan, *Sodom on the Thames,* 166–223. On the Wilde trials, see Ed Cohen, *Talk on the Wilde Side: Toward a Genealogy of a*

Discourse on Male Sexualities (London and New York: Routledge, 1993), esp. 97–214; Kaplan, *Sodom on the Thames*, 224–51.

23. Houlbrook, *Queer London*, 195–218.

24. Cook, *London and the Culture of Homosexuality*, 122–42; Seth Koven, *Slumming: Sexual and Social Politics in Victorian London* (Princeton, N.J., and Oxford: Princeton University Press, 2004), 228–81.

25. For nuanced accounts of these ideas and their uneven take-up among both British intellectuals and queer men, see Cook, *London and the Culture of Homosexuality*, 73–94; Waters, "Havelock Ellis, Sigmund Freud and the State."

26. Houlbrook, *Queer London*, 66–67.

27. See ibid., 191–94, 205–6.

28. For an excellent account of this program in relation to specific "problem" categories of the individual, see Swanson, *Drunk with the Glitter*.

29. The most sustained analysis of this mode of governance and its structural role in the perpetuation of mid-twentieth-century capitalism was undertaken by the French sociologist Henri Lefebvre. In almost all of his work on "everyday life," Lefebvre analyzed how a specific set of social contradictions brought about by the modernization of France in the wake of the Marshall Plan required an intensive reorganization of quotidian space and time. Although his work remains firmly rooted in its own national context, his basic theoretical perspective remains essential to the present book. See, for instance, his *Critique of Everyday Life: Volume 1*, trans. John Moore (London: Verso, 2008); *Critique of Everyday Life: Volume 2*, trans. John Moore (London: Verso, 2002); *Everyday Life in the Modern World*, trans. Sacha Rabinovitch (London: Athlone, 2000).

30. T. H. Marshall, "Citizenship and Social Class" (1950), in T. H. Marshall and Tom Bottomore, *Citizenship and Social Class* (London: Pluto, 1992), 33.

31. Ibid.; my emphasis.

32. Ibid., 34–35.

33. Alison Light, *Forever England: Femininity, Literature, and Conservatism Between the Wars* (London and New York: Routledge, 1991); see also David Matless, *Landscape and Englishness* (London: Reaktion, 1998).

34. George Orwell, "England Your England," in *"England Your England" and Other Essays* (London: Secker and Warburg, 1953), 196; on Mass-Observation, see Nick Hubble, *Mass-Observation and Everyday Life: Culture, History, Theory* (Basingstoke: Palgrave Macmillan, 2006).

35. Marshall, "Citizenship and Social Class," 7; my emphasis.

36. Ibid., 36.

37. Patrick Abercrombie and J. H. Forshaw, *The County of London Plan* (London: Macmillan, 1943), 103.

38. Marshall, "Citizenship and Social Class," 47.

39. Nicholas Bullock, *Building the Post-war World: Modern Architecture and Reconstruction in Britain* (London: Spon Press, 2002), 69–75; Barry Curtis, "One Continuous Interwoven Story (the Festival of Britain)," *Block*, no. 11 (1985–86): 48–52; Owen Gavin and Andy Lowe, "Designing Desire—Planning, Power and the Festival of Britain," *Block* no. 11 (1985–86): 53–69.

40. Frank Mort, "Fantasies of Metropolitan Life: Planning London in the 1940s," *Journal of British Studies* 43 (2004): 120–51.

41. Gavin and Lowe, "Designing Desire," 57.

42. "Spiv," *Time,* August 4, 1947. See also David Hughes, "The Spivs," in Michael Sissons and Philip French, eds., *Age of Austerity* (Oxford: Oxford University Press, 1996), 69–88; Alistair O'Neill, *London—After a Fashion* (London: Reaktion, 2007), 116–18.

43. See Paul Willetts, *North Soho 999: A True Story of Gangs and Gun-crime in 1940s London* (London: Dewi Lewis Publishing, 2007).

44. Robert Murphy, *Realism and Tinsel: Cinema and Society in Britain, 1939–1948* (London and New York: Routledge, 1999), 146–47; see also Tim Pulleine, "Spin a Dark Web," in Steve Chibnall and Robert Murphy, eds., *British Crime Cinema* (London and New York: Routledge, 1999), 27–36.

45. Peter Scott, "A Clinical Contribution," in Norwood East, ed., *The Roots of Crime* (London: Butterworth and Co., 1954), 59.

46. Gavin and Lowe, "Designing Desire," 58.

47. Ibid., 59.

48. Marshall, "Citizenship and Social Class," 44.

49. See Swanson, *Drunk with the Glitter,* esp. 13–72.

50. Scott, "A Clinical Contribution," 60; my emphasis.

51. Ibid., 59.

52. Ibid., 69.

53. Ibid., 70.

54. Gordon Westwood, *Society and the Homosexual* (London: Victor Gollancz, 1952); D. J. West, *Homosexuality* (London: Duckworth, 1955). "Gordon Westwood" was a pseudonym used by the sociologist Michael Schofield, who would later publish studies of male homosexuality under his own name.

55. Peter Wildeblood, *Against the Law* (London: Weidenfeld and Nicholson, 1955).

56. Mary Renault, *The Charioteer* (London: Longmans, Green and Co., 1953); Audrey Erskine Lindop, *Details of Jeremy Stretton* (London: Heinemann, 1955); James Courage, *A Way of Love* (London: Jonathan Cape, 1959).

57. Rodney Garland, *The Heart in Exile* (London: W. H. Allen, 1953); see also Matt Houlbrook and Chris Waters, "*The Heart in Exile:* Detachment and Desire in 1950s London," *History Workshop Journal* no. 62 (2006): 142–65; Simon Ofield, "Cruising the Archive," *Journal of Visual Culture* 4, no. 3 (2005): 351–64.

58. Houlbrook, *Queer London,* 243; see also Houlbrook and Waters, "*The Heart in Exile*"; and Richard Dyer, "*Victim:* Hegemonic Project," in *The Matter of Images: Essays on Representations* (London and New York: Routledge, 1993), 71–88.

59. See Swanson, *Drunk with the Glitter,* esp. 32–53.

60. John Wolfenden et al., *Report of the Committee on Homosexual Offences and Prostitution* (London: Her Majesty's Stationery Office, 1957), 67, para. 196.

61. Patrick Abercrombie, *The Greater London Plan, 1944* (London: His Majesty's Stationery Office, 1945), 18–19.

1. Reconstructing Everyday Life in the Atomic Age

1. Abercrombie and Forshaw, *The County of London Plan.*

2. Abercrombie, *The Greater London Plan.*

3. Marshall, "Citizenship and Social Class," 35–36.

4. Jonathan M. Woodham, "*Britain Can Make It* and the History of Design," in Patrick J. Maguire and Jonathan M. Woodham, eds., *Design and Cultural Politics in Post-war Britain: The* Britain Can Make It *Exhibition of 1946* (London: Leicester University Press, 1997), 19.

5. 3d "Plan" to the *South Bank Exhibition* (London: His Majesty's Stationery Office, 1951).

6. Bullock, *Building the Post-war World,* 69–75; see also Gavin and Lowe, "Designing Desire," 53–69.

7. Donald L. Foley, *Controlling London's Growth: Planning the Great Wen, 1940–60* (Berkeley and Los Angeles: University of California Press, 1963), 79; Alison Ravetz, *Remaking Cities: Contradictions of the Recent Urban Environment* (London: Croom Helm, 1980), 63–97; Steve Humphries and John Taylor, *The Making of Modern London, 1945–1985* (London: Sidgwick and Jackson, 1986), 88–93 and 146–68.

8. Judy Attfield, "Inside Pram Town: A Case Study of Harlow House Interiors, 1951–61," in Judy Attfield and Pat Kirkham, eds., *A View from the Interior: Women and Design* (London: Virago, 1995), 215–38.

9. See, for instance, "A Plan for Britain," a special themed edition of *Picture Post* 10, no. 1 (January 4, 1941); Ralph Tubbs, *Living in Cities* (Harmondsworth: Penguin, 1942); E. J. Carter and Ernö Goldfinger, *The County of London Plan* (Harmondsworth: Penguin, 1945).

10. Films produced to showcase the principles of postwar planning included *Proud City* (Ralph Keene, 1945); *Planned Town* (Welwyn Garden City Co., 1948); and *New Town* (John Halas and Joy Batchelor, 1948). For a discussion of these and other films, see the twin articles by John R. Gold and Steven V. Ward: "'We're Going to Do It Right This Time': Cinematic Representations of Urban Planning and the British New Towns, 1939 to 1951," in Stuart C. Aitken and Leo E. Zonn, eds., *Place, Power, Situation, Spectacle: A Geography of Film* (London: Rowman and Littlefield, 1994), 229–58; and "Of Plans and Planners: Documentary Film and the Challenge of the Urban Future, 1935–52," in David B. Clarke, *The Cinematic City* (London and New York: Routledge, 1997), 59–82. A *Guide* to the Festival's *Exhibition of Architecture, Town-Planning and Building Research,* ed. H. McG. Dunnet (London: His Majesty's Stationery Office, 1951), was also produced.

11. Mort, "Fantasies of Metropolitan Life," 120–51.

12. See, for instance, Peter Hall, *Cities of Tomorrow: An Intellectual History of Urban Planning and Design in the Twentieth Century* (Oxford: Blackwell, 1988); Stephen V. Ward, *Planning and Urban Change* (London: Paul Chapman Publishing, 1994); Helen Meller, *Towns, Plans, and Society in Modern Britain* (Cambridge: Cambridge University Press, 1997); Gordon E. Cherry, *Town Planning in Britain since 1900: The Rise and Fall of the Planning Ideal* (Oxford: Blackwell, 1996).

13. See Hall, *Cities of Tomorrow*, 94–108, 123–26.
14. Abercrombie and Forshaw, *The County of London Plan*, 20.
15. Ibid., 43–44.
16. Ibid., 105.
17. Abercrombie, *The Greater London Plan*, 36.
18. Abercrombie and Forshaw, *The County of London Plan*, 140.
19. Ibid.; see also 103.
20. Ibid., 140.
21. Ibid., 31.
22. Ibid., 37
23. See Hall, *Cities of Tomorrow*, 140–43; Simon Rycroft and Denis Cosgrove, "Mapping the Modern Nation: Dudley Stamp and the Land Utilisation Survey," *History Workshop Journal* no. 40 (1995): 91–105.
24. Abercrombie and Forshaw, *The County of London Plan*, 39; Abercrombie, *The Greater London Plan*, 35–36.
25. For instance, this is Abercrombie on the need to conserve the Lee Valley: "in the hands of a skilful landscapist this valley, with its streams, disused gravel pits and water reservoirs could in places be turned into a miniature Norfolk Broads: there is still time to rescue it and to make it an open space of artificial beauty contrasted with primeval Epping Forest" (*The Greater London Plan*, 11). This approach also reworked and extended Geddes's earlier linkage between a healthy social order and its aesthetic appreciation of the holistic natural environment; see Rycroft and Cosgrove, "Mapping the Modern Nation."
26. Abercrombie and Forshaw, *The County of London Plan*, 5.
27. Ibid., 4.
28. Ibid.
29. Ibid., 96; Abercombie, *The Greater London Plan*, 24.
30. Abercrombie and Forshaw, *The County of London Plan*, 30.
31. See Marion Roberts, *Living in a Man-made World: Gender Assumptions in Modern Housing Design* (London and New York: Routledge, 1991).
32. Abercrombie and Forshaw, *The County of London Plan*, 102.
33. Ibid.
34. Abercrombie, *The Greater London Plan*, 98.
35. See Matless, *Landscape and Englishness*, 62–100; S. G. Jones, *Sport, Politics, and the Working Class: Organised Labour and Sport in Interwar Britain* (Manchester: University of Manchester Press, 1992).
36. Abercrombie and Forshaw, *The County of London Plan*, 122.
37. Ibid., 28.
38. Ian Cox, *The South Bank Exhibition: A Guide to the Story It Tells* (London: His Majesty's Stationery Office, 1951), 7. Such descriptions neatly overlooked the experience of those former inhabitants of the South Bank site, forcefully removed to make way for its redevelopment; see Gavin Stamp, "The South Bank Site," in Elaine Harwood and Alan Powers, eds., *Festival of Britain* (London: Twentieth Century Society, 2001), 11–24.

39. The best accounts of such intricate coordinations can be found in a number of edited collections: Maguire and Woodham, *Design and Cultural Politics in Post-war Britain;* Mary Banham and Bevis Hillier, eds., *A Tonic to the Nation: The Festival of Britain 1951* (London and New York: Thames and Hudson, 1976); and Harwood and Powers, *Festival of Britain.*

40. *Architect's Journal* (May 1951), cited in Becky Conekin, "'Here Is the Modern World Itself': The Festival of Britain's Representations of the Future," in Conekin, Mort, and Waters, *Moments of Modernity,* 238; emphasis in the original.

41. Similar strategies had been developed in the United States around this time, notably in Bel Geddes's *Futurama* show, part of the General Motors Highway and Horizons Exhibit at the 1939 New York World's Fair. At *Futurama,* however, visitors were carried in trains along a motorized conveyor belt, a device more in accordance with the exhibit's projection of mechanical modernity. See Edward Dimendberg, "The Will to Motorization: Cinema, Highways, and Modernity," *October* no. 73 (1995), 116–22.

42. John Nicholas, "A Triumph of Showmanship," *Art and Industry* 41, no. 246 (December 1946): 163.

43. Herbert Read, "Britain Can Make It," *The Listener* (October 3, 1946): 429. Peristalsis is the involuntary muscular contractions by which food is passed along the intestines.

44. 1d *Guide* to *Britain Can Make It.*

45. "The Exhibition as Landscape," *Architectural Review* 110, no. 666 (August 1951): 80.

46. "The Exhibition as a Town Builder's Pattern Book," *Architectural Review* 110, no. 666 (August 1951): 108; emphasis in original.

47. Cox, *The South Bank Exhibition,* 8.

48. "Let's Celebrate Ourselves!" *Picture Post* (May 12, 1951): 25.

49. Cox, *The South Bank Exhibition,* 8.

50. Gavin and Lowe, "Designing Desire," 68–69.

51. "Exterior Furniture or Sharawaggi: The Art of Making an Urban Landscape," *Architectural Review* (January 1944): 8; cited in Bullock, *Building the Post-war World,* 35. See also Andrew Law, "English Townscape as Cultural and Symbolic Capital," in Andrew Ballantyne, ed., *Architectures: Modernism and After* (Oxford: Blackwell, 2004), 202–26. Ironically, the same orchestration of surprise and contrast had recently been used in Nazi Germany by the landscape architects of the Reichsautobahn; see Dimendberg, "The Will to Motorization," 106–10.

52. Becky Conekin, *"The Autobiography of a Nation": The 1951 Festival of Britain* (Manchester: University of Manchester Press, 2003), 45.

53. J. M. Richards, "The Exhibition Buildings," *Architectural Review* 110, no. 666 (August 1951): 132.

54. See, for instance, J. B. Boothroyd, "Report on the South Bank, V: More Water With It," *Punch* (May 30, 1951): 665.

55. J. B. Priestley, "On with the Festivals!" *The Listener* 45, no. 1158 (May 10, 1951): 740.

56. Critic, "Festival Diary," *New Statesman and Nation* (May 5, 1951): 497.

57. Geo M, "'Of Course We Shall Put It Back after the Festival Is Over,'" *Punch* 220, no. 5766 (May 9, 1951): 582.

58. Gavin and Lowe, "Designing Desire," 58.

59. See, for example, Sylvia I. Jenkinson, "A Wonderful Day for £5," in Banham and Hillier, *A Tonic to the Nation*, 186.

60. See *Brief City: The Story of London's Festival Buildings*, a film made by the *Observer* newspaper in 1952.

61. Mass-Observation, "A Report on *Britain Can Make It*" (December 1946) (Design Council Archive [DCA]/ID/903), Section B, 33.

62. Cited in Mass-Observation, Summary of Findings on *Britain Can Make It* (1946) (DCA/ID/903), 2.

63. Council of Industrial Design, "Rooms Made to Fit: Notes for the Press on the Furnished Rooms," IDN 44 (1946) (Mass Observation Archive [MOA]/TC26/1/B), 1.

64. Gordon Russell, "Furnished Rooms," *Art and Industry* 41, no. 247 (January 1947): 13; emphasis in the original.

65. Mary Schoeser, "Fabrics for Everyman and the Elite," in Maguire and Woodham, *Design and Cultural Politics in Post-war Britain*, 49.

66. Ward, *Planning and Urban Change*, 80–86.

67. Philip Ziegler, *London at War, 1939–1945* (London: Pimlico, 2002), 337; Jerry White, *London in the Twentieth Century: A City and Its People* (Harmondsworth: Penguin Viking, 2001), 39.

68. Angus Calder, *The Myth of the Blitz* (London: Cape, 1991).

69. Ministry of Information, *Front Line, 1940–1941: The Official Story of the Civil Defence of Britain* (London: His Majesty's Stationery Office, 1942), 68.

70. Ibid., 57.

71. Quoted in ibid., 26. Although the heroic myth of the blitz has been challenged by subsequent historians, this narrative of normalization has persisted. When Tom Harrisson published his *Living through the Blitz* in 1976, a book based on the ordinary accounts of wartime life collected in the Mass-Observation archive, he too found evidence of "a process taking place all over London: the slow and steady acclimatization of the population to life under bombardment" ([London: Collins, 1976], 66).

72. The Finsbury Health Centre opened in 1938. Its significance as an iconic fusion of both social and architectural modernism is explored by Elizabeth Darling in her *Re-forming Britain*, 72–80.

73. See Eric Newton, "The Poster in War-time Britain," *Art and Industry* 34 (June 1943): 8–9. Ironically, this particular poster—one of three similar designs that Games produced for the Army Bureau of Current Affairs—was never seen by a wide audience. On viewing it prior to distribution, Prime Minister Winston Churchill thought it to be "exaggerated and distorted propaganda"—particularly for its implications of social neglect by the interwar government—and ordered all copies to be destroyed. On this, see Catherine Moriarty, "Abram Games: An Essay on His Work and Its Context," in Naomi Games, Catherine Moriarty, and June Rose, *Abram Games, Graphic*

Designer: Maximum Meaning, Minimum Means (Aldershot: Lund Humphries, 2003), 65–68.

74. See "From Mud to Festival," *Picture Post* 51, no. 5 (May 5, 1951), 11–15; Simon Rycroft locates the South Bank reclamation as a crucial expression of wider reconstruction ideologies of efficient land utilization: see his "The Geographies of Swinging London," *Journal of Historical Geography* 28, no. 4 (2002): 569.

75. My thinking in this paragraph has been informed by the connections Freud makes between uncathected wartime trauma and repetitive spatial mastery in his 1920 essay "Beyond the Pleasure Principle" (trans. James Strachey, in Angela Richards, ed., *The Pelican Freud Library*, vol. 11: *On Metapsychology, the Theory of Psychoanalysis* [Harmondsworth: Penguin, 1984], 269–338). In this piece, Freud considers the "traumatic neurosis" suffered by soldiers returning from the trenches, a state that he roots in the experience of an intense shock coupled with the lack of any injury through which this could be cathected. Such neuroses, he claims, were characterized by the patients' refusal to let their trauma impinge on their everyday consciousness ("[p]erhaps they are more concerned with *not* thinking of it" [282; emphasis in the original]) and became manifest instead through a continual replaying of the incident in dreams. Freud then uses these remarks to frame his discussion of what has now become known as the "*fort-da* game," a behavior he observed in an eighteen-month-old boy who, in the absence of his mother, would throw and retrieve a wooden reel tied to a piece of string over the edge of his cot. Upon its disappearance from view, the boy would make an "o-o-o-o" sound, interpreted by Freud as an attempt to say "*fort*"—a German word that James Strachey translates into English as "gone." The boy would then pull the reel back over the edge of the cot while "hail[ing] its reappearance with a joyful '*da*' ['there']" (284; second brackets Strachey's own). For Freud, this game sustained the boy's ability to cope with his mother's absence—reenacted by the reel's disappearance—without suffering excessive pain or crying. As Freud surmises: "At the outset he was in a *passive* situation—he was overpowered by the experience; but, by repeating it, unpleasurable though it was, as a game, he took on an *active* part. These efforts might be put down to an instinct for mastery that was acting independently of whether the memory was in itself pleasurable or not" (285; emphasis in the original). Yet, it is interesting to note that the word "*fort*" not only translates as "gone" (as in "*geh fort!*" [go away!]), but also comes close to the English prefix "pro-" (as in "*Fortschreiten*" [progress] and "*Fortschreiben*" [to update or to project forward]). Throwing the reel, therefore, becomes a psychic mechanism by which the boy resolves—but in some way relives—his anxiety through mastering his own spatial environment. Only by actively and repeatedly reproducing the space around him—suddenly made terrifying by the absence of his mother—can he continue to cope with his normal daily life, albeit in a state of continued mild anxiety.

Certain instructive parallels can be drawn with those forceful visions of postwar life propagated during the reconstruction, particularly considering its heavy cultural investment in repetition and routine as ways of producing a new spatial order impervious to historical trauma. In fact, it is interesting to note just how frequently reconstruction events and texts reworked motifs and themes made familiar during the blitz. Thus the very title of *Britain Can Make It* was a reworking of "Britain Can Take It," the famous *Daily Mail* headline from the morning after the initial bombing raids in December 1940—but it turned a feminized state of passive receptivity into a proclamation of proud masculine activity. Likewise, the exhibition's opening section, "From War to Peace," took the visitor from an underlit blitz scene into a bright, clean display space to emphasis how the modern products of the postwar age were only made possible by the materials and techniques developed during the war. The exhibition's Furnished Rooms must also have seemed uncannily close to that once-shocking sight of ordinary houses torn open to the public by the force of the bombs; yet here, their tatty and dust-covered contents had been miraculously replaced by the very latest in bright and functional furniture. Even the South Bank's Skylon may have been implicated here; when John Betjeman visited, he confessed: "I am for ever wanting to pull it by its end on elastic and see if it shoots to the moon" ("The Festival Buildings," *Time and Tide* [May 5, 1951]; reprinted in *Coming Home: An Anthology of His Prose, 1920–77* [London: Vintage, 1998], 279). Much like a child's wooden reel, this piece of functionless technology could cathect a desire to actively colonize space—a falling V-2 rocket stopped milliseconds before impact and inverted to point skywards in the opposite direction.

76. *Experiment with Death,* British Pathé Newsreel, August 12, 1946; see also the popular Pelican paperback *Atomic Energy,* ed. J. L. Cramer and R. E. Peierls (Harmondsworth: Penguin, 1950), which carefully divides essays between the horrors of the bomb and the benefits of atomic power.

77. *The Mighty Atom,* British Pathé Newsreel, August 16, 1945.

78. *The Fifth Warning,* British Pathé Newsreel, August 12, 1946.

79. "Designs inspired by Crystal Structure Diagrams," *Architectural Review* 109, no. 652 (April 1951): 237. For the full story of the Festival Pattern Group, see Lesley Jackson's beautifully illustrated *From Atoms to Patterns: Crystal Structure Designs from the 1951 Festival of Britain* (Shepton Beauchamp: Richard Dennis Publications, 2008).

80. Rycroft, "The Geographies of Swinging London," 566–88; see also David Matless, "Appropriate Geography: Patrick Abercrombie and the Energy of the World," *Journal of Design History* 6, no. 3 (1993): 167–78; G. Dix, "Patrick Abercrombie, 1879–1957," in Gordon Cherry, ed., *Pioneers in British Planning* (London: Architectural Press, 1981), 103–30.

81. J. Bronowski, *The Exhibition of Science: A Guide to the Story It Tells* (London: His Majesty's Stationery Office, 1951), 25.

82. Ibid., 23.

83. Important here are two exhibitions produced in the early 1950s by members of the Independent Group (an association of young artists, designers, and architects associated with the Institute of Contemporary Arts). *Growth and Form,* organized by Richard Hamilton in July 1951, and *Parallel of Life and Art,* organized by Nigel Henderson, Eduardo Paolozzi, and Alison and Peter Smithson in September 1953, both used microscopic photography to reveal the essential forms of the natural world and to explore their significance within contemporary art and design. In the United

States, similar ideas were being explored by Gyorgy Kepes and the contributors to his edited collection, *The New Landscape in Art and Science* (Chicago: Theobold and Co., 1956). Both groups were deeply interested in microbiological forms and in images of molecular crystallography. Of course, the atomic model presented within the texts and exhibitions of the British reconstruction remained far more simple and mechanistic than the atomic imagery causing excitement elsewhere.

84. Cox, *The South Bank Exhibition*, 61.

85. Ian Cox, "About This Exhibition," in Bronowski, *The Exhibition of Science*, 6.

86. Bronowski, *The Exhibition of Science*, 10.

87. Ibid., 7.

88. Ibid., 144.

89. B. Taylor, "Science at South Kensington," in *The Official Book of the Festival of Britain* (London, 1951), 14.

90. Ibid., 13.

91. See Mark Hartland Thomas, "Festival Pattern Group," in *The Souvenir Book of Crystal Designs: The Fascinating Story in Colour of the Festival Pattern Group* (London: His Majesty's Stationery Office, 1951), 5.

92. See Rycroft, "The Geographies of Swinging London," 567; the term "recapitalization" is his.

93. Abercrombie, *The Greater London Plan*, 160.

94. Ibid., 40.

95. Abercrombie and Forshaw, *The County of London Plan*, 118.

96. Denis Judd, *Empire: The British Imperial Experience from 1765 to the Present* (London: HarperCollins, 1996), 314–19.

97. See David Watt, "Withdrawal from Greece: The End of Balance-of-Power Diplomacy and the Beginning of the Cold War," in Michael Sissons and Philip French, eds., *Age of Austerity* (Oxford: Oxford University Press, 1996), 89–113; Kenneth O. Morgan, *The People's Peace: British History, 1945–1989* (Oxford: Oxford University Press, 1990), 43–60; David Childs, *Britain since 1945: A Political History*, 5th ed. (London and New York: Routledge, 2001), 28–46; Keith Robbins, *Great Britain: Identities, Institutions, and the Idea of Britishness* (Harlow: Addison Wesley Longman, 1998), 297–314.

98. Cited in Judd, *Empire*, 287.

99. Abercrombie and Forshaw, *The County of London Plan*, 20, 136.

100. Ibid., 136; see also Mort, "Fantasies of Metropolitan Life."

101. Schoeser, "Fabrics for Everyman and the Elite," 73.

102. Cox, *The South Bank Exhibition*, 43; see also Bill Schwartz, "Reveries of Race: The Closing of the Imperial Moment," in Conekin, Mort, and Waters, *Moments of Modernity*, 189–207.

103. Abercrombie and Forshaw, *The County of London Plan*, 33.

104. Ibid., 78.

105. See, for example, the material recorded by Patrick Trevor-Roper for the Hall-Carpenter Archives [British Library Sound Archive/C456/89/01]; Tom Driberg, *Ruling Passions* (London: Quartet, 1978), 144; Quentin Crisp, *The Naked Civil Servant*

(Glasgow: Fontana, 1977), 154–55. See also Hugh David, *On Queer Street: A Social History of British Homosexuality, 1895–1995* (London: HarperCollins, 1997), 146–50.

2. The Perversity of the Zigzag

1. Douglas Warth, "Evil Men," *Sunday Pictorial,* May 25, 1952, 6; emphasis in the original.

2. See Cook, *London and the Culture of Homosexuality,* 50–63. On "The Maiden Tribute of Modern Babylon," see Walkowitz, *City of Dreadful Delight,* 81–134; on the Cleveland Street scandal, see Cocks, *Nameless Offences,* 144–53, and Kaplan, *Sodom on the Thames,* 166–223; on the Wilde trials, see Cohen, *Talk on the Wilde Side,* esp. 97–214, and Kaplan, *Sodom on the Thames,* 224–51.

3. Waters, "Disorders of the Mind, Disorders of the Body Social," 139.

4. Warth, "Evil Men" (June 1, 1952), 12.

5. Houlbrook, *Queer London,* 273 and 35–36.

6. See Mort, "Scandalous Events," 106–37.

7. For an account of this opposition, see Frank Pearce, "The British Press and the 'Placing' of Male Homosexuality," in Stanley Cohen and Jock Young, eds., *The Manufacture of News: Deviance, Social Problems, and the Mass Media* (London: Constable, 1981), 305.

8. For the work done by the queer scandals of the 1880s and 1890s in defining the norms of English behavior and London's imperial image, see Cook, *London and the Culture of Homosexuality,* 71–72, and Cohen, *Talk on the Wilde Side.* Matt Houlbrook traces the similar work done by the paper *John Bull* in its presentation of the "painted boy menace" around 1925 (see his *Queer London,* 225).

9. Michael Balcon, *Michael Balcon Presents . . . a Lifetime in Films* (London: Hutchinson, 1969), 159; ellipsis in the original.

10. Sigmund Freud, *The Interpretation of Dreams,* trans. James Strachey (Harmondsworth: Pelican, 1976), esp. 414–19.

11. See, for instance, *Whisky Galore* (dir. Alexander Mackendrick, 1949) and *Passport to Pimlico* (dir. Henry Cornelius, 1949). These films were also based on fanciful and harmless collective crimes that are ultimately foiled within a general reassertion of the wider social order.

12. Ian Green, "Ealing: In the Comedy Frame," in James Curran and Vincent Porter, eds., *British Cinema History* (London: Weidenfield and Nicolson, 1983), 301.

13. Balcon, *Michael Balcon Presents . . . ,* 159.

14. Charles Barr, *Ealing Studios,* 2d ed. (London: Studio Vista, 1993), 17.

15. "Unreal City / Under the brown fog of a winter dawn / A crowd flowed across London Bridge, so many, / I had not thought death had undone so many" (T. S. Eliot, "The Waste Land," in *Selected Poems* [London: Faber and Faber, 1961], 53). See Adrian Rifkin, "Benjamin's Paris, Freud's Rome: Whose London?" *Art History* 22, no. 4 (November 1999): 624.

16. Barr, *Ealing Studios,* 117.

17. By at least the seventeenth century, usury and sodomy had become linked as illegitimate corruptions of monetary and sexual production, respectively (see Will

Fisher, "Queer Money," *ELH: English Literary History* 66, no. 1 [1999]: 1–24). Such homologies were also prevalent during the nineteenth century. Young men's popular education manuals, for instance, were saturated with a semenal economics that presented sperm as a finite resource not to be squandered on illicit or unproductive acts (see Ben Barker-Benfield, "The Spermatic Economy: A Nineteenth-Century View of Sexuality," in Michael Gordon, ed., *The American Family in Social-Historical Perspective* [New York: St. Martin's Press, 1972], 336–72). Similarly, Stephen Heath (in *The Sexual Fix* [Basingstoke: Macmillan, 1982], 14) has noted the significance of "to spend" as a common Victorian euphemism for ejaculation and highlights a passage in Walter's *My Secret Life* (ca. 1890) in which the protagonist fills a prostitute's vagina with eighty silver shillings. It is my contention that this conceptual homology is, in some form, reworked within the narrative of *The Lavender Hill Mob*.

18. Joseph Brayshaw, "Should They Be Blamed?" *Daily Herald,* November 5, 1953, 4; emphasis in the original.

19. Warth, "Evil Men" (May 25, 1952), 15. See also his use of quotations from "the great psychiatrist Clifford Allen" in "Evil Men" (June 8, 1952), 12.

20. "Riddle of Lord Montagu's Passport," *Daily Mirror,* December 16, 1953, 5–6; "Lord Montagu Found Not Guilty on One Charge," *News of the World,* December 20, 1953, 2; "Lost Diplomats: Mr. Morrison to Make Statement," *News of the World,* June 10, 1951, 1.

21. Brayshaw, "Should They Be Blamed?" 4; emphasis in the original.

22. Warth, "Evil Men" (June 1, 1952), 12.

23. For a more detailed account of this working-class bachelor culture, see Houlbrook, *Queer London,* 167–94.

24. Warth, "Evil Men" (June 1, 1952), 12.

25. "Lord Montagu on Trial," *The Times,* March 16, 1954, 5.

26. See "Wildeblood 'Was Crucified,'" *Daily Herald,* March 23, 1954, 5, and Waters, "Disorders of the Mind, Disorders of the Body Social," 134–51.

27. "Montagu: Story of a Party," *The People* (January 24, 1954): 5.

28. Warth, "Evil Men" (May 25, 1952), 6.

29. Houlbrook, *Queer London,* 186–87.

30. See ibid., esp. 43–46 and 85–89.

31. "Judges Are Shocked," *News of the World,* November 1, 1953, 2; ellipsis in the original.

32. "Home Office Inquiries into Importuning," *The Times,* November 13, 1953, 8.

33. "Offences with Male Persons," *The Times,* November 14. 1953, 3.

34. Hughes, "The Spivs," 72, 77.

35. See Robert Murphy, "The Spiv Cycle," in *Realism and Tinsel,* 146–67.

36. "Montagu: Story of a Party," 5.

37. "'My Social Life'—by Wildeblood," *Daily Mirror,* March 19, 1954, 9.

38. Marshall, "Citizenship and Social Class," 3–51.

39. "Charges against Three Men," *The Times,* March 24, 1954, 4.

40. "Wildeblood speaks of 'My lonely moments,'" *Daily Mirror,* March 19, 1954, 6.

41. "Q.C. Questions Wildeblood," *Daily Express,* March 19, 1954, 2.

42. "Wildeblood speaks of 'My lonely moments,'" 6.

43. "Wildeblood: It Was a Foolish Letter to Write," *Daily Herald,* March 19, 1954, 7.

44. "Wildeblood speaks of 'My lonely moments,'" 6.

45. On March 24, 1954, all three of the defendants were found guilty as charged. Wildeblood and Pitt-Rivers were sentenced to eighteen months in jail; Montagu received twelve months.

46. Cited in "Five Troopers Punished by Court-Martial," *News of the World,* April 29, 1951, 2.

47. Warth, "Evil Men" (June 1, 1952),12.

48. Hughes, "The Spivs," 71.

49. Duncan Webb, "Male Vice Clean-up Has Now Started," *The People* (November 1, 1953): 1.

50. Warth, "Evil Men" (June 1, 1952), 12.

51. "It All Started 'When Two Men Met and Smiled,'" *Daily Mirror,* March 16, 1954, 6; emphasis in the original.

52. "'My Social Life'—by Wildeblood," 9.

53. Warth, "Evil Men" (June 1, 1952), 12.

54. Wolfenden et al., *Report of the Committee on Homosexual Offences and Prostitution,* 47, para. 129.

55. Police Constable (PC) Butcher, oral evidence to the Wolfenden Committee (December 7, 1954) (The National Archives [TNA]: Public Records Office [PRO]/ HO/345/12/CHP/TRANS/8), 2.

56. "Police Story of Box & Cox Watch on M.P. in West End," *News of the World,* January 18, 1953, 7.

57. William Field MP, cited in "M.P. to Appeal against Bow Street Conviction," *News of the World,* January 25, 1953, 7.

58. PC Butcher, oral evidence to the Wolfenden Committee, 11.

59. T. E. B. Clarke, "The Lavender Hill Mob," in Roger Manvell, ed., *The Cinema, 1952* (Harmondsworth: Penguin, 1952), 44.

60. Cox, *The South Bank Exhibition,* 8.

61. Hughes, "The Spivs," 77.

62. Abercrombie and Forshaw, *The County of London Plan,* 10.

63. Warth, "Evil Men" (June 1, 1952), 12.

64. "Lord Montagu for Trial: He Declares His Innocence," *News of the World,* November 22, 1953, 4.

65. "No More Trifling with Men Who Corrupt!" *Sunday Pictorial,* October 25, 1953, 5.

66. Gavin and Lowe, "Designing Desire," 60–62; Matless, *Landscape and Englishness,* 234–64.

67. 1d *Guide* to *Britain Can Make It.*

68. The most pertinent statement of this principle was made through a series of illustrated books called *The Things We See,* published by Penguin Books Ltd. throughout the late 1940s and supported by the COID. The various issues covered topics

such as "Houses," "Gardens," "Furniture," and "Public Transport"—and all repeated the hegemonic line about how functional and truthful design was vital to all parts of the material fabric of everyday life. In Alan Jarvis's volume *Inside Out* (Harmonds-worth: Penguin, 1946), for instance, the "vulgar" and "coarse" decoration on a piece of gaudy pottery was presented alongside what appeared to be an overly made-up young woman but was, in fact, an image of a transvestite by the photographer John Deakin. This was one of the clearest intimations of how the aesthetic principles of good design spilled over into a reactionary concern about nonnormative and sexual-ized metropolitan display; see Matless, *Landscape and Englishness*, 263–64.

69. For a discussion of Burton's and the "classless" aspirations of postwar mens-wear, see Frank Mort, *Cultures of Consumption: Masculinities and Social Space in Late Twentieth-Century Britain* (London and New York: Routledge, 1996), 134–45.

70. Hughes, "The Spivs," 76; see also Gavin and Lowe, "Designing Desire," 60.

71. Warth, "Evil Men" (May 25, 1952), 6.

72. Ibid.

73. Quoted in "Montagu: Story of a Party," 5.

74. "I Wasn't Ashamed, Airman Tells Peer's QC," *Daily Mirror*, March 17, 1954, 6.

75. Cited in "Q.C. and the 'Missing' 7 Witnesses," *Daily Mirror*, March 23, 1954, 6.

76. Warth, "Evil Men" (May 25, 1952), 6.

77. Eve Kosofsky Sedgwick has written of this epistemology as that of "it takes one to know one," and has found it central to the organization of knowledge of male same-sex desire in the West since the late nineteenth century; see *Epistemology of the Closet* (Harmondsworth: Penguin, 1994), 100–101 and 222.

78. Tom Tullett, "Yard Picks the Men to Fight Vice," *Sunday Pictorial*, December 13, 1953, 4.

79. Matt Houlbrook has found the systematic deployment of plainclothes officers within London's streets, parks, and public urinals to have been a regular practice since at least the 1920s. See his *Queer London*, 25–36.

80. Wolfenden et al., *Report of the Committee on Homosexual Offences and Prosti-tution*, 43–44, para. 121; see also Frank Mort, "Mapping Sexual London: The Wolf-enden Committee on Homosexual Offences and Prostitution 1954–7," *New Formations* no. 37 (spring 1999): 92–113.

81. Tom Harrisson and BW, "Plan for Investigation on *Britain Can Make It* by Mass-Observation for the Council of Industrial Design" (October 8, 1946) (Mass Observation Archive [MOA]/TC26/1/A), 3.

3. Trial by Photobooth

1. Gordon Westwood, *Society and the Homosexual* (New York: E. P. Dutton and Co., 1953), 21. Schofield would later go on to publish work on male homosexuality under his own name.

2. See also Mary Renault's *The Charioteer* (1953), James Courage's *A Way of Love* (1959), and Rupert Croft-Cooke, *The Verdict of You All* (London: Secker and War-burg, 1955).

3. Richard Dyer explores this idea of the hegemonic project in his essay "*Victim: Hegemonic Project,*" 71–88.

4. Waters, "Havelock Ellis, Sigmund Freud and the State," 165–79.

5. Gavin and Lowe, "Designing Desire," 59–61.

6. See Waters, "Havelock Ellis, Sigmund Freud and the State."

7. Westwood, *Society and the Homosexual,* 72.

8. Wolfenden et al., *Report of the Committee on Homosexual Offences and Prostitution,* 7, para. 1.

9. Ibid., 24, para. 61.

10. Bacon's 1967 painting *Four Studies for a Self-Portrait* marks something of a departure in the artist's oeuvre. A single tall, thin canvas, the four component images of Bacon's head and shoulders are stacked one on top of the other, each contained within its own pictorial frame, in a way that expressly mimics the photobooth format. This effect is further underscored by the visual replication between the portraits, their common dark red background and the minor variations in the artist's pose (as if each successive image involves a time lapse of just a couple of seconds). Of course, Bacon may have drawn on photobooth imagery in earlier canvases, but on this I am unable to speculate.

11. Simon Ofield, "Cecil Beaton: Designs on Francis Bacon," *Visual Culture in Britain* 7, no. 1 (2006): 21–38.

12. David Sylvester, *Interviews with Francis Bacon* (London and New York: Thames and Hudson, 1975), 70.

13. Ibid., 71–72.

14. See O'Neill, *London—After a Fashion,* 101–25.

15. Quoted in "Survivors," *Time* 54, no. 21 (November 21, 1949): 28.

16. Westwood, *Society and the Homosexual,* 107. Subsequent references are given in the text.

17. Ibid., 28–30. Kinsey had published his groundbreaking study *Sexual Behavior in the Human Male* in 1948, although its take-up by homosexual reformers in Britain was marked by its uneasy tension with competing sexological models of inversion and psychoanalytic etiologies; see Waters, "Disorders of the Mind, Disorders of the Body Social," 134–51.

18. Houlbrook, *Queer London,* esp. 167–94.

19. Westwood, *Society and the Homosexual,* 116.

20. Ibid., 85.

21. Houlbrook and Waters, "*The Heart in Exile,*" 142–65.

22. Westwood, *Society and the Homosexual,* 125. Subsequent references are given in the text.

23. For accounts of the HLRS, see Jeffrey Weeks, *Coming Out: Homosexual Politics in Britain from the Nineteenth Century to the Present,* rev. ed. (London: Quartet, 1990), 169–78; Antony Grey, *Quest for Justice: Towards Homosexual Emancipation* (London: Sinclair-Stevenson, 1992).

24. Commander A. Robertson, Oral evidence to the Wolfenden Committee (December 7, 1954) (The National Archives [TNA]: Public Records Office [PRO] HO/345/12/CHP/TRANS/7), 6–7.

25. PC Darlington, Oral evidence to the Wolfenden Committee (December 7, 1954) (TNA: PRO/HO/345/12/CHP/TRANS/8), 10.

26. Leslie J. Moran, *The Homosexual(ity) of Law* (London and New York: Routledge, 1996), 136.

27. Houlbrook, *Queer London,* 139–40, 156–58.

28. Matt Houlbrook, "'The Man with the Powder Puff' in Interwar London," 145–71.

29. Cited in Moran, *The Homosexual(ity) of Law,* 122.

30. Waters, "Disorders of the Mind, Disorders of the Body Social," 134–51; Mort, "Mapping Sexual London," 92–113; Houlbrook, *Queer London,* 256–60.

31. Peter Wildeblood, oral evidence to the Wolfenden Committee (May 24, 1954) (TNA: PRO/HO/345/13/CHP/TRANS/24), 29.

32. Waters, "Disorders of the Mind, Disorders of the Body Social."

33. Wildeblood, oral evidence to the Wolfenden Committee, 7.

34. Wildeblood, *Memorandum to the Departmental Committee on Homosexual Offences and Prostitution,* 1. See Mort, "Mapping Sexual London."

35. Wildeblood, *Memorandum to the Departmental Committee on Homosexual Offences and Prostitution,* 1.

36. Wildeblood, *Against the Law,* 13.

37. Wolfenden et al., *Report of the Committee on Homosexual Offences and Prostitution,* 25, para. 64.

38. "Statement by the Directors of the Photomaton Parent Corporation Limited, issued for public information," *The Times,* April 11, 1928, 17.

39. On the *carte-de-visite,* see Peter Hamilton and Roger Hargreaves, *The Beautiful and the Damned: The Creation of Identity in Nineteenth-Century Photography* (London: Lund Humphries in association with the National Portrait Gallery, 2001), 43–49; John Tagg, *The Burden of Representation: Essays on Photographies and Histories* (Basingstoke: Macmillan, 1988), 48–53; Beaumont Newhall, *A History of Photography from 1839 to the Present* (London: Secker and Warburg, 1982), 64–66.

40. Tagg, *The Burden of Representation,* 64; see also Hamilton and Hargreaves, *The Beautiful and the Damned,* 57–107.

41. For accounts of the Bertillonage system, see Allan Sekula, "The Body and the Archive," *October* no. 39 (1986): 3–64; Martine Kaluszynski, "Republican Identity: Bertillonage as Government Technique," in Jane Caplan and John Torpey, eds., *Documenting Individual Identity: The Development of State Practices in the Modern World* (Princeton, N.J.: Princeton University Press, 2001), 123–38; Hamilton and Hargreaves, *The Beautiful and the Damned,* 7, 66–67, 105–7.

42. It was in 1966 that the British Passport Office finally sanctioned photobooth portraits as a legitimate image for use within its passports. This can be seen as the final dovetailing of two forms of portraiture that had, since their inception, been closely linked—aesthetically, if not yet administratively.

43. Jonathan Crary, *Techniques of the Observer: On Vision and Modernity in the Nineteenth Century* (Cambridge: MIT Press, 1992), 39.

44. Siegfried Kracauer, "The Mass Ornament," trans. Barbara Correll and Jack Zipes, *New German Critique* no. 5 (1975): 67–76.

45. Marshall, "Citizenship and Social Class," 35.

46. See David Alan Mellor, "Realism, Satire, Blow-ups: Photography and the Culture of Social Modernisation," in Chris Stephens and Katherine Stout, eds., *Art and the 60s: This Was Tomorrow* (London: Tate Publishing, 2004), 83.

47. Rowena Agajanian, "'Nothing like Any Previous Musical, British or American': The Beatles' Film, *A Hard Day's Night*," in Anthony Aldgate, James Chapman, and Arthur Marwick, eds., *Windows on the Sixties: Exploring Key Texts in Media and Culture* (London: I. B. Tauris, 2000), 105.

48. Ibid., 98.

49. Ofield, "Cruising the Archive," 351–64.

50. Garland, *The Heart in Exile*, 40; Stuart Lauder, *Winger's Landfall* (London: Eyre and Spottiswood, 1962), 103.

51. Wildeblood, oral evidence to the Wolfenden Committee, 23.

52. Wildeblood, *Against the Law*, 188.

53. "Wildeblood speaks of 'My lonely moments,'" 9.

54. See Alan Sinfield, *The Wilde Century: Effeminacy, Oscar Wilde, and the Queer Movement* (London: Cassel, 1994).

55. See Cook, *London and the Culture of Homosexuality*, 61. In addition, Gill Davies notes how late-nineteenth-century writers on London's East End were preoccupied with the mouth of the working-class woman as a synecdoche for a greedy sensual appetite that troubled the ideological sensibilities of bourgeois restraint ("Foreign Bodies," 64–80).

56. Wildeblood, *Against the Law*, 8.

57. For more on the place of Weimar Germany in the imagining of mid-twentieth-century British homosexuality, see Simon Ofield, "Wrestling with Francis Bacon," *Oxford Art Journal* 24, no. 1 (2001): 113–30.

58. Wyndham Lewis, "Round the London Art Galleries," *The Listener* (November 17, 1949): 860.

59. John Russell, *Francis Bacon* (London and New York: Thames and Hudson, 1971), 38.

60. O'Neill, *London—After a Fashion*, 113.

61. Sir John Nott-Bower, *Memorandum to the Departmental Committee on Homosexual Offences and Prostitution* (November 22, 1954) (TNA: PRO/HO/345/7/CHP/10), unpaginated.

62. Sir John Nott-Bower, oral evidence to the Wolfenden Committee, (December 7, 1954) (TNA: PRO/HO/345/12/CHP/TRANS/7), 24.

63. Ibid.

64. "Murder Check Again on A6," *The Times*, August 30, 1961, 6.

65. "Identification Parade," *The Spectator* no. 6949 (September 1, 1961): 277.

66. Paul Foot, *Who Killed Hanratty?* (London: Jonathan Cape, 1971), 49.

67. Louis Blom-Cooper, *The A6 Murder, Regina v. James Hanratty: The Semblance of Truth* (Harmondsworth: Penguin, 1963), 70–71.

68. Nick Hopkins and Owen Bowcott, "40 Years after His Execution, Appeal Judges say DNA Is Certain Proof of Hanratty's Guilt," *The Guardian,* May 11, 2002, 5.

4. Of Public Libraries and Paperbacks

1. Wolfenden et al., *Report of the Committee on Homosexual Offences and Prostitution,* 67, para. 196.

2. Edward Glover, "Introduction," to Westwood, *Society and the Homosexual,* 11.

3. Westwood, *Society and the Homosexual,* 149, 158–59.

4. See Roger Chartier, "The Practical Impact of Writing," in Roger Chartier, ed., *A History of Private Life,* vol. 3: *Passions of the Renaissance,* trans. Arthur Goldhammer (Cambridge, Mass., and London: Belknap Press, 1989), 111–59; Alain Corbin, "The Secret of the Individual," in Michelle Perrot, ed., *A History of Private Life,* vol. 4: *From the Fires of Revolution to the Great War,* trans. Arthur Goldhammer (Cambridge, Mass., and London: Belknap Press, 1990), esp. 534–47.

5. See, for instance, Kevin Porter and Jeffrey Weeks, eds., *Between the Acts: Lives of Homosexual Men, 1885–1967* (London and New York: Routledge, 1991), 24, 36, 61, 86, 127; Hall Carpenter Archives, *Walking after Midnight: Gay Men's Life Stories* (London and New York: Routledge, 1989), 33, 60, 170. For similar moments in the postwar period, see National Lesbian and Gay Survey, *Proust, Cole Porter, Michelangelo, Marc Almond, and Me* (London and New York: Routledge, 1993), 35–36, 39, 83, 86, 92; Brighton Ourstory Project, *Daring Hearts* (Brighton: QueenSpark, 1992), 90–92.

6. Stuart Laing, "The Production of Literature," in Alan Sinfield, ed., *Society and Literature, 1945–1970* (London: Methuen, 1983), 139.

7. See ibid., 135–41; Thomas Kelly, *History of Public Libraries in Great Britain, 1845–1975,* 2d ed. (London: Library Association, 1977).

8. Abercrombie and Forshaw, *The County of London Plan,* 140.

9. Swanson, *Drunk with the Glitter,* esp. 54–72.

10. See, for instance, W. A. Munford, *Penny Rate: Aspects of British Public Library History, 1850–1950* (London: Library Association, 1951); W. J. Murison, *The Public Library: Its Origins, Purpose, and Significance* (London: George G. Harrap & Co., 1955).

11. W. A. Munford, "The Public Library Idea," *Library Association Record* 57 (1955): 348. See also John Minto, *A History of the Public Library Movement in Great Britain, and Ireland* (London, George Allen & Unwin, 1932), esp. 79.

12. Lionel R. McColvin, "Public Libraries Today," *Library Association Record* 52 (1950): 331.

13. James D. Stewart, "The London Borough Libraries," in Raymond Irwin and Ronald Staveley, eds., *The Libraries of London,* 2d ed. (London: The Library Association, 1964), 118–21.

14. Ibid., 110.

15. Ibid., 111.

16. Michel Foucault, "Different Spaces," in James D. Faubion, ed., *Aesthetics, Method, and Epistemology* (Harmondsworth: Allen Lane, 1998), 182.

17. See Sigmund Freud, "The Unconscious," trans. James Strachey, in Angela Richards, ed., *The Pelican Freud Library,* vol. 11: *On Metapsychology, the Theory of Psychoanalysis* (Harmondsworth: Penguin, 1984), 167–210.

18. Cited in J. P. Lamb, "Teaching the Use of Books and Libraries: A Sheffield Experiment," *Library Association Record* 51 (1949): 102; emphasis in the original.

19. Freud, "The Unconscious," 175.

20. Cited in F. S. Green, "The Missing Three Quarter," *Library Association Record* 57 (1955): 392.

21. Charles A. Elliott, "The Library's Public," *Library Association Record* 53 (1951): 223; emphasis in the original.

22. J. E. Morpurgo, *Allen Lane: King Penguin* (London: Hutchinson, 1979), 80.

23. "The Aristocrat of Paperbacks," *Liaison: Library Association News-Sheet* (October 1959): 85.

24. Ibid.; emphasis in the original.

25. "The Gay Look (or Just Plain Nasty?)," *Liaison: Library Association News-Sheet* (October 1959): 91.

26. Foucault, "Different Spaces," 182.

27. Desmond Flower, "The Paper-back: Its Past, Present and Future," *Library Association Record* 62 (1960): 180.

28. Wolfgang Schivelbusch, *The Railway Journey: The Industrialization of Time and Space in the Nineteenth Century* (Berkeley: University of California Press, 1986), 64–69.

29. Hans Schmoller, "The Paperback Revolution," in Asa Briggs, ed., *Essays in the History of Publishing: In Celebration of the 250th Anniversary of the House of Longman, 1724–1974* (London: Longman, 1974), 289; Rachel Bowlby, *Just Looking: Consumer Culture in Dreiser, Gissing and Zola* (London: Methuen, 1985), 86–89. For the anxieties around "railway reading," see Tony Davies, "Transports of Pleasure: Fiction and Its Audiences in the Later Nineteenth Century," in *Forms of Pleasure* (London and New York: Routledge, 1983), 46–58.

30. Richard Hoggart, *The Uses of Literacy* (Harmondsworth: Penguin, 1958), 211.

31. Cited in C. H. Rolph, ed., *The Trial of Lady Chatterley: Regina v. Penguin Books Limited* (Harmondsworth: Penguin, 1961), 27.

32. Ibid., 230.

33. Kenneth Tynan, "Lady Chatterley's Trial," *The Observer,* November 6, 1960, 21–25; Peter Lewis, "The Day of the Penguin: . . . and It's Lunch with the Legal Lady in W1," *Daily Mail,* November 11, 1960, 9.

34. "What London Read Yesterday . . . : Second Printing of 'Lady C.' in Hand," *Guardian,* November 11, 1960, 16.

35. Cited in Rolph, *The Trial of Lady Chatterley,* 39.

36. Ibid.

37. Rachel Bowlby, "'But She Could Have Been Reading *Lady Chatterley*': the Obscene Side of the Canon," in *Shopping with Freud* (London and New York: Routledge, 1993).

38. Cited in Rolph, *The Trial of Lady Chatterley,* 18–19. Subsequent references are given in the text.

39. The irony here is that, contrary to the resolutions of the trial, Lawrence's novel ambiguously celebrates anal sex, rather than procreative coitus, as the ultimate achievement of sexual intimacy. See chapter 12 of D. H. Lawrence, *Lady Chatterley's Lover* (Harmondsworth: Penguin, 1960), esp. 171–85.

40. Kenneth Walker, *The Physiology of Sex and Its Social Implications* (Harmondsworth: Penguin, 1940), 124–25.

41. Kenneth Walker and Peter Fletcher, *Sex and Society* (Harmondsworth: Penguin, 1955), 72.

42. Anthony Storr, *Sexual Deviation* (Harmondsworth: Penguin, 1964), 12.

43. Walker and Fletcher, *Sex and Society,* 72.

44. West, *Homosexuality* (Harmondsworth: Pelican, 1960), 133.

45. Ibid., 13.

46. Walker and Fletcher, *Sex and Society,* 11.

47. G. M. Carstairs, "Editorial Preface," in Storr, *Sexual Deviation,* 7.

48. Richard Dyer, "Coming Out as Going In: The Image of the Homosexual as a Sad Young Man," in *The Matter of Images,* 73–92.

49. West, *Homosexuality,* 50, 181; see also Houlbrook and Waters, "The Heart in Exile," 142–65.

50. Susan Stryker, *Queer Pulp: Perverted Passions from the Golden Age of the Paperback* (San Francisco: Chronicle Books, 2001).

51. Dyer, "Coming Out as Going In," 84.

52. Alexander Connell, "A Successful Prosecution," *Library Association Record* 65 (1963): 102.

53. D. A. Miller, *The Novel and the Police* (Berkeley: University of California Press, 1988).

54. Cited in John Lahr, *Prick Up Your Ears: The Biography of Joe Orton* (Harmondsworth: Penguin, 1980), 95–96.

55. Simon Shepherd, *Because We're Queers: The Life and Crimes of Kenneth Halliwell and Joe Orton* (London: Gay Men's Press, 1989), 14.

5. Life in the Cybernetic Bedsit

1. Houlbrook, *Queer London,* 19–37.

2. Westwood, *Society and the Homosexual,* 157, 42.

3. See Swanson, *Drunk with the Glitter.*

4. Mass-Observation, "A Report on *Britain Can Make It,*" Section C, 42; emphasis in the original.

5. Ibid.

6. Mass-Observation, "Furnishing," *Mass-Observation Bulletin* no. 49 (March–June 1953): 3. Sally McDonald and Julia Porter have since challenged M-O's findings, claiming that reactions to contemporary interior design were far more complex and fluid both among and between classes; see Sally MacDonald and Julia Porter, *Putting on the Style: Setting up Home in the 1950s* (London: Geffrye Museum, 1990).

7. Mass-Observation, "Furnishing," 4.

8. Ibid., 5.

9. Ibid.

10. John Ruskin, *The Works of John Ruskin*, vol. 8: *The Seven Lamps of Architecture,* ed. E. T. Cook and Alexander Wedderburn (London: George Allen, 1903), esp. 38–39.

11. Michael Hatt, "Space, Surface, Self: Homosexuality and the Aesthetic Interior," *Visual Culture in Britain* 8, no. 1 (2007): esp. 106–11.

12. See Cook, *London and the Culture of Homosexuality,* 55–59; Cohen, *Talk on the Wilde Side,* 179–80. In 1948, these logics were brought back into public attention by H. Montgomery Hyde's publication of his transcripts of the trial, *The Trials of Oscar Wilde* (London: William Hodge, 1948); see also H. Montgomery Hyde's short article "Oscar Wilde and His Architect," *Architectural Review* 109, no. 651 (March 1951): 175–76, in which Wilde's fastidious overinvestment in the decor of his Tite Street home is presented as destabilizing and eventually undermining its ability to function as a support for a healthy, loving bourgeois family.

13. Christopher Reed, "Design for (Queer) Living: Sexual Identity, Performance, and Décor in British *Vogue,* 1922–1926," *GLQ* 12, no. 3 (2006): 377–403; see also his *Bloomsbury Rooms: Modernism, Subculture, and Domesticity* (New Haven: Yale University Press, 2004).

14. Jean Baudrillard, *The System of Objects,* trans. James Benedict (London: Verso, 1996), 15–17. This book was first published in French in 1968.

15. Walter Benjamin found something similar in the drawing rooms of nineteenth-century Paris, in which a profusion of casings and coverings retained the imprinted marks of the inhabitants' respectable bodily life. See Walter Benjamin, *Charles Baudelaire: A Lyric Poet in the Era of High Capitalism,* trans. Harry Zohn (London: Verso, 1983), 167–69.

16. Garland, *The Heart in Exile,* 44–45.

17. Ibid., 39.

18. Ibid., 40.

19. For a reading of this passage in relation to the wider sexual ambiguities of the photograph in postwar visual culture, see Ofield, "Cruising the Archive," 351–64.

20. Mary Renault, *The Charioteer* (1953; London: New English Library, 1977), 186–87.

21. Ibid., 194.

22. Ibid., 192–93. For an alternative reading of these interiors in relation to the sexualized postwar dichotomy between "serious" fine art and trivial decoration, see Ofield, "Cecil Beaton," 21–38.

23. Renault, *The Charioteer,* 194.

24. Council of Industrial Design, *Furnishing to Fit the Family* (London: Council of Industrial Design, 1947), 46.

25. See Richard Dyer, "Homosexuality and Film Noir," in *The Matter of Images,* 56–57.

26. Council of Industrial Design, "Design for a Housewife's Home," in *New Home, No. 2* (London: Council of Industrial Design, 1948), 3.

27. Council of Industrial Design, *Ideas for Your Home* (London: His Majesty's Stationery Office, 1950), 2.

28. Council of Industrial Design, "Design for a Housewife's Home," 2.

29. Margaret Llewellyn, *Design and Our Homes* (Loughborough and London: COID and the Co-operative Union Ltd., 1951), 7; my emphasis.

30. Council of Industrial Design, *Furnishing to Fit the Family,* 4.

31. Ibid., 45–46.

32. In the same way, more conventionally "family" interiors were perpetually couched in terms of how much cleaning they saved for the housewife, while defining what that housework was and where it would take place. See, for example, Council of Industrial Design, "Design for a Housewife's Home," 2–5.

33. Alan Jarvis, "How to Make the Most of What You Have," in Gordon Russell and Alan Jarvis, *How to Furnish Your Home (with a Shopping Guide by Veronica Nisbet)* (London: Newman Neame, 1953), unpaginated.

34. Council of Industrial Design, *Furnishing to Fit the Family,* 5–6.

35. Good Housekeeping, *Furnishing To-day* (London: National Magazine Co, n.d. [1946?]), unpaginated.

36. Baudrillard, *The System of Objects,* 18.

37. Ibid., 25.

38. Veronica Nisbit, "Shopping Guide to Light and Colour," in Russell and Jarvis, *How to Furnish Your Home,* unpaginated.

39. Ibid.

40. Baudrillard, *The System of Objects,* 26.

41. Nisbet, "Shopping Guide to Light and Colour."

42. Llewellyn, *Design and Our Homes,* 35.

43. Margaret Llewellyn, *Colour and Pattern in Your Home* (Loughborough and London: Co-Operative Union Ltd. and COID, n.d. [after 1956]), 23.

44. See Baudrillard, *The System of Objects,* 35.

45. T. Kilburn, "The University of Manchester Universal High-Speed Digital Computing Machine," *Nature* 164 (October 22, 1949): 684–87; T. Kilburn, "The New Universal Digital Computing Machine at the University of Manchester," *Nature* 168 (July 1951): 95–96; School of Computer Science, University of Manchester, *50th Anniversary pages* (available at www.computer50.org; accessed 03.02.08).

46. *Faster Than Thought: The Ferranti Nimrod Digital Computer* (Hollinwood: Ferranti, 1951).

47. See Alan M. Turing's two essays "On Computational Numbers, with an Application to the *Entscheidungsproblem,*" *Proceedings of the London Mathematical Society* 2, no. 42 (1937): 230–65, and "Computing Machinery and Intelligence," *Mind* 59, no. 236 (1950): esp. 436–37. For a contextualization of these essays, see Andrew Hodges, *Alan Turing: The Enigma* (London: Vintage, 1987), esp. 96–110.

48. See Jon Agar, *Turing and the Universal Machine* (Cambridge: Icon, 2001), 140–49.

49. Turing, "Computing Machinery and Intelligence," 436.

50. Laplace proposed that if the state of the universe was known in its entirety at one moment in time, then it would be possible to predict all its future states. Turing felt his model to be "rather nearer practicability than that considered by Laplace." See ibid., 440.

51. Council of Industrial Design, "Ask Yourself," in *New Home* (London: Council of Industrial Design, 1946), 15.

52. Nisbet, "Shopping Guide to Light and Colour."

53. See, for instance, Llewellyn, *Colour and Pattern in Your Home*, 15–18.

54. Council of Industrial Design, "Setting the Stage," in *New Home* 6; emphasis in the original.

55. Council of Industrial Design, *Rooms Made to Fit: Notes for the Press on the Furnished Rooms* (Mass Observation Archive [MOA]/TC26/1/B), 1–2.

56. ML's report on *Britain Can Make It* (October 22, 1946) (MOA/TC26/4/E). ML was one of Mass-Observation's observers.

57. Turing, "Computing Machinery and Intelligence," 433–34.

58. See John Marshall, "Pansies, Perverts and Macho Men: Changing Conceptions of Male Homosexuality," in Ken Plummer, ed., *The Making of the Modern Homosexual* (London: Hutchinson, 1981), 133–54; Sinfield, *The Wilde Century.*

59. Tyler Curtain, "The 'Sinister Fruitiness' of Machines: *Neuromancer*, Internet Sexuality, and the Turing Test," in Eve Kosofsky Sedgwick, ed., *Novel Gazing: Queer Readings in Fiction* (Durham, N.C.: Duke University Press, 1997), 139.

60. Turing, "Computing Machinery and Intelligence," 434. Ironically, later commentators on Turing's article have argued that the Turing Test's attempt to make a distinction between the physical and the intellectual is wishful thinking, because a machine would only be able to convince the interrogator that it could think if it truly *experienced* the world in a human way, that is, with the same material construction and sensory apparatus as a human being. See Robert M. French, "Subcognition and the Limits of the Turing Test," *Mind* 99, no. 393 (1990): 53–65; Peter Bieri, "Thinking Machines: Some Reflections on the Turing Test," *Poetics Today* 9, no. 1 (1988): 163–86.

61. Turing, "Computing Machinery and Intelligence," 435.

62. On the postwar British "social problem" film, see John Hill, *Sex, Class, and Realism: British Cinema, 1956–1963* (London: British Film Institute, 1986), 67–95. See also Dyer, "*Victim:* Hegemonic Project," 93–110.

63. F. J. Camm, "Our Free Advice Bureau—A Complete Service," *Practical Householder* 2, no. 16 (March 1957): 281.

64. See, for instance, "Making the Best of It," in *New Home*, 26–29.

65. See, for instance, "Colour Schemes for Interior Decoration," *Practical Householder* 2, no. 21 (August 1957): 765–66; D. G. J., "Colour in the Home," *Do It Yourself* 3, no. 4 (April 1959): 335–36.

66. F. J. Camm, "D.I.Y. Advertisements," *Practical Householder* 3, no. 29 (April 1958): 443.

67. Council of Industrial Design, "6d Guide" to *Design Fair: A Travelling Exhibition* (London: His Majesty's Stationery Office, n.d. [late 1940s]), unpaginated.

68. Arthur Marwick, *The Home Front* (London and New York: Thames and Hudson, 1976), 92. See also Paul Atkinson, "Do It Yourself: Democracy and Design," *Journal of Design History* 19, no. 1 (2006): 1–10.

69. See, for instance, Jarvis, "How to Make the Most of What You Have"; Oxford House, *Setting Up Home for Bill and Betty* (London: Whitechapel Art Gallery in

association with Oxford House, 1952); M. Pleydell-Bouverie, *The Daily Mail Book of Post War Homes* (London: Daily Mail, 1944).

70. "It's So Quick and Easy to Brighten Your Home for Winter With . . . ," advertisement for Brolac and Murac P·E·P paints, *Practical Householder* 2, no. 23 (October 1957): 1026.

71. See Janet Finch and Penny Summerfield, "Social Reconstruction and the Emergence of Companionate Marriage, 1945–59," in David Clark, ed., *Marriage, Domestic Life, and Social Change: Writings for Jacqueline Burgoyne (1944–88)* (London and New York: Routledge, 1991), 7–32.

72. Jen Browne, "Decisions in DIY: Women, Home Improvements and Advertising in Post-war Britain," in Maggie Andrews and Mary M. Talbot, eds., *All the World and Her Husband: Women in Twentieth-Century Consumer Culture* (London: Cassell, 2000), 134; see also MacDonald and Porter, *Putting on the Style,* unpaginated.

73. "It started on the 8.14 . . . ," advertisement for Asbestolux fire-safe board, *Practical Householder* 3, no. 35 (October 1958): 1072.

74. Matt Cook, "Homes Fit for Homos: Joe Orton and the Domesticated Queer," in Sean Brady and John Arnold, eds., *What Is Masculinity? Historical Perspectives and Arguments* (Basingstoke: Palgrave Macmillan, forthcoming [2010]).

75. Jane Gaskell, "Joe Has a Colourful Way with Words . . . ," *Daily Sketch,* November 30, 1966, 17.

76. Brian Silk and Peter Burden, "Jealousy Theory in Playwright's Murder," *Daily Sketch,* August 10, 1967, 1.

Conclusion

1. Although this image has conventionally been cited as the work of Richard Hamilton, recent debates have questioned the extent to which the artist John McHale (Hamilton's collaborator on *This Is Tomorrow*) conceived, assembled, and produced the collage; see John-Paul Stonard, "Pop in the Age of Boom: Richard Hamilton's *Just what is it that makes today's homes so different, so appealing?*" *Burlington Magazine* 149, no. 1254 (2007): 607–20. For the sake of this conclusion, I have followed tradition and cited Hamilton as its sole creator.

2. Richard Hamilton, *Collected Words, 1953–1982* (London and New York: Thames and Hudson, 1982), 24; see also David Mellor, "The Pleasures and Sorrows of Modernity: Vision, Space and the Social Body in Richard Hamilton," in the Tate Gallery, ed., *Richard Hamilton* (London: Tate Gallery Publications, 1992), 33; and Isabelle Moffatt, "The Labyrinth, the Laboratory and the Labyratorium," *Third Text* 20, no. 2 (2006): 269–77.

3. Stonard, "Pop in the Age of Boom," 618–19.

4. For two excellent overviews of the Independent Group, see Anne Massey, *The Independent Group: Modernism and Mass Culture in Britain, 1945–59* (Manchester: Manchester University Press, 1995), and David Robbins, ed., *The Independent Group: Postwar Britain and the Aesthetics of Plenty* (Cambridge, Mass., and London: MIT Press, 1990).

5. See Massey, *The Independent Group,* 57–60, and Victoria Walsh, "'Real Imagination Is Technical Imagination,'" in Matthew Gale and Chris Stephens, eds., *Francis Bacon* (London: Tate Publishing, 2008), 78–80.

6. Lawrence Alloway, "City Notes," in Richard Kalina, ed., *Lawrence Alloway: Imagining the Present; Context, Content, and the Role of the Critic* (London and New York: Routledge, 2006), 66. This essay was originally published in the journal *Architectural Design* 29 (January 1959): 34–35.

7. Ibid., 67.

8. Ibid., 66, 67.

9. See, in particular, MacInnes's essays "Young England, Half English: The Pied Piper of Bermondsey" (1957); "See You at Mabel's" (1957); "Pop Songs and Teenagers" (1958); "Sharp Schmutter" (1959); and "A Taste of Reality" (1959). These and several others were later anthologized as Colin MacInnes, *England, Half English: A Polyphoto of the Fifties* (Harmondsworth: Penguin, 1966), which also contains an interesting preface, "Notes for the Penguin Edition," in which MacInnes draws together some of his themes and concerns.

10. Tony Gould, *Inside Outsider: The Life and Times of Colin MacInnes* (London: Allison and Busby, 1993), esp. 93–108.

11. Erwin Fieger, in Erwin Fieger and Colin MacInnes, *London—City of Any Dream* (London and New York: Thames and Hudson, 1962), vii.

12. Colin MacInnes, "City of Any Dream," in ibid., xviii; my emphasis.

13. MacInnes, in Fieger and MacInnes, *London—City of Any Dream,* facing page 72.

14. MacInnes, "City of Any Dream," xxxii.

15. Colin MacInnes, *Absolute Beginners* (Harmondsworth: Penguin, 1986), 55.

16. Ibid.

17. Ibid., 131.

18. Ibid., 53; emphasis in the original.

19. Lawrence Alloway, "'Pop Art' since 1949," *The Listener* (December 27, 1962): 1085–87.

20. Simon Ofield, "Comparative Strangers," in Gale and Stephens, *Francis Bacon,* 64–73.

21. Jeffrey Weeks, *Coming Out: Homosexual Politics in Britain from the Nineteenth Century to the Present,* rev. ed. (London: Quartet, 1990), 191–92.

22. See Lucy Robinson, *Gay Men and the Left in Post-war Britain: How the Personal Got Political* (Manchester: Manchester University Press, 2007), 73–75.

23. Mark W. Turner, "Gay London," in Joe Kerr and Andrew Gibson, *London: From Punk to Blair* (London: Reaktion, 2003), 54.

INDEX

Abercrombie, Patrick, 6, 33, 39, 105, 182, 271n25; neighborhood concept of, 14, 20–21, 41, 71–74, 77, 97, 170–71, 258; remodeling of roads by, 74–75; trajectories structured by, 23, 85–86; vision of, 14, 46–47, 49, 52, 54, 61, 99, 115, 224–25. *See also County of London Plan; Greater London Plan, The*
Absolute Beginners (MacInnes), 255, 257–58, 260
adolescents. *See* youth
advertising: DIY, 234–40; mass-market, 248
Against the Law (Wildeblood), 28–29, 118, 138, 139, 152, 153–55, 164
Agajanian, Rowena, 146
Agar, Jon, 224
age, 45, 49, 115
Aldus Manutius (printer), 176; book covers patterned after, 182, 186
Alloway, Lawrence, 252, 253, 254, 258
"amusing" style, 211, 216
architects: homosexual, 28, 29; modernist, 5, 26; Nazi Germany, 272n51; postwar, 16–17, 21, 22, 23, 252; wartime, 33, 59
archive, library as, 170–74, 177–78, 180, 182, 194. *See also* libraries, municipal branch

A6 murderer, 36, 158–60
Assheton, Ralph, 17
Assize courts, 94–95
Atlantic Charter (1941), 75
atom, motif of, 34–35, 44, 68–76, 78, 275n83

bachelors, 86, 207; middle-class, 7-8, 100, 134; model furnished rooms for, 4, 204–6, 229; perceived as threat, 84; working-class culture of, 7–8, 94. *See also* bedsitting rooms
Bacon, Francis, 117, 258–59; paintings, 121, 150, 281n10; personal appearance, 155, 157; photobooth portraits, 36, 121, 122, 125, 127, 128–29, 149–51, 158. *See also Head II; Head VI; Heads I–VI*
Balcon, Michael, 85, 86
Balfour Declaration (1926), 75
Bantam Books (publisher), 175
Barr, Charles, 86
Barthes, Roland, 117
Baudrillard, Jean, 211–12, 221, 223
Bayswater, 6, 7
Beatles, the, 146
bedsitting rooms, 217–18; model, 204–6, 229; Orton and Halliwell's, 242, 243, 244–45, 247, 250. *See also* furnished rooms
behavior, English norms of, 11, 277n8

293

behavior, queer male: detecting, 114,
    158; as feminized, 7, 9, 10, 93,
    274n75; moral significance of, 28,
    118–19; perceived threats from, 3, 90–
    91; plurality of, 9, 266n19; urban, 3,
    25–30, 105, 138, 163–64. *See also* queer
    activities; queer men; tabloids:
    campaigns against male vice
Bel Geddes, Norman, 272n41
Benjamin, Walter, 287n15
Bentley, Nicholas: cartoons by, 17, 18,
    63, 206, 207
Bermondsey, 69; public library, 170
Bertillonage system, 142, 143, 146
Betjeman, John, 274n75
biography: homosexual identity built
    on, 138–39, 140, 157
Birch, R. E. T., 157–58
Birley, Arthur, 99, 100, 133–34, 206
Blackburn, Raymond, 69
blitz, the: aftermath of, 3, 4, 39, 202;
    everyday life during, 65–68, 70,
    274n75; "myth" of, 44, 65, 273n71
Blom-Cooper, Louis, 160–61
Blue Lamp, The (film), 22–25, 35, 101,
    230, 255
bodies: criminal, 138; interior design
    related to, 218–21, 227, 240, 242,
    287n15; laboring male, 33, 216, 238;
    male, 9, 195, 197, 240, 258–59; spivs',
    9, 19, 20–21; urban planning related
    to, 47, 109, 110; working-class, 9, 134.
    See also cells: biological; prostitution
book covers: *Lady Chatterley's Lover*,
    180, 181, 182, 189; mass-market
    paperbacks, 177, 189, 192, 194; Orton
    and Halliwell's defacement of, 194–
    200; Pelican, 190, 191; Penguin,
    176–77, 178
books: geographies of, 36–37, 166–67,
    176–77; Orton and Halliwell's
    defacement of, 167, 169, 194–200,
    244, 247, 250, 261; readers' relation-
    ship to, 37, 194, 197, 198–99;

timelessness of, 171–72, 173, 174, 175,
    176, 177, 178. *See also* libraries,
    municipal branch; mass-market
    paperbacks; novels; readers/reading
borstal boys, 82, 94, 99
Boulton, Ernest, trial of, 7
bourgeoisie, the. *See* middle classes
Bowlby, Rachel, 183
boys: origins of homosexuality in, 116,
    202; sex education for, 31, 165–66,
    277n17. *See also* youth
Brayshaw, Joseph, 90, 91, 92
Britain: centrality of, 78; culture of, 13,
    86; postwar, 4, 6, 17, 59, 61, 75–77;
    values of, 31, 58, 117, 131–32, 169.
    See also Festival of Britain; London
Britain Can Make It (exhibition,
    COID), 14–16, 34, 41–44, 52–55, 61,
    96, 110; architects portrayed in, 17,
    18, 22; exhibition guide, 39, 53, 54–55;
    families depicted in, 32, 77, 79, 100,
    248; Furnished Rooms display, 63–65,
    97, 201, 203, 204–7, 212, 216–18, 229,
    258, 274n75; Mass-Observation's
    survey for, 114–15, 206, 226–27;
    message of, 73, 178; time spent at,
    55, 56; visitors to, 76, 102, 109, 251.
    See also Council of Industrial
    Design
British Museum, 9
British Nationality and Status of Aliens
    Act (1914), 142
broken homes, 26, 27, 30
built environment: individual's
    relationship to, 33, 42, 50, 57–58, 63,
    109; management of, 39, 48, 261;
    moving through, 3, 16, 44, 54, 84,
    116; planned, 42, 118
Burgess, Guy, 91
Butcher, Police Constable, 106

cafés, 82, 101–2, 104, 108
Calder, Angus, 65
camera obscura, 143–44

Campaign for the Preservation of Rural England, 6

capital: accumulation of, 33, 168; flows of, 75, 76, 77

capitalism: consumer, 33–34; laissez-faire, 21, 40; management of, 12–13, 34, 203, 235; mid-twentieth-century, 10, 268n29; Victorian, 4. *See also* economy

carte-de-visite photography, 141, 142

Carter, E. J., 252

cells: biological, 70, 72–73; as metropolitan structure, 71

Charing Cross Road, 180, 182, 214

Charing Cross Underground Station, exhibit in. *See Register Your Choice*

Charioteer, The (Renault), 29, 214–16, 227, 242, 257

Charlotte Street shootings, 19, 22

children: corruption of, 210, 211; effects of color on, 223; origins of homosexuality in, 116, 119–20, 130–31, 138–39, 163–64, 187–88, 202; social investment in, 16, 115. *See also* boys; youth

Children's Play Streets, 48

choreographies: illicit, 35, 79; of photobooths, 150; of public spaces, 102, 137; sexual, 194, 195; urban, 15, 42–43, 52–65. *See also* movement

Churchill, Winston, 273n73

cigarette box, symbolism of, 213–14, 230

circuits/circulations: prescribed, 23, 24, 44, 59, 103, 105, 112; queer, 242, 260; repetitious, 42, 52, 72, 73–74, 76, 77. *See also* cycles

citational logics. *See* criminality: queer citations of; sign systems: queer

citizenship: in *Britain Can Make It*, 205; built environment's relationship to, 33, 42, 50, 57–58, 63, 109; domestic environment as preparation for, 30, 201–3, 235; library's role in, 171, 173, 174, 180, 197; managed, 101, 224;

national, 58, 110, 145; as participation, 44, 118, 150, 198; photobooth's portrayal of, 143, 144, 145, 154; post-war, 17, 20–22, 23, 32, 35; reformist, 96, 211; social, 13, 14–15, 28, 36, 97, 115, 125, 194; spatial, 16, 35, 42, 50, 57–58, 79, 84, 105; urban, 3, 15, 26, 115; wartime, 234

citizenship, model for homosexual, 31, 33–34, 115–18, 128–40, 149–61, 163–64, 188; Wolfenden Committee's portrayal of, 29–30, 36, 120–21, 259

"Citizenship and Social Class" (essay, Marshall), 11–14, 21, 41, 97, 98, 145, 171

Clarke, T. E. B., 35, 106

classes: disparities among, 4, 12, 22, 41, 49; exploitation of, 8; hierarchies of, 14, 46, 64, 86, 91; intermingling of, 14, 25, 51, 96–100, 116, 253; queer encounters among, 36, 92–93, 128, 135; transgression of boundaries, 98, 115, 183, 258, 266n19. *See also* middle classes; sociality: interclass; upper classes; working classes

Cleveland Street affair (1890-91), 8, 82

clothing: Beatles', 146; in *The Lavender Hill Mob*, 110; queer, 7, 137, 158, 161; spivs', 19, 20, 26, 96; wartime, 109–10

Clouds of Witness (Sayers), defacement of, 198

Code Napoléon, 91

cohesion: in interior design, 221, 222, 225, 235; metropolitan, 40, 51, 73; national, 14–15, 42; social, 26; spatial, 53, 261. *See also* classes: intermingling of; communities: integration of

collages: Orton and Halliwell's, 37, 195, 197, 199, 242–44, 247–48, 250, 259

color: in interior design, 206, 215, 218, 221–24, 226–27, 234

commodities, 192, 199, 236; in *Britain Can Make It*, 54, 63; movement of, 75, 76, 77; semiotic fidelity of, 109.

See also consumption; decoration; furnishings; mass-market paperbacks

Commonwealth, British, 75–77; London as center of, 40, 76, 89–90

communication: cybernetic, 229; queer codes of, 112–14, 137, 140

communities: balanced, 14; civic, 86; hierarchies of, 24; integration of, 40, 46, 63, 64, 97; local, 31; national, 15, 21, 64, 145, 258; queer, 115; urban, 45, 52, 127, 258. *See also* cohesion; design for community living; neighborhoods

commuters/commuting, 49, 50, 104, 105, 240

computer science, 223–27

"Computing Machinery and Intelligence" (Turing), 227–29, 289n60

Conekin, Becky, 59

conflict: preclusion of, 14, 89, 97, 172. *See also* dissent: preclusion of

Connell, Alexander, 195

consensus, 11, 15, 46, 50, 86, 178; social, 2–3, 12, 44; urban, 47, 48, 97, 145

conservatism, 14, 51–52, 64

conspiracies, queer, 108–16

consumption: bourgeois forms of, 4, 5; bureaucratization of, 168, 175, 200, 203, 235; destabilizing effects of, 33–34, 178, 235–36; inappropriate acts of, 19, 20, 25, 35, 93, 96, 99–100; orgies of, 115, 206; queer male, 200, 247, 248; urban, 169, 259, 260, 261

"contemporary" style, 204–17, 234, 248; abstract principles of, 219, 244; in France, 221; freedoms brought to queer men, 32, 204, 229, 232–33; reactions to, 222, 286n6; as social management, 37, 203

control, 203–4, 227, 229, 257

Cook, Matt, 242, 266n19

Cornelius, Henry, 19, 277n11

corruption: changing views of, 130; "contemporary" style symbolic of, 210, 211–12, 214; perceived queer,

93–94, 95, 112, 277n17; of youth, 8, 100, 233

Council of Industrial Design (COID), 11, 111, 224, 279n68; "contemporary" style advocated by, 32, 33, 211, 216–17; design advice from, 37, 203–4, 229-31, 232, 234, 235, 236. *See also Britain Can Make It;* Festival of Britain

County of London Plan (Abercrombie and Forshaw), 14–16, 34, 42–52, 59, 71, 79; message of, 64–65, 75–76; neighborhoods in, 87; order to be brought by, 73, 104, 107–8, 252; public libraries in, 168, 169; suburbs in, 40

Courage, James, 29

courts, judicial, 94–95, 167, 186, 199. *See also* law(s)

Coward, Noël, 163

Crary, Jonathan, 143

Crichton, Charles, 35, 84

crime, 19–25, 35, 95–96, 120, 201

criminality: improper use of space perceived as, 104–5, 136–38; lack of movement perceived as, 102, 103, 109; of queer acts, 84, 89, 99, 108; queer citations of, 140, 153, 157–61, 213, 229, 230, 231, 244–45, 259

Criminal Law Amendment Act (1885), 82, 129

criminology: photography used for, 36, 142–43, 146, 158-60; psychiatry and, 20, 26, 30, 118, 138, 160–61

culture: American mass, 6, 20; bachelor, 7–8, 94; bourgeois, 4–6, 9, 29–30, 173; British, 13, 86; reconstruction, 43, 44; state policies toward, 31, 168; street, 92, 134; timelessness of, 86, 171; urban, 144, 146, 250, 255, 260; youth, 253, 257–58. *See also* London: queer culture in

Curtain, Tyler, 228

cycles: atom as motif for, 73; of display and consumption, 178; of repetition,

34, 49–50, 52; of routines, 16, 63, 79. *See also* circuits/circulations; movement

Darling, Elizabeth, 5
Darlington, Police Constable, 137, 182
Davies, Gill, 283n55
Day, Robin, poster by, 77, 78
Deakin, John, 279n68
Dearden, Basil, 22, 32
decency, 132, 140, 151
decoration: bourgeois influences, 64, 168; "contemporary style," 217–18, 232, 233; Victorian era, 210, 211, 216, 233. *See also* display; furnishings
delinquency, 28, 201, 257. *See also* spivs
democracy, 59, 252; role of libraries in, 169, 172, 173, 174. *See also* social democracy
design. *See* decoration; interior design; reconstruction, postwar; town planning
Design and Industries Association (DIA). *See Register Your Choice*
design for community living, 10–16
Design Reform movement, 210
desire, 11, 24–25, 86, 195, 240; homosexual, 3, 132, 137–38, 163–65, 202, 280n77; illicit, 101, 197–98; queer male, 89–101, 118, 169, 266n19; selfish, 21, 108
Details of Jeremy Stretton (Lindrop), 29, 118
deviation, 21, 35, 111, 189, 240; interior decoration as indicator of, 210, 216; queer, 164, 213, 244–45; sexual, 106, 187, 190; signs of, 139, 153; spatial, 58, 105, 106, 108, 183. *See also* masculinity, deviant; pleasure, textual (perverse); spivs
Dilly Boys, 137
discipline: through interior design, 204, 229; in libraries, 197, 198

discretion, 8, 29, 30, 36, 101; bourgeois codes of, 21, 135–36, 151, 164, 202–3, 206, 283n55
disharmony: elimination of, 10–11, 12, 14, 15
disorder: aesthetic, 39; leisure-related, 26; preclusion of, 10–11; public, 9, 131, 132, 164–65, 202; queer, 83, 131, 132, 137; sexual, 8, 50, 108, 164–65; social, 35, 115; spatial, 86, 103, 108; temporal, 102, 105; urban, 6–7, 89, 98, 134. *See also* order
displacement: Freud's concept of, 85
display, 178, 189, 252, 259, 261, 279n68. *See also* decoration; furnishings
dissent: preclusion of, 11, 12, 15, 22, 86. *See also* conflict: preclusion of
distractions: at interstitial times, 102, 104, 108; of mass-market paperbacks, 169, 183, 195; urban, 76, 174, 259
dockyards, 4, 8
Do-It-Yourself (DIY), 37, 204, 233–45, 247; advertisements for, 234–240, 241; companionate aspects of, 236, 237; homosocial ambiguity of, 33, 236, 238, 239
Do It Yourself (magazine), 234–40
Dome of Discovery *(South Bank Exhibition)*, 69, 72
domestic environment: confinement of homosexual activities to, 8, 136, 151, 164, 202, 216; criminality vs. virtue of, 230–31; as formative space of citizenship, 30, 201–3, 235; interior design of, 37, 64, 211–12, 236; queer, 33, 211, 212–16, 244–45, 247–48, 250; reformation of, 32, 77, 118, 201–4, 219–21; sanctity of, 100–101, 115. *See also* home, the
Du Maurier, George: cartoons of, 210
Dyer, Richard, 192, 194

Ealing Studios: films by, 19, 22, 35, 84, 85
East End, the, 9, 45, 139, 283n55

economy: consumer, 248, 259; disparities in, 4, 10, 12, 39, 44, 115; exchange
in, 84; expansion of, 5–6, 7, 21, 76;
leisure, 26; urban, 34, 97, 127. *See also*
capitalism; moral economy; welfare
state
education, 266n19. *See also* sex
education
electrons, 73–74. *See also* atom, motif of
Eliot, T. S., 89
Elliott, Charles A., 174–75, 177
emotions: homosexual, 91, 120, 130, 151,
160, 164, 213, 214; in *Lady Chatterley's
Lover*, 189; maturation of, 166, 169,
187, 204
England. *See* Britain
English, Arthur, 17
ephemera, 174–79, 218, 259. *See also*
mass-market paperbacks
epistemology, queer, 113, 280n77
Eros (Gilbert), 103
eroticism, 184–85, 216; queer, 19, 25, 90,
149–50, 190, 195
ethnicity, 253, 266n19
eugenics, 26
everyday life: carried on during blitz,
65–68, 70, 274n75; of homosexuals,
136, 165; interior design for, 217, 221,
225, 279n68; management of, 3, 10–
16, 42, 48, 50–51, 54, 77; mass-market
paperbacks' invasion of, 168–69;
prescriptions for, 63, 64, 89; routines
of, 32, 44, 47; spatialization of, 15, 31,
35, 220, 224, 268n29; urban, 252–53
*Everything You Always Wanted to Know
about Sex* (Reuben), 260–61
"Evil Men" (newspaper series, Warth),
81, 82, 90–92, 94, 101, 102, 104, 110,
112, 113, 117
exhibitionism, 21, 27
Exhibition of Science, 69, 70, 71, 72–73,
74, 223; poster for, 77, 78
exhibitions. *See* Britain Can Make It;
Festival of Britain; Futurama; *Parallel
of Life and Art; Register Your Choice;
South Bank Exhibition; This Is
Tomorrow*

facial expressions, 137, 153. *See also* glad
eyes; smiles
factories, 5, 47–48
factory workers, 49, 50
fairground, motif of, 177–78
families: in *Britain Can Make It*, 63–64;
as cause of male homosexuality, 119,
202; interior design for, 203–4, 210,
218-19, 220, 287n12, 288n32; social
investment in, 16, 17, 77, 79; wartime
disruptions of, 83–84; working-class,
45. *See also* broken homes; domestic
environment; home, the
feminization, 7, 10, 216, 274n75
Festival of Britain (exhibition), 15, 41,
69–70, 76, 81, 252
Festival Pattern Group, 69
fetishism, 27
Fieger, Erwin, 253–55
Field, William, 105–6
films: postwar British, 86; "spiv cycle,"
20, 22–25, 96; town planning, 44,
270n10. *See also* Ealing Studios, films
by; *and individual films by title*
Finsbury Health Centre, 67, 68, 273n72
First World War, 13
Fletcher, Peter, 188, 189–90
Flower, Desmond, 178
flowers: as decoration, 218
Fontana Press (publisher), 175
Foot, Paul, 160
Fordist era, 7, 144
Forshaw, J. H., 14, 39, 40, 47, 48, 50, 51,
105. *See also County of London Plan*
fort-da game (Freud), 274n75
Foucault, Michel, 171, 177
Four Square (publisher), 192
Four Studies for a Self-Portrait (painting,
Bacon), 281n10
fragmentation, 39, 42, 54, 125, 146, 259

France, 91, 221, 268n29, 287n15
freedom, 32, 42, 52, 72, 74; individual, 57, 75, 85–86; intellectual, 170. *See also* interior design: freedoms brought to queer men
Freeman, Robert: poster for *A Hard Day's Night*, 146–47
freemasonry: queer community as, 113–14, 116
Freud, Sigmund: descriptions of human psyche, 172, 173, 274n75; displacement, 85; models of homosexuality, 9; psychology of, 138, 187, 202
Front Line, 1940-1941 (Ministry of Information), 65–66
furnished rooms, 6, 7, 235. *See also Britain Can Make It;* Furnished Rooms display
furnishings: "contemporary" style, 205–6, 232, 234; for everyday life, 217, 221; guide for deciding on, 223, 225; inherited, 219, 233, 234; moral significance of, 203–4, 211–12. *See also* decoration
Furnishing to Fit Your Family (booklet, COID), 218–19, 220
Futurama (exhibition), 272n41

Games, Abram, 176; poster by, 67–68, 273n73
Garden City Association, 45
Gardner, Helen, 185–86
Garland, Rodney, 29, 118
Gaskell, Jane, 244, 247
Gavin, Owen, 16, 20, 58–59, 61, 109, 118
Gay Liberation Front (GLF), 260–61
gay men, use of term, 266n19. *See also* homosexual, the; queer men
Geddes, Patrick, 47, 70, 271n25
gender: identities, 10, 127; inversion of, 7, 138, 210, 228, 229, 281n17; transgression of boundaries, 49, 183, 258, 266n19; working-class systems of, 92

General Motors Highway and Horizons Exhibit, 272n41
gentlemen's clubs, 4, 135
geographies: of books, 166–67, 176–77, 178, 180; illicit, 24, 25, 79; of male vice, 102; of photobooths, 150; prescriptive, 31, 36–37; queer, 35, 95, 118, 189, 240; of reading, 183, 194–95
Gielgud, John, 83, 95, 102
Gilbert, Albert, 103
glad eyes, 137, 153, 155, 157
glandular inverts, 139
Glover, Edward, 166, 167
Goldfinger, Ernö, 252
Gould, Tony, 253
Great Britain. *See* Britain
Greater London Plan, The (Abercrombie), 14–16, 34, 40, 42–52, 59, 64–65, 73, 79
greed, 92, 93–94, 96. *See also* selfishness
Green Belt, 6, 40, 47, 49, 50, 52, 74
Gregston, Michael: murder of, 158
guardsmen, 82, 92, 94, 100, 206
guidance: terminology of, 55, 57

Halliwell, Kenneth, 253; collages by, 195, 197, 199, 242–44, 259; defacement of books by, 169, 194–200; trial of, 37, 167, 199
Halperin, David, 266n19
Hamilton, Richard, 248, 250, 275n83, 290n1
Hampstead: branch libraries in, 37, 167, 194, 197
Hanratty, James, 160–61
Hard Day's Night, A (film), 146–47
Harlow (new town), 43
harmony, 2–3, 10, 14, 42, 86, 164
Harrisson, Tom, 273n71
Havelock Ellis, Henry, 2, 9
Head II (painting, Bacon), 124, 125
Head VI (painting, Bacon), 123

Heads I–VI (paintings, Bacon), 121, 125, 127, 128–29, 140, 151, 155, 157, 158, 160, 161
health, 4, 5, 10. *See also* homosexuality: as medical condition
Heart in Exile, The (Garland), 29, 118, 150, 164; cover of, 192, 193; interior decoration in, 212–14, 227, 229
Heath, Stephen, 277n17
Henderson, Nigel, 250, 275n83
heteronormativity: of DIY, 236, 242, 244–45; of interior design, 32, 204; of reading, 37, 180, 189, 194
heterosexual-homosexual binary, 10, 132
heterosexuality: companionate, 236, 237; confinement of to private spaces, 135, 140; contrasts in, 24–25; as norm, 132, 186–89, 190, 197
hierarchies, 74, 199; class, 14, 46, 64, 86, 91; economic, 21, 97; neighborhood, 24, 258; social, 51; within the welfare state, 115
history, 173, 224; halting flow of, 34, 52, 59, 61, 63, 77, 89, 171–72, 274n75
Hoggart, Richard, 179, 185, 253
home, the: confining of homosexual acts to, 32, 132, 135; dangers of mass-market paperbacks in, 32, 180, 182; privacy of, 121, 197; sanctity of, 108, 109, 115, 179; as source of male homosexuality, 119, 202; working-class, 43, 64. *See also* broken homes; domestic environment; interior design; living rooms
Home Office Departmental Committee on Homosexuality and Prostitution, 120
homophobia, 260, 261
homosexual, the: freedom brought by interior design, 227, 232–33; genuine, 30, 132–35, 139–40, 153; in literature, 166–67, 212–15, 230; metropolitan, 25–30, 35–36, 119; public visualization of, 127, 157–58; respectable, 29, 138,

151, 163–64, 202, 212, 233, 255, 257; secret knowledge shared by, 113–14, 240; society and, 119–21, 131, 260; spivs compared to, 26–28, 119–21, 131; use of term, 93, 266n19. *See also* citizenship, model for homosexual; novels, homosexual themes in; queer men
homosexual-heterosexual binary, 10, 132
homosexuality: acceptance of, 121, 129–32; adolescent, 187, 188; authentic, 151, 157; decriminalization of, 29, 140; environmental factors of, 30–34, 36–37, 119–20, 163–65, 187–88, 189; as gender inversion, 7, 138, 228; as medical condition, 1–2, 9–10, 25–26, 28, 29, 83, 190; metropolitan, 28–29, 116, 161, 189, 258; models of, 8, 36, 92, 266n19; ontology of, 27–30, 131, 138–39; psychiatric theories of, 83, 84, 94, 116, 118, 165; psychoanalytic theories of, 29–30, 129–30, 138–39, 199, 281n17; as psychological disposition, 116, 118–19, 132, 140, 151–52, 163–64; public visibility of, 28–29, 137–38, 139, 231; respectable, 116, 135, 161, 229, 259. *See also* tabloids: distortion of homosexuality in
Homosexuality (West), 28, 188, 190, 192, 194; cover of, 191
Homosexual Law Reform Society (HLRS), 135
homosexual offences, 1, 31, 82, 94–95, 114, 131, 157; laws relating to, 120, 135, 138, 140, 233, 257. *See also* policing; vice, male
homosociality, 236, 238, 239, 240
Houlbrook, Matt, 7, 82, 94, 137, 280n79
Housing Act (1930), 4–5
Hughes, David, 95, 107, 110
Hume, Kenneth: trial of, 83, 108
Hyde, H. Montgomery, 287n12
Hyde Park, 9

Identikit pictures, 36, 158–60
identity. *See* gender: identities; self, the
imitation game (Turing), 227–33
immaturity: psychic, 164; in reading,
177, 189, 197; sexual, 134, 194, 195,
199; of spivs, 95. *See also* maturity
immorality, 30, 84, 130, 131. *See also*
moral economy; morality
indecency: acts of, 1, 82, 95, 131, 132, 151
Independent Group, 38, 250–51, 252,
253, 255, 258, 275n83
individual, the: autonomy of, 22, 75,
85–86, 105, 108, 252; as basis of
London reconstruction plans, 45–47,
49, 52, 61; photography and, 142,
144–45; relationship to the built
environment, 33, 42, 57–58, 63, 109,
152, 225–26; urban, 115, 254. *See also*
self, the
industrial areas, 4, 48, 75
inequalities, 12, 13, 14, 260
infanto-homosexual, 132–33, 139
Inside Out (Jarvis), 279n68
insincerity, 177, 210, 211, 215, 233
instability: of consumption, 33–34, 178,
235–36; homosocial, 103–4, 240;
library-related, 173–74; metropolitan,
31, 111; of photobooths, 146; sexual,
248; social, 50, 86; spatial, 108, 178–
79; temporal, 180, 182. *See also*
stability
Institute of Contemporary Arts (ICA).
See Independent Group
integrity, civic, 23, 109, 111
Interdepartmental Committee on
Physical Deterioration, 4
interior design: bodies' relationship
to, 218–21, 227, 240, 242, 287n15;
computer science applied to, 224–27,
229, 230; freedoms brought to queer
men, 32, 34, 37, 226, 227, 229, 233;
modern, 210, 218, 230, 233, 234, 247;
moral economy of, 182, 217, 222–23,
229, 230; role in family life, 203–4,

210, 287n12, 288n32; semiotic aspects
of, 218, 221, 225, 229; sexual morality
and, 204–17, 230. *See also* "contemporary" style; Council of Industrial
Design; Do-It-Yourself
internationalism, 253, 258, 260
Interviews with Francis Bacon
(Sylvester), 121, 127–28, 140, 150, 151
intimacy: of photobooths, 141, 149, 150;
sexual, 151, 286n39
Islington, 6; branch libraries in, 37, 167,
194, 195, 197; Orton and Halliwell's
bedsit in, 37, 242, 244, 259

Jarvis, Alan, 220, 279n68
Jennings, V., 177, 178, 183
jobs, 46, 64, 98
journalism. *See* new journalism; press,
the; tabloids
*Just what is it that makes today's homes so
different, so appealing?* (poster image,
Hamilton), 248–50

Kensington, 69, 103, 128, 212, 258,
259. *See also* Britain Can Make It;
Exhibition of Science
Kepes, Gyorgy, 275n83
Kinsey, Alfred, 133, 281n17
Knack and How to Get It, The (film),
147–49
knowledge: books as repositories of,
176–77, 182–83, 186, 199; flows of,
77; heternormative structures of,
180, 190, 197; secret homosexual,
113–14, 240; timelessness of, 171–72,
175, 189
Kracauer, Siegfried, 144
Krafft-Ebing, Richard von, 9

Labourchère Amendment, 82
Lady Chatterley's Lover (Lawrence), 179–
89, 199, 286n39; cover of, 180, 181,
182, 186, 189; Penguin edition of, 37,
163, 167, 180–89

Lancaster, Osbert: cartoons by, 17, 18, 19
Land Utilisation Survey, 47
language: in *Lady Chatterley's Lover,* 185–86; secret queer, 112–13, 115; semiotic, 221
Lansbury Estate (exhibition), 43
Laplace, Pierre-Simon, 288n50
Laski, Harold, 174
Latham, Lord, 44
Lauder, Stuart, 150
Lavender Hill Mob, The (film), 35–36, 84–91, 99–100, 103–4, 106, 107, 110–14, 255, 277n17
law(s), 7, 16, 23, 87, 95, 117. *See also* homosexual offences: laws relating to
Lawrence, D. H., 37, 163, 185, 186. *See also Lady Chatterley's Lover*
leering, 137, 153
Lee Valley, 271n25
Lefebvre, Henri, 268n29
Leicester Square, 92, 102, 103, 105, 259
leisure, 5, 26, 48, 50
lesbians, 192, 257
Lester, Richard, 146, 147
Lever, Arnold, 70
Lewis, Wyndham, 155
libertarianism, British, 57. *See also* freedom
libraries, municipal branch, 31, 36–37, 169–74; discipline in, 197, 198; as heterotopias, 186; *Lady Chatterley's Lover* in, 184; layout of, 171, 173, 195; mass-market paperbacks in, 175–76, 182–83; timelessness of, 172, 173, 177, 178. *See also* archive, library as; readers/reading
Light, Alison, 13
Lindrop, Audrey Erskine, 29, 118
Liverpool Street Station, 178
living rooms, 211, 216–27, 229, 248; outmoded vs. "contemporary," 208–12, 215, 222
living spaces, 46–47

Llewellyn, Margaret, 219–20, 223, 234
loitering, 24, 105, 116, 150, 215; of books, 31, 179, 192; perceived as criminality, 102, 103, 109
London: as ancient network of villages, 14, 40, 45, 51–52, 59, 73–74; as center of Commonwealth, 40, 76, 89–90; interwar years, 3–10; male vice in, 81–84, 93–95, 97; public library network, 167, 169–74; queer culture in, 6–10, 15–16, 34–35, 103, 116–17, 131, 133–35, 192, 257–58, 261; recapitalization of, 74–76, 95. *See also County of London Plan; Greater London Plan, The;* metropolis, the; queer men: metropolitan; reconstruction, postwar; *and individual London districts*
London-City of Any Dream (Fieger), 253–55
Londoners: plans built around, 45–47, 49, 52, 61
London Underground: expansion of, 5
Lowe, Andy, 16, 20, 58–59, 61, 109, 118
lower classes. *See* working classes
lunch hours, 50, 102, 105

MacInnes, Colin, 1, 38, 253, 255, 257–58, 260
Mackendrick, Alexander, 277n11
Maclean, Donald, 91
make-do-and-mend, 234, 235
male perversion: use of term, 93. *See also* perversion
management of mind, 172–73, 177
Marshall, T. H., 11–14, 21, 41, 97, 98, 145, 171
Marshall Plan, 75, 268n29
Marwick, Arthur, 235
masculinity: austere, 213, 242; deviant, 19, 199, 210–11, 231; laboring, 33, 215, 216, 230, 238; normal, 8, 28
mass-market paperbacks, 36–37, 167, 175–79, 184–85; covers of, 168–69, 189, 192; destabilizing effects of, 33,

180, 195; seductiveness of, 182, 197, 200; vulgarity of, 31–32, 210

Mass-Observation surveys, 13, 55, 56, 63, 208, 211, 222. *See also Britain Can Make It*: Mass-Observation's survey for

mass ornament, the, 144

masturbation, 27, 133, 137, 187, 188

maturity, 31, 166, 169, 187–88, 190. *See also* immaturity

Maxwell Fyfe, Sir David, 1

Mayfair, 121, 250; male vice in, 82, 102, 105; reconstruction of, 45, 99–100; upper-class flats in, 4, 206; working-class housing in, 49

McColvin, Lionel, 170

McDonald, Sally, 286n6

McHale, John, 290n1

McNally, Edward, 83; homosexual encounters of, 103, 109, 150, 153, 240; at Montagu trial, 93–94, 96–98, 113

media, 83, 146, 248, 259. *See also* books; films; press, the; tabloids

medicine. *See* health; homosexuality: as medical condition; psychiatry; psychoanalysis; psychology

memory, 214, 224, 274n75; collective, 65, 68, 172, 173

metropolis, the: bustle of, 103, 143, 149–50, 168–69, 178–79, 180, 192; cellular structure of, 71, 72–73; instability of, 31, 178–79, 252–53; management of, 2–3, 10–16, 34, 42, 49, 132; movement through, 25, 257, 258, 260; networks of, 43, 49, 82, 252; postwar, 73, 77, 253–54, 255; remapping of, 47–48; semiotics of, 109, 111, 260; time-lessness of, 59, 61, 74. *See also* homosexual, the: metropolitan; homosexuality: metropolitan; London; perverts, metropolitan; queer men: metropolitan; reconstruction, postwar; renewal: urban; street corners

Metropolitan Joint Fiction Reserve, 170

Metropolitan Police, 22, 82–83, 115, 136, 153, 157

middle classes, 5, 97, 100, 118, 168, 208, 260; codes of privacy and discretion, 21, 135–36, 151, 164, 202–3, 206, 283n55; culture of, 4–6, 9, 29–30, 173; decorative influences of, 64, 168; domestic assumptions of, 32, 43, 168; queer activities among, 8, 9, 10, 28–29, 92, 202

Miller, D. A., 197

mobility, 11, 146; class-related, 21, 96; metropolitan, 34, 42, 49, 52; social, 84, 115, 257. *See also* movement

modernism, 5, 10, 18, 26, 41, 42, 84, 233. *See also* "contemporary" style

modernity, 130, 147, 272n41; civic, 26, 43; narrative of, 5; of reconstruction plans, 51–52, 61

monogamy, 8, 187, 257, 259

Montagu, Lord, 91, 100, 138; trials of, 1, 83, 93, 96–98, 103, 108, 109, 113, 233

moral economy, 32, 119, 134, 182, 212, 214, 217, 222–23, 229, 230

moral imperatives, 2–3, 10, 42, 116, 167, 266n19

morality, 134, 204–17, 222–23, 230, 253

Moran, Leslie, 137

Mort, Frank, 43, 83

movement, 65; atom as motif for, 70, 73; through built environment, 3, 42, 44, 55; of capital, 75, 76, 77; circuits of, 50, 52, 63; deviant, 105; through exhibitions, 54, 55, 57–59; of homosexual desire, 137–38; lack of perceived as criminality, 102, 103, 109; logics of, 34, 87; management of, 23–24, 61; through the metropolis, 25, 36, 114, 257, 258, 260; of people, 49, 76, 77, 224; of readers, 37, 180; transient, 143, 150, 197. *See also* chore-ographies; commuters/commuting;

metropolis, the: bustle of; mobility; trajectories; zigzagging
Munford, W. A., *169*
Murphy, Robert, 20

narrative, 5, 58–59; homosexual identity built on, 138–39, 140, 161, 165
nationality, 266n19
neighborhoods: Abercrombie's concept of, 14, 20–21, 40–41, 71–74, 97, 170–71, 258; centers of, 51, 77, 134; interclass, 45, 46, 64, 97; model, 23, 43. *See also* communities; zoning strategies
Nelson's Column, 61
New English Library (publisher), 175
new journalism, 8, 25, 81–82, 133
New Left writers, 253
newsagents, 175, 177, 194, 197; sale of mass-market paperbacks, 31, 168, 182
News of the World (tabloid), 99, 100, 105–6
new towns, 40, 43, 74
Nicholas, John, 54
nineteenth century. *See* Victorian Era
Nisbet, Veronica, 221–22, 223, 225–26
Nott-Bower, Sir John, 81, 157
Notting Hill, 257, 258
novels, 166, 174; homosexual themes in, 29, 118, 134, 150, 190, 192, 212–16, 230, 253, 254, 255. *See also* mass-market paperbacks
nuclear energy, 69
nucleus, 71, 73–74, 75, 76–77, 78

Obscene Publications Act (1959), 180
obscenity, 180, 182, 186
Ofield, Simon, 127, 150, 258
O'Neill, Alistair, 155
order: civic, 30, 42, 115, 164, 254–55; class, 86; communitarian, 75; domestic, 32, 216, 232; maintenance of, 3, 11; metropolitan, 30–31, 47, 85;

natural, 73; spatial, 40, 48, 108, 138, 178, 185, 224, 274n75; threats to, 22, 23–24, 116. *See also* disorder; harmony; social order
organic formalism, 70
Orton, John (Joe), 253; collages by, 195, 197, 199, 242–44, 259; defacement of books by, 169, 194–200; plays by, 167, 244; trial of, 37, 167, 199
Orwell, George, 13

Paddington, 6, 7, 22, 23, 107
"painted boy menace," the, 6–7, 277n8
Pall Mall Gazette, 81–82
pansies, 29, 110, 139
Paolozzi, Eduardo, 250, 275n83
Parallel of Life and Art (exhibition), 250–51
Park, Frederick: trial of, 7
parklands, 40, 43, 48, 50, 51. *See also* Green Belt
parkways, 14, 49. *See also* roads
passing as heterosexual, 152, 153, 154
passports, 142–43, 282n42
Passport to Pimlico (film), 19, 277n11
pathways: of electrons, 74; in homes, 221; in libraries, 177, 183, 186, 195; metropolitan, 52, 54, 254
peace, 3, 52, 77, 118
pederasts, 139
Pelican books, 186, 192
Penguin Books Ltd., 31, 175–77, 179; covers of, 176–77, 178, 199; publication of *Lady Chatterley's Lover,* 180–89; trial of, 37, 167, 180, 182–86, 188, 189
people: movement of, 49, 76, 77, 224. *See also* commuters/commuting
peristalsis, 272n43
Perry, Clarence, 45
perversion: interior decoration as indicator of, 206, 216; male, 9, 28, 92–96, 105, 130, 132–34; use of term, 93, 187

perverts, metropolitan: affluent, 82; as a conspiracy, 112, 113, 240; criminality of, 35, 83, 84; spivs compared to, 26, 95–96, 110, 115; tabloid distortions of, 29, 79, 133–34, 210
photobooths, automatic, 36, 117, 121–29, 140–52, 154, 281n10, 282n42; Bacon's portraits from, 121, 122, 125, 127, 128–29, 149–51, 158
photography, 36, 141, 142–43, 146, 158–60
Piccadilly Circus, 4, 252; queer activities in, 6, 92, 103, 106, 240; Underground station, 150, 153. See also "Policeman at Piccadilly Circus"
picturesque tradition, 42, 59, 252
Pimlico, 6, 255. See also Passport to Pimlico
Pitt-Rivers, Michael: trial of, 1, 83, 233
planning. See regional planning; town planning
play spaces, 46–47, 48
pleasure, 6, 89, 91; covert, 79, 86; erotic, 90, 149, 216; of laboring bodies, 33, 239; prescriptive, 15, 21, 23; sexual, 167, 169, 197; textual (perverse), 32, 174, 177–80, 182–86, 189, 192, 194, 197–99
pluralism, 9, 252–54, 257–58, 261, 266n19
"Policeman at Piccadilly Circus" (photograph, Fieger), 255, 256
policing, 24, 94, 113–115, 137, 202, 280n79. See also homosexual offences; vice, male
politics, 38, 41, 75, 76, 260–61
poofs, 92, 257
pop artists, 258. See also Bacon, Francis; Independent Group
pornography, 182, 186
Porter, Julia, 286n6
poverty, 4, 5, 6, 9, 12, 41
Practical Householder, The (magazine), 234, 238, 239–40

preconscious, the, 173
press, the, 108, 113. See also tabloids; and individual newspapers and magazines
Priestley, J. B., 59
"Prince of the Wide Boys" (TV show), 17
privacy: bourgeois codes of, 29, 101, 151, 164, 203, 206; domestic, 32, 64, 121, 197; homosexual behavior confined to, 36, 91, 132, 136, 194, 202, 233; interior design for, 203–4; of photobooths, 141, 143, 149, 150; of psyches, 26–27, 172, 197
progress, 21, 61
projection, 129
prostitution, 1, 82, 120, 133–34, 187
Proud City (film), 44
pseudo-homosexuals, 93, 133, 139
psyche, human, 26–27, 164, 167, 172, 197
psychiatry, 1–2; criminal, 20, 26, 30, 118, 138, 160–61; theories of homosexuality, 83, 84, 94, 116, 118, 165
psychoanalysis, 32, 37, 172, 173, 186; theories of homosexuality, 29–30, 129–30, 138–39, 199, 281n17
psychology, 28, 30–31, 138, 187, 202, 234, 260–61. See also homosexuality: as psychological disposition
public houses (pubs), 101, 134–35, 139, 157

queans/queens, 7, 9, 10, 30, 92, 257, 259
queer, use of term, 266n19
queer activities, 7–8, 77, 83, 130, 133, 250; decriminalization of, 120; middle-class, 8, 9, 10, 28–29, 92, 202; perceived criminality of, 89, 92–94, 99, 108, 163–64; working-class, 7–10, 96, 100, 115, 133–34, 137
queer men, 200, 253; affluent, 7, 8–9, 15, 82, 92, 100, 153, 257; blamed for declining birth rate, 90–91; choreographies of, 58, 79, 102, 166;

conspiracies of, 108–16; diversity of, 116, 261, 266n19; freedoms brought by interior design, 32, 34, 37, 204; metropolitan, 25–30, 36–38, 83–85, 198, 210, 253–55, 258–60; in novels, 190, 192, 212–15; in postwar reconstruction, 77, 114, 131, 200, 255; in public spaces, 121, 130–37, 139, 151–52, 158, 161, 194, 202; scandals involving, 8, 83, 277n8; spivs compared to, 22–28, 131; use of term, 266n19; working-class, 7–10, 30, 92, 94, 96, 100, 115, 133–34, 137. *See also* citizenship, model for homosexual; homosexual, the; homosexuality; London: queer culture in; self, the: queer formulation of

race, 258, 260
railway reading, 179
railway stations, 102, 143, 197; sale of mass-market paperbacks in, 168, 178, 179, 182
Ramblers' Association, 50
Read, Herbert, 54
readers/reading, 36–37, 166–68; maturing of, 31, 188–89; proper, 169, 179, 180, 183, 185, 189, 199; supervision of, 174, 175. *See also* books; libraries, municipal branch; mass-market paperbacks; pleasure: textual (perverse)
reconstruction, postwar, 17, 41, 79, 91, 115; atom motif used in, 68, 70, 72, 74; cultural influence of, 16, 43, 44; early period of, 2–4, 20, 165, 203; ideologies of, 29, 87, 274n74; interior design programs, 216, 219; logics of, 35, 85, 89, 102, 151, 252; queers' place in, 77, 114, 131, 200, 255; social, 9–16, 42, 86, 201, 224, 254–55; vision of, 34, 178, 274n75, 275n83. *See also* County of London Plan; Greater London Plan, The; renewal: urban

Reed, Christopher, 211
reform/reformers: bourgeois, 260; citizenship and, 96, 211; domestic, 10, 32, 201–4; homosexual, 118–21, 128, 130–36, 163–64, 215, 230, 255, 257, 281n17; legal, 29, 203, 233; social, 5, 10–13, 26, 252; urban, 14, 30–31, 39–40. *See also* Abercrombie, Patrick; welfare state
Regent Street, 103
regional planning, 47
Regional Planning Board, 33
Register Your Choice (exhibition, DIA), 208–10, 211, 212, 213, 215, 217, 222
Renault, Mary, 29
renewal: national, 53; social, 6, 11, 84, 115, 116, 129, 200, 201; urban, 10, 15, 63, 79, 101, 109, 118, 266n12. *See also* reconstruction, postwar
repetition, 35, 65, 94, 114; as antidote to wartime trauma, 68, 274n75; circuits of, 42, 52, 72, 73–74, 76, 77; cycles of, 34, 49–50, 52; ephemeral, 178, 197; gratuitous, 184–85, 186; in interior decor, 226–27. *See also* history: halting flow of; routines
responsibility, 28, 86, 199
restraint, 85–86, 202. *See also* discretion
Reuben, David, 260
Reynolds, John: at Montagu trial, 83, 93–94, 96–98, 113
Richards, J. M., 59
rituals, 31, 194
roads, 49, 51, 74–75
Robertson, Commander, 136–37
Rolph, C. H., 182
routines: atomized, 15, 240; computational, 224; cycles of, 15, 33, 79; of everyday life, 32, 44, 47; library-related, 171, 172, 173, 180; maintained during blitz, 65–67, 70; management of, 50, 63, 74, 220–21; prescribed, 23, 42, 104–5; urban, 44, 89. *See also* repetition

Royal Parks, the, 45
Ruskin, John, 210, 211
Russell, Gordon, 64
Russell, John, 155
Rycroft, Simon, 70, 274n74

Sayers, Dorothy L., 198
Schmoller, Hans, 176–77, 178
Schofield, Michael. *See* Westwood,
    Gordon
schools: as neighborhood centers, 51,
    77; as source of male homosexuality,
    119, 130
science. *See* psychiatry; psychoanalysis;
    psychology; technology
Scott, Peter, 20, 26–28
scrapbook: motif of, 230, 258–59
Second World War: aftermath of, 2, 5,
    13, 65–68, 274n75. *See also* blitz, the;
    reconstruction, postwar
Sedgwick, Eve Kosofsky, 280n77
seduction: changing views of, 130. *See
    also* youth: seduction of
Seen Any Good Films Lately? (Zinsser):
    defaced cover of, 195, 196
self, the, 146, 258; creation of, 146, 236,
    244–45, 258; homosexual, 127, 128,
    138; management of, 132–33, 145, 165;
    presentations of, 110, 125, 140–50,
    211; queer formulation of, 7, 28–29,
    33–34, 169, 200, 259, 261; urban, 38,
    253–54
selfishness, 21, 25, 91, 107–8. *See also*
    greed
semiotics: of deception, 108–16, 240; of
    fidelity, 109, 110, 195, 197; of truth,
    143
sensibilities: bourgeois, 283n55; civic, 21,
    23, 42; queer spatial, 119, 242, 253,
    259; reconstruction-oriented, 128, 131,
    132; urban, 25, 34, 172, 178, 252, 258
Settlement House movement, 9
Sex and Society (Walker and Fletcher),
    189–90

sex education, 31, 165–66, 190, 277n17
sexologists/sexology, 138, 166, 199;
    Pelican books on, 186–87, 189–92;
    theories of homosexuality, 9–10, 28,
    29, 92, 93, 116, 266n19, 281n17
    Sexual Behavior in the Human Male
    (Kinsey), 281n17
Sexual Deviation (Storr), 190
sexuality, 27–28, 32, 79, 189, 190, 202,
    258. *See also* heterosexuality; homo-
    sexual, the; homosexuality
Sexual Offences Act (1967), 260
Shakespeare, Arden editions: deface-
    ments of, 199
Shepherd, Simon, 199
Shoreditch, 69; public library, 174
Signet Classics (publisher), 175
sign systems: queer, 35, 112–13, 137,
    140, 153. *See also* criminality: queer
    citations of; glad eyes; smiles
sin, 9, 28, 120, 187, 188
single men. *See* bachelors
"skippers," 104
Skylon *(South Bank Exhibition)*, 59–61,
    62, 274n75
slums, 6, 21, 43, 202; renewal in, 4–5,
    14, 26, 40, 44–46, 49
smiles, 103, 106, 109, 116, 117, 136, 137,
    153; in photographs, 145, 147, 149
Smithson, Alison and Peter, 250, 275n83
social democracy, 16, 51, 64, 77, 132,
    201; contradictions of, 21, 61;
    renewed, 40, 91. *See also* citizenship:
    social; democracy; welfare state
sociality: civic, 79, 98–99, 118; interclass,
    35, 45, 46, 63, 64–65, 97; queer, 7,
    8–9, 115, 257, 259; spaces of, 50,
    101–2, 135, 179; urban, 38, 44, 51–52
social order, 118, 138, 200, 201, 271n25;
    management of, 3, 15, 65, 97, 203–4,
    257; stable, 33, 52, 77, 168, 172, 252
Society and the Homosexual (Westwood),
    28, 117–18, 119, 120, 129–36, 166, 188,
    202

sodomy, 133, 277n17
Soho, 107, 128, 155, 157, 261
South Bank, the, 21, 54, 86, 87, 271n38, 274n74
South Bank Exhibition, 15, 34, 44, 52–63, 81, 171, 173; Dome of Discovery, 69, 72; exhibition guide, 57, 106–7; Gavin-Lowe article on, 16; interior design in, 32, 251; message of, 41–43, 73, 131–32; movement through, 55, 57, 74, 115, 252
space: atom as motif for, 72, 73; controlled participation in, 15, 251; domestic, 27, 63, 77, 120, 221, 248; everyday, 2–3, 35, 41, 89, 116; library-related, 37, 167, 171–73, 176–77, 197; logics of, 34, 35, 36, 87, 106, 132, 180, 188, 220; management of, 3, 10, 23, 33, 46–47, 54–55, 116, 165, 204, 227, 257, 274n75; mapping, 47–51, 70; organization of, 48, 50, 53, 185, 224, 261, 268n29; private, 32, 98–99, 120–21, 233, 248; psychic, 27, 30; public, 31, 58, 99, 101, 109, 120, 175, 179; public-private dichotomy, 149, 150, 151, 167; queer, 134, 215; sterile, 229; totalized, 53; transgressions of, 101–8, 183–85; urban, 111, 148–49, 194, 240. *See also* citizenship: spatial; domestic environment; home, the; living spaces; play spaces; queer men: in public spaces
sperm, squandering, 90, 91, 278n17
spivs, 16, 17, 19–25, 101, 199, 210, 218; clothing of, 19, 110, 178; homosexuals compared to, 26–28, 131; perceived criminality of, 24, 32, 107, 160, 202; perverts compared to, 26, 95–96, 110, 115. *See also* delinquency
sportsman, 207; model room for, 204–6, 212, 218, 220
stability, 75, 224, 261; interior design's role in, 203–4, 210; of knowledge, 171–72; of matter, 70, 72–73, 74;

postwar, 21, 42, 68, 73; of routines, 220–21; social, 23, 34–35, 41, 52, 77, 115, 168, 201, 252; threats to, 2–3, 116. *See also* instability
Stamp, Lord, 172
"steamers," 102
Stevenage (new town), 43
Stewart, James D., 170–71
Stiles, Corporal, 99
St. James's, 4
Storie, Valerie: attack on, 158
Storr, Anthony, 187, 190
street corners, 82–83, 134, 135
Stryker, Susan, 192
subjectivities: human, 224, 229; queer, 3, 7, 8, 16, 42, 140, 259
suburbs, 5, 6, 40, 45, 240. *See also Greater London Plan, The*
suggestion: terminology of, 55, 57
Swanson, Gillian, 26
Sylvester, David, 121, 140, 149–50

tabloids: campaigns against male vice, 30, 35, 81–85, 87, 91–94, 99, 101, 104, 115, 116, 206; distortions of homosexuality in, 25–26, 29, 79, 84–85, 117–19, 129, 131, 133–34, 153, 163
Tagg, John, 142
Taylor, Alfred, 153, 210–11
technology, 2, 141, 158, 204, 274n75
teenagers. *See* youth
temporality, 52, 59, 73, 74, 171–72, 178. *See also* time; timelessness
testimonials: homosexuality built on, 28, 118, 138–39
Things We See, The (Penguin Books), 279n68
This Is Tomorrow (exhibition), 248, 249, 290n1
Tiller Girls (dance troupe), 144
time: atom as motif for, 34–35, 72, 73; interstitial, 49–50, 104, 105, 182; logics of, 34, 87, 132; management of, 3, 10, 55, 59; mapping of, 70;

organization of, 48, 50–51, 268n29; transgressions of, 183–85. *See also* temporality

timelessness: of books, 173, 174, 176, 177, 178; of knowledge, 171–72, 175, 189

toilets, public, 82–83, 92, 102, 105, 136–37, 198

total planning schemes, 14, 41

town planning, 59, 65; films about, 44, 270n10; ideology of, 2, 63, 70, 252; movement built into, 15, 55; postwar, 35, 88, 120, 165; reformist, 26, 39–40. *See also* reconstruction, postwar

traffic lights, 2, 3, 24, 108, 247

trajectories, 15, 35, 42, 65; Abercrombie's, 74, 85–86; deviant, 105, 106, 108, 111; within exhibitions, 53, 58; individual, 52, 104; management of, 63, 76, 252; of reading, 37, 177. *See also* movement

transportation. *See* commuters/commuting; parkways; roads

transvestism, 27, 279n68

trophies, as decoration, 217–18

truth, 186, 190, 197; semiotic, 109, 115, 116, 143

Tube stations, 103, 104, 105, 108, 143, 150, 153, 240

Turing, Alan, 37, 223–24, 227–29, 247, 288n50, 289n60

unconscious, the, 173

Underground stations. *See* Tube stations

United States: postwar ascendancy of, 75, 76, 77

Unwin, Raymond, 45

upper classes, 4, 206; queer activities among, 7, 8–9, 15, 82, 92, 100, 153, 257

urban areas. *See* metropolis, the; renewal: urban; town planning

urinals. *See* toilets, public

usury, 277n17

vice, male, 8, 9, 97–98, 102, 130, 150; policing, 113–14, 163–64. *See also* tabloids: campaign against male vice

vice squad (Scotland Yard), 102, 114. *See also* policing

Victim (film), 32, 229–33, 242, 258

Victorian era: economy of, 4, 21, 40; interior decoration of, 210, 211, 216, 233; legacies of, 25, 83–84, 118, 129, 130; neighborhoods from, 139; photography in, 142. *See also* new journalism; slums

visual fidelity, 87, 178

Walker, Kenneth, 186–87, 188, 189–90

Walpole, Corporal, 99

wars. *See* First World War; London: interwar years; Second World War: aftermath of

Warth, Douglas, 99. *See also* "Evil Men"

Waters, Chris, 138

Way of Love, A (Courage), 29

Weeks, Jeffrey, 260

welfare state, 21, 97; citizenship in, 11–14, 125; computer's relationship to, 224; ideologies of, 45, 115, 260; legislation, 203. *See also* social democracy

West, D. J. *See Homosexuality*

West End, the, 4, 6–7, 9, 45, 49, 141, 255; queer activities in, 8, 103, 114, 119, 139, 242; vice in, 82, 94–95, 105, 106

Westwood, Gordon, 28, 36, 138, 151, 166, 200, 269n54. *See also Society and the Homosexual*

Whisky Galore (film), 277n11

W. H. Smith & Son, 179, 260

Wilde, Oscar: home decoration, 287n12; trials of, 8, 82, 97, 153, 210

Wildeblood, Peter: biography of, 157, 161; homosexual encounters, 103, 109, 150, 240; photographs of, 36, 153–54, 156, 160; testimony to Wolfenden

Committee, 1–2, 29, 138–39, 152; theory of homosexuality, 94, 151, 200; trial of, 1, 83, 96–98, 153, 233. *See also Against the Law*

Williams, Kenneth, 163

Wilson, Angus, 201

Winger's Landfall (Lauder), 150–51

Wolfenden Committee, 1–3, 31, 106, 114, 136–40, 157, 202; model of homosexual, 29–30, 36, 120–21, 259; Report of, 104–5, 132, 165, 216; Wildeblood's testimony, 1–2, 29, 138–39, 152

women: as objects, 27; railway reading by, 179; reading *Lady Chatterley's Lover*, 182, 183; working-class, 253, 283n55

working classes, 4–5, 6, 12, 41, 185; homes of, 64, 202; interior design preferences, 211, 244; leisure activities of, 26, 50; queer activities among, 7–10, 30, 92, 94, 96, 100, 115, 133–34, 137; railway reading by, 179; reading

Lady Chatterley's Lover, 182, 183; removal from slums, 43, 45–46, 49. *See also* spivs

World War II. *See* Second World War

Wormwood Scrubs (prison), 139

Your Britain (poster, Games), 67, 273n73

youth: culture of, 253, 257–58; laddish workingmen, 30; metropolitan, 255, 260; mobility of, 146; origins of homosexuality in, 187, 188; photobooth use by, 125; protection of, 233; railway reading by, 179; seduction of, 8, 82, 100, 102, 108, 206. *See also* boys; delinquency; spivs

zap, the, 260

zigzagging, 58, 106–7, 108, 111, 116

Zinsser, William K., 195, 196

zoning strategies, 44, 49, 63, 65; discipline through, 48, 50, 54, 101, 102; functionalism of, 43, 79

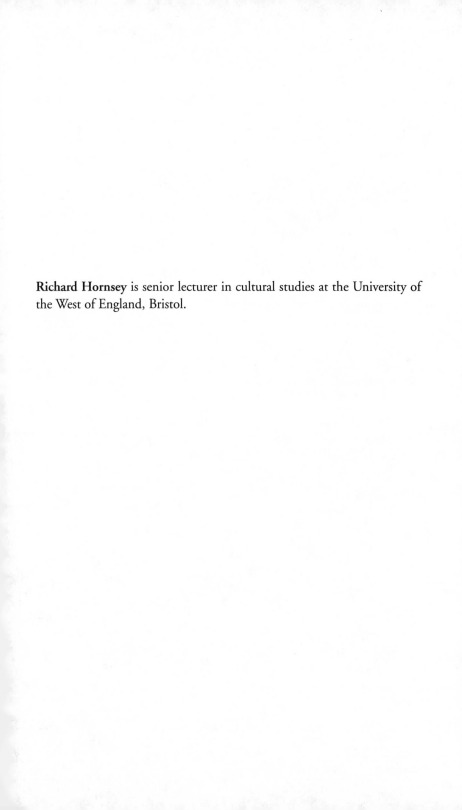

Richard Hornsey is senior lecturer in cultural studies at the University of the West of England, Bristol.